T5-CGA-872

History and trends
of professional nursing

History and trends of professional nursing

GRACE L. DELOUGHERY, R.N., M.P.H., Ph.D.

Head, Department of Nursing
Winona State College
Winona, Minnesota

with a special unit on Legal Aspects by

EILEEN A. O'NEIL, J.D.

Minneapolis, Minnesota

EIGHTH EDITION

with 43 illustrations

THE C. V. MOSBY COMPANY

Saint Louis   1977

EIGHTH EDITION

Copyright © 1977 by The C. V. Mosby Company

All rights reserved. No part of this book may be reproduced
in any manner without written permission of the publisher.

Previous editions copyrighted 1943, 1950, 1955, 1959, 1965, 1969, 1973

Printed in the United States of America

Distributed in Great Britain by Henry Kimpton, London

The C. V. Mosby Company
11830 Westline Industrial Drive, St. Louis, Missouri 63141

Library of Congress Cataloging in Publication Data

Deloughery, Grace L   1933-
   History and trends of professional nursing.

   Seventh ed. by G. J. Griffin.
   Includes bibliographies and index.
   1. Nursing—History.   I.   Griffin, Gerald Joseph.
History and trends of professional nursing.   II.   Title.
[DNLM: 1.   History of nursing.   WY11.1 D362h]
RT31.J4   1977   610.73'09   77-386
ISBN 0-8016-1974-2

VH/VH/VH   9   8   7   6   5   4   3   2   1

Preface

This edition is a revision of material prepared by Griffin and Griffin and published previously. A consolidation is undertaken not to devalue the extensive historical presentation by the previous authors, but to emphasize those portions of history that have the greatest impact on the modern nurse and to permit updating of the history and more discussion of trends that project from the historical material.

Change, although perceived as slow when an urgency is present, occurs at such a rate that individuals aspiring to be nurses must be more than minimally prepared to cope with its dynamic process. A recurring theme throughout the book is the parallel evolution of the role of women and modern professional nursing in our Western society. Along with the achievement of greater status and independence, nurses must be prepared also to carry the responsibility that goes with it. To be knowledgeable about legal aspects involving their professional activities is absolutely essential. Legal aspects could be incorporated throughout the body of the book, but the separation in this edition is continued at the request of instructors and other users who distinguish that content to give it special emphasis.

Acknowledgment is given to the human desire to look back periodically in a moment of nostalgia, for although one is eager to rise to a new challenge, it is often pleasant to reflect on days gone by. To encourage this, pictures are included that portray the history of nursing as it was in earlier eras. After reflecting on the past, one often achieves new heights of courage and assurance, better prepared to meet the challenges ahead.

Sincere thanks are extended to those individuals who have contributed by their careful study of nursing history, particularly Gerald and Joanne Griffin. Special acknowledgment is due Deborah MacLurg Jensen, whose ideas and dedication originally made this book a reality. It is hoped that the changes made in this edition will enhance the efforts of those authors and will be found useful and interesting by the readers. It is also hoped that the history of nursing will take on real meaning, with themes being identified throughout the discussions and later explored separately as they evolve to the point of being current trends.

It also seems imperative to acknowledge those twentieth century pioneers in nursing education who are admired by many of their former students and preceptors for their world-wise view. Through rich life experience they have gained a perspective of history and trends that should be a valuable contribution to the present generation of young men and women entering the profession of nursing.

Thanks is given to three special people—Donna Doyle, Theresa Johnson, and Phyllis Malotka. Their extraordinary interest and support was a continued encouragement during manuscript preparation. To my husband and children is extended additional gratitude for their patience and understanding while this project was being completed.

Grace L. Deloughery

Contents

UNIT ONE
Early history of nursing

1 • Ancient beginnings

It has been said that we are a product of the past. This is true in part. If one rejects the past (history), even unconsciously, one also eliminates the possibility of planning for a future that can provide outward and inward peace and satisfaction to individuals and to communities. The past has much to teach us; without a genuine sensitivity and acceptance of the past, we leave the future to chance and intuition.

To study the history of nursing is to study world events, as well as trends of thought and action as they have influenced nursing's evolution. The rise and fall of men and nations and the battles they waged are events less important than the principles that underlie the conflicts. These principles can be seen within every struggle for money, status, title, and other forms of power. Strategies to gain monetary power or strength remain the province of economists; tactics of battle belong to the student of military science. Means of elevating social status or title may draw on the expertise of the sociologist or political scientist. It is possible to better understand the outcome and impact of all these various events and conflicts if one realizes that they all affect political thinking, economics, and religion. These, in turn, either directly or indirectly affect nursing.

Though each human being in some way adds to history, it is necessary to identify those persons, events, and principles that had the most critical impact. The impact of any one factor depends on the total circumstances surrounding it. Measurement of that impact depends on the perspective and judgment of the observer and his written or unwritten account. Records are sometimes scanty, and one cannot always be sure that the scarcity is indicative of any lack of actual importance.

While studying history, it is difficult to distinguish between conflicts that are classical examples of power politics and those which can be readily isolated as great movements that surge through our civilization as a whole. The conflicts that now rage between nations are evidence of the significance of power politics. In the eyes of the future historian, however, they may seem like incidents when compared to the great social changes that, today, sweep across the entire world. These social changes are characterized by government's assumption of greater responsibility for all citizens, concomitantly limiting every individual's freedom of action, avowedly for the common good. These global changes are so profound that any country resembles any other country more than it resembles itself as it was a century ago.

In addition to being a product of the past, we are the product of our time. Characteristics of any social group are determined by the greater movements occurring around it. Therefore, in order to understand the development of any group, some time should be devoted to studying the movements on which it depends for its origin and growth. We speak of history in the sense of growth and change, not in the chronology of names and dates.

To understand and plan change, it is necessary to clarify the facts that serve as the base. For example, data was presented in June, 1975, at the International Conference on Women in Health sponsored by the federal Department of Health, Education, and Welfare. Discussion focused on a definition of the role of women within the medical profession (Cimons). Nurses were included in that discussion as part of the medical profession, but nursing is not a product of modern medicine in the same sense that social service, dietetics, and occupational therapy are.

Medicine and nursing had independent origins and existed for many centuries without much contact. The practice of medicine and surgery was relatively simple and undeveloped, requiring essentially no technical skill. During the Middle Ages, nursing needs were met by a group of uneducated or untrained women, by members of the family, or by religious or military groups whose prime function was not nursing. The evolution of medicine, surgery, and public health into complex technologies required specially trained persons with an understanding of scientific principles; thus the two professions were brought closely together. By the time the need became urgent, nursing reforms were well under way, motivated from within the nursing profession, to coincide with social demands and conditions.

Today the two major health professions are becoming more distinct as a result of the promulgation by state legislators of the legal distinction of nursing as a profession. The New York State definition, a landmark achievement, was signed into law on March 15, 1972. The New York State legal definition of nursing established the professional status of nurses. It distinctly described the nursing function for the first time in the his-

tory of the profession, and it established full legal authority for the implementation of the independent role of the nursing practitioner. Because of the increasing professionalism, the public will expect, and rightly so, far more accountability on the part of all nurses. It is imperative, therefore, that nurses become involved in matters relating to nursing and health care, but that they do so only after having as a basis for their involvement an increased conceptual understanding of their action.

Evolution of professional nursing

To understand the evolution of nursing we should understand other important developments that have profoundly conditioned and influenced its growth. Primarily, these are the Crusades, the Renaissance, the Reformation, the Industrial Revolution, the development of modern science and health facilities, two World Wars, various types of research in social and basic science areas, social welfare, and the Equal Rights Movement. Perhaps more important than any one of these, the liberation of women served as a catalyst and critical component of the evolution of the nursing profession.

Women's new freedom enabled them to develop and participate without old constraints in various areas in which they had interest and ability to contribute. Women demonstrated that they could develop a profession and they achieved recognition. They continued to strive for, and were granted by society, additional freedom so that they might be better able to develop their individual and professional potential.

Though separate and distinct from medicine, nursing is closely allied to medical progress and practice. Just as one cannot understand modern nursing without some understanding of medicine and surgery, one cannot understand the evolution of nursing without an awareness of the primitive beginnings of medicine. The phases progress from witchcraft, through the birth of the scientific method introduced by Hippocrates and through the Dark Ages, until the Hippocratian principles were rediscovered by the English clinicians of the seventeenth century. It is important to understand that modern medicine rests on the physiological principles that Harvey discovered and the correlation of symptoms with organic changes that Morgagni taught. When these great principles became integrated with clinical medicine, they gave to it the impetus under which we still progress in the understanding, cure, and prevention of disease.

The Industrial Revolution and the growth of medicine inevitably led to the need for hospitals. When poor people crowded together in tenements, it became necessary to segregate the sick in institutions designed for their care. Communities gradually began to assume some responsibility for the relief of their sick and unfortunate members. The growing medical science demanded working conditions and special facilities that the tenement did not offer. The aggregation of many patients under one roof favored specialization among the physicians. The outcome was the modern metropolitan hospital with hundreds or thousands of beds separated into departments according to medical specialty.

As medical knowledge grew, the demands on the individual physician increased and his training became more complicated. A need arose for an entirely new group of persons who could tend the sick and carry out many procedures formerly done by the physician. This need was met by the modern nurse.

When medicine was passing into its modern phase, nursing was at a low ebb. Originally, nursing had developed to satisfy a fundamental need in all families. This impulse to care for the sick and weaker members of the group took different forms of expression among different peoples, influenced largely by the form of religion they practiced, their intelligence, and their humanitarian interests. Among all early peoples the dominating influence in nursing was the religious one. It is difficult at times to differentiate between religious ceremonies and purification and medical and nursing measures.

There is little evidence that any organized group of women nurses existed before the Christian Era. The ideals of brotherhood, service, charity, and self-sacrifice were preached by the early Christian church. Thus groups of workers whose main function was to care for the sick and needy developed and organized as deacons and deaconesses. Often nursing of the poor was a way of atoning for sin. Nursing as a function of the church, linked to this old ascetic idea, prevailed until after the development of nursing as a secular activity. The concept of nursing as an economic, independent, and secular vocation, an art requiring intelligence and technical skill as well as devotion and moral purpose, was first developed by Florence Nightingale.

Nurses in the early nineteenth century had much practical experience in looking after the sick, but they had no concept of scientific medicine and no social standing or responsibility. The physician needed an assistant who could work scientifically and could observe and assist intelligently without relinquishing the qualities of common sense and sympathy. The concept of this being a woman's role remained, although the new nurse needed specialized training, and as the craft grew into a profession, began to require professional education. The modern development of the "physician assistant role" and "the nurse practitioner role" results in part from the dichotomous struggle of women to win acceptance of their new independence and men's struggle to avoid the embarrassment of doing what society had clearly labeled women's work.

A distinction is drawn between "nursing" and "modern nursing." Nursing in the sense of caring for the sick dates back to prehistoric times, when those who had proved themselves most adept in caring for the sick naturally were called on to nurse friends or acquaintances and some even acquired the reputation of establishing a practice of nursing. This is the usual state of affairs in primitive societies. The concern here is with the evolution of an organized group within a society, whose members have specific preparation for their work, devote the major part of their time and effort to the systematic pursuit of a task, and are given recognition as a social group devoted to that task.

Viewed historically, the development of modern nursing, particularly from the perspective of the American reader, seems to fall into three periods: (1) from the earliest times to the latter part of the eighteenth century; (2) from the latter part of the eighteenth century through the establishment of the first modern school for nurses at St. Thomas's Hospital, England, in 1860; and (3) from 1860 to the present.

The first period was a long preparatory one; there was no special training or education in nursing. The obvious and most pressing needs of the patient, a natural adaptation or liking for this work, and occasionally some kind of appointment by a religious group started the nurse in her work. The practical experience which was received at the patient's bedside constituted the training.

The second period was much shorter and was marked by definite attempts at reform and at beginning actual training for those wishing to equip themselves to care for the sick. Many far-reaching discoveries in the field of science and in social thought occurred during this period. The foundations for the tremendous activities of the nineteenth century were being laid in all fields as well as in nursing and nursing education. For example, in 1798 Dr. Valentine Seaman began a series of lectures for nurses in New York Hospital. In 1833 Pastor Fliedner founded his noted Institute of Deaconesses, where Miss Nightingale received her only formal education in nursing.

The third period is characterized by the establishment of schools for nurses—college schools, both undergraduate and graduate—and associate degree nursing programs; by the development of specialization in nursing; by the growth of nursing organizations; by the beginning of study and research; by expanding opportunities for the graduate nurse; by legislation affecting nurses and nursing; and by the development of community interest in activities related to improvement of health and health care for all people in our society.

In studying the history of nursing, it is obvious that the fight for professional advancement is entangled with the struggle for the political, social, economic, and educational freedom of women. In no other field has the emancipation of women been of greater or more practical importance. This struggle evolved from the philosophy of the eighteenth century, was nourished by the revolutions of 1789 and 1848, and culminated in the general reaction against the Victorian era. The result has been a newly won freedom that has enabled the modern woman to reach achievements of which her mother scarcely dreamed.

This new freedom is further enhanced by the women's liberation movement, with revolutionary repercussions that affect us educationally, socially, economically, and politically. An acceptance of newer life styles includes pairings as well as marriage. Recent magazines deal with newer concepts of mothering and child rearing. Modern contraceptive methods make it possible for the first time in the history of civilization for women to control, with almost absolute certainty, what was once considered their primary function—childbearing and childrearing. The Supreme Court decision on abortion has legalized the elimination of unwanted pregnancies. This ruling has led some states to discuss elimination of required parental consent when abortions are performed for young women under what is defined as legal age. This circumstance holds implications for nursing care and raises questions for large groups of nurses. It has made staffing difficult in some clinics because nurses have traditionally been educated and trained to preserve life. Some nurses find it physically and emotionally impossible to work in units where they feel life is being destroyed, and they find themselves unable to carry out what is expected of them.

Neither nursing nor medicine has remained within the confines of the hospital or the sickroom. As both professions developed, their purpose spread beyond cure to the maintenance of health and the prevention of disease. Disease prevention required work among the healthy in the community, schools, factories, and military establishments. Laboratories that control the development and spread of disease need not be part of hospitals. Thus a new science arose—public health. Its aim was to protect the population as a whole by instituting relatively simple preventive measures. Once these measures were devised and standardized, the nurse became the ideal agent for putting those measures into action. Since its very recent birth, public health nursing has grown into a field of unequaled opportunities. These opportunities reach far beyond the traditional public health structure into pioneering unstructured approaches to meeting today's health needs. The simple technical tasks that were carried out by the early public health nurse evolved into an art and science of caring for individuals of all ages in the context of their family, community, and society. The focus broadened to incorporate physical as well as psychosocial measures. The right of all persons to an optimal level of health encouraged not only health restoration but also disease prevention and attainment and maintenance of health in its broadest sense.

Regardless of the magnitude of change, and although almost 80% of all health care personnel in the United States are women, they are not the decision-makers. Physicians and administrators remain the decision-makers, even though laboratory technicians, nurses' aides, and laundry workers make up the bulk of that 80% (Cimons).

The story of modern nursing's evolution must be understood against the background of the Industrial Revolution, the evolution of modern science and health care, and the emancipation of women. When this background is comprehended, the history of nursing can be traced from antiquity through the Dark Ages to the rise of the great nursing leaders of the preceding and present centuries. The results of their lifework may then be traced in Europe, North America, and elsewhere. Though sometimes obscured by today's events and trends it is possible to discern real efforts expended by women and nurses to achieve international cooperation and understanding. If it is accepted that one mark of "profession" is meeting the needs of society, then perhaps the work that results from these efforts will prove eventually to be nursing's greatest achievement.

Egyptian medicine

Medicine originated in the practice of magic. In early Egypt certain empirical knowledge regarding sickness slowly accumulated from the witchcraft. The practice of medicine never entirely outgrew the superstitions that surrounded its origin. Today even the very educated patient looks toward his physician for something more than the logical application of a technical science. Medicine in Egypt reached a surprisingly advanced stage of knowledge. The custom of embalming enabled the Egyptians to become well acquainted with the organs of the human body. From clinical observations they learned to recognize some 250 different diseases; to treat these they developed a great number of drugs and procedures, including surgery. At the time of Herodotus, about 484-425 B.C., neurosurgery was advanced to a point beyond the imagination of the visiting Greeks. However, their ignorance of normal and pathological physiology and of experimental investigation limited their theories.

Egyptian medical practice centered around Imhotep, chief physician to Pharoah Zoser of the Third Dynasty about 3000 B.C. Not only chief physician and by far the most trusted advisor to Pharoah Zoser, one of his major contributions was in architecture. He made a major contribution in the care of the sick and left behind much wisdom in the formulation of his wise proverbs. People sang these proverbs for centuries after his death. His fame was such that he became a demigod almost immediately on death and was raised to the honor of full deity centuries later. A temple was erected to Imhotep on the Isle of Philae, and actual worship to him continued into the sixth century of the Christian Era.

With the decline of Egyptian civilization, medicine came under Greek influence. Al-though the Greeks brought their own ideas regarding medicine, they undoubtedly absorbed much of the knowledge found in Egypt, thus becoming bearers of some of the ancient truth to our own time.

Greek medicine and hospitals

Hippocrates (about 460 to 370 B.C.) stands out as a real person surrounding early Greek medicine. The chief contribution of his school was to change the magic of medicine into the science of medicine. Hippocrates taught physicians to use their eyes and ears and to reason from facts rather than from gratuitous assumptions. His writings on frac-

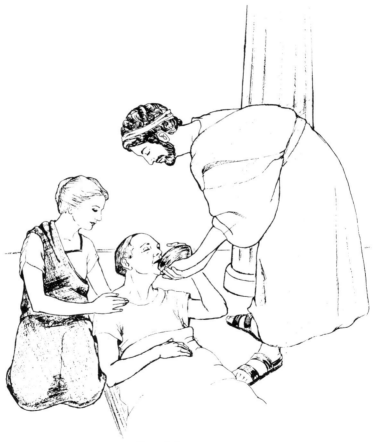

Special training

Specially trained care of the sick has been a characteristic of highly civilized peoples. The ancient Greeks had several centers for such care—among them the Temple of Hygeia, named for the goddess of Health, the daughter of Aesculapius.

tures and dislocations remained unexcelled until the discovery of the x ray. The Oath of Hippocrates possesses such a vitality that even today many are admitted to the practice of medicine with it, and the Hippocratian school has perhaps erroneously been given credit for the first ethical guide on medical conduct.

In ancient Greece we distinguish between two refuges for the sick: the secular and the religious. Physicians directed the secular, which corresponded roughly to spas or health resorts of today. Some were endowed and had outpatient departments, and some were used for the instruction of medical students. The secular places of healing and the sanctuaries of the gods, especially Aesculapius, were closely associated; of these, the one at Epidaurus, his birthplace, is the most famous. Most important here was the play on the patient's emotions by a complicated ritual. Other practices that may have been more effective in bringing about cure were rest, wholesome food, physiotherapy, and fresh air and sunshine on porches overlooking the blue Mediterranean while the patient awaited the appearance of the god in his dreams. There were more than eighty such sanctuaries throughout ancient Greece. One of the most famous is the Temple of Cos, the birthplace and later seat of activity of Hippocrates.

The first suggestion of women being associated with the healing arts is found in Greek mythology in the person of Aesculapius, who eventually became deified as the God of Healing. One of his five children, Hygeia, became the Goddess of Health, and another, Panacea (from which comes our word for "cure-all"), the Restorer of Health. Aesculapius is represented by the familiar caduceus. Later most Greek healing centered around shrines in which many patients congregated. Among the attendants were the so-called "basket bearers" and those who were supposed to look after the sick somewhat in the manner of nurses. The writings of Hippocrates make many references to procedures that

would be undertaken in modern hospitals by nurses but no reference to a nursing vocation as such. In ancient Greece and Rome the nursing of the sick and wounded was probably an incidental household duty, since there is no reference to any organized nursing group.

Early Christian church and hospitals

The great element of altruism contained in the Jewish religion later became further emphasized by Jesus Christ in His teachings of love. Its practical expression appeared in the early Christian church in the form of succor to the orphans, the poor, the travelers, and above all, the sick. The deaconesses of the early church visited the sick, much like modern visiting nurses. They were laywomen appointed by the bishops. These appointments were highly esteemed and were given to women of good social standing. Gradually their work was assumed by the various orders, and their activities declined. One of the best known deaconesses of the early Christian church was Phoebe, a Greek lady who is also remembered as the bearer of St. Paul's epistle to the Romans. Visiting nursing soon became an important part of the work of these early deaconesses, and Phoebe is often referred to as the first visiting nurse as well as the first deaconess. During the fourth and fifth centuries the names of three Christian matrons of patrician Rome —Fabiola, Paula, and Marcella—were associated with charitable work—the care of the sick.

In the early days of the Christian Era the Roman Empire was at its peak. At the height of its splendor Claudius Galen (A.D. 130-201), physician to the Emperor Servetus, wrote voluminously. His writings, containing anatomical and physiological observations, encompassed virtually all the medical knowledge of his day—knowledge that only through his industry survived the destruction of the Roman Empire. The translation of his writings into the Arabic chiefly accounted for their preservation; therefore, until the time

Greek Christian physician of the fourth century reading in front of a library cabinet. On top is a surgical instrument case.

(Courtesy Bettmann Archive, New York, N.Y.)

of the Crusades, Arabian physicians became the standard bearers of medical knowledge.

Although early Christendom at first encouraged women to visit the sick and to nurse them, refuges for the sick made an early appearance. Patients were sheltered in the bishops' houses, but when this proved impractical, special institutions were established by endowments throughout the Roman Empire. In Rome the first large hospital was established by Fabiola, a beautiful, worldly woman, who thereby did penance for her second marriage. She administered this hospital so well that her death was mourned by all Rome.

In the eastern Roman Empire several large hospitals were established; the Emperor Constantine founded one at Constantinople, A.D. 330; however, the largest of them all was the one that St. Basil of Athens built on land granted him by the Emperor Valerian near the city of Caesarea in Asia Minor. It was tremendous, constituting a town all of its own, with separate hospitals for lepers, children, the aged, and strangers. These hospitals, however much contemporaries may have been impressed by them, did not continue into the later centuries.

A few centuries later in the Western world the first hospitals immediately under the auspices of the Roman Catholic Church were founded; these still exist. In Lyons the Hôtel Dieu was established in A.D. 542 by Childebert; it is now the hospital with the longest record of continuous service. Detailed records were kept of the Hôtel Dieu in Paris, which was founded about A.D. 650-651 by St. Landry, bishop of Paris. It was greatly enlarged in the thirteenth century by St. Louis and was the prototype of the medieval hospital. The records of this hospital constitute a principal source of information regarding nursing in those days.

Moslem hospitals and medicine

During the eighth to the tenth centuries magnificent hospitals were erected throughout the Moslem world. For the times they had excellent endowments. One in Bagdad received about $1,200 a month, and the physician-in-chief served gratuitously. In addition, these hospitals had a great advantage over their European contemporaries, for they were staffed by physicians superior to any in the world. Greek knowledge had been preserved by the Moslems.

One large hospital in Bagdad had a staff of twenty-four physicians. In A.D. 869 its superintendent published the first known pharmacopeia. By A.D. 1160 there were some sixty medical institutions in that city. Best known to Western lands, however, were the big institutions in Damascus and Cairo. The hospital in Cairo was founded by the sultan of Egypt in 1276 as a thank offering for having been cured of the colic.

It was endowed with an income of 25,000 pounds [$63,500], and contained four great Courts, each with a fountain in the centre, wards for each separate disease, a lecture room, and a department for attending patients at their own homes. Musicians and storytellers were provided for the amusement and benefit of those troubled with sleeplessness, and the convalescent patient received, at his departure, five pieces of gold, about 50 shillings [about $4.25] that he might not be obliged to return to work immediately.°

Such was one of the hospitals of the "infidels," whom the Crusaders tried so hard to exterminate. These structures were in marked contrast to the rather gloomy Gothic Hôtel Dieu in France of a few centuries before.

Physiology and hygiene were studied by the Arabian scientists, knowledge in materia medica was expanded, and surgeons used

various drugs as anesthetics, but Moslem belief in the uncleanliness of the dead forbade dissection. The following names stand out: Rhazes (A.D. 860-932), noted for his study of communicable disease, and Avicenna (A.D. 980-1037), who wrote extensively —his *Canon of Medicine* was used long after his death.

Medieval medicine and nursing
Military orders

During the Middle Ages medicine in Europe was under two influences—the lay medicine that followed (left from Roman traditions) and the ecclesiastical medicine (existed in the monasteries) around which most of the existing hospitals were built.

For 1,000 years after Christ there were no attempts to organize nursing. As the Middle Ages advanced, three organizations developed that either have persisted in some form to the present day or established certain principles still recognized as important. These organizations were the military, regular, and secular orders. All worked under the auspices of the church, which, as we know, profoundly influenced all activities of the Middle Ages.

The most spectacular product of the feudal system was the Crusader, a man who was supposed to combine a lofty spirit devoted to the service of God with a fierce, belligerent temper, ready to fight the infidel wherever he was to be found so that the holy ground on which Christ trod might again belong to His followers. He carried the principles and the glory of knighthood to their fullest as he traveled over the continent of Europe and throughout the Mediterranean basin. When he traveled in the Near East, he learned much from the enemy, including the idea of the organized hospital from the Arabs. The natural places for the establishment of hospitals were the outposts, particularly Jerusalem itself, where those wounded in battle sought refuge while they recovered. The hospital had to be staffed by physicians and nurses who were members

---

°British Medical Journal, p. 1448, 1908.

of the regular orders. Men went to battle and then retired to nurse the sick. They were called "night hospitalers." In later years they devoted themselves entirely to nursing. Two great influences shaped nursing practice in the Middle Ages—the military and the religious. Gradually the care of the sick was considered more and more to be a religious duty.

Three nursing orders became preeminent: Knights of St. John, Teutonic Knights, and Knights of St. Lazarus. Corresponding with these were three orders for women who tended female patients in special hospitals.

Knights of St. John. About 1050, Italian merchants of Analgi founded two hostels in Jerusalem, one for men and the other for women. The former was dedicated to St. John the Almoner; the latter to St. Mary Magdalene. Some 50 years later the Order of St. John became prominent, and it is generally assumed that this order originated in the nursing staffs of these two hospitals. Peter Gerard, an intensely devout man, was active in the organization of the order on a high religious plane under the grand master. The members were divided into three classes: the priests, the knights, and the serving brothers. The women's branch of the order, organized under Agnes of Rome, devoted itself to religion and nursing; they gave up the latter pursuit, however, when the order was driven from Jerusalem.

The Order of St. John proved a huge success; branches were established everywhere, and its extraordinary vitality is shown by the fact that it has persisted to the present day and is active in England. St. John's Ambulance Association and the National Association for the Aid of the Sick and Wounded During War are activities of the order. The order was active in the organization of the International Red Cross, which carries its insignia as its mark.

A prominent, affluent, and important factor in medieval Christendom, the order established many customs that remain the heritage of nursing today. Being military in character, the discipline was strict, and modern nursing traces its tradition of obedience to superiors to the Order of St. John. The order also established the organization of rank and the principles of complete and unquestioned devotion to duty.

Teutonic Knights. The Teutonic Knights made up the German equivalent of the Order of St. John. They date back to a hospital founded by Germans in Jerusalem soon after 1100. They took an active part in the subsequent wars in the Holy Land, especially the siege of Acre in 1190, when they established a tent hospital for wounded crusaders. Their organization, modeled on the Order of St. John, gradually came into possession of great property, especially in Sicily. They eventually moved to Germany where they became primarily a military order. The nursing of this order was largely done by men; women were not admitted to full membership but retained a secondary position. Sisters of this order were, however, engaged in nursing as late as the end of the fifteenth century.

Knights of St. Lazarus. The Knights of St. Lazarus were established primarily for the nursing of lepers in Jerusalem after this city had been conquered by the Christians. Later, Boigny near Orleans became their main seat, but as leprosy became less prevalent by the end of the fifteenth century, the order was dissolved and its property was absorbed by the Order of St. John.

Regular orders

As the early Christian church developed, those who devoted their lives to the service of God followed the example of Christ, and the very spirit of the church led it to care for the fatherless, the poor, and the sick. When people could travel safely the deaconesses went to people's homes to nurse their sick. Later, because of the insecurity of the early Middle Ages, men sought protection behind moats and walls. The men and women of God established monasteries in which they organized hospices to house their charges. In the beginning, travelers, paupers, and patients were housed under the same roof; the modern words of hostel, hotel, and hospital, now with different meanings, all have the same origin—hospice or hospitium, a place of refuge. The early hospital was called a "Hôtel Dieu." Soon, however, it became advisable to care for the sick separately; with the knowledge the crusaders gained from the Arabs, the hospital as we now know it had its origin. As society again became better organized, and with the growth of cities, hospitals tended to become separate institutions apart from monasteries, although many of them continued to be staffed by the regular orders.

The sisters who took charge of the Hôtel Dieu in Paris are best known because their records are the most complete. They began about A.D. 650 as a small group of volunteers who looked after the sick in the hospital. They remained primarily a nursing order called the Augustinian Sisters. For the first 600 years of their existence as a nursing order they were without severe restrictions, but about 1250, Innocent IV caused them to become cloistered under the rigid rules of St. Augustine. The Augustinian nun wore a white robe, and when she became a full sister, a hood was added to her habit. In Hôtel Dieu she worked very hard, both early and late, with no recreation, and apprenticeship the only method of instruction.

In spite of very inadequate medicine and nursing during the Middle Ages, there began to be an increase in the institutions for the care of the sick. Sometimes this was stimulated by epidemics. The number of individuals, mainly volunteers, who devoted themselves to nursing also increased. During the fourteenth century one of the outstanding and devoted women whose activities were linked with the care of the sick was St. Catherine of Siena (1347-1380). At night her lamp represented to the sick of Siena what Florence Nightingale's lamp was to mean in the Crimea. Catherine was not of noble birth; she had been trained in what we would call a middle-class home to help with

housework, as was the custom of the day. She taught herself to read and, some years later, to write. Because of her great homeliness, it was considered safe for her to nurse and visit in the homes of sick patients. In 1372 the plague came to Siena, and Catherine worked day and night at nursing. She became particularly well known about the hospital at La Scala; it stands as a memorial to her today.

St. Hildegarde (1099-1179), a Benedictine abbess in Germany, is associated more with medicine than with nursing, since she actually prescribed cures and was supposed to perform miracles. However, she trained young noblewomen in the care of the sick in her abbey.

In the sixteenth century the Ursulines, an order that emphasized the care of the sick and the education of girls, was founded. It is of great interest to nurses and teachers in the United States because some of the early schools and hospitals were staffed by Ursuline Sisters.

Nursing provided in the Middle Ages was simple, consisting mostly of providing for the patient's physiological needs, giving medications, and bathing and dressing wounds and ulcers. Ideas concerning cleanliness and ventilation differed considerably from ours: windows were often placed so high that they were difficult to reach; bathing and changing of bed linen would not measure up to modern standards. Heating, lighting, and plumbing arrangements were either very primitive or nonexistent. The mother superior made her evening rounds by the light of a torch. Nursing appliances were also primitive. Much equipment now considered essential, such as thermometers and hypodermic syringes, were entirely missing; rubber was unknown and accessories like bed rings were made of leather stuffed with hair; drawsheets were made of leather and later of oiled cloth. At the Hôtel Dieu there were no washing machines; nurses carried the dirty linen down to the river on washdays. Many of the activities of the sisters were limited by prejudices. Because the human body was considered inferior and unclean, it was thought improper for nurses to undertake certain procedures, such as giving enemas to men or vaginal douches to women. An important duty of the sisters was to minister to the spiritual needs of the patients; in an age when religious considerations dominated every activity, this took a great deal of time.

The nursing order was structured so that the sisters advanced from the stage of probationer to wearing the white robe to receiving the hood. They were all under a "superintendent of nurses" or director of nursing; in those days she was called a prieure or maîtresse. In the beginning there was no uniformity of dress; nurses wore their regular clothes when on duty. Clothes became gaudy as the Middle Ages advanced; and because the church secluded itself from the more worldly aspects of life, there was a tendency to adopt a uniform dress that eventually became entirely standardized. We have thus studied the first organization devoted to nursing; now let us consider its strong and its weak points.

The strength of the nursing order was its organization into an institution under the immediate guidance of the strongest spiritual and secular power of the time, the church. The Augustinian Sisters at Hôtel Dieu in Paris can look back upon its record of over twelve centuries of uninterrupted service. The nursing order was not firmly associated with the medical profession for two reasons: it was sponsored and dominated by the church, and the medical profession in the Middle Ages had not developed into a profession capable of exerting leadership over nursing.

However, the strength of the nursing orders was also their weakness. By being so closely attached to the church, they had to share the vicissitudes of that organization; because the church later suffered censure for practices that were at variance with its professed purpose and ideals, the nursing orders suffered with it. They were sent out

of countries in which the Protestant Reformation had gained the upper hand, and their property was confiscated. Those countries then passed into what has been called the "dark age" of nursing. Their close attachment to the church also sometimes prevented them from enjoying the advantages of the medical progress that did occur. When the interests of church and medicine conflicted, the church prevailed, often to the detriment of the patient. As time passed, and as the Catholic church recovered from weaknesses occurring during the Middle Ages and adopted broader policies of modern days, these difficulties were largely solved.

Secular orders

Some of the drawbacks of the nursing orders were apparent also to their contemporary observers. Demands for complete and perpetual devotion to God would not always attract those best suited or inclined to care for the sick. Consequently, organizations developed for the primary purpose of nursing. Many of them prospered under the auspices of the church, often as lay branches of the regular holy orders, but some of them remained relatively independent. On the whole the tendency in the course of time was to make the secular orders approach the regular ones by requiring temporary vows, uniformity in dress, and religious observances. Many of these orders possessed extraordinary vigor and have persisted to the present time. They were very numerous but similar; this description will be limited to six of the more interesting ones.

Third Order of St. Francis. A lively, carefree young man in Assisi in northern Italy about the year 1200, St. Francis was struck with illness and encountered an argument with his father. This prompted him to seek seclusion and make a decision to devote his life to the service of God and man. He began by rebuilding a local church, attempting to lead a life as similar as possible to that of Jesus. Soon he was joined by friends, all of whom devoted their lives to poverty and service to the poor. When the group numbered twelve, they obtained papal sanction as an order and dressed in brown or gray woolen hooded robes ("Gray Friars") with ropes around their waists. They traveled from place to place spreading the Gospel and teaching the better way of life they had learned to live. Eventually their number increased, and they became a great and powerful order with branches throughout the countries of Europe. They were the First Order of St. Francis.

Among those watching the work of St. Francis was a young girl from his home town named Clarissa. She was so influenced by his work that one night she ran away from home and joined the small band of Francis and his friends. Francis consecrated her at the altar and cut off her beautiful hair as a sign that she had abandoned vanity and devoted herself to God. She dressed in a simple robe similar to that of the brethren and lived in a Benedictine convent for protection. Eventually, she established an abbey of her own, and the sisters who gathered around her grew into a regular nursing order, "The Poor Clares." These were the Second Order of St. Francis.

St. Francis served as such a powerful influence on the people of his time that it became necessary to limit the number admitted to his order. He then instituted the third or tertiary order, which was secular in the sense that the members did not give up their social relationships or take vows of chastity, but devoted their lives to the order in their home town without neglecting their duties as citizens. These people improved their communities as they served the order. One of their most important duties was nursing. For centuries male and female nurses belonging to the Third Order of St. Francis could be found in hospitals and homes.

Order of St. Vincent de Paul. Nearly 400 years later, about 1600, another inspired priest, St. Vincent de Paul, founded with prophetic vision another nursing order that has become very important. St. Vincent lived in Paris, France, where he joined in the care of the sick of a neighboring hospital. Here he discovered that charity was often poorly directed, being bestowed to excess on some, while others equally deserving went without aid; therefore St. Vincent organized charity wherever he could. He devoted special attention to begging, which was rampant at the time, and whenever possible he tried to guide tramps and beggars into useful occupations. His greatest work, however, was done in companionship with Louise de Gras (Saint Louise de Marillac). She was a widow of a noble family who had devoted herself to visiting nursing and directed a group of volunteer women devoted to this purpose. She was a rare woman, for along with her feeling of social responsibility she was highly educated, being conversant with the Scriptures, Latin, philosophy, and painting. Under the guidance of St. Vincent she studied closely the various lay organizations of charity devoted to the care of the poor and the sick all over France. Finally, on her return to Paris, she organized the "Dames de Charité" (the Ladies of Charity), an institution devoted to social work.

Soon she found that these ladies had difficulty in establishing the right kind of contact with the poor of the slums of Paris; also, their duties as ladies of charity conflicted too often with their domestic duties. Louise then decided to train her own social workers. In 1633 she opened her home to young peasant girls who as "The Community of the Sisters of Charity" became the foundation of one of the most important of nursing orders. To be accepted, the girls must be of good family and of good character, entering with the consent of a male relative. Each year on March 25 they dedicate and rededicate themselves to do their work, but if they do not wish to do so, they are free to resign from the order to marry or to take up some other occupation.

In their training and practice they have made every endeavor to overcome the difficulties that were noted in the discussion of the regular orders, and by working closely with physicians and by assuming all nursing duties, they have spread all over the world and set a fine example of what a nursing order should be. One of their greatest services was in the Crimean War, for here they not only nursed the French wounded but also, by their example, indirectly stimulated the discontent in the British army that eventually resulted in Florence Nightingale's great work.

The Beguines. The Beguines are a most interesting group of lay nurses originally organized in Liege, Flanders, about 1170 by the priest Lambert le Begue. The concept of their organization was that it should be liberal but devoted to the service of suffering mankind. Groups of women lived together in little houses, four or five in each. (If they occupied a number of houses, these might be surrounded by a wall; however, in small communities this was not the case.) These women were available for all kinds of household aid, especially nursing of the sick, but they also sewed, made lace, or taught. They did not beg but supported themselves by their wages and fees for services to those who could pay, as well as by special funds provided for them by the community. They made no vows but accepted certain standards as long as they belonged to the order. For instance, they could not marry and remain Beguines. The adoption of a uniform was optional; when a group designed one for themselves, it was generally in accordance with contemporary dress. Immensely popular, the order spread from West Flanders into the Netherlands, France, and Germany. At its height about the middle of the fourteenth century it numbered approximately 200,000 members. They staffed hospitals where necessary but generally devoted themselves to work throughout the community.

Similar groups have from time to time come under the domination of the regular orders as tertiaries. Such a fate overcame the entire Order of the Visitation of Mary that was established in Dijon, France, by St. Jane de Chantal with the help of St. Francis de Sales. They began as an order of visiting nurses, with activities like those of the Beguines, but because the church insisted on cloistered seclusion, they had to change their activities and to restrict themselves to offering succor to those who could come to them.

The Oblates. The Oblates evolved during the twelfth century as an important group of individuals in Florence, Italy. Like the Beguines, they were dedicated to serving the community. They became an order and gained distinction by the manner in which they staffed the hospitals of Florence (of which there were now thirty) and by the broad training that they received for this task. They still remain an established order.

Order of the Holy Ghost (Santo Spirito). The Order of the Holy Ghost originally had branches for both men and women, although this order is remembered chiefly as a male nursing order. It was founded in Montpellier, France, in the twelfth century by Guy de Montepellier. The numerous "Holy Ghost" hospitals, churches, and streets may be traced back to the activities of this order.

The medieval hospital

Moslem ideas about hospital construction and administration were adopted by the Crusaders and influenced the great hospitals of the military nursing orders in Jerusalem. Later, as these orders were driven west, the Moslem influence appeared in the hospitals that they constructed in Rhodes (near Turkey) and Malta (south of Sicily). Inspired by what he had learned in the East, Pope Innocent III about A.D. 1200 decided to build a modern hospital in Rome. He called on Guy de Montpellier of the growing Order of the Holy Ghost to establish this hospital on the bank of the Tiber. Because of its architecture, efficient management, and nursing care, it remained in operation until destroyed by fire in 1922.

When this hospital was finished, the Pope begged the bishops from foreign lands to come and to inspect it and then to go back

The hospital of St. Matthews
(Courtesy Bettmann Archive, New York, N.Y.)

and to construct similar hospitals in their home dioceses. During the next 100 years literally thousands of such hospitals under the Order of Santo Spirito, Heiligen Geist, or Holy Ghost were spread all over Europe. Street names bear witness to their locations down to the present day. The best of these hospitals were architecturally beautiful with painted Gothic doors, window and wall coverings, and high carved wooden ceilings: privacy of the beds was secured by partitions that could be removed when Mass was said.

Not until the present day has the wholesome effect that pleasant architectural designs and attractive furnishings have on the patient's morale been appreciated. Some medieval hospitals were so attractive that even well-to-do citizens who were left alone in the world would move into them bag and baggage and turn over all their property to the hospital in return for carefree old age.

In this period a distinction must be made between the two types of hospitals in the medieval towns. There were city hospitals, built within or actually in the walls of the city to care for the sick and elderly. There were also isolation hospitals placed outside the city for persons with communicable diseases, called "plague houses" or "leper houses" that served as refuges for those unfortunate outcasts of society. Nursing in them was largely provided by the Order of St. Lazarus. When the bubonic plague ("Black Death") swept Europe in the fourteenth century, it seemed like a fire to consume all who were weak and ailing; following it, leprosy almost disappeared, with consequent neglect and decay of the leper houses.

The better hospitals had resident and visiting physicians who were also often professors of medicine. If they had known a little more medicine, the hospitals would have been a setup for fine medical services, for nursing by religious orders was then at its height, its devotees being enthusiastic servants of Christ.

Medical schools and medicine

The establishment of the famous medical school in Salerno, Italy, was a great medical event of the ninth century. Until the fourteenth century this school was the center for all medical teaching and was not primarily dominated by the church. It was abolished by a Neapolitan decree in 1811, but had been in a decline for a long period before that. In the twelfth and thirteenth centuries, many famous universities were established in Europe. The growth of medieval cities with the corresponding increase in wealth and power influenced this development. The medical school at the University of Montpellier established in the twelfth century was the most famous medical school for several centuries, probably because it was practically independent. The University of Paris had a medical faculty at the same time, but within the department of philosophy. In Italy the medical school at the University of Padua was gaining a favorable reputation, as was the University of Bologna. By the end of the fifteenth century there were well-organized medical schools in many European countries and in Great Britain. Laws governing the practice of medicine were in effect in these same countries. It was to these centers of medical learning that the great medical men of the Renaissance turned for information and inspiration.

Physicians or doctors of medicine at that time considered the practice of surgery inferior and beneath the dignity of scholars. In the fourteenth century the student of medicine in Paris had to swear that he would not do any surgical operations. Surgeons of that period often traveled from place to place performing operations for carbuncles, hernia, and cataract, as well as blood-letting, pulling teeth, applying cups, and giving enemas. In England the Union of Surgeons and Barbers lasted until 1745, and in 1800 the present Royal College of Surgeons was founded.

By the end of the fifteenth century the newly invented technique of printing resulted in the rapid increase in both the number and variety of medical books that before then could only be reproduced painstakingly by copyists.

Although names such as Paracelsus (1493-1541) are recorded as outstanding in their time, they do not represent any fundamental advance of physicians; medicine was deeply involved in superstitions and erroneous assumptions. Patients who recovered often did so because their desire to live overcame not only the disease but also the treatment to which they were subjected.

Lay nurses with or without uniforms, self-supporting and fee for service, evolved from the Beguines, a lay group of nurses in Flanders, Netherlands. What followed was the apparent origin of the visiting nurses and at the middle of the fourteenth century numbered about 200,000 members.

The Moslem ideas on construction and decor of hospitals along the Order of the Holy Ghost (a mainly male nursing order) were instigators of the construction of thousands of hospitals which stood and were used for centuries.

Medicine during the Renaissance

Leonardo da Vinci, Andre Vesalius, Ambroise Paré. Forerunner in the great medical developments of this period is Leonardo da Vinci, whose anatomical studies and sketches remain classical. Vesalius (1514-1564) is credited with developing anatomy as a science and Harvey is credited with founding medical science based on fact rather than on tradition. The work of these sixteenth century anatomists enabled surgeons to work on a more solid basis. Ambroise Paré (1510-1590), a military surgeon, wrote a great book on natural history in general and on surgery in particular in which he emphasized that it was not necessary to dress wounds with boiling oil and that bleeding could be controlled with ligatures as well as by red-hot cautery. He also devised artificial limbs for the victims of war. During this period nursing reached a high level of organization and efficiency in the religious and military orders.

William Harvey (1578-1657). One ordinarily associates William Harvey's name with the discovery of the circulation of the blood, but his contribution to medicine is much greater than the discovery of a single physiological fact, however important: he established the principle of the physiologi-

Sixteenth century hospital scene. At right, a mentally ill person being chained to the wall.

(Courtesy Bettmann Archive, New York, N.Y.)

cal experiment. He received his anatomical training at Padua and returned to the St. Bartholomew's Hospital in London where he served as demonstrator of anatomy at the Physicians' College in Amen Street. Here he completed his great discovery, which he communicated in a lecture in 1616. His book was not published until 12 years later. While in Oxford during the reign of Charles I, the city was beseiged during a civil war, his home in London was searched, and all of his manuscripts and notes were destroyed. What loss medicine thereby suffered can only be surmised, for some of the titles were of great promise, including "The Practice of Medicine Conformable in the Thesis of the Circulation of the Blood" and "Anatomy in Its Application to Medicine."

Following several decades of political dis-

turbance, which led ultimately to the beheading of King Charles I in 1649, Harvey returned to London and became one of the scientific leaders of his day. He donated his library to the College of Physicians and established a lectureship that has continued to this day and to which is owed, among others, Osler's marvelous oration of 1905 on the founder himself. Harvey exhorted the fellows and members of the college to study the ways of nature by means of experiment.

Thomas Sydenham (1644-1689). Sydenham was first to set the example of true clinical methodology. His independent and unprejudiced spirit, combined with great powers of observation, made him the prototype of the clinical investigator. Referred to as the English Hippocrates, it was he who resurrected the great but simple methods and principles taught by Hippocrates many centuries earlier. He emphasized the need to observe phenomena and let observations logically lead to conclusions. This Puritan by birth and outlook expounded, "We should not imagine or think out, but find out, what nature does or produces." This sounds obvious now, but only because Sydenham succeeded to such an extent that his teaching has become commonplace. In his time medical science carried a superstructure of wanton speculations and theories so complicated and cumbersome that it became deprived of real value. In fact, Sydenham was attacked because he made the practice of medicine too simple and easy. In modern times his name is most commonly associated with his description of chorea, although his description of gout was much more of a masterpiece. His philosophy was to utilize probability as a guide, thus eliminating fantasies and vagaries that tend to distract the mind.

Sydenham had much in common with and was a friend of John Locke (1632-1704), the physician-philosopher and private physician to Lord Shaftesbury. Locke, a proponent of common sense and straight thinking, was the forerunner of Hume and Kant.

Views that Sydenham held met with great opposition. He did not participate in the activities of the Royal Society of Medicine. Even during his lifetime he was considered one of the great physicians. The true magnitude of his accomplishments, however, was not appreciated for several generations.

During the seventeenth century, London abounded in quackery of all kinds. Quacks, mountebanks, chemists, apothecaries, and even surgeons, who in those days were not supposed to treat internal diseases but nevertheless did, joined in exploiting the healing crafts. Druggists copied prescriptions they were supposed to fill and sold the drugs privately over the counter. One was said to have profited a hundred times as much out of a single prescription as did the doctor

Visiting the sick

(Seventeenth century copper engraving; courtesy Bettmann Archive, New York, N.Y.)

who wrote it. It was considered that medicine was overstocked with students graduating from the universities. He who began practice must have had to resolve to be a perpetual slave and servant to the meanest and basest all the days of his life. More than any time before, increased taxes, polls, large fees for houses, servants, and entertainment were imposed on physicians. In those days, the main requirements for beginning a practice were to have a good understanding with the druggist and to be seen regularly at church (Payne).

People began to ask questions to which they expected to find rational answers based on facts alone. The scientific method of inquiry was born. This method of reasoning led to objective observation and to the physical and physiological experiments that form the basis for the modern natural sciences. The writings of Locke, Roger Bacon, and Hobbes guided people's thoughts. Suffice it to mention that Gilbert of Rochester assembled all knowledge pertaining to magnetism and introduced the word electricity; Newton invented calculus and discovered laws governing optics and the law of gravity; and Boyle introduced the atomic theory. Thus, through hundreds of observations and discoveries, which often in the most unexpected way gained practical importance, the foundations for sciences were established. It was the scientific attitude that led to the discovery of steam power and the construction of the steam engine and somewhat later to the discovery of electromagnetism and the construction of the electric motor. Without it the modern engines would hardly have come into being, and the Industrial Revolution would have remained unborn. In the course of time, the scientific attitude also laid the foundations for modern medicine; the fundamental work of Harvey and Sydenham was its direct outgrowth. Thus clearing the air for straight thinking eventually led to the construction of the engine by which entire lives of subsequent generations were to be altered.

SUMMARY

The first evidence that any organized group of women were nurses was in the early Christian Era when the status of women was improved significantly. Nursing then was one of few acceptable means for self-actualization that women could choose. The religious and maternal aspects of the role predominated over the healer role. At this point in time, the nurse was to nurture her patients as a mother nurtures her children and show deference to the physician as a wife to a husband. It was no wonder that nursing should evolve as the nurse-mother, the first nonphysician health worker, and that while resented by physicians as a colleague, the nurse was nonetheless valued as an aide.

2 • Nursing from the Reformation to the Industrial Revolution

A dark period in nursing and the social setting for reform dates roughly from the end of the seventeenth to the middle of the nineteenth century. This dark period was characterized by nursing conditions so terrible that some time must be spent on an analysis of how such conditions could come about. It should be noted that during the same period were established the principles on which modern medicine was built and remarkable progress was made in other fields of human endeavor. Medicine developed rapidly during these years. One great man after another made important contributions, not only to detailed medical knowledge but also to its basic principles. As in all areas, there has always been a lag between medical discoveries and their practical adoption. In our modern day this lag has become relatively shorter. One notes, for example, the rapid adoption of insulin or the sulfonamides, but in the old days when postgraduate communication was slow and medical instruction proceeded along primitive lines, physicians persisted tenaciously for long periods in old habits.

The general practitioner and most specialists practiced as did their medical predecessors until well into the eighteenth century. During the years that followed, the changes were not great. The doctor of those days simply was not in a position to demand good nursing, for he did not know what comprised good nursing. Good nursing is predicated on a knowledge of anatomy, physiology, hygiene, and bacteriology, a knowledge that in those days was nonexistent. Assumed knowledge and superstition, the details of which are now practically forgotten, occupied the place of scientific knowledge. Therefore, in the practice of medicine, in spite of the growth of medical knowledge, nothing existed to stimulate the evolution of nursing as a profession. The new knowledge was not to bear practical fruits for many years to come.

The guiding principle of ecclesiastic nursing was charity; there was no concept of medical progress or of medical efficiency. Nursing services therefore were as good as the organization within the church that supported them; some orders continued nursing efficiently until the present time and experienced no "dark age." In Catholic countries, nursing remained more or less on the same level, ready to take advantage of progress when it appeared.

The emergence of any organized group can be understood only if one understands its background. Organized nursing as it is known today was greatly influenced in its professional development by the social and economic change of the Industrial Revolution. In referring to this change as an industrial revolution, it is not intended that attention be focused on one element—the mechanical change that occurred in Western civilization. One must realize that the entire process was fostered by economic change.

Economy originally meant the rules governing housekeeping; here it is used in the sense of producing or procuring the essentials of life. As this activity changed, it altered people's entire lives, including their environment, their thinking, and their political philosophy and conduct. Out of this setting emerged the world of today. The present world must be accepted as the outcome of the past and the beginning of the future. There is nothing static about it, nor anything permanent.

One must understand the most important elements of the past as well as those that are likely to dominate the future. In other words, nursing must be regarded as fulfilling the needs of society at any given time.

Religion's attitude

Nursing sank to its lowest levels in the countries in which the Catholic organizations were upset by the Reformation. The state closed churches, monasteries, and hospitals. In England alone it was said that over a hundred hospitals were closed, and for a while there was little or no provision for the institutional care of the indigent sick. When the demand became too great to be ignored, lay persons were appointed to run the hospitals. For example, this was done in the case of St. Bartholomew's Hospital in London and in St. Giles in the Fields and St. Katherine's Hospitals. These hospitals were not run because of the principle of charity but because of a social necessity. There was no honor attached to running a hospital or to being on its staff. At St. George's Hospital a man and his wife were engaged at salaries of £8 and £10 per annum to be messenger and matron, respectively. The matron remained there in charge of the nurses, and a nurse in charge of a ward or a division was called a "sister," possibly because it was thought that by retaining the title, some of the devotion and dignity of the old days might be retained also. This, however, was not the case, for when deprived of the dignity of the church, nursing somehow lost its social standing. Nurses were no longer recruited from the respectable classes of the community but from the distinctly lower classes. The new Protestant church abhorred cloisters and religious institutions and did not feel the same responsibility to the sick that had characterized the early Catholic church. Nurses were drawn from among the discharged patients or from the lower strata of society—women who could no longer eke out a living from gambling or vice often turned to nursing.

Another factor in this situation was the status of women in the social structure of 200 or 300 years ago. From the antiquity of Rome to the Middle Ages the Catholic church had assigned to woman a place in society that afforded her much freedom and opportunity to move about in the world. Thus women of ability could carve out careers for themselves, and the lay nursing orders especially offered them great opportunities to contribute to the life of the times.

The Protestant church, although it stood for religious freedom and freedom of thought, did not think much of freedom for women. In the seventeenth and eighteenth centuries and into the Victorian era the place of the average respectable woman was in the home—a "career woman" would have been next to unthinkable around the year 1700. Men performed all teaching, secretarial work, and literary endeavors; work then unsuitable for men, such as nursing, was entirely out of the reach of the average woman, even if she had wanted to do it. Housework demanded infinitely more effort than nowadays, and those women who had enough servants to free themselves from domestic tasks gave their efforts entirely to the shallow and superficial life of society. The only profession open to women was acting, and that was not respectable. So women faced with the necessity of earning their own living were practically forced to enter domestic service; nursing was considered a type, although not a very desirable type, of domestic service. After all, the chief duties of a nurse in those days were to take care of the physical needs of the patient and to make sure that he was reasonably clean, although this was not considered essential in the early municipal hospitals. Dressings were applied by dressers or by surgeons; the dispensing of medicines was the responsibility of the doctors and the apothecary.

Nursing existed in a low and dismal state indeed. It existed without organization and without social standing. No one who could possibly earn a living in some other way performed this service. Those who did so lost caste thereby, for, as one is judged partly by the company one keeps, a woman who began to practice nursing was almost certain to become corrupted if she was not so already. Most nurses were venal, drunken, and given to even worse vices than these. They expected and took bribes wherever these could be obtained, and liquor was their chief solace.

There were reasons why the nurse should fall a victim to these vices. Her pay was poor; if she had to provide only for herself, she could perhaps eke out a miserable living; but if she had children or other dependents to support, her pay was entirely insufficient, and she was forced to supplement it by any means available in order to survive. Her hours were so long and her work so strenuous that she had no opportunity to supplement her income by additional work. Her work was cheerless and depressing if she thought about it. If she worked in the hospitals, she was dealing with riffraff and the scum of creation; if she was lucky enough to be admitted to nurse respectable persons, she was considered the most menial of servants. Besides the long hours (sometimes nurses worked 24 or 48 hours at a stretch), they received poor food and sometimes none at all during the long night shift. There was no future toward which these women could look; this was the end of the road. They should therefore not be judged too harshly if they turned to the chief source of comfort that was open to them—alcohol.

Emancipation of women

The torch of liberation was carried largely by the intellectuals who continued to follow the views on the human right to happiness that had been championed by the humanitarian liberals of the eighteenth century. Recognizing the deplorable conditions, Parliament reformed the Poor Laws in England in 1832, but even this left much to be desired, and when Dickens, Carlyle, and others of their school revealed the social evils of their time, they met with a ready response among their readers. A sense of social responsibility and a desire to give this feeling a practical response developed among the well-to-do classes. Owen's sociological experiments are an example of this movement, but of greatest interest is its expression in the lifework of Florence Nightingale, which was entirely devoted to the relief of the classes in society that could not help themselves. One of the most important accomplishments of this era was the entire reform of nursing education, which is the main topic of this book.

The beginning of the evolution of the nursing profession was primarily the private work of philanthropic persons; it was not sponsored by the state. In time the women who had done nursing in religious or military orders and those untrained and uneducated women who did nursing for money were replaced by the new profession. The government sponsorship of causes that so greatly increase the fields and scope of nursing is of still more recent origin and has developed out of trends that we have yet to explain.

The emancipation of women may be traced ultimately to the trend toward personal freedom, which was one of the factors in the Industrial Revolution. It is part of the fight for human rights, which was first audibly expressed in the eighteenth century and which became one of the principles of the French Revolution. It is a step without which nursing might have developed as a craft but never into the profession as we know it today. Therefore the emancipation of women forms part of the background required to understand the evolution of nursing. Many attitudes of Miss Nightingale appear peculiar to us if we do not appreciate the difference between the social position of women a hundred years ago and now. Furthermore, the emancipation of women can no more be considered a completed process than can the Industrial Revolution, the evolution of modern medicine, or even the very evolution of nursing with which we are principally concerned.

The word "moral" comes from the Latin *mos, moris,* custom, and to use the word in its original sense we may say that the emancipation of women is fundamentally a moral process, its various practical manifestations —suffrage for women, legal rights, and educational and occupational opportunities—are secondary to the moral aspect.

Society's attitude

The customary social attitude toward women a few hundred years ago was one that was almost as old as Christendom and that, in fact, had been dictated by the church—not by Christ, for his attitude toward women was, as far as can be judged, quite liberal—but by the early church, especially as influenced by Paul. During the sixth to eighth century the stern attitude toward women was relaxed somewhat, but it was generally believed that woman's place was in the home only.

There were practical reasons for this: the work of housekeeping, like that of producing the necessities of life, was so complicated that it left little time for other pursuits. One part of housekeeping was the rearing of children; because of the high rate of infant mortality, it was a most inefficient process. It was not uncommon that out of ten or twelve pregnancies, labors, and months spent taking care of infants, there resulted but two or three effective citizens for the community. The energy lost in this manner of procreation was appalling, especially when compared with modern marriages. Young couples today are often lim-

ited to two to four pregnancies, but nearly all result in effective citizens. By an effective citizen we mean one who grows to productive manhood or womanhood. Thus there was a good physical reason which would have restrained all but a small privileged class of women from enjoying any measure of freedom even if it had been granted them; even if the Machine Age had reduced the time required for domestic work, the professional woman as a social class still would not have been possible.

A fundamental factor in the emancipation of woman was the changing attitude of society toward her. When, during the period of the French Revolution, Condorcet upheld the right of women and Mary Wollstonecraft wrote her *Vindication of the Rights of Women*, it is doubtful if many understood that these were the germs of a movement that eventually was to transform society. Few realized that women needed any "rights." In fact, the rights that women already had (such as the franchise , which women had in the United States under the first constitution of New Jersey from 1776 to 1807 and in England prior to the Reform Act of 1832) were not used and consequently were abrogated without contest.

Until the middle of the nineteenth century there was no place for women in the professions or in public life; whatever they wished to do had to be accomplished behind the scenes, hence "the little war office" at Burlington Hotel where Florence Nightingale worked out the army reforms with Sir Sidney Herbert and Dr. John Sutherland. As we shall see later, this failure to recognize women in public life may have been the real reason for Miss Nightingale's illness. Those few who bravely broke the bonds of tradition, such as Elizabeth Blackwell, the first woman doctor, and Miss Dorothea Dix, faced a great resistance purely because they were women.

The real difficulty in securing for women a place of equality with men was the negative attitude of society; its members took refuge in all types of rationalizations. The meeting of the argument therefore did not change the fundamental attitude of the opponents. The passing of laws or the exercise of previously unused constitutional privileges or rights does not accomplish much as long as these efforts are not in accord with the emotional attitude of the dominant citizenry, for our moral or customary attitudes are fundamentally determined by emotions. This has best been illustrated in our own country by the failure of the Eighteenth Amendment and the partial failure of the Fifteenth Amendment in the South, attributable to this cause. The relative inertia of our emotional attitudes, together with our social structure, is still effective in maintaining certain social handicaps for women long after they have legally and politically been given rights practically equal to those of men.

In spite of the fact that the professions are open to women, few enter the medical, legal, and, especially theological schools or attain high executive positions. On the other hand, society has expected some professions to be staffed preponderantly by women, for example, those of nursing, elementary school teaching, and social work. In the evaluation of the progress of the movement for the equalization of women with men, these two distinct aspects must be borne in mind. Nevertheless, the fact that women can now enter almost any career open to men on a more nearly equal basis is an indication of the trend of the times even though the lag is still markedly felt.

Seen through the eyes of history, nursing was a blot on seventeenth and eighteenth century society, but the contemporary attitude was one of inertia and complacency. The high ideals of the Middle Ages were gone, and a demand for adequate nursing had not yet risen. However, when men with the inquisitive spirit of the eighteenth century began to look into social evils, nursing was examined along with the rest of them.

Hogarth's cartoons and later Dickens' description of Sairey Gamp were caricatures that had their effect. In a more serious vein the writings of John Howard in the eighteenth century have become famous.

Judicial emancipation

If it had not been for the Reformation, which really was a product of the Renaissance, and great scientific discoveries, feudalism might have gone on for centuries. Feudalism was a social state in which class relationships were defined by insurmountable barriers. Life was strictly localized; it centered around the manor, which offered a measure of protection and exercised a crude but effective form of law and justice in return for hard work so that the individual could obtain the bare necessities of life. So much work was required to obtain food, clothes, and shelter for the present that there was very little chance of obtaining reserves for the future or for barter. There was little time for education or for leisure, and freedom to pursue them became, of necessity, restricted. Limitations became further imposed by social order on the right of movement as well as on political and religious thinking. It was a conservative, patriarchal state of society, offering few of what we today consider the amenities of life. The individual lived in continuous fear of famine, pestilence, and the figments of his own imagination, such as witchcraft and other superstitions.

Out of the social stall of feudalism emerged the Industrial Revolution. The Crusades also acted as a catalyst. Knights returning from the Middle East yearned for the knowledge, pleasures, gracious living, and comforts they had enjoyed so briefly. Out of the ferment came the sixteenth century with its great changes. New, rich lands were discovered beyond the seas, and men began to emigrate and to bring back treasures to the old centers of population. The immediate effects of this were tremendous: the treasures from the new lands made for a richer life, a "surplus economy" was being created, transportation was encouraged, and the center of gravity was shifted from the Mediterranean to the Atlantic seaboard, a change that was to chiefly benefit England.

During the time that followed, there was progress in domestic agriculture. Under the feudal system it had been, to a certain extent, communal; it now became more individualistic, and methods were improved. This led to a better yield, fewer men were required to till the ground, and with better food more men survived to a productive age. This agricultural surplus population moved to the cities in which industries had begun to develop in response to the growing wealth. These industries did not offer attractive careers; at first they had few, if any, machines, and it was long before they utilized power other than that of man and beast. There were the guilds but their range was narrow, and the early industrial worker was limited by fixed wages, inability to move, and many social customs. Essentially the feudal outlook was carried into the early industrial community.

Equal political rights for women were advocated since antiquity, but autocratic forms of government, which prevailed in ancient times and under feudalism during the Middle Ages, restricted suffrage even among men so that enfranchisement of women became a major political issue. Women's suffrage movements came into their own only after the male population won those rights as a consequence of the democratic revolutions of the eighteenth and nineteenth centuries.

It is questionable whether this Industrial Revolution would have extended very far had it not been stimulated by new thought that may immediately be traced to the Reformation.

Benefits of industry

Although the religious aspects of the Reformation Movement are most spectacular,

more important than these fundamental elements is the new stimulus to thought provided by the freedom that generated from the Reformation and eventually transformed ideas regarding government, politics, business, and philosophy. The right of private judgment was established, which later led to individualism in politics and in business and to the concept of free contract and the right to property. In the feudal order the right to property, by custom, was vested in the sovereign who could, in all ways, abrogate the rights of an individual to hold and to utilize that individual's property. The thinking of Locke, especially, established individual prerogative: the individual's right of property antedates that of the state, and he cannot be deprived of it without his consent (or "due process of law"). With the right of free contract it follows inevitably that the individual is also privileged to acquire and to hold as much property as he can within the limits of the law. This is the fundamental Protestant ethic, and without it the Machine Age of the nineteenth century would have been unthinkable. Unless one understands this, it is impossible to understand subsequent modifications that profoundly influenced the development of nursing.

Before women can hope to advance as a group, they must be equal with men before the law. The original concept of the family was that of a unit ruled by a head; the change in legal concept has been to recognize the members of the family as equivalent members of society. This change has been wrought by many individual laws, some of which pertain to franchise or occupation, others to the civil standing of women in the community. Some of these changes may be mentioned: women are now capable of and allowed to acquire and hold property, something they could not do before; prior to 1925 a mother in England did not possess the same rights as the father did of guardianship of her children; and divorce laws were changed in favor of the wife. Reciprocity is increasingly reflected in divorce laws. In some cases custom has changed ahead of the law.

Although laws placing women at a disadvantage have gradually been displaced by others giving women the same status as men, the increasing participation of women in trade and industry has led to the introduction of many laws protecting, but at the same time limiting, the activities of women. These laws are justified insofar as they take into account the physical difference of women, but not if they limit their rights and privileges, as, for instance, the discrimination which allows lower wages or salaries for women performing the same service as men.

Enfranchisement

In recent history the vote has proved to be a most powerful means to change when used by an organized group. This was appreciated by the early champions of women's rights. If a woman could vote, she could enforce the correction of many injustices. In spite of Condorcet's efforts, suffrage was not extended to women through the French Revolution; and because this movement soon became unpopular in the Anglo-Saxon countries, the cause did not gain impetus until about the middle of the nineteenth century.

The agitation for women's vote was more intense in the United States than in England. There are isolated examples before the Revolution of women's participation in political decision-making. Women who were property holders in Massachusetts voted as early as 1691. The Continental Congress debated the issue at length, but finally decided that the decision regarding women's right to vote should be left with the individual states. Through the years individuals and groups consistently advocated the enfranchisement of women; among them were the American Quakers; the American patriot Thomas Paine; clergymen Henry Ward Beecher and Wendell Phillips, and writer Ralph Waldo

Emerson. The antislavery movement accelerated the suffragist activities. It was led by Lucretia Mott and Elizabeth Cady Stanton and supported by the Quakers. As a result of their activity, the first Women's Rights Convention met in Seneca Falls, New York, in 1848. During the next few years the movement continued to gain strength. It received wide publicity in the press, and soon other leaders joined in. Most famous among these was Susan B. Anthony who remained actively interested until her death in 1906.

Suffragists were called "the shrieking sisterhood," labeled as unfeminine, and accused of such features as immorality. This may sound quite familiar to readers who hear such terms as "women's libber" with negative connotations.

After the Civil War the Abolitionists pushed for a constitutional amendment that would grant voting rights to all male Americans including ex-slaves. For fear that the amendment would suffer defeat, feminist leaders such as Elizabeth Stanton interpreted the law to extend voting privileges to women but were unsuccessful in a subsequent election to cast a ballot. Susan Anthony's subsequent arrest and trial aroused widespread public visibility and lent impetus to the feminist movement. Much effort was invested at state and federal levels to gain support. Beginning with the state of Wyoming in 1890, individual states granted women the vote, but it was not until after World War I that the Nineteenth Amendment to the Constitution was ratified and became law.

A parallel movement took place in Great Britain but as its height was a more vigorous and violent battle. Bombing, boycotting, picketing, and other forceful and provocative behavior prompted incidence of manhandling by the police. Subsequently most of the nations of the world have granted the franchise to women. As a result, women's rights have broadened throughout the world. Feminist groups have moved to gain the right to serve on juries, to retain earnings and property after marriage, to retain citizenship after marriage to an alien, and to equal pay and equal job opportunity. The latter has been of great concern to nurses.

In England early efforts were made between 1840 and 1850 when suffrage for women was advocated by such men as Cobden, Disraeli, and Hume. The most potent protagonist, however, was John Stuart Mill, who entered Parliament in 1865, having placed women's suffrage in his election address. Later he published his *Subjection of Women,* which had a tremendous influence. Women now began to organize themselves and to present petitions to Parliament. When a reform bill was to be introduced in 1884, they thought that they stood a good chance of achieving their goal; however, Gladstone killed the bill through the treason of 104 liberal members. The movement became greatly discouraged, although at this time women gained the right to participate in local government.

The movement had to pass through more troubled waters in England. After the setback in 1884 it grew without any dramatic events until 1897 when a national union was formed of the various smaller societies. This step strengthened the effort. In 1903 the Women's Social and Political Union was formed; this was the famous organization that for the next decade, under the leadership of Mrs. Pankhurst, was to obtain such notoriety. Offhand the new union changed tactics. Formerly each candidate for office had been questioned on his views, but this method had achieved nothing. Now the union applied directly to the government, and as the liberal party came into power in 1906, it was hoped that it would be more favorable than the previous conservative rule. Instead the new government handled the suffragettes roughly, and when they attempted to hold a meeting, they were brutally thrown into the street and eventually into prison. The ensuing notoriety gave a

tremendous impetus to the movement; they now began to adopt "militant" tactics with parades, heckling of ministers when they appeared on public platforms, and general disturbances—all in the name of propaganda. Their efforts showed the world what determined propaganda could do: everybody all over the world was talking about them, and the papers carried pictures of their activities, with the result that the movement became tremendously popular. New societies sprang up everywhere, and the membership grew by leaps and bounds. In 1907 they organized their first public demonstration, and on a rainy afternoon 3,000 women marched through London; soon one mass meeting followed another, and no one could move anywhere in England without encountering their propaganda.

After a while the suffragettes became so violent that they had to be arrested; in prison they went on hunger strikes and had to be released, and immediately they resumed their tactics. To combat hunger strikes the "cat and mouse" act was passed, whereby prisoners who refused to eat could be rearrested when they had recovered their health. A few efforts on the part of individual members to introduce bills failed, and finally in 1910 a committee was organized under Lord Lytton for the purpose of drafting an acceptable bill. Even this effort came up against the unyielding resistance of the government under H. H. Asquith. The struggle reached its climax when the government, in 1911, proposed to introduce a new franchise bill, "for male persons only." New and violent protests followed, but in decisive matters Parliament supported the government, and seemingly the suffragettes made no progress.

The suffragettes now decided to support the party that would further their cause. This happened to be the labor party. By 1913 they believed that they had public opinion behind them, and they did. The government's cause was virtually lost; Brit-

ish women would probably have been en-
franchised if World War I had not begun in
1914 and all efforts turned toward winning
the war. The Women's Social and Political
Union was dissolved, and the National Union
undertook war relief work; the women thus
gained even greater favor in public opinion. Finally in 1917 a conference called by
the Speaker of the House of Commons
(that is, the government) recommended
that the vote be given to householders and
wives of householders. A bill drafted along
these lines was passed in the House of Commons by a majority of 7 to 1 and soon became law. The next year women became
eligible to run for Parliament, and in 1919
Viscountess Astor was elected. The experience with women's franchise was so entirely
favorable during the next ten years that by
1928 women were given voting rights similar to those of men, and the movement came
to a successful close.

Women's suffrage apparently has not ma-
terially altered the course of Anglo-Saxon
civilization, but it has given to women a potential power with which they can support
any movement in which they choose to
take interest. Although women's suffrage
may never be given any bias as a whole
(the women's vote has in general been divided along party lines similar to those of
the male vote), protecting the rights of
women before the law in the professions
and in the labor market is always extant. A
movement such as the state (or national)
registration of nurses would always receive
a more favorable treatment in the hands of
legislators if it were to be backed by nurses
as voters rather than by a disfranchised profession. Therefore this whole movement,
now successfully completed, has been of
the greatest value and may be of still
greater potential value in the progress of
American nursing.

Education

The placing of women on an equal foot-
ing with men, before the law, had politically enabled them to seek careers comparable to those of men. Furthermore, it became
necessary to give them educational facilities
equal to those that were offered to men.
Early in the nineteenth century it was difficult for a young woman to obtain an education except through private tutoring, which
was very expensive and therefore limited to
a privileged few. Thus Miss Nightingale received much of her education from her father and by travel and social contact. There
was no "college" to which she could have
been sent. If there had been, the evolution
of nursing might have developed quite differently. As it is, the growth of colleges and
universities for women has profoundly affected nursing education; therefore a short
review of this is in order.

Before 1800 occasional schools in America had been open to girls, but educational
opportunities for women were practically
nonexistent until 1821, when Emma Willard
opened a Female Seminary at Troy, New
York. "Academies" and "seminaries" soon
followed in various parts of the East, and
about the middle of the century the public
high schools, which were coeducational,
were extensively established. Higher education for women, however, lagged somewhat
behind; the first colleges open to women
were Oberlin in Ohio (1833) and Wheaton
at Norton, Massachusetts (1835). Mount
Holyoke also dates from this early period,
having been established in 1857. A number
of other colleges were established during
the next thirty or forty years. Outstanding
among them was Vassar, which opened in
Poughkeepsie, New York, in 1865; it is remarkable for its high educational standards,
which have been maintained from the first.

During the latter part of the century,
when higher education for women became
more generally recognized, large numbers
of institutions all over the country admitted
women. Some of them were separate colleges for women; others were established
within already existing universities, some of
these being coeducational. Among colleges

for women established during this period, Smith, Wellesley, and Bryn Mawr became outstanding. Mount Holyoke also obtained a college charter (1888). Simmons College in Boston was established in 1899 for the specific purpose of preparing women for independent professional careers. Tulane University in New Orleans and Western Reserve in Cleveland were the first universities to open their doors to women (1887 and 1888) and soon others followed their example. The University of Chicago was established in 1893 on the basis that it should be open in equal measure to men and women. To mention them all would be tedious; in general, not only did the number of women admitted to college increase but also the educational standards of institutions admitting them advanced rapidly during this period.

These colleges and universities have maintained very high standards. All the good ones have had their pick of students, with the result that their material to start with was superior; they had been led by educators of vision who had emphasized the liberal arts education as applied to the individual, with the result that more and more of their graduates have sought and qualified for distinguished professional careers. The American Association of University Women, established in 1915, has been active in creating opportunities, often by establishing fellowships for the advanced education of women, with the result that an increasing number of women have obtained the degree of doctor of philosophy. Most of these women enter advanced teaching or research in the physical sciences, where they are beginning to occupy more of the important posts.

The participation of the nursing profession as a whole in the development of the education of women will be extensively discussed later; in addition, we may note that an increasing number of women seeking professional education go into nursing.

Thus it will be clear that the advances made in the education of women form an important integral part of the professional evolution of nursing.

Occupational emancipation

Perhaps some of the early emancipators of women visualized a world in which woman took a place in society in all respects similar to that of man. Obviously that dream has not been and is not likely to be realized. As long as the family remains the unit of Western Civilization, the larger proportion of women's efforts will be concerned with homemaking and child rearing. Therefore, although the growing freedom of women has resulted in their admission to most occupations, this movement has encountered certain countercurrents of considerable power.

Experience has shown that, physically and temperamentally, women are less suited than men for certain pursuits although they are eminently fitted for others. In certain professions women still constitute a small percentage, and it is of great significance that this percentage in some instances tends to decrease proportionately to men. There are still perhaps fewer women physicians in private practice now than there were a few decades ago. It has also been found necessary to protect women in the labor market by limiting their participation in certain activities by law; for instance in England women may not be employed in mines below ground, and they are protected by special hour and wage regulations. On the other hand, some professions are unique. It must be acknowledged that in nursing, for example, women have maintained a status of superiority in the sense that positions in the profession, even in the highest national offices, remain largely occupied by women.

Thus, as far as the participation of women in occupations and professions is concerned, the movement is finding a level consistent with the compatibility of women for the various tasks.

Another important countercurrent is survival of the old attitude toward women—"prejudice", it is often called—although it is not strictly so, but rather survival of a view that formerly was both justifiable and proper. This, however, is waning steadily, and it is slowly being realized that women should be admitted to any place or career in society for which they are constitutionally and educationally fitted without the handicap of old custom.

Rise of socialism

The social reformers of the early part of the nineteenth century were promoting ideas of philanthropic enterprises on the part of those who were privileged to be in a position in which they could carry them out. The power of the organized lower classes was not prominent in the reforms that they suggested, although an awareness of the powers of the French Revolution existed, as is evidenced in the writings of both Carlyle and Dickens. The impulse that eventually was to stimulate action by the workers themselves was to come from another source. About the middle of the century Karl Marx wrote *Das Kapital,* and he and Engels founded the socialistic movement that was directly or indirectly to influence so much political thinking and action. The socialistic way of thinking shifted the center of gravity in society. The industrial system, so far, had acknowledged individual freedom to act and to extract from one's fellowmen whatever one could within the law. The state was for the protection of the individual, but it had no obligation to him. According to the socialistic doctrine, it is the duty of the individual to give his work to the state; in return this state will see that he receives his full share of the proceeds of his labors. In the socialistic state all are politically equal. As this aimed at abolition of political and economic privilege, the masses had but one means to enforce their demands: to organize.

Organized labor movements began to develop in Europe during the second half of the nineteenth century, slowly at first, but gradually gaining momentum. Organized labor advanced in Europe much more quickly than in America, where the labor unions are of relatively recent origin. Consequently the by-products of labor organization, with which we are particularly concerned, developed more gradually in America than in Europe. The chief enemies of the laboring man are old age, sickness, exploitation, and unemployment. It is therefore reasonable that requests for protection from these enemies would soon be added to demands for improved working conditions and would become important objects of social legislation.

Social legislation

At the same time, retained from feudalism was the concept of sovereignty of the head of the state—"L'etat, c'est moi," proclaimed Louis XIV—and that was the view to which most persons acquiesced. It was therefore the monarch or his representative who personified more than anyone else the practical aspects of this philosophy. The common man is the principal asset of the state, and the personification of the state is the monarch; this is the absolute monarchy. The state became a dynamic entity that, depending chiefly on the industrial centers of the cities, competed with other states for trade monopolies and far-flung colonies. This was the era in which colonial empires were built.

This political philosophy had one interesting result: since it was realized that the power of the monarch ultimately depended on the number and opulence of his subjects, the monarch became concerned for their welfare. This led to the enlightened monarchy, which was one of the most efficient forms of government ever devised by man. Its defect was the lack of checks and balances that would become effective when the monarch ceased to be benevolent, and that was the cause of its ultimate doom.

There were other currents of thought that were to influence people in the future. The philosophers of the seventeenth century who had accepted the right of property and of free contract soon began to ask by what right the sovereign owned the state and by what right he collected tax monies to be spent on his own personal ambitions rather than on the common good. The answer soon was found—by the acquiescence of his subjects. This doctrine of consent of the governed led directly to the political philosophy of the eighteenth century engendered by Rousseau, Voltaire, and Hume.

These political philosophies led to a reevaluation of human rights and to the new concept of political liberty. Once the people understood that concept, the Boston Tea Party was inevitable, leading as it must to the American Revolution and then to the French Revolution. The citizen is no longer the chattel of the sovereign; he is the state, and "citizen" became in France an appellation of honor. The French Revolution and the American Revolution were not revolutions in the sense that the proletariat was placed in power, as occurred in the Russian Revolution a century later. The absolute power of the head of the state was abolished and replaced with a constitutional form of government—immediately in America and eventually in Europe—in which the real power was placed in the hands of the bourgeoisie, the propertied classes.

Among the problems that society faced during the early industrial era was the condition in hospitals. The advances in medicine were so far largely theoretical and had not yet borne practical fruits; while medicine definitely was advancing, it was still proceeding slowly and without the dramatic developments that were to mark the end of the nineteenth century. The hospitals were large and crowded, and the conditions of nursing, which were brought about by the Reformation when the Catholic institutions were closed, had been steadily aggravated until they reached an all-time low.

Patients with mental diseases had been treated with cruel restraint, and it was thought proper to exhibit them to spectators for a small fee. So a visit to see the sights of London included a visit to "Bedlam," as the Hospital of St. Mary of Bethlehem was eventually called in common parlance. The building was wrecked in 1676 and a new and magnificent structure took its place, which lasted until 1812 when a last and final structure was commenced.

For many years Bedlam played an important part in London life. Fiction writers sent their characters to languish within its walls, and artists painted its terrors; probably Hogarth's final state of *A Rake's Progress* was as pictorial a representation of lunacy as was ever accomplished. Awe was inspired by a public exhibition, the horrors of which exceeded the imagination.

The first moves for sickness and unemployment legislation were not initiated by the labor movement iself but by Bismarck in Germany, who thought that by anticipating the demands of labor he could control its development. The passing of legislation in Germany protecting labor against sickness and unemployment has progressed even during the more recent periods when the electorate was relatively impotent. Another effect of Bismarck's reform, one that he perhaps did not anticipate, was that it established a precedent and acknowledgment of the obligation of the state to the underprivileged. From this time the reevaluation of the rights of man, which had been going on throughout the century, became rapidly accentuated. The right of life, liberty, and the pursuit of happiness was given an even more liberal interpretation, except perhaps as far as liberty was concerned. The modern era has seen industry increasingly regulated: hours have been shortened, health and safety requirements regarding workshops have been steadily improved and better enforced, and there has been a steady trend in wage increase. Altogether the present age has been one of social and industrial reform foreshadowed in the preceding century; these reforms are still far from completed.

Extension of medical care

The seventeenth century had seen two great principles established: (1) disease is to be observed like any other natural phenomenon and (2) the functions of the human body can be investigated by means of physiological experiments. A third great principle was to be added: symptoms and disturbances of function are associated with changes in the organs of the body and this relation is frequently very specific. It is to Giovanni Morgagni (1682-1771) that we owe this contribution.

His principal work, *On the Seats and Causes of Disease*, appeared in 1761 when he was 79 years old. He insisted on examining every organ, as well as the one that he suspected of being chiefly affected. Only after exhaustive investigation would he allow the inference that the organ referred to either was or was not the seat of the disease. He created a work of classical importance and beauty, which even today delights the mind of the scholar.

Morgagni came to reap the highest honors bestowed on living men. He was a friend of popes and princes, honored by all the scientific groups of importance in Europe, sought by every student of medicine; he died beloved by his family in his eighty-ninth year. Twice when hostile armies invaded his town, their commanders gave strict orders that no harm come to Morgagni and that his work be not hampered. His wife, who could not have been surpassed in judgment or affection, bore him eleven children—eight daughters who all became nuns, one son who died young, one son who became a Jesuit priest, and one son who married and reared a family.

In Delft, Holland, an unlettered man had the honor of first using the microscope systematically and of perfecting its construction. Anton van Leeuwenhoek (1632-1723) lived quietly, pursuing his microscopic studies and communicating most of his observations to the Royal Society.

In spite of the great leaders who had risen in the seventeenth century, British practice and the teaching of medicine and surgery fell to a low ebb by the middle of the eighteenth century. Obstetrics as a science was just being founded through the efforts of William Smellie (1669-1763). But that was about all. Then suddenly anatomy, surgery, and obstetrics received a great impetus through the efforts of the brothers John and William Hunter. Alike in their zeal and industry for the advancement of science, they otherwise differed most strikingly.

William (1718-1783), the elder, was born in 1718 near Glasgow, where he received his early classical and professional education. Still in his youth he, like so many celebrated Scots, gravitated to London. He became associated with Dr. Smellie, the first male-midwife, founder of obstetrics. He was one of those fortunate few who early in life were placed exactly in the situation for which they were best suited by nature and by education. Given the opportunity to teach anatomy, he soon found himself in charge of the most famous school in the country, and turning to obstetrics he advanced rapidly and eventually became obstetrician to the queen. In spite of his success, he never let financial considerations crowd out his professional ideas. He realized that a man may do infinitely more good for the public by teaching his art than by practicing it because the influence of the teacher extends over a whole nation and descends to posterity. So Hunter continued to combine in himself the qualities of a polite scholar, an accomplished gentleman, a complete anatomist, and a most perfect demonstrator as well as lecturer. *The Pregnant Uterus* is his main work, which for all time will stand as a landmark in medical literature.

In contrast to the polished William, John Hunter (1728-1793), ten years younger, was considered a misfit for the first twenty years of his life. Not until his brother had introduced him to the art and science of anatomy did his native ability assert itself, but from that day John developed into one of the greatest geniuses of all time. His great intellectual powers triumphed over his early defective training, and he marched onward step by step, despite vast obstacles, to the highest achievements. After serving a term in the army, he became surgeon to St. George's Hospital, and he gradually acquired the leading surgical practice in London. In contrast to his brother, his progress was slow, for he did not possess the charming manners of William but had to advance by sheer ability. In fact, to the end of his days he remained crude in his expressions and highly undiplomatic; for instance, he generally gave precedence to his poorer patients, saying they had no time to spare, whereas the wealthy ones, having nothing to do, could afford to wait.

Although he had never read Bacon, his mode of studying was as strictly Baconian as if he had. Characteristic is his answer to Edward Jenner (1749-1823), his student: "But why think? Why not try the experiment?" Yet he himself was so busy in his search for knowledge and so cautious in his estimate of it that he always delayed to publish what he knew. He was 43 years old when he published his first work, and at his death he left many valuable manuscripts and notes, which, to the inestimable loss to the world, were destroyed by his brother-in-law.

A wave of enthusiasm was apparent in France after the French Revolution. Young men now advanced by ability and no longer by privilege and nepotism. This also applied to medicine, and in that century medical science advanced as never before. Beginning with Napoleon's own physician, Jean Nicolas Corvisart (1755-1821), the list runs through François Xavier Bichat (1771-1802), the pathologist, who unfortunately died young; Réné Laennec (1781-1826), to whom we owe the stethoscope and our knowledge of diseases of the chest; to Pierre Louis (1787-1872), who first introduced statistical methods into medicine and who, more than the others, attracted young American students, especially the pathetic figure of James Jack-

son, Jr., whom he considered almost like a son. The famous school of Dublin, which soon was to shine with the names of Robert Graves (1796-1853); William Stokes (1804-1878), Robert Adams (1791-1875), and Dominic Corrigan (1802-1880), had not yet reached its climax; on the continent Karl Rokitansky (1804-1878) and Rudolf Virchow (1821-1902) were not yet famous. By the middle of the eighteenth century interest in real clinical medicine was being stimulated; for example, decisions were based on examination of the patient and the diseased organs rather than on the study of classical texts and the use of metaphysical discussion.

One of the most successful clinicians of the century was William Heberden (1710-1801). Among other things for which he is remembered is the description of angina pectoris, which has been made available to modern student in reprints. He also described the rheumatic nodules on the fingers called "Heberden's nodes."

William Withering (1741-1799) is remembered for the discovery of the use of foxglove (digitalis) for dropsy.

While nursing was in a very bad condition during this period, medicine was advancing rapidly. During the first part of the eighteenth century Hermann Boerhaave (1668-1738) of Leyden, the Netherlands, was easily the most famous physician of Europe. Princes and statesmen alike crowded his waiting room. When he appeared after he had been sick, the whole town was illuminated, rejoicing in his recovery. A letter from a Chinese mandarin, addressed "To the illustrious Dr. Boerhaave, Physician in Europe," found him without difficulty. His greatest contribution was his pupils. There was hardly a prominent physician in Europe and North America who had not at some time studied under him. He occupied several university chairs at the same time and excelled in wisdom and classical knowledge. He was one of the first great physicians who appreciated music. When he died in 1738, he left a large fortune of about 2 million florins.

Although Bedlam presented the horrors of maltreatment of mental disease, it was also responsible for the first rays of the new dawn. It was in connection with the tortures sustained by one American, James Norris, that William Tuke, a York tea merchant in 1792, suggested that mental disease be treated along humane lines. His plea was without immediate effect, but it was the next year that the Frenchman Pinel introduced the famous reform of the treatment of mental patients. When reform did occur, the Bethlehem Hospital was again in the vanguard and has taken its place among modern hospitals devoted to the treatment of mental disease. Tuke's work did have an important effect in the United States, for when the Bloomingdale Asylum was opened in 1821 in connection with the New York Hospital, it was modeled after Tuke's "York Retreat" and emphasized the mild and humane treatment of the patients.

The study of the laws of population growth was one extension of earlier medical care and was a part of the new field of public health (this will be discussed later in this chapter). The study of population is but a short step away from the study of economics. This, however, was not accepted without public scrutiny and criticism. Gresham founded the science of public finance, and soon the men who guided the new thinking arrived at certain conclusions that, by their general acceptance, were to exert a fundamental influence on subsequent proliferation of social legislative programs, medical care programs, and industry and public health efforts.

An ever-increasing demand for hospitals and medical and nursing services followed. This demand had an economic aspect: to increase interest in the cost of medical care in its broadest sense. Efforts continue to find means by which health care can be distributed in such a manner that families are not financially crippled in case of severe illness and those in society who cannot afford medical care can receive it in a properly orga-

nized manner without having to accept it as a more or less accidental charity. The attempts to distribute the cost of medical care have led to the development of numerous programs; the Krankenkasse system in Germany, the panel system in England, and group hospitalization and sickness insurance by private insurance companies in the United States are but examples of a field so vast that it requires special study to be understood in its entirety. Extending medical care has been met with resistance, the chief and general argument being that it would lead to "socialized" medicine.

By this is meant that it interfered with professional freedom and initiative of those engaged in the healing art. This conflict has many aspects. In Western Civilization as a whole such schemes have progressed at an accelerated pace. Suffice it to say that this evolution of the healing art is of the greatest significance for nursing, for it continuously widens the scope of nursing practice: new and larger hospitals are built, public health activities continue to expand, and new categories of positions continue to become available. In later chapters these developments will be discussed further against the background just described.

Industrial Revolution

During this same eighteenth century, industrialism, which so far had been very primitive, developed into the Machine Age; the steam engine had now been invented. It multiplied man's power in the factory, and eventually the railroad and the steamship revolutionized transportation. Now factories could be placed near the chief source of their raw materials.

Machines still had to be tended laboriously by men and were not the laborsaving devices of today. The chief motor power was manpower; therefore the men of mercantilism began to welcome increases in population, because these increases in manpower would eventually mean increases in wealth.

England became the first great nation of factories, but certain elements that were part of that development later had to be discarded. Views on the right of property and on national ambition led to an economic and political philosophy that had been called mercantilism. Property was the watchword, especially property represented by holdings of precious metals or bullion. To obtain these metals foreign trade had to be encouraged, even at the cost of domestic trade. Because trade flourishes when a country has a product to sell, preferably a manufactured product, the importance of manufacturing was stressed. To be able to produce finished goods was considered preferable to producing the raw materials from which these goods were manufactured because the profit was greater.

All during the eighteenth century and at an accentuated pace during the nineteenth century, England forged ahead of the industrial countries. There were many reasons for this: her capitalists had apparently been more awakened by the new philosophies than had been those of her continental confreres; she understood first what production for the masses really implied; her isolated position had largely protected her against the devastation of wars; she was traditionally a nation of sailors; and when it came to getting colonies, she got the lion's share, including the plum of them all—India. The greatness of the British Empire was to a large extent built on the riches of India. And so England is looked on as the leader of the Machine Age and consequently as the source of many of the movements that were direct results of this age.

Within the society of the United States, social reforms are premised on the ability of the industrial system to carry its share of the burden. One needs to consider how industrialism became so prosperous. During feudalism, most people were occupied full-time simply in obtaining food and other basic commodities. With the advent of the machine, there was greater emphasis on the sav- ing of time that could be used for other work or for leisure ("leisure" being defined as any activity other than productive labor, that is, education and engaging in luxury trade). As machines became increasingly efficient, this saving of time increased at an almost incredible rate. A quotation from A. J. Todd serves as an example:

It has been calculated that to copy by hand a volume of 100,000 words would require 14 days and cost approximately $54.40; to write 1,000 copies would require 44 years, 45 weeks and 2 days and cost $54,400. To do the same work with a modern power press would require some preliminary work which the author estimates would occupy 96 days and cost some $1,780, but once that was done, 1,000, and as many additional thousands of copies could be run off at less than a cent a copy in less than 10 hours. This example could be amplified by thousands more all showing how the machines increase efficiency and save time.[*]

This tremendous advance applies not only to the production of goods but also to their transportation. For example, modern transport renders it more profitable to carry letters at 13¢ than it was to carry them at a dollar each when mail service was first established.

Further study makes it clear that a striking difference exists between poverty of feudalism and poverty of the modern Machine Age. Feudal poverty was inevitable, for the work of all the people could produce commodities barely above subsistence level, while the productive power of the modern industrial structure is such that it can produce ample commodities for all the people living under Western civilization if converted into production at full capacity. In present industrial society there are two causes of poverty: (1) society fails to provide an adequate distribution of its commodities or (2) the citizens at the bottom of the economic scale lack the capacity or education to acquire a reasonable share of the communal wealth.

---

[*]Todd, A. J.: Industry and society, New York, 1933, Henry Holt & Co., Inc., p. 109.

Public health

Along with studying the laws of nature, the philosophers of this era began to ask questions regarding the conduct and the rights of man. The right of contract earlier referred to was but one of their conclusions. They studied the laws that seemed to govern the growth of population; Petty founded the science of vital statistics, and Malthus showed that the population increased in a geometric ratio but that this increase was checked by various factors. These, in turn were studied by Davenant and de Mandeville. All this eventually led to the sciences concerning trends in population that are now fundamental to the field of public health. Although purely theoretical in the beginning, this knowledge is now of the greatest importance to the modern public health nurse.

Defective distribution of commodities, however intriguing, is too complex and outside the scope of this discussion. The second cause of poverty is, however, definitely our direct concern.

A certain measure of public health was appreciated by the proponents of mercantilism, but these concepts of public health were limited by restricted medical knowledge and furthermore were partly ignored when the absolute monarch disappeared; in fact, they were largely squeezed out by the aggressiveness of the new capitalist. As a type he was so impressed with the right of free contract and the right to acquire and to hold property that he forgot that when a man has only the choice between absolute starvation and starvation wages he is not really a free agent. The result was the early dark years of the Machine Age when the capitalist was protected by law in his exploitation of the worker under the guise of free contract. The result was child labor, sweatshops, unhygienic factories, and hours of labor fixed only by the limits of human endurance. This led to the gin shop (factory) and all the social evils that soon were to be graphically described by their reformers.

There is now general agreement that failure to achieve a reasonable standard of living can be traced in many cases to an unhygienic environment with resulting disease that is preventable or curable. The whole subject of hookworm anemia and the deficiency diseases as causes of chronic illness is pertinent. The prevalence of pediculosis and ringworm among the less-favored classes is another example. Gradually, although slowly, society accepted an ever-increasing responsibility for alleviating these problems. What resulted was the formulation of the first notions of public health.

Although factory towns of the eighteenth century may have appeared dingy by today's standards, nevertheless, they were far in advance of the dirty, smelly cities of the century before. Wealth accumulated, and many strata of the population improved their living conditions. It was also this outlook that, together with the rapid growth of the cities, was responsible for the rapid increase in hospital construction of this era.

Society's acceptance of responsibility was furthered by enlightened self-interest and an increasing realization that the wealth of a state depends primarily on the number and opulence (including health) of its citizens. This became particularly evident in the examinations of recruits for World War II. The practical realization of this truth led the government to assume a greater share in the prevention and treatment of preventable diseases. Consequently, medical care in city insitutions, veterans hospitals, or other governmental institutions increased both in the number of beds available and the quality of services offered.

The field of public health, sponsored by public and/or semipublic bodies, continued to expand. Corporations followed suit either because of pressure of public opinion, ever the severest taskmaster, or because they found it to their advantage to maintain a high standard of health and safety on their premises in order to avoid damages and compensations that they had paid in the past. As public goodwill became more important, many corporations and governmental bodies prided themselves in making known the health measures they sponsored. Organized health measures required more and better nursing; the Industrial Revolution and its collateral economic, political, and philosophical developments may be considered the soil that nurtured the growth of all the healing arts.

Medicine during the nineteenth century

A new development in our social structure, the rise and evolution of capitalism and industrialism, influenced the construction and administration of hospitals in the eighteenth and nineteenth centuries. Wealth was created by the manufacture of natural resources brought to the industrial countries from faraway colonies. Manufacture demanded factories, factories required workers, and the profits from individual enterprise went into relatively few pockets; therefore large numbers of people congregated in the new cities, and the gulf between the new-rich industrial employers on the one hand and the laborers on the other grew even wider. The result was that extensive sections in industrial cities were inhabited almost entirely by laborers. In sickness, these individuals required ever larger hospitals, and as a direct result of the Industrial Revolution the demand grew for bigger, but not always better, hospitals. Great city hospitals such as the London Hospital in the East End of London, the Grosse Charité in Berlin, and the Allgemeines Krankehause of Vienna originated during the eighteenth century. This development continued through the nineteenth century with the growth of the great cities.

The following notes, taken from the catalogue of the London Hospital, give an interesting account of its progress.

The first course of lectures on surgery was delivered in 1749. In 1772 iron bedsteads were first introduced. In 1780 surgeons were henceforth to be members of the company of surgeons in London. In 1781, Mr. Blizard was granted permission to deliver courses of lectures on anatomy and surgery. In 1791 a thermometer was purchased. In 1820 feather beds were bought for special cases. In 1833 gas was installed in the corridors, though not in the wards. In 1838 an ordinance was passed that medicine was to be administered only by nurses who could read and write. In 1842 special wards were set aside for Jewish patients. In 1849 a microscope was bought. In 1852 the committee held that the apothecary was not the fit person to administer chloroform. In 1856 Miss Florence Nightingale was elected life governor. In 1896 x-rays were introduced.

The pavilion system of hospital construction, introduced in the French Academy of Sciences in 1788, became generally accepted both in Europe and in this country. As implied in the name, the hospital consists of pavilions and is not built in large blocks as was hitherto the case. Examples include the outstandingly beautiful Bispebjerg Hospital in Copenhagen and the first buildings of the Johns Hopkins Hospital in Baltimore. The eighteenth century also saw the introduction of better hygiene throughout hospitals, from the nursing service to the plumbing and heating, because the old hospitals had been very cold and unsanitary places. Florence Nightingale, although she failed to appreciate the significante of bacteriology, thoroughly understood the value of fresh air, soap and water, and sunshine. This all preceded the antiseptic and aseptic operating room.

During the nineteenth century there was also a tendency to develop hospitals for various specialties. This reached its height in London where the start was made with the Royal London Ophthalmic Hospital, which was founded in 1804 and which was followed by many others, including the Royal Free Hospital run for women by women doctors, St. John's Hospital for diseases of the skin, and the Royal Victoria Hospital for diseases of the chest. Some appeared in this country until the disadvantages of such specialization appeared. The trend has now been modified so that separate departments are developed within the same hospital, easily accessible to each other.

As hospitals developed, it also became apparent that the hospital's responsibility toward the patient did not always end with his discharge. Aftercare for the ambulatory or availability of experienced hospital staff to those not sick enough to gain or able to afford admittance to the ward became logical reasons to establish outpatient departments in connection with the hospitals. Although dispensaries, that is, clinics in which poor patients could be seen free and could obtain medicine at cost or free, had been organized in the beginning of the eighteenth century, the outpatient department idea was not thoroughly developed until near the end of the nineteenth century. When it was developed, the possibilities for medical teaching that it offered were first grasped and best developed in England. The United States was slower to appreciate the excellent source of clinical material found in the outpatient department.

The vigorous intellectual, political, and social activity of the nineteenth century affected medicine, resulting in a remarkable development in America as well as in all the European countries. Some of the outstanding men and their contributions will be outlined briefly, but the reader is referred to books on the history of medicine for the complete discussion of this fascinating period. During this period the tendency to specialize in a single clinical field had its beginning. General physicians practicing in all branches of medicine became proportionately fewer in number; this trend was encouraged.

Ignatz Philipp Semmelweis (1818-1865). One of the most tragic figures of medicine—Semmelweis—was the genius who banished childbirth fever from maternity hospitals. Hungarian by birth, he was assistant at the second Vienna clinic about 1845 when the death rate from puerperal sepsis had reached the appalling figure of 10% of all those delivered. At the same time, it was only about 3%

Ignatz Philipp Semmelweis

Ignatz Semmelweis had a share in the "emancipation of women" by helping to free them from the specter of puerperal fever.

at the first clinic. Medical students were taught at the second clinic, pupil midwives at the first. Semmelweis proved that the high rate of death at the second clinic was caused by the filthy habits of the students. They were dissecting and doing postmortem work at the same time that they took their obstetrical work. Often they walked directly from the postmortem room and proceeded to examine a women in labor without washing their hands. Rubber gloves were not used in those days. Semmelweis showed that this practice was the cause of the appalling mortality; the fever was caused by decomposing organic matter that had gained access to the mother's system through the generative organs that were traumatized during childbirth. He also showed that other sources could cause it—the examining hand could carry the infection from woman to woman and from infections occurring elsewhere in the body of other patients. Most important, he demonstrated that the infection could be prevented by cleaning the hands with a solution of chlorinated lime before examinations. This work was done before Pasteur began his great task.

Semmelweis died young, at the age of 47 years. His biography is the story of the fight to gain recognition of an idea. In having to wait long years for the victory of his discovery, Semmelweis shared the fate of Harvey, Jenner, and many others. Semmelweis was met by his contemporaries not only with antagonism but also with derision—he was called "the fool from Pesth."

In America, Oliver Wendell Holmes (father of the chief justice of the Supreme Court) has been extolled as the hero who with Semmelweis conquered the scourge. In fact, the contagiousness of puerperal fever had been suggested by him, before Semmelweis published his papers, in a paper *On the Contagiousness of Puerperal Fever* (1843). Holmes was agreeable to his friends and clever with his pen, whereas Semmelweis was difficult to get along with and an awkward writer. Although Holmes held the professorship of anatomy at Harvard and Dartmouth, he is now remembered mainly for his wit and clever pen. His work on pueperal sepsis was his most important contribution to medicine.

Another person with whom it is tempting to compare Semmelweis is Lord Lister (1827-1912), who in 1883 visited Pesth where he learned of the fate of this unfortunate man. Studying the lives of these two men offers a good opportunity to learn the effect of circumstance on the association of fame and genius. Why should Semmelweis's life have been such a tragedy while Lister's was a triumph? The work of Semmelweis was advanced for his time; he died in 1865 before Pasteur's great work was accepted, the year Lister began his researches. Semmelweis had a small and unimportant promoter. Lister's promoter was his father-in-law, the master surgeon of his day in Great Britain, Mr. James Syme (1799-1870). "There are few things more encouraging to aspiring youth than a strong and triumphant master; few things more discouraging than an unpretentious or timorous one." Semmelweis died at the age of 47 years; Lister did not experience his final triumph until 1879 when he was 52 years old. Semmelweis had difficulty with his environment; Lister was never known to speak a sharp word to a house surgeon, dresser, or anyone in his employ. Lister was fortunate in finding prompt support. If circumstances had been different, Semmelweis might have attained a fame as great as that of Lister.

Joseph Lister (1827-1912). Joseph, Lord Lister, the father of modern surgery, was born in 1827, the son of a well-to-do Quaker merchant. He received his early medical training in London, after which he went to Edinburgh and became the house surgeon of Syme, whose daughter he afterward married. In due course, partly through Syme's influence, he became professor of surgery in Edinburgh. In 1877 he came to London where he worked until his retirement.

When Lister entered the surgical wards he found a condition as bad as that found by Semmelweis in the obstetrical wards. Particularly, he was impressed by the huge mortality from sepsis following compound fracture

Joseph, Lord Lister

This photograph was taken about the time Lister discovered antisepsis. (From Smith, Alice Lorraine: Principles of microbiology, ed. 6, St. Louis, 1969, The C. V. Mosby Co.)

and amputation. After much thought and experimentation, he discovered that if wounds were cleansed with carbolic acid and were kept clean, sepsis did not occur. Out of these observations he developed his antiseptic surgical technique. Although his results were conclusive, his methods were accepted slowly, for it not only takes a great man to make an important discovery but it also takes a great man to be the next to adopt it. Saxtorph of Copenhagen was, in this case, the first to adopt Lister's method, and soon it spread to Germany, France, and elsewhere. England and America were very slow to appreciate Lister's methods. However, by 1879 the evidence in Lister's favor was so overwhelming that it enforced the acceptance of Lister's principles, which since then have guided all surgical work.

Lister, on every occasion, recognized his debt to the genius of Louis Pasteur (1822-1895), whose germ theory supplied the missing link in his reasoning. The assumption of pathogenic bacteria made everything clear. If this effect of great minds on each other could have happened a few years earlier, another of the greatest catastrophes of history could have been avoided, that is, the casualties from wound infections during the Franco-German war when for the first time the modern war machine was unleashed.

Rudolf Virchow (1821-1902). In 1881 an international medical congress was held in London under the presidency of Sir James Paget. Among the many thousands attending were some already famous and many destined to become so later. Among them were these four, each of a different national heritage: the Latin Pasteur, the Teuton Virchow, the Anglo-Saxon Lister, and the young and relatively unknown Celt Osler, who had come from Montreal with his chief, Palmer Howard.

Eldest of these was Virchow. Born in 1821, he soon displayed an interest in natural history which, as so often happens, became supplanted by the love of medicine. He combined a brilliant mind with great in-

Rudolf Virchow

Rudolf Virchow is justly famed for his many contributions to medical knowledge. His greatest work was probably as a pathologist.

dustry, and in his twenties the young professor occupied the chair of pathology at the University of Berlin. With the exception of a few years spent at Würzburg, largely for political reasons, he remained in this position until his death at the age of 81. The mind of this intellectual giant was enormous. His fame is founded in his many different contributions to medicine, but he is famous in his own right in many different sciences. He is possibly the greatest pathologist who ever lived. His conception of the cellular changes of disease transformed the entire outlook of the scientific world. Besides his fundamental contribution, he founded or contributed to our knowledge of leukemia, thrombus formation, tumors, septicemia, and much else. Under his direction about 50,000 postmortem examinations were performed. He founded and personally edited the first 170 volumes of his *Archives.* He was also active in politics; he became associated with the liberal movement of 1848 and suffered for his views.

After the age of 50, at the time when most men willingly slow down, Virchow became active and famous in the fields of anthropology and archeology. His knowledge and contributions were so great that people wondered how he could do this work and still remain a leader in pathology. He contributed to the science of public health; he studied the epidemics of typhus and did much to stamp them out. He helped plan the system of sewage disposal of Berlin. It was partly a result of his efforts that Germany for a while was leading the world in public health research. Virchow was active in the sanitation program of the German army in the war of 1870, in the heating and lighting of schools, in the organizing of the duties of school physicians, in the training of nurses, and in the organization of the medical profession into national and local associations. In short, his mind was encyclopedic.

Louis Pasteur (1822-1895). The son of a country tanner in moderate circumstances, he did not show any promise of genius at first. His father was one of Napoleon's veterans and instilled into his son a wholesome respect for truth and industry, love of family, and appreciation of the glory of his beloved France. Pasteur traveled one road from his youth to his death, but it was a mountainous one leading him, like the youth in "Excelsior," to ever-greater achievements. He began by solving the molecular structure of racemic acid. He then discovered the true nature of the fermentation of wine and of vinegar and of the production of beer. The relation of these substances to infectious processes and certain fortuitous circumstances led him to the study and eventual conquest of silkworm disease, anthrax, "swine fever," chicken cholera, and finally to the greatest of all his achievements—the preventive treatment of hydrophobia. Any one of these conquests would have assured him immortal fame.

He gave all his attention to his work; thus his wife wrote: "Your father is absorbed in his thoughts, he talks little, sleeps little, rises

Louis Pasteur

The genius of Pasteur, first evidenced by his discovery that polarization of light could be related to the structure of crystals, carried him to the solution of many problems: the spoilage of beers and wines with accompanying pasteurization process; the discovery of anaerobic bacteria, virus vaccines, and attenuation of virulence; and studies of spontaneous generation. His studies in immunology have rightly earned him a position as father of the science. (From Carpenter, P. L.: Microbiology, ed. 3, Philadelphia, 1972, W. B. Saunders Co.)

at dawn, and in one word continues the life I began with him 35 years ago." But with it all, Pasteur upheld the highest ideals. As he himself expressed it: "Blessed is he who carries within himself a God, an ideal, and who obeys this ideal of art, ideal of science, or ideal of gospel virtues; therein lie the springs of great thoughts and great actions. They all reflect light from the infinite." This was the man who established the science of bacteriology—and yet he never possessed a physician's diploma.

James Simpson and others. In 1847 James Simpson in Scotland discovered the use of chloroform, which was the leading anesthetic for many years until it was replaced by newer and safer drugs.

Psychiatry was first considered a separate branch of medicine toward the end of the eighteenth century. The most famous doctor associated with modern reform in the treatment of patients with mental illness was Philippe Pinel (1745-1826).

Concern for community hygiene and public health began to emerge during the eighteenth century. At that time there were no city sanitation departments, and open sewers ran through the streets into which people dumped all their garbage and waste. English doctors and medical societies became interested in trying to control communicable diseases as well as in treating them.

At about the same time that Dr. Jenner (1749-1823) discovered a vaccination against smallpox and initiated a first step in prevention of disease in England, Johann Peter Frank (1745-1821), an Austrian physician, was outlining the whole structure of modern systematic hygiene. He maintained that the government (state) should be responsible for the public health at all times rather than only during periods of serious epidemics or disaster. This was supported in the writings and activities of many nineteenth century social reformers.

Antituberculosis legislation was begun in Italy toward the end of the seventeenth century. Important in the dissemination of medical knowledge among practitioners was the development of medical journals, which began to appear in all countries during the eighteenth and nineteenth centuries. No longer were physicians attached only to the courts of princes; they also began to practice in towns and to appear in localities all over the civilized world.

Early reforms in nursing

Nurses participated in social reforms during the late nineteenth and early twentieth centuries. At the same time, nursing began to evolve beyond being only a set of skilled techniques necessary in scientific medicine to also providing community service in the areas of health and welfare. Following is a brief discussion of early reform and nursing as part of this evolution.

During the medieval era, men provided nursing care in military settings while women provided nursing care in religious settings. The inpatient duty of sisters was to minister to the spiritual needs of patients. As early as the sixteenth century, Ursuline Sisters emphasized care of the sick and the education of girls. This had its carryover into the United States as some of the earliest hospitals and schools were Ursuline.

The torch or lamp and night duty dates from the 1300s. Religious prejudice often determined lack of hygienic practices. Strong power of the church prevailed over nursing, while medicine had not developed sufficiently to have the control over nursing at that time. Nurses felt the impact of censures; the dark ages in religious history were also the dark ages in nursing. Whenever there was controversy, the religious dictates won out whether or not in the best interest of the patient.

The oath taken by nurses dates at least to about 1633. An annual rededication of oneself was planned by the community of the Sisters of Charity if the nurse did not wish to marry or carry on some other occupation but wanted to continue to nurse.

The secular nursing uniform followed naturally from the characteristic uniformity of dress common in religious orders.

Nursing sisters. It was realized that nursing, in and out of hospitals, was thoroughly unsatisfactory both in England and on the Protestant continent. Meanwhile, social liberation progressed slowly. Many men were lost in the frequent wars and women unable to find husbands were naturally looking for careers. Among them was Mrs. Elizabeth Gurney Fry (1780-1845), an outstanding social reformer in England, working to improve conditions in prisons.

In the British Isles the first efforts at systematic lay nursing institutions were made in Ireland by the Irish Sisters of Charity and the Sisters of Mercy. They antedate the modern deaconesses and orders sponsored by the Anglican church by a number of years and are more closely related to the Sisters of Charity of de Paul than to the later English orders.

The Irish Sisters of Charity was started by Mary Aikenhead (Sister Mary Augustine). In 1812 she and a friend went to the Convent of the Blessed Virgin Mary at York where they studied the work of nuns who practiced visiting among the poor, and in 1815 they began similar work in Dublin. Some years later they sent three sisters to study nursing at the Hôpital de la Pitié in Paris. When they came back, the sisters got their own house and hospital in Dublin, which later expanded into St. Vincent's Hospital, suggesting a relationship to the French order of Sisters of Charity.

The Sisters of Mercy was a similar order founded by Catherine Macaulay. It began as a home for destitute girls but soon included visitation of the sick and, by 1830, increasingly emphasized nursing. This order also sent branches to different parts of the world, and from the branch in Bermondsey near London some sisters went with Miss Nightingale to the Crimea. The order was brought to the United States in 1843 by Mother Warde. Among outstanding hospitals established from her efforts are the Mercy Hospitals in Chicago and Pittsburgh.

These orders are important as being the first modern nursing orders in the British Isles; they are, however, Catholic and derived from the French orders. They did not in their original conception embody the modern training school for nurses. This idea was first propounded by Dr. Robert Gooch, who around 1825 suggested that lay nursing orders should be established for women. The applicants should first be entered as pupil nurses in the big hospitals in London and Edinburgh, should be supplied with regular textbooks adapted to their needs, and should be regularly examined so that

their progress could be checked. After graduation they should, following the manner of the Beguines, go into the country or districts where they were to live together in small houses. This plan, excellent as it was, did not materialize for many years. Having worked to improve prison conditions, and following a discussion with him, Mrs. Fry became increasingly interested in nursing and established the order that inspired the Fliedners. With Dr. Gooch being a friend of Mrs. Fry's, it is not impossible that some of these ideas were conveyed to Mr. Fliedner and thus first materialized in Germany. Mr. Fliedner has been labeled the father of the deaconess movement.

Deaconesses at Kaiserswerth. The need for better nursing was being acknowledged in Germany. In Hamburg, Amelie Sieveking had organized 'The Friends of the Poor," who did home visiting and nursing. Efforts were being made to improve nursing in the hospitals and nursing manuals were being written. Still, it all lacked the spark of genius that was eventually to overshadow all similar efforts in Europe.

This spark was contributed by Theodor Fliedner and his wife, Fredericka. As a young minister Mr. Fliedner was called to Kaiserswerth near Düsseldorf. He found a community in the throes of an economic depression and little prospect of earning even a modest livelihood. However, in spite of tempting offers elsewhere, he decided to remain at his post and to travel abroad to raise funds necessary to work where he was.

In 1822 he traveled through Holland and England, and because he had introductions to all kinds of influential people, he was soon able to solve his financial problem. He also had the opportunity to study first-hand many efforts at relieving shame and suffering; in Holland he observed the work of the deaconesses, and in England he formed a close friendship with Elizabeth Fry, who allowed him to study her work in the prisons. He investigated schools, hospitals, almshouses, and other eleemosynary institutions so that he returned to Kaiserswerth one of the best-informed men in his field.

It took his wife and him many years to materialize their plans, and not until 1833 were they able to open their first refuge for discharged prisoners. However, the problem of the deaconesses lay closest to their hearts. They had seen what the Sisters of Mercy were able to do, and they appreciated the intrinsic value of the deaconesses. They also realized that a nursing organization such as they had in mind must be modernized to meet the demands of the times. The training had to be more systematic than it had been in the past, and the organization had to be more closely knit, although elastic enough to meet the most varied demands.

In 1836 they bought the biggest house they could find in Kaiserswerth, hoping somehow to pay for it later—which they did. Soon afterward their first patient, a servant girl, arrived, and Mrs. Fliedner persuaded her friend, Gertrude Reichardt, to enter as the first deaconess. Mrs. Reichardt was a doctor's daughter, middle-aged, who had already had extensive experience dealing with sick people in assisting her father with his practice. She arrived at the Kaiserswerth Hospital expecting little in the way of equipment, but even that was not there. Four bare walls and a patient were about all the new institution had to offer, and Gertrude Reichardt was just about ready to give up and go home when the first load of equipment unexpectedly arrived, and somehow the young hospital got started. By the end of that year there were six more deaconesses; eventually there were 120 deaconesses, and by 1842 the hospital had 200 beds.

Fredericka Fliedner had a marvelous talent for organizing, and soon each girl found herself in charge of her own autonomous department. To complete their training, the deaconesses rotated from service to service, all the while receiving systematic instruction. Mr. Fliedner instructed them in ethics and religious principles, and Mrs. Fliedner instructed them in the principles of practical nursing. A physician gave them theoretical training and bedside instruction in the care of the sick, and they learned enough pharmacology to pass the state examinations for pharmacists. These trained deaconesses could nurse sick and convalescent patients, manage children, and dispense medicines. They were familiar with occupational therapy, parish or district visiting, and religious theory and instructions.

The organization that accomplished so much was managed very strictly. No student could assume a privileged position; all were equal before their instructors. In this way they differed markedly from the later English and American orders. To be admitted to the course, a girl had to be at least 18 years of age and had to present letters from a clergyman and a physician certifying both her moral standing and her health. She would then be admitted for three months' probation; later this probation was replaced by required attendance at a preparatory school, sometimes for as long as a year. She received a regular, small allowance of pocket money. Rotating through the various services, she in turn became a junior, senior, and finally head sister. The student received, besides practical instruction, regular theoretical classroom instruction. The course took three years, and required wearing a uniform. This was indeed the first complete modern training school for nurses with the essential components.

The modern training school was a huge success, and it grew rapidly. The Fliedners already had a normal school for the preparation of deaconesses, and soon a lunatic asylum for female patients was added to the hospital and in 1842 an orphanage for Protestant girls. They also organized an infant school and a day school for girls. Finally they organized an asylum for released female prisoners and for wayward girls in an attempt to help them readjust to society.

When the hospital was fully developed, its facilities included, besides wards for male and female patients and children, a unit for communicable diseases, one for convalescents (which is remarkable for this period), and one for sick deaconesses. There were also an apothecary shop, administrative offices, a chapel that took care of burials, and a garden that furnished vegetables.

Not only did the institution prosper in Kaiserswerth but it also received calls for branches from all over Europe and from America. In addition Fliedner had founded an institution to train male nurses at Duisberg in 1844. As early as 1846 he went to London with four deaconesses to begin nursing in the German Hospital there. In 1850 he took a group to Pastor Passavant in Pittsburgh, and at the same time a deaconess home and hospital were founded in Milwaukee. Branches were established throughout the Near East in such cities as Jerusalem, Smyrna, Constantinople, and Alexandria, and by the time Fliedner died in 1864 there were about 1,600 deaconesses working in 400 different fields, and they had 30 motherhouses. Since that time the organization has continued to grow and expand in some communities.

The growth of the organization was a result of the urgent need for such an organization and the incessant industry of the Fliedners. Along with her enormous task, Fredericka Fliedner found time to bring into the world five children before she died in 1842. Theodor Fliedner was fortunate in marrying Caroline Bertheau, a former pupil of Amelie Sieveking, a year later. Caroline had been in charge of nursing in the female surgical department of the Hamburg Hospital. She was able to carry the mantle of Fredericka and did not neglect the domestic side of life; being a good wife, she had eight children before he died in 1864. After his death she continued to direct Kaiserswerth until 1882.

Primarily religious, this order was modern, basically practical, and democratic.

Not all clergymen possessed Fliedner's wide vision, and sometimes interference by the clergy hampered efficiency in spite of the principle that doctor's orders should prevail. Exaggerated idealism on the part of the girls would occasionally lead to excessive self-negation, and at times they were exploited by unscrupulous leaders. Some opposition to the order resulted, manifest in the appearance of "free sisters" who later became organized, but, on the whole, deaconesses weathered the storms and continue as the outstanding Protestant religious nursing organization. The security of the motherhouse, which meant so much to the European girl, was somewhat modified in America. They still offer a unique opportunity for serious-minded young women to do good in the world. No vows are required. A deaconess may retire or marry, but in return for a life of faithful service can look forward to retirement security during old age.

British nursing orders. Fliedner's work made a great impression on interested persons, especially in England and on the European continent. Florence Nightingale received much inspiration from his work, visited the institution repeatedly, and for a while even participated in the Fliedners' activities. This will be discussed more in Chapter 3. Mrs. Fry also followed the work closely, and finally in 1840, largely under the inducement of Dr. Gooch and the poet Robert Southey, she organized the first Protestant nursing order in England, the Protestant Sisters of Mercy or the Nursing Sisters, as they were lated called. The order is still in existence.

These women received some training in their preparation for the care of the sick; they visited Guy's Hospitail in London for several hours each day where they received some instruction from the doctors and ward nurses. Largely uneducated, these doctors and nurses could not be very valuable instructors. Students received neither classroom nor theoretical instruction; they were trained entirely for practical home nursing.

Early nursing organizations in England were sponsored by the Church of England. As a result, these organizations were dominated by the clergyman's conception of nursing as primarily an act of mercy and of religious devotion, including the belief that such service must be free to the patient.

The concept of professional services, rendered for remuneration by trained, devoted women, was slow in becoming accepted. Refined and capable women were attracted to this new profession for women. More nursing activities were being sponsored by the upper classes, and more nurses were recruited from the middle classes of the country.

The Park Village Community, established in 1845 by Pusey, was the first of the Anglican nursing orders. Its emphasis was largely on friendly visiting of the sick in their homes; there was no emphasis on systematic training or care of patients. About the same time, Miss Sellon organized a similar group, the Sisters of Mercy in Devonport. These orders were established for the purpose of home nursing and did not participate in the reform of hospital nursing that took place in the next few years.

A primary factor in this reform was St. John's House, started by the Church of England in 1848. Its purpose was to establish systematic training of nurses in the hospitals and to attract young ladies of the middle classes into nursing. Like the nurses of the Hôtel Dieu, they were to advance through three stages. For the first two years they were to be probationers, after which they were to qualify as "nurses," when they would receive board and lodging as well as a salary. After having worked for five years as nurses, they could advance to become "sisters," who had the privilege of living at home with their families. Women of the better classes could enter as "nurses." Training in obstetrics was not included until 1861. St. John's House became identified with nursing activities in most of the important London hospitals at one time or another. At first the probationers were trained at Middlesex and Westminster Hospitals, and then, from 1849, at Kings College Hospital where in 1856 they took over the entire nursing service until the hospital established a school of nursing of its own in 1885. The order also practiced in Charing Cross Hospital and was finally taken over in 1919 by St. Thomas's Hospital. The order is now known as the St. John's and St. Thomas's House and is maintained on a cooperative basis as an institution for private nurses. The order contributed twenty-six nurses to Miss Nightingale's expedition.

A similar order, the Sisterhood of All Saints, was founded in 1851 by Miss Byron. This order also concerned itself with the training of nurses in hospitals. It was especially connected with University College Hospital; from 1857 it was responsible for the nursing of a few wards, and from 1862 to 1899 for nursing in the entire hospital. The order assumed direction also of St. John's House from 1883 to 1893.

Finally, St. Margaret's Order, established by the Rev. Dr. Neele in East Grimstead in 1854, should be mentioned. Although this order emphasized nursing, the training offered its members was not outstanding.

In the United States the Protestant Episcopal church established similar nursing orders patterned after the English. A branch of the English order, the Sisterhood of St. Margaret, practiced at the Children's Hospital in Boston from 1872 to 1912. The Sisterhood of the Holy Communion has practiced in St. Luke's Hospital in New York since 1854, and the Sisterhood of St. Mary has practiced in St. Mary's Free Hospital for Children in New York since 1870.

La Source. One development on the Continent should be mentioned. In 1859, Comtesse Agenor de Gasperin and her husband established L'école Normale Évangelique de Gardesmalades Indépendents, briefly called "La Source," in Lausanne, Switzerland. They endowed this school of nursing and provided it with a building. The students received instruction for six months during a preliminary course, after which they practiced in the homes of the poor. Since 1891 the institution has had its own hospital. The order, if it may be called that, was based on the principle of personal liberty. The nurses were salaried and made no vows. Although the quality of nurses issuing from this institution was sometimes questioned, it served as a new departure in the form of an endowed school for nursing.

International Nursing Movement. Change is not realized in one moment but results from ideas that germinate and are moved forward in incremental steps by pressures and counterpressures which have taken place and are taking place concurrently. So it was with the International Nursing Movement, formally begun by Mrs. Bedford-Fenwick (Chapter 11). Her early life experiences influenced her attitudes and activities. Her country was at the time enjoying a period of peace and tranquility under the reign of Queen Victoria. The Suez Canal had just been completed so that world trade would expand to unknown limits. The unknown continent of Africa was opened by the explorer Stanley between 1874 and 1877. Alexander Graham Bell developed the telephone between 1876 and 1896. During that same twenty years, Thomas A. Edison invented the microphone and phonograph, Edison and Swan invented the incandescent light, and Marconi developed the telegraph.

Similar discoveries were taking place in the medical area. Pasteur discovered how vaccines work, Eberth discovered the bacillus that causes typhoid fever, and Pasteur did his first inoculation against rabies. A serum to counteract diphtheria was developed by Roux and von Behring, the x ray was discovered by Roentgen, and radium was discovered by the Curies.

This was indeed a period of creativity in many areas. Darwin published the *Origin of Species* in 1859 and *Descent of Man* in 1871. Authors of that period included Ibsen, Tennyson, Hugo, Twain, Renoir, Offenbach, and César Auguste Franck. In 1891 A. Conan Doyle published his first account of Sherlock Holmes in London.

Parallel in time to all this the development of an international organization of nurses was fed by an awakening, restlessness, and rebellion among women against their role in society. It was during this period that the suffragist movement was born and grew. The American woman journalist Elizabeth Seaman, using the name Nellie Bly, decided she would challenge the record of Phileas Fogg who supposedly traveled around the world in 80 days. The woman challenger successfully completed the trip by rail and steamer in 72 days, 6 hours, and 11 minutes.

3 • Florence Nightingale

EARLY LIFE AND EDUCATION

The dominant figure in the development of organized nursing is Florence Nightingale. The previous chapter discussed (1) the evolvement of medicine into a scientific practice that would soon require more than menial labor from nurses, (2) the general state of society as well as improvement of hospital facilities seeming to be amenable to the new profession, and (3) realization on the part of Protestant ministers in various countries that an organization was needed similar to Catholic nursing orders with more freedom in various ways.

---

*This pledge was formulated in 1893 by a committee of which Mrs. Lystra E. Gretter, R.N., was the chairman. It was first administered to the 1893 graduating class of the Farrand Training School, now the Harper Hospital, Detroit, Mich.

The training and organization of lay Protestant nurses had begun before Florence Nightingale made her contribution to nursing, but with her powerful personality, her vision, and her practical organizing ability she took the lead in the movement, placed it on a powerful foundation of organization, on sound educational principles, and on high ethics, and inspired it with an enthusiasm that gave to it an impetus under which it is still progressing. A few years before Miss Nightingale's time there was no such thing as professional nursing. At the time of her death nursing was a profession, administered by women and offering them nursing and educational opportunities, formerly unthinkable.

However, Florence Nightingale devoted only a part of her life to the advancement of nursing; she also contributed greatly to

Florence Nightingale in the hospital ward at Scutari

(Courtesy Bettman Archive, New York, N.Y.)

reforms in the Army, improved sanitation in India, and public health in Great Britain. Her full stature cannot be comprehended unless attention is given also to these accomplishments.

On May 12, 1820, a daughter was born to Mr. and Mrs. William Edward Nightingale. She was their second girl, and because the family was then staying in Florence, Italy, she was named after the city of her birth. Her family was of considerable wealth, of good social standing, and highly cultured; therefore they could afford to give their children the best education available. Florence was brought up with a broad outlook and knowledge of French, German, and Italian. Her father took a very active part in her education by personally instructing her in mathematics and the classics.

When the Nightingale family returned to England, they built a new house at Embley Park, Hampshire, and most of their time was spent there or at the old family home at Lea Hurst, Derbyshire. Each year during the season an extended visit was made to London, and the young ladies grew up with opportunities to make the best social contacts, which later were to be of the greatest value to Florence.

In 1837 the family again went abroad, touring France, Italy, and Switzerland. In the winter of 1838 they traveled to Paris where Florence was introduced to the salons in which she made acquaintances that she was to treasure throughout her life. When she returned to London, she was a young lady and was supposed to take her place in society. However, Florence was too serious to be satisfied with such a life. She felt a calling for something greater, although it took some years before her yearnings became articulate. From time to time she made inquiries into the possibilities of becoming a nurse, but knowing the social attitudes toward these women it is no wonder that Mrs. Nightingale fought such ideas. Nevertheless, Florence had definite plans to become a nurse at the Salisbury

Hospital not far from her home. Although these did not materialize, her purpose became even firmer.

In 1844 Miss Nightingale met the American philanthropist, Samuel Gridley Howe, and his wife, Julia Ward Howe, who later became known as the author of "The Battle Hymn of the Republic." They stayed at Embley, the Nightingale home. Miss Nightingale was very much impressed with an institution for the blind that Dr. Howe had founded in New York in which he had worked out a plan to make medical care and nursing available without payment to elderly or ill American citizens. During their stay Miss Nightingale discussed with them the feasibility of working in English hospitals as Catholic sisters did. At that time, no English women of any social standing would have sought a vocation outside the home, except to enter the church as a Catholic sister. During this year she felt she had reached the turning point of her life and it was clear to her that her vocation was to be the care of the sick in hospitals. However, her family would not even discuss the possibility of her entering the hospital, so far was it removed from any of their thinking.

Until 1845 she had believed that qualities such as tenderness, sympathy, goodness, and patience were all that a nurse required. After experience in caring for some members of her own family during their illnesses, she recognized that knowledge and skill were also necessary and that acquisition of these required education and training.

It is not surprising that her family was shocked whenever she mentioned going to a hospital, either for training or to nurse, because in the middle of the nineteenth century, hospitals were at a low level of degradation and squalor. Dirt and lack of sanitation were common. They were crowded, and the patients who were dirty when they came to the hospital were likely to remain that way during their stay.

In 1847, after a busy "social summer," she set out for Rome with Mr. and Mrs. Bracebridge, close friends of the family—a visit that was to result in two important experiences. She went into retreat for ten days in the Convent of the Trinita dei Monti, where she absorbed much of the spirit of the church and where her religious belief greatly matured. Although she was much impressed with the practical endeavors of the Catholic church, she did not become converted to Catholicism; in fact, it could never be said that she strongly preferred any particular branch of the church, although she remained deeply religious throughout her life. By tradition she remained within the Church of England.

Her second important experience was the meeting of Mr. and Mrs. Sidney Herbert. Mr.—later Sir—Sidney Herbert was to have the greatest influence on her life; it was through him that she was to go to the Crimea, and with him (and Dr. Sutherland) that she was to form "the little war office." For the present their contact was largely social, consisting of parties and visits to the galleries. There was some talk of nursing, for there were plans to establish a nursing home when they returned to England. It is interesting to note at this time that Mr. and Mrs. Sidney Herbert and many of their friends were beginning to be interested in hospital reform. Public opinion was being awakened, and Miss Nightingale, who had been collecting facts on public health and hospitals for several years, was able to give this group a great deal of information. Gradually she became known as an expert in hospital reform.

When Miss Nightingale returned to England, she was about 28 years of age, and it was about time for her to marry. In fact, marriage was seriously considered repeatedly but did not materialize. The next year she once more accompanied the Bracebridges abroad to Egypt and Greece. In the meantime she had grown considerably, both emotionally and intellectually so that she studied intently all that she saw; she paid much attention to institutions for the sick and the poor. She had learned about the institution at Kaiserswerth. Through some friends she had received the Yearbook of the Institution of Deaconesses at Kaiserswerth in 1846. She studied it very carefully and realized that here she could receive the training she so keenly wanted. Because the institution was under religious auspices and the character of the deaconesses and pastors above reproach, she could go there without the stigma attached to the English hospitals.

On the return journey she paid it a visit. She was greatly impressed and became very eager to return to participate in the training. Miss Nightingale was so impressed with Kaiserswerth that on her return she issued anonymously a pamphlet called *The Institution of Kaiserswerth on the Rhine for the Practical Training of Deaconesses Under the Direction of the Rev. Pastor Fliedner, Embracing the Support and Care of a Hospital, Infant and Industrial Schools, and a Female Penitentiary.* This was a 32-page pamphlet and was printed by the Inmates of the London Ragged Colonial Training School at Westminster where Miss Nightingale had taught and in which she had a great deal of interest.

She was well aware that to become a good nurse a thorough training was essential, and when in 1851 her mother and sister went to Carlsbad to "take the cure," she finally contrived to accompany them with the intention of paying an extended visit to Kaiserswerth. She spent three months at the Fliedners' institution and derived from it a great deal of instruction. She participated in the nurses' instruction even to the point of scrubbing floors and left much impressed with the organization and high purpose of the place. Her opinion of the actual training of the nurses was not so high. The experience at Kaiserswerth strengthened her purpose, but as yet she failed to give it practical expression.

In 1851 she met the famous woman doctor, Dr. Elizabeth Blackwell, through the Herberts. Dr. Blackwell visited Miss Nightingale at Embley, and although Miss Nightingale did not approve of women doctors in general, they had many discussions about hospitals and medical care. In the spring of 1853 she was in Paris again researching hospitals and infirmaries; finally she arranged to enter the Maison de la Providence for a course of training with the Sisters of Charity. An attack of the measles, however, promptly forced her to receive nursing care instead of dispensing it. Her illness more or less put an end to this undertaking.

In the meantime she had entered into negotiations with the committee supervising an "Establishment for Gentlewomen During Illness." This was a type of nursing home in London for governesses who became ill, and after appearing before the committee she was appointed superintendent. In 1853 the establishment moved into an empty house at No. 1 Upper Harley Street, and here for the next few years Florence Nightingale found a limited expression for her desire to nurse. She had a number of difficulties with her committee, all of which she negotiated with tact, and she soon had the nursing home running smoothly.

As soon as Miss Nightingale had reorganized the institution, she again began visiting hospitals and collecting data for reforming conditions for nurses. In the middle of the nineteenth century, social reform was becoming increasingly popular, and people like the Herberts and many of their friends became interested in the reform of medical and social institutions. Miss Nightingale realized that before any nursing reform could be launched, some type of school for the training of reliable and qualified nurses must be organized. At this time, she realized that her first task was to help produce a new type of nurse. Because of her knowledge of hospitals, she was being consulted by social reformers and by many doctors who were beginning to recognize the need for the trained nurse. For example, Dr.

Bowman, a well-known surgeon of that day, had performed a difficult operation on a patient anesthetized with chloroform, which was just beginning to be used as an anesthetic, and Miss Nightingale has assisted as his nurse. He was very eager for her to accept the position of superintendent of nurses in the King's College Hospital. However, when rumors of this reached her family, the objections they had always had to Miss Nightingale's going into large hospitals were again brought forward.

She remained in charge of the nursing home at No. 1 Upper Harley Street until her departure for Scutari, with the exception of a vacation to her home and a short leave of absence for the purpose of nursing at the Middlesex Hospital during an epidemic of cholera.

CRIMEAN WAR

The Crimean War broke out and the British, French, and Turks were fighting the Russians, chiefly near the Black Sea and the Crimean Peninsula. As the war dragged on, it became apparent that there were some serious defects in the organization of the British army, particularly in the handling of the sick and wounded soldiers. The letters of the war correspondent W. H. Russell to the *Times* stirred up emotion at home. His comparison of nursing in the French army to that in the British brought things to a climax, which resulted in the letter to the *Times* containing the famous question: "Why have we no Sisters of Charity?"

Many inquiries were made about town in a similar vein, and Miss Nightingale's name was mentioned repeatedly in this connection. Miss Nightingale herself was turning the matter over in her mind and finally wrote to Sir Sidney Herbert, who now was secretary of war, offering to take a group of nurses into the Crimea. Curiously enough, a letter from Sir Sidney requesting that she do so crossed hers. Her family consented, and she was soon hard at work enlisting thirty-eight nurses. Among these were ten

Roman Catholic sisters, partly from Bermondsey, eight of Miss Sellon's sisters from Devonport, and six from St. John's House. These were the best she could obtain at short notice, but several were inadequately trained and later had to be returned.

On October 21, 1854, the party set out for Scutari on the steamer Vectis. The problems that awaited Miss Nightingale were prodigious. The equipment for the hospital was defective or nonexistent; the staff already there looked on the expedition as a slur on their own capabilities and were not kindly disposed to this arrangement of admitting female nurses into a military hospital. So her job required both organizing ability and tact.

The interested reader may refer to Miss Nightingale's biography for detailed descriptions of the conditions at Scutari. This discussion is concerned mainly with her contribution to organized nursing; therefore details of the conditions are omitted. Plumbing and sewage disposal were next to nonexistent. The simplest means of hygiene and civilized living were lacking. There were no knives and forks, no bedclothes, no scrubbing brushes, no operating room—in fact, hardly anything but a crowded space full of suffering, dying, verminous, undernourished soldiers, attended by inexperienced orderlies and supervised by men who were largely inefficient and who considered the intruders with hostility.

At first Miss Nightingale and her nurses were ignored by the doctors. Although the patients were in great need and Miss Nightingale could get supplies for them, only one doctor would use her nurses and her supplies. She realized that before she could accomplish anything, she must obtain the cooperation and confidence of the medical staff. She was determined to stand by and wait until she was asked to help. This required a great deal of restraint because the need for nursing care and for the supplies that she could get was evident. She was determined that the doctors would ask for her

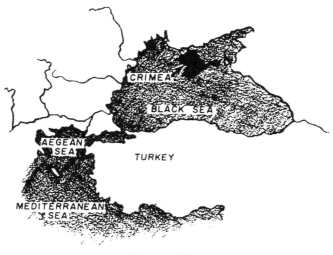

Crimean War

The Crimean War dragged on for many years while the English, French, and Turkish fought the Russians. The English lacked the organization and personnel to care for their wounded until Miss Nightingale came to Scutari.

help and was equally determined that no nurse would take care of patients unless she was reliable.

At last, as the fighting increased and the sick and wounded came in ever-increasing numbers, everyone—even visiting representatives from the British government—was pressed into service. At last the doctors turned to Miss Nightingale and her nurses. The medical staff and the hospital officials gradually became aware that Miss Nightingale was the one person who had money at her disposal and who had contacts with influential people who could help in critical situations.

Miss Nightingale and her nurses set to work at once. They had the authority from the War Office, and they began by requisitioning several hundred scrubbing brushes. Before the war was over, there was a reasonable measure of cleanliness, special diet kitchens had been established, and the rats had been brought under some control. In brief, out of a shambles Miss Nightingale had established a hospital.

The manner in which she handled her staff is also interesting. They were there to cooperate, not to take charge. Miss Nightingale's nurses were strictly instructed not to undertake nursing except when requested by medical officers and to take orders regarding patients from the doctors only. Furthermore, she established herself in the hearts of the men, dividing her time between administration and personal attention to patients. Famous are her nightly rounds when the day's work supposedly was done. Then with her lantern she made her tour of inspection past the long lines of cots, with a friendly word for some and a smile for others; in all she inspired a feeling of comfort that someone was sympathizing with them and striving to make their hard lot a little less hard. Of all her activities in Scutari, these nightly rounds are perhaps the most famous; they have been immortalized by Longfellow in his poem *The Lady With the Lamp*.

All this was achieved, but not without difficulties. One of the worst was that she was informed one day that forty-six nurses were on their way to Scutari under the direction of Miss Mary Stanley. It has never been explained who initiated this move or how it was made without consulting Miss Nightingale. They were not sent to assist her but were instructed to report to the inspector general. Considering the importance of the experiment that Miss Nightingale was performing, her distress at such an attempt at dual control can easily be imagined. She protested vigorously to Sir Sidney Herbert, and eventually the nurses came into her organization. Other nurses were added from time to time, and at the end of the war she had a staff of 125 nurses.

Miss Nightingale's interest extended beyond nursing. She was in the best sense a social worker. The army in those days had no recreational facilities for the soldiers when they were off duty. The only choice was such entertainment as they might find outside the camp. This entertainment was not of the best and was usually designed to part them from their hard-earned pay with the least possible effort. Many soldiers had brought their wives; these women were painfully neglected, especially during sickness or childbirth. Miss Nightingale did much to relieve the lot of these poor women. She established reading rooms, games, and other entertainments for the soldiers in an attempt to direct their attention away from the dramshop (barroom) and immorality. She also established in her own office a type of savings bank through which the soldiers might transmit money to relatives in England. She was eminently successful in all these pursuits.

She gained the sympathy of the medical staff by furnishing them out of her own pocket with a dissecting room and the necessary instruments. In addition to all this, she spent the better part of her nights writing; she wrote long official reports and private communications to Sir Sidney Herbert and did much of the work now incumbent on the army chaplain by writing to the families of sick and dying soldiers.

She had hardly begun to get things into shape when a new and formidable task loomed before her. Her work so far had all been done at Scutari, across the Straits of Bosporus from Constantinople. The war itself was fought across the Black Sea at the Crimean Peninsula, and she felt it incumbent on her to investigate conditions at the actual theater of war. So in the spring of 1855 she went to Balaklava in the Crimea and worked on the reorganization of the few hospitals there. Here she encountered great obstacles: the roads were dreadful, often nonexistent, and the official attitude of jealous superior officers caused her much grief. However, the commander of the British forces supported her, and she had done much toward achieving her purpose when she was taken sick with the Crimean fever (probably typhoid or typhus). For a few days her condition was critical. Her convalescence was slow and she never recovered entirely. She refused a leave of absence to recuperate and returned to work too soon. She stayed until the very end of the war and left with the last contingent of nurses from Scutari.

At the end of the Crimean War two figures are prominent: the common British soldier and the nurse. However, at the beginning of the war most British soldiers were the drunken, immoral dregs of society, and the status of the women doing nursing was not much better. Miss Nightingale, because of her experiment in the Crimea, did much to set the pattern for the improvement of conditions for these two groups.

NIGHTINGALE ENDOWMENT FUND

The significance of Miss Nightingale's work in Scutari became known and understood far and wide in England: in the future, nurses must be properly trained, and the nursing care of the sick must take its place beside the surgical and medical care. Accordingly a public meeting was held in London on November 25, 1855, under the presidency of the Commander-in-Chief, the duke of Cambridge; a fund, called the "Nightingale Endowment Fund," was established for the purpose of furthering nursing education. Some $220,000, of which $35,000 was subscribed by the army, was collected within a short time in England and in the Dominions. The medical profession, which ultimately was to benefit so greatly from this undertaking, remained critical of it and did not enter it wholeheartedly.

When Miss Nightingale heard of this fund, she accepted it with the proviso that it would be some time before she could utilize it, and she expressed concern that her health might not permit her to accomplish the task. In fact, several years elapsed before she established the first school of nursing.

MISS NIGHTINGALE'S ILLNESS

In August, 1856, she returned from Scutari, six months after the end of the war and began the most difficult period of her life. Her brilliant ambitions were hindered by her lack of physical strength. Although there is no record that she was suffering from any organic disease, she never regained her stamina. During the first few months after her return to England she was so weak that she was not expected to live. When new problems arose in 1857 she rallied to the occasion. For many years she displayed the greatest vigor of mind and undertook the most sustained mental efforts —and yet she was never well enough to see anyone who came to call out of curiosity or on trivial errands. By thus excluding herself from the superficialities of society, she managed to concentrate her energies on the truly great tasks of her life. Much has been written about her "illness." It cannot simply be dismissed as neurasthenia. It could possibly be considered an exhaustion neurosis from which she never recovered because she never afforded herself sufficient rest. It may also be considered an escape through which she, unconsciously perhaps, avoided certain conflicts that would have

been inevitable if she had moved about in society hale and hearty. In mid-Victorian England it would have been unthinkable for her to obtain the official position in public life to which she might have legitimately aspired. As it was, she was an invalid. Those who wished her advice had to come to her; and by living in almost total seclusion, she found time and opportunity to gather the tremendous amount of data and information with which she filled the reports that emanated from her rooms.

Miss Nightingale's first aim was the permanent rectification of the defects that had become glaringly apparent during the Crimean War. This was to be achieved through extensive reforms of the army. She accomplished this by working through a committee, the principal members of which were Sir Sidney Herbert and Dr. Sutherland. This committee, often called the "little war office," sat usually in her rooms, at first at the Burlington Hotel, later in various rented houses. This work was progressing when it was severely upset by the death of Sir Sidney (then Lord Lea) in 1861 and by changes in the government. The reforms were being made slowly; the origins of many reforms carried out years later can still be traced to the activities of Miss Nightingale.

In 1856 the result of Miss Nightingale's conferences and deliberations was published as *Notes on Matters Affecting the Health, Efficiency and Hospital Administration of the British Army*. This was a volume of nearly 1,000 printed pages. In 1859 she published a small book called *Notes on Hospitals*. This was so successful that a second edition was published in 1860 and a third, rewritten and with many additions, in 1863. After the publication of this book she was constantly being asked for advice on hospital administration and construction. The plans for many hospitals were submitted to her.

In 1858 she was elected a member of the Statistical Society, and at the Statistical Congress of 1860 she presented a paper for discussion called "Miss Nightingale's Scheme for Uniform Hospital Statistics." Until this time each hospital had used its own method for naming and classifying diseases and keeping other statistics.

Although Miss Nightingale's interest in nursing and nursing reform had never diminished, her activities for reforms in the army had pushed it into the background.

In 1859 her book, *Notes on Nursing,* was published and caused quite a sensation for that day. Habits of personal hygiene taken for granted today were completely foreign to the mid-Victorian days. This book was very widely used and thousands of copies were distributed to factories and schools. It was also translated into French, German, and Italian.

About 1860 she found time to devote herself to the establishment of a school of nursing to be financed by the Nightingale Fund. St. Thomas's Hospital was finally selected, and for many years Miss Nightingale took a most active part in all details concerning her school. This interest was slackened only by feebleness of old age.

For the remainder of her life Miss Nightingale's interests were divided among "the Nightingale Nurses," the construction of hospitals, reforms in workhouses, public health measures throughout England (and other countries), and the promotion of public health reforms in India. Because of her powerful personality and her vast knowledge, her advice was sought on most subjects in which she was expert, but she never stood out in an official capacity. Somewhat later she became interested in the development of district nursing, and during the Franco-German war she was frequently consulted by both belligerents regarding the care of sick and wounded.

In only two respects was she judged wrong by history. First, she did not appreciate the significance of the bacteriological discoveries that occurred during that period. In spite of her interest in public health and her good judgment regarding hygienic

measures, wherever bacteriological facts conflicted with her ideas regarding hygiene, the facts were ignored. Second, she did not appreciate the importance of a central registry for nurses, similar to that for medical men. She thought that the reputation of nurses could be established better through their schools and that a central registry would lead to standardization that would have a detrimental effect on the profession as a whole. Experience, of course, has shown that this was not the case, but she did manage to delay this reform for many years.

In her writings Miss Nightingale dealt with many aspects of the fields in which she was interested. She wrote about the care of the sick in hospitals, workhouses, army camps, city tenements, and rural districts. She also discussed problems in the public health field, such as housing and sanitation, and was interested in health teaching. She wrote extensively on sanitary problems in India, of racial questions, and of the uses of statistics. Her writings appear in books, pamphlets, papers, addresses, articles, and many letters. The Adelaide Nutting Historical Nursing Collection at Teachers College, Columbia University, New York, probably contains the finest collection of her writings to be found anywhere. Following is a chronological list of some of the writings of Miss Nightingale:

1. The Institution of Kaiserswerth on the Rhine for the Practical Training of Deaconesses under the Direction of the Rev. Pastor Fliedner, Embracing the Support and Care of a Hospital, Infant and Industrial Schools, and a Female Penitentiary. Printed by the Inmates of the London Ragged Colonial Training School, 1851.
2. Letters from Egypt. Privately printed, 1854.
3. Statements Exhibiting the Voluntary Contributions Received by Miss Nightingale for the Use of the British Hospitals in the East, with the Mode of Their Distribution, in 1854, 1855, 1856. Harrison & Sons, 1857.
4. Notes on Matters Affecting the Health, Efficiency, and Hospital Administration of the British Army. Founded Chiefly on the Experience of the Late War. Presented by Request to the Secretary of State for War. Privately

printed for Miss Nightingale. Harrison & Sons, 1858.

5. Subsidiary Notes as to the Introduction of Female Nursing into Military Hospitals in Peace and in War. Presented by Request to the Secretary of State for War. Privately printed for Miss Nightingale. Harrison & Sons, 1858.
6. A Contribution to the Sanitary History of the British Army During the Late War With Russia. Harrison & Sons, 1859.
7. Notes on Hospitals. John W. Parker & Sons, 1859. 3rd edition, almost completely rewritten, 1863. Longmans, Green & Co.
8. Notes on Nursing: What It Is, and What It Is Not. By Florence Nightingale. Harrison & Sons, 1859.
9. Suggestions for Thought to the Searchers after Truth Among the Artisans of England. Privately printed for Miss Nightingale. 3 vols. Eyre & Spottiswoode, 1860.
10. Army Sanitary Administration and Its Reform Under the Late Lord Herbert. M'Corquodale & Co., 1862.
11. Observations on the Evidence Contained in the Stational Reports Submitted to the Royal Commission on the Sanitary State of the Army in India. By Florence Nightingale. (Reprinted from the Report of the Royal Commission.) Edward Stanford, 1863. "The Observations."
12. Introductory Notes on Lying-In Institutions. Together With a Proposal for Organising an Institution for Training Midwives and Midwifery Nurses. By Florence Nightingale. Longmans, Green & Co., 1871.
13. Life or Death in India. A paper read at the meeting of the National Association for the Promotion of Social Science, Norwich, 1873. With an Appendix on life or death by irrigation, 1874.
14. The Zemindar, the Sun and the Watering Pot as Affecting Life or Death in India. Unpublished, proof copies among the Nightingale papers, 1873-1876.
15. On Trained Nursing for the Sick Poor. By Florence Nightingale. The Metropolitan and National Nursing Association, 1876.
16. Miss Florence Nightingale's Addresses to Probationer-Nurses in the "Nightingale Fund" School at St. Thomas's Hospital and Nurses Who Were Formerly Trained There, 1872-1900. Printed for private circulation.
17. Florence Nightingale's Indian Letters. A glimpse into the agitation for tenancy reform, Bengal, 1878-1882. Edited by Priyaranja Sen. Calcutta, 1937.°

°Woodham-Smith, Cecil: Florence Nightingale, New York, 1951, McGraw-Hill Book Co., pp. 368-369.

Thus for about 40 years Miss Nightingale was actively interested in some of the most important reforms of the times, but at about the turn of the century her powers waned— she was then nearly 80—and the last ten years of her life she spent in a state of decline until she died quietly in her sleep on August 13, 1910. It was proposed that she be buried in Westminster Abbey, but in accordance with her wish she was interred in the family burying place at Willow, Hampshire.

INFLUENCE ON NURSING EDUCATION

It is hard for us to realize that recognized preparation for modern nursing and the real beginning of nursing education began with the establishment of the Nightingale School at St. Thomas's Hospital.

The cardinal prinicples on which she established that first school were the following:

1. Nurses should be technically trained in hospitals organized for that purpose.
2. Nurses should live in "homes" fit to form their moral lives and discipline.

The direction of her school was largely accomplished through the efforts of others, but she was consulted often about what was being done in the school. She rebuked head nurses who were not giving enough time and thought to teaching students. She also recognized the need for appointing a nurse instructor for classroom teaching. Some of the following points that she made are quite modern.

1. In addition to her salary received from the hospital, the Ward Sister should be paid by the fund (The Nightingale Endowment Fund) for training these probationers.
2. It was recorded that remuneration was to be paid also to medical instructors.
3. Weekly records of the work of the probationers were to be kept by the head nurses and monthly records by the matron.
4. Diaries (as previously noted) were to be kept by probationers.
5. Miss Nightingale emphasized the need for cor-

relation of theory and practice (although she did not use that phrase).

6. Probationers, she said, must be taught to know symptoms—and the reasons why and they must be given time to learn "the reason why."[*]

Miss Nightingale established the custom of sending an annual letter to her students. In some respects similar messages are now given at commencement time. Quotations from these letters demonstrate that they contain not only helpful ideas but also encouragement and inspiration. Many of them are applicable to students in nursing schools today.

> A women who takes a sentimental view of nursing (which she calls "ministering" as if she were an angel) is, of course, worse than useless. A woman possessed with the idea that she is making a sacrifice will never do; and a woman who thinks that any kind of nursing work is "beneath a nurse" will simply be in the way.
>
> For us who nurse, our nursing is a thing which, unless in it we are making progress every year, every month, every week, take my word for it we are going back. The more experience we gain the more progress we can make. The progress you make in your year's training with us is as nothing to what you must make each year after your training is over. A woman who thinks of herself "Now I am a full nurse, a skillful nurse. I have learnt all there is to be learnt," take my word for it, she does not know what a nurse is, and she will never know: she has gone back already. Conceit and nursing cannot exist in the same person.[†]

The principles on which this first school of nursing was established exerted great influence as the need for trained nurses increased. These graduates went out to establish schools and to become matrons in hospitals throughout England and her colonies and in the United States. Because of inadequate financial arrangements, few schools remained separate from the hospitals even if they had been organized as distinct units.

[*]Roberts, Mary: Florence Nightingale as a nurse educator, American Journal of Nursing 37:775, July, 1937.

[†]Pavey, Agnes E.: The story of the growth of nursing, London, 1938, Faber & Faber, Ltd., p. 296.

They were all soon part of the hospital and controlled by its administration. This important principle of Miss Nightingale's—that the school be considered as an educational and not as a service institution, is being revived today in the recent reorganization of nursing schools.

It was natural that there should have been opposition to Miss Nightingale. There was a growing need for nurses, and many believed that the type of training demanded, the close supervision, and the strict regulations insisted on would never produce enough nurses to meet the need. In 1866 a committee of the Hospital Association proposed that an independent body of examiners should be created to set an examination and that when a nurse had passed it, her name would be placed on a register of nurses. Thus the public would be protected from incompetent or unscrupulous nurses. Miss Nightingale opposed this step because she thought nursing was still too young and too unorganized for such a standard examination and because she did not believe that any examination could test the character of the nurse, which she held to be so very important. She believed that only a certificate from the matron in the nursing school would be a guarantee that the nurse had the necessary qualities of character as well as the technical skill. An examination conducted by strangers, she thought, could never test this important aspect of the nurse's qualifications. This controversy continued between Miss Nightingale and a few of her British matrons for some years. Later the British Nursing Association was granted a royal charter but not in the terms they had sought, so that actually neither side won.

SUMMARY

Notwithstanding her great contribution in other fields, Miss Nightingale's greatest and most enduring work was done in nursing.

From her youth she believed that her

calling was to nurse the sick, and as her purpose in life gradually evolved, she increasingly concentrated her efforts on the organization of hospitals and the training of nurses. She availed herself of the training that was then available and always deplored that it had not been better. Although she accepted most of the good aspects of Kaiserswerth, she was keenly aware of the defects in the nurses' training. When she was sick in Paris, she criticized the nursing care that she received. When she was placed in charge of a nursing home, its greatest defect in her opinion was that it gave her no opportunity to train nurses. The lack of trained nurses was at the root of the evils of Scutari and Balaklava, and her greatest single contribution in the Crimean War was the organization of nursing care and such training of nurses as she could effect. The next logical step in her career would have been the administration of the "Nightingale Endowment Fund," and it was only because of the pressure of the army reforms and her poor state of health that the establishment of a school of nursing under her direction was delayed. However, the time was not wasted, for in 1859 she published two books, *Notes on Hospitals*, which advocated better construction of hospitals and better nursing care, and *Notes on Nursing; What It Is, and What It Is Not*. In the latter book she set forth the fundamental principles of nursing, and it became widely read; it was followed by a "popular edition" in 1861, called *Notes on Nursing for the Laboring Classes*, which include a chapter on infant care. Her *Notes on Nursing* was really one of the first nursing texts and was widely used as such by nurses. It was first published in 1859 and translated into several languages. The first American edition was published in 1860.

Finally, in 1859 a committee was appointed to select a hospital for Miss Nightingale's training school, and, as previously noted, St. Thomas's Hospital was selected. The medical officer, Mr. R. G. Whitfield,

was sympathetic to the plan, and the matron, Mrs. Wardroper, was a most capable woman. In 1860 fifteen probationers were admitted for a year's training. Miss Nightingale was consulted on all details of selection of pupil nurses, instruction, and organization. Throughout this chapter emphasis has been placed on Miss Nightingale's appreciation of the necessity for training of nurses. This is so obvious to us that it is hard to understand that she had to fight to establish this principle. Most people, including many medical men, thought that nursing could be done "by intuition." If that attitude is understood, the magnitude of Miss Nightingale's contribution is better appreciated. Furthermore, she made it clear that she did not advocate a new "nursing order." She wanted to establish a secular career for women, similar to law and medicine for men. And she succeeded. If it had not been for Miss Nightingale, the elevation of nursing from a lowly craft to a respected profession might have been delayed many years, to the detriment of the progress of medicine and hospital administration.

As it was, Miss Nightingale placed the emphasis on the education of women in an endowed school; in fact she was less concerned with the production, in the first place, of practical nurses than with a group of educated women who could go into outlying areas and establish similar centers of training elsewhere, acting as leaders who would help raise the level of nursing everywhere. Again she succeeded. More nursing pupils were admitted, more instruction was instituted, and gradually the old type nurses were replaced by younger women to whom nursing was a career and not a last resort.

Along with all this she personally kept in touch with her nurses. She rarely went out, but they came to see her in her home at South Street where she lived for many years. Aided by her acute judgment of human character, she quickly sized them up and her notes made at the time bear witness to her shrewd powers of observation. During her lifetime she became an almost legendary figure in English nursing. The growth of her reputation was not hampered by the eventual decline of her frail body. Her name continues to be the beacon light for our profession.

In 1893 she prepared a paper on "Sick Nursing and Health Nursing," which was read at the Chicago Exhibition of Women's Work at the World's Fair.

Many memorials have been erected to Miss Nightingale. National Hospital Day is celebrated on her birthday; on the Sunday nearest that date nurses all over America hold memorial services. In 1912 it was proposed at the International Council of Nurses in Cologne that an international memorial be developed; a Florence Nightingale Foundation was set up for this purpose. Before World War II a group of nurses from many countries lived at Florence Nightingale International House in London for one year and acquired a better conception of international understanding while studying together in three courses: (1) public health, (2) nurse administration and teaching, and (3) social work. The courses were given at Bedford College in cooperation with the College of Nursing.

Although Florence Nightingale contributed a great deal toward the improvement of the image and competence of nurses as well as eliminating some of the demeaning and handmaiden activities of the nursing occupation, which existed before her time, she failed to recognize one factor. While providing for more education for nurses, she failed to provide for additional independence of thought that the education produced. Her training emphasized the submissive role and did not make clear a new relationship with physicians, which would result from the improved educational preparation for nurses of which she was the proponent. Florence Nightingale nourished the religious calling to which many nurses testified. The religious component of nursing continues with a significant proportion of students still considering nursing to be a "calling."

References for unit one

A century of nursing; reprints of four historic documents, including Miss Nightingale's letter of September 18, 1872, to the Bellevue School: Foreword by Elizabeth M. Stewart and Agnes Galinas, for the National League of Nursing Education, New York, 1950, G. P. Putnam's Sons.

Andrews, Mary R.: A lost commander: Florence Nightingale, New York, 1938, Doubleday & Co., Inc.

Austin, A. L., and Stewart, Isabelle, M.: History of nursing, ed. 5, New York, 1962, G. P. Putnam's Sons, pp. 23-64.

Baker, Rachael: The first woman doctor (Elizabeth Blackwell), New York, 1944, Julian Messner, Inc.

Banworth, Calista: A living memorial to Florence Nightingale, American Journal of Nursing 40: 491-497, May, 1940.

Blackwell, Elizabeth: Pioneer work for women, New York, 1914, E. P. Dutton & Co., Inc.

Cimons, Marlene: A 2nd look at women, health, Milwaukee Journal, Aug. 10, 1975.

Cook, Sir Edward: The life of Florence Nightingale (2 vols. in 1), New York, 1942, The Macmillan Co.

Deutsch, Albert: Dorothea Lynde Dix: Apostle of the insane, American Journal of Nursing 36: 987-997, Oct., 1936.

Doyle, Ann: Nursing by religious orders in the United States, American Journal of Nursing 29: 775-786, July, 1929 (Part I, 1809-1840); 29: 959, 1929 (Part II, 1841-1870); 29:1085, 1929 (Part III, 1871-1928); 29:1197, 1929 (Part IV, Lutheran deaconesses, 1849-1928); 29:1466-1484, Dec. 1929 (Part VI, Episcopal Sisterhoods, 1845-1928).

Editorial—Dedication of the American Nurses' Memorial, Florence Nightingale School, Bordeaux, France, American Journal of Nursing 22:799-804, July, 1922.

Editorial—The dedication of the Bordeaux School Building, American Journal of Nursing 36:491-492, May, 1936.

Extracts from letters from the Crimea, American Journal of Nursing 32:537-538, 1932.

Ferguson, E. D.: The evolution of the trained nurses, American Journal of Nursing 1:463-468, April, 1901; 1:535-538, May, 1901; 1:620-626, June, 1901.

Fishbein, Morris: History of the American Medical Association, Philadelphia, 1947, W. B. Saunders Co.

Florence Nightingale is placed among mankind's benefactors, American Journal of Nursing 50: 265, 1950.

Frank, Sister Charles Marie: Foundations of nursing, ed. 2, Philadelphia, 1959, W. B. Saunders Co.

Gallison, Marie: The ministry of women: one hundred years of women's work at Kaiserswerth, 1836-1936, London, 1954, Butterworth & Co., Ltd.

Hamilton, Samuel W.: The history of American mental hospitals. One hundred years of American psychiatry, New York, 1944, Columbia University Press.

Hume, Edgar Erksine: Medical work of the Knights Hospitallers of Saint John of Jerusalem, Baltimore, 1940, The Johns Hopkins Press.

Jones, Mary Cadwalader: The training of a nurse, Nov., 1890, Scribner's.

Lee, Eleanor: A Florence Nightingale collection, American Journal of Nursing 38:555-561, May, 1938.

McGinley, Phyllis: Saint-watching, New York, 1969, The Viking Press, Inc.

Noyes, Clara D.: American nurses complete fund for Memorial School in France, American Journal of Nursing 29:1189-1191, Oct. 1929.

Nightingaliana: American Journal of Nursing 49: 288-299, May, 1949.

Payne, Joseph Frank: Thomas Sydenham, New York, 1900, Longmans, Green & Co.

Pavey, Agnes E.: The story of the growth of nursing, London, 1938, Faber & Faber, Ltd., pp. 267-298.

Robb, Isabel Hampton: Educational standards for nurses, Cleveland, Ohio, 1907, E. C. Koechart.

Roberts, Mary M.: Florence Nightingale as a nurse educator, American Journal of Nursing 37:773-778, July, 1937.

Scovil, Elisabeth R.: Florence Nightingale's notes on nursing, American Journal of Nursing 27: 355-357, May, 1927.

Seymer, Lucy: St. Thomas' Hospital and the

Nightingale Training School, International Nursing Review **11**:340-344, 1937.

Sharp, Ella E.: Nursing during the pre-Christian era, American Journal of Nursing **19**:675-678, June, 1919.

Stephen, Barbara: Florence Nightingale's home, International Nursing Review **11**:331-334, 1937.

Strachey, Lytton: Eminent Victorians, New York, 1963, G. P. Putnam's Sons.

Trevelyan, George Macaulay: History of England, London, 1928, Longmans, Green & Co., Ltd.

Whittaker, Elvi W., and Olesen, Virginia L.: Why Florence Nightingale? American Journal of Nursing **67**:2338-2341, Nov., 1967.

Woodham-Smith, Cecil: Florence Nightingale, New York, 1951, McGraw-Hill Book Co., Inc.

UNIT TWO
American beginnings

4 • Expansion of nursing

PIONEER DAYS IN AMERICA

The humanitarian impulse that developed at the dawn of the Christian Era resulted in many hospitals' being established. The industrialization of the community emphasized the need for hospitals and the training of personnel as both a community and a religious obligation. The concept of group responsibility for the individual was beginning to develop.

The time of the great discoveries in medicine and the early immigration to America was also the time of the Reformation, which split the European nations into either Catholic or Protestant states. The early Spanish explorers and the French were Catholic and brought with them as missionaries Dominicans, Franciscans, and Jesuits and, later, the nursing orders. The care of the sick and the wounded among friend and foe in the missions and in the wilderness was largely their task. The old term for quinine, "Jesuits' bark," is reminiscent of those days when medical knowledge was in the hands of the clergy. In the Spanish civilization nursing continued to be the responsibility of the monks, and any high degree of efficiency was never reached. During the eighteenth century, when the great European hospitals began to develop, American hospitals were also beginning to be established. Mexico City can justly claim the first American hospital to be built by the white man—established by Cortez in 1524; also the early French immigrants built hospitals in Quebec, New Orleans, and St. Louis.

Beginnings of hospitals and organized nursing service

The Charity Hospital of New Orleans established in 1737 is considered by many authorities to be the oldest hospital still existing in America for the care of the sick. In 1737 a sailor, Jean Louis, died in New Orleans and left a bequest of 10,000 liras "to serve in perpetuity and the founding of a hospital for the sick of the City of New Orleans and to secure the things necessary to succor the sick."* The contract for this hospital gives the following description: "A hall measuring 45 feet in length, by 24 feet in breadth, and 14 feet in height including the foundation, the whole in walls of well conditioned brick."*

This building was completed in 1737 and named St. John's Hospital. In official records it is mentioned as "L'hôpital des pauvres de la charité," and it is considered the original Charity Hospital of New Orleans. The institution served both as a hospital and as an asylum, most of the early hospitals performed both functions. The school for nurses, however, was not established until 1894.

The Ursuline Sisters came to Canada from France in 1639 to teach. They were

---

*Sister Henrietta: A famous New Orleans hospital, American Journal of Nursing 39:249, March, 1939.

accompanied by three Augustinian nuns who were to nurse in a hospital in the new land. However, nursing care was needed so badly that they all did nursing at first until the new Hôtel Dieu was built in Quebec in 1658. These early settlements of New Orleans and farther up the Mississippi were to have great influence on American nursing. The early Ursuline Sisters in France had done nursing as well as teaching, and in 1727 a small group of them came to New Orleans where even then colonial life had achieved certain standards of luxury in a civilization based on slavery. However, the people living in the settlement were swept by epidemic diseases, most important of which were yellow fever and smallpox; all the scourges of a seaport town were encountered. During the nineteenth century the Ursuline Sisters were active throughout the entire territory of Louisiana. They opened many hospitals and performed many heroic deeds, which were climaxed in the nursing done during the Battle of New Orleans. Soon after this they practically gave up nursing and restricted themselves to teaching.

As the growth of settlements in the new country proceeded, the need for nursing became urgent; the various Catholic nursing orders responded to the call. The Sisters of Charity were among the first; in 1809 Mother Elizabeth Bayley Seton in Emmitsburg, Maryland, established the Sisterhood of St. Joseph as a branch of the Sisters of Charity. In 1849 the Sisters of Charity became affiliated with the Order of St. Vincent de Paul. In 1830 the Sisters of Charity established the first hospital west of the Mississippi River—a log cabin in St. Louis. Almost at once it proved insufficient for the demands made on it, and in 1831 a larger hospital was built on Spruce and Fourth Streets. This came to be known as the Mullanphy Hospital; in 1874 it moved to bigger quarters, and in 1930, during its centenary, it was replaced by the DePaul Hospital, one of the most modern and certainly

Mother Elizabeth Bayley Seton

Mother Seton founded the American branch of the Sisters of Charity of St. Vincent de Paul.

one of the most beautiful hospitals in St. Louis at that time. The Sisters contributed some of the best nursing during the Civil War. Sister Anthony O'Connell, a Sister of Charity from Cincinnati, is remembered in the history of this period as the "Angel of the Battlefield."

The Sisters of Mercy, the Sisters of the Holy Cross, and also the Irish Sisters of Mercy came to America during the 1830s and 1840s and extended their orders throughout the new country, establishing hospitals everywhere and practicing the highest standards of nursing of the times.

Early nursing in Protestant hospitals

Protestant settlements did not fare as well. We have previously seen the havoc that was wrought during the Reformation to the Catholic nursing orders and to all for which they stood. The result was that wherever Protestant pioneers advanced, there was no organized effort to take care of the sick and wounded. The task was done by

Bellevue Hospital, 1848

Originally Bellevue Hospital was established as the New York Public Workhouse. The name was taken from its second site, Belle Vue on Kip's Farm, where it still stands.

persons who felt inclined thereto; although these persons apparently performed their task with kindness, their skill was limited by their inherent ability. As the colonies grew and as settlements became better established, they followed the pattern of their homeland and organized institutions for the care of the sick and the poor, not so much out of Christian charity as for social convenience—something had to be done with the unfortunate ones. The result, according to the descriptions that have reached us of these early refuges of poverty, sickness, and immorality, was a fair match for what Mrs. Fry found in British workhouses and hospitals during the same era. For in those early days the poorhouse and hospital were under a common roof, and no one who could possibly be nursed elsewhere would go to a hospital. Consequently the public developed a fear of hospitals, remnants of which survive even today, long after hospitals have ceased to be dens of horror and torment.

The most accurate information about nursing in American hospitals before the reform movement is found in the records of an investigation made in 1837 of conditions at Bellevue in New York. Later, the Bellevue Hospital Visiting Committee was cre-

ated as an agency of the New York State Charities Aid Association; yet little improvement was seen in the care of the sick.

Dirt and squalor were predominant factors; no money was available with which to accomplish anything; everybody lived, or died, close to a subsistence level. There was neither ventilation nor hygiene; plumbing was defective. The "nurses" were ill-paid individuals from the lower strata of the community, they were venal to a degree and were tempted to supplement their meager pay with bribes and extortions from the patients. They could be trusted with nothing—neither with administration of medicine nor with gifts of food for the patients. Often they were so deficient in number or health that the sicker patients had to receive most of their nursing from other patients who could move about or from prisoners or inmates of the workhouse. No proper provisions were made for the maintenance of the nurses. Their food was poor, and there is record that they even had to sleep in the barns on bundles of straw. Now we realize that "hospital" and "nursing" had a different connotation in those days from that of today. Only the utterly destitute went to the hospital. Any others who had a home or place to stay remained there when they were sick, and nursing was provided by the mother of the home, or the grandmother, or in well-to-do homes by trusted servants. The "Mrs. Gamp" of English life, portrayed by Charles Dickens in *Martin Chuzzlewit* as a benevolent character who nurtured the sick in this manner, does not seem to be quite as prevalent in early American days. In many neighborhoods certain women gained reputation in being especially good in nursing and were sought out for cases of sickness and confinement. These were called monthly nurses. Most of them were respectable women; many had a great deal of experience and, considering the limitation of medical experience of the period, were fully a match for the family doctors. Thus, considering the general state of medical knowledge and practice a hundred or more years ago, nursing of the sick in the middle and upper classes was not bad.

To present a few definite landmarks, we may remember that the Pennsylvania General Hospital was established in 1751, the New York Hospital in 1781, and the Massachusetts General Hospital in 1821. Two other institutions, the Philadelphia General Hospital and the Bellevue Hospital in New York, had their early beginnings before these came into being.

In 1713 the Quakers of Philadelphia established an almshouse for Quakers only. It demonstrated the value of such an institution as well as the need for one that was not restricted to Quakers.

Accordingly, in 1731 the town established a general almshouse and, in connection with it, a hospital ward. This institution repeatedly outgrew its quarters, new buildings were constructed outside the city in Blockley Township. In 1834 it was transferred and henceforth assumed the name Blockley, later "Old Blockley." During this period it had become less and less of an almshouse and more and more of a hospital, and an increasing amount of instruction of medical students took place within its walls. Many famous medical teachers, the best known

of whom is Dr. Osler, walked its wards. But all that did not prevent the standards of medical and nursing care at Old Blockley from sinking to a very low level until attempts were made to improve conditions during the early period of nursing reforms. Eventually Old Blockley developed into what is now known as Philadelphia General Hospital, still one of the leading hospitals in the country. Its early origin can probably be traced back farther than any of the other early American hospitals.

About the same time as Philadelphia General Hospital emerged, Bellevue Hospital originated as the New York Public Workhouse. When the New York Workhouse was erected in 1736, where the city hall now stands, one large room in the west end of the building was set aside to be used as an infirmary, and a medical officer, Dr. John Van Buren, was employed at a salary of £100 a year to look after the sick inmates. By the end of the century the institution had outgrown its quarters and was moved to Belle Vue on Kip's farm. Its name was taken from the place, and it has remained there since then, gradually changing its character from that of a workhouse and almshouse to that of a hospital. By 1825 a fever hospital was added, and from 1836 to 1838 the prisoners were moved to Blackwell's Island, after which Belle Vue continued as one of the leading American hospitals. The leading part that it took in the development of American schools of nursing will be discussed in Chapter 4.

The first hospital to be organized as such was the Pennsylvania Hospital. It was built in response to a petition presented in 1751 before the Colonial Assembly by a committee of Philadelphia citizens. Prominent men on the committee included Dr. Thomas Bond and Benjamin Franklin. The governor granted a charter for the hospital and provided £2,000 to be paid in two annual installments toward its construction, provided a like amount be raised by private contributions. This was rapidly done, and

Pennsylvania Hospital

The first hospital to be organized as such in America was Pennsylvania Hospital, whose first administrator was Benjamin Franklin.

after some negotiations, a site was acquired and the cornerstone was laid in 1755. The first patients were admitted by the end of the following year. The first president of the organization, Joshua Crosby, died within a month of the laying of the cornerstone. His place was taken by Benjamin Franklin, who remained in the post until he was appointed provincial agent at London in 1757. Among his many other accomplishments, Franklin was thus our first hospital administrator, and his views and organization here, as in his other projects, were quite progressive. The hospital has since continued its outstanding development.

When the Pennsylvania Hospital was being organized, New York City was still for many years to remain without a regular hospital for its citizens—during a time when all the great cities in Europe were building large institutions for their sick. That the defect was keenly felt was evidenced in the commencement address made by Samuel Bard to medical graduates at King's College in 1769: "It is truly a reproach, that a city like this should want a public hospital." This address immediately stimulated a movement that was heavily backed by Sir Henry Moore, governor of the colony. It resulted in 1771 in the granting of a royal charter to the Society of the Hospital, in the City of New York. A site was acquired on the west side of Broadway, opposite Pearl Street. The necessary funds were procured, and construction was begun on a fine hospital. It was almost finished in 1775 when, accidentally, a fire destroyed the entire inside of the building. However, the men behind the movement, including the new governor, renewed their efforts; new funds were raised, partly by a grant of £4,000 from the Colonial Assembly. The rebuilding was completed before the Revolutionary War broke out less than a year later. With the occupancy of New York City by the British, the hospital was used as a barracks and occasionally as a military hospital. There followed, after the war, a prolonged period of reconstruction, and not until the year 1791 was the hospital finally opened for regular medical service.

The Philadelphia Dispensary established in 1786 was the forerunner of our modern outpatient department and clinic for ambulatory patients. It was independent of any hospital and supported by civic-minded citizens in Philadelphia. The Philadelphia Dispensary for Out-Patients was so successful that the idea soon spread to other early American cities.

American medicine was still in its infancy in the eighteenth century. Many doctors came from Europe to settle in America, and many students went from this country to study in the European centers. Benjamin Franklin influenced American medicine not only by inventing bifocal glasses but also by preaching the use of fresh air and by helping in the foundation of the Pennsylvania Hospital.

Too, in America, medical teaching was for the most part at a low ebb. Only Philadelphia had attained any reputation; New York and Boston were still struggling into existence as medical centers. It was therefore simple and logical that American doctors should be divided into two groups: (1) those with the ambition and resources that enabled them to visit Edinburgh, London, and Paris, from which they returned to become leading surgeons and physicians, mostly in the larger cities of the East, and (2) those content with the preceptorship of an older practitioner—by far the majority.

The first medical schools in the United States were organized in the second half of the eighteenth century, the first one being the college of Philadelphia, now the University of Pennsylvania, founded by John Morgan, modeled after the Edinburgh School. The first American doctor of medicine degree was conferred in 1771 at the King's College School in New York, now the College of Physicians and Surgeons of Columbia University, founded in 1767. Harvard did not start a medical school until 1773. Other medical schools founded in this century were the Dartmouth College and School and the Transylvania College School in Kentucky.

It is no wonder that with a few exceptions medical practice in the United States 100 years ago was very bad; it could not have been otherwise. It is remarkable that

in America, largely through the efforts of the American Medical Association, the profession has been raised to the level at which it stands today and that in spite of all handicaps, Americans have been able to make important and fundamental contributions to the science.

One such contribution was McDowell's operations on ovarian tumor. Having had his attention drawn to the problem when he was a student in Edinburgh under John Bell, Ephraim McDowell (1771-1830), when he became a backwoods practitioner in Kentucky, had the courage to perform the operation. He was successful and gained fame by several repetitions of his feat. So incredible was his achievement that when reports first reached Europe, they were simply not believed.

Because of the growth of medical knowledge and of the hospital as a social institution, the deficiencies of nursing became glaringly apparent. As we have pointed out, the growth of modern medicine really began to gain momentum about the year 1800; there were doctors, then, who realized that properly trained nurses would be a great asset. In 1798 Dr. Valentine Seaman, attending surgeon to the New York Hospital, gave regular courses to nurses in anatomy, physiology, obstetrics, and pediatrics. He did not restrict instruction to lectures; he gave practical demonstrations also. He published a synopsis of these lectures, probably one of the earliest attempts at preparing nursing texts.

NURSING DURING EARLY AMERICAN WARS

The need for nurses has always been felt, but even more keenly in time of war. In America the crisis of the Revolutionary War occurred before Miss Nightingale's day, but it is interesting to note that George Washington asked Congress for a matron and for nurses to care for the sick and wounded. However, we know that the number of women with any nursing experience was pitifully small and that many laywomen volunteered their services more on a community level than anything else. The Catholic orders were the only organized groups with any actual knowledge of nursing, and they placed their hospitals and personnel at the disposal of the army. As was the custom of the time, wives, sisters, and mothers followed the men in the army and took care of them when they were sick and wounded.

During the Revolutionary War the Continental Army Medical Corps was not very successful at the beginning, and conditions were not improved until 1781 when Dr. John Cochran was appointed general director. Anesthesia and modern aseptic technic were unknown, the hospitals were unsanitary, and there was a shortage of food, medicine, and trained personnel. Epidemics were common in the army, and preventive medicine was unknown. It is interesting to note that during the Revolutionary War, chaplains from both the Catholic and Protestant faiths were appointed not only to improve morale but also to "recommend cleanliness as a virtue conducive to health." These conditions were common during all the wars of the nineteenth century and were not brought to the attention of the public in any organized and penetrating way until Miss Nightingale's efforts during the Crimean War.

Some Americans had begun to hear about the Red Cross and Florence Nightingale's work during the Crimean War. When the Civil War started, little organized information was available and independent of M. Dunant's efforts at that time, the United States Sanitary Commission was established in April, 1861. A branch of this commission opened a bureau in New York for the examination and registration of nurses for war service; about 100 applicants were offered as nurses to the federal army.

When the war finally broke out, this arrangement was totally inadequate, and the Surgeon General agreed to the organization of its own sanitary commisison as part of the army. The nurses for this arrangement were supplied largely by the Catholic orders: Sisters of Charity, Sisters of Mercy, and Sisters of St. Vincent. The Holy Cross Sisters, an Anglican Order, also supplied some.

Protestant nursing orders, including deaconesses, did good work in the war. All that organized nursing units could do proved insufficient, however, in the face of conditions that existed. After the big battles, experiences similar to those depicted in *Gone With the Wind* were reenacted throughout the war-ridden area. The descriptions by Louisa May Alcott in her *Hospital Sketches* serve as a classic example of one woman among thousands who were anxious to aid the cause and signed up as nurses without prerequisities other than a warm heart and an eager hand. She vividly described her feelings when she was first faced with the invasions of bloody, filthy, smelly human wrecks, whose wounds were covered by remnants of uniforms matted with filth and clotted blood. Victims came in numbers far exceeding the capacity of the accommodations prepared for them. Somehow everybody had to go to work with soap and brushes and try to clean them up to get them ready for surgical attention. Food had to be provided, and when the confusions of the first rush had subsided, there were hundreds of little jobs, apparently trivial, yet important to the patients or those they had left behind—letters to be written and valuables to be received and kept or transmitted to relatives.

Thus, in the American as in other armies, two types of nursing developed; a regular army nursing service, which was placed under the direction of Miss Dorothea Dix, and an organization sponsored by private citizens, at first tolerated, later supported, by the government.

Dorothea Lynde Dix (1803-1887) was known for her interest and activity in the field of reform for the mentally ill. She studied in England and on the Continent and was a friend of both Elizabeth Fry and Mr. Rathbone. Returning to America, she had worked unceasingly to improve conditions for the care of the mentally ill.

In 1861 a meeting of interested women resulted in the formation of the Women's Central Association of Relief. Out of this activity grew the Sanitary Commission. Influential laywomen and physicians became interested because it was necessary that they have some central organization through which supplies could be distributed. The Sanitary Commission attempted to bring together the relief work of many scattered organizations and groups. It was interested in recruiting and in everything associated with the health and welfare of the troops. It studied ways and means of supplementing government appropriations from private funds.

In some ways it might be said that this organization was a forerunner of the Red Cross. The Confederacy had no such type of organization, but as we know from official and unofficial stories, valiant work was done by laywomen and religious groups. In 1861, although Dorothea Dix was not a nurse, she was appointed superintendent of female nurses, and then she proceeded to organize the first nurse corps of the United States Army. At this time Miss Dix was about 60 years of age, and by some her standards were considered very rigid and inflexible. She would not have any nurses less than 30 years of age, and they were preferably to be homely. Although no uniform was designated, somber colors were insisted on—black or brown. An allowance of $12 a month was paid these nurses, Miss Dix herself serving without remuneration. Miss Dix found, as Miss Nightingale did in the Crimean War, that most of her nurses came from religious orders, both Protestant and Catholic.

Although eventually some 2,000 nurses participated in the Civil War, their number was entirely inadequate. Their equipment was worse than primitive, and hospital facilities were whatever could be found, although in this respect the Civil War con-

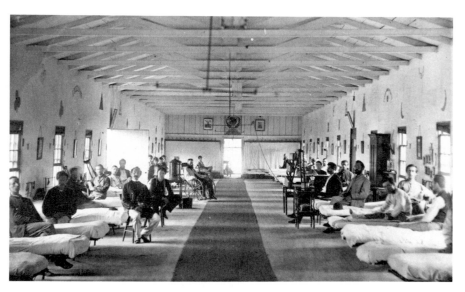

Armory Square Hospital, Washington, D.C., during the Civil War
(From The Granger Collection, New York, N.Y.)

tributed one thing: hospital ships were first placed in service at this time. Not only were hospital and nursing facilities insufficient, but also the hygiene was atrocious; there were in that war about 6 million medical hospital admissions, mostly from epidemic or contagious diseases, and only about 425,000 surgical cases, from actual war casualties. It is no exaggeration to state that in those days war claimed more victims from disease than from bullets.

This experience made clear, especially in the light of what Miss Nightingale had done, the desperate need for organized schools of nursing; such schools were accordingly started in New York City, Boston, and New Haven.

At the turn of the century when trouble between America and Cuba was imminent, Congress authorized employment of nurses under contract. This was necessary because military nursing had not developed at all since the Civil War and because no mecha-

Spanish-American War nurse

nism existed by which the surgeon general could find nurses if needed. However, by 1898 when the Spanish-American War began, schools of nursing had been training young women for this profession for about twenty years. More than 500 schools of nursing had graduated about 10,000 nurses by the year 1900.

Dr. Anita McGee, at that time vice-president of the Daughters of the American Revolution, had interested the Surgeon General, George M. Sternberg, with a plan for a nurse corps, which was to be organized with the D.A.R. acting as an examining board or a clearinghouse for all applications. Congress gave him authority to employ as many nurses by contract as would be needed. Nurses in the Spanish-American War received $30 a month, plus ration allowances. In spite of the great need, not all medical officers were willing to accept army nurses in the beginning. Since they were carefully selected by Dr. McGee, assistant to the surgeon general, and they gave satisfactory service, the army doctors became increasingly dependent on them. More than 1,500 nurses were accepted as army nurses during the Spanish-American War.

The Nurses' Associated Alumnae of the United States and Canada were disturbed with the nursing conditions at the outbreak of the Spanish-American War, and at a meeting its president, Mrs. Isabel Hampton Robb, suggested that the association offer its services to the government in an attempt to obtain more and better nurses. When this suggestion was taken to Washington, it was found that Dr. McGee had already been appointed and had set up her own standards. Several prominent superintendents of nursing schools volunteered to help in the organization of army nursing, among them Anna C. Maxwell, superintendent of nurses, Presbyterian Hospital in New York City. Miss Maxwell was appointed chief nurse at the hospital at Chickamauga Park, Georgia.

In 1900 there were 202 nurses remaining

in the nurse corps, and the Army Reorganization Bill presented to Congress in that year provided for a permanent nurse corps as part of the medical department of the army. The Army Nurse Corps was created by law on February 2, 1901.

THE RED CROSS

All over the world the symbol of the Red Cross stands for help in wars or in civilian disasters. What is the history behind such a unique organization?

In reviewing the life of Florence Nightingale, it was noted that her first great task was to care for the sick and the wounded of the battlefield. That accomplished, her attention turned to the general welfare of the men in the army. They had more coming to them than a cot, three meals a day, and small pay, and she began to organize all those recreational facilities that, as we know today, add greatly to the comforts of army life. Finally, after the war she turned her attention to many activities concerned with the health of the civilian population. In many respects the life of Miss Nightingale after 1854 epitomizes the later development of the Red Cross, which she inspired.

The story of this institution begins on June 24, 1859, near the town of Solferino in Northern Italy. About 300,000 men, Italians and French, were locked in mortal combat, and the carnage was incredible. Yet the work of Florence Nightingale but a few years previously had gone unheeded, and the provisions for taking care of the wounded were woefully insufficient. Hundreds died from inadequate attention. The appalling situation struck a tourist who accidentally happened to be there, to the point that he assembled such volunteers as he could gather, mostly woman of Solferino, for the work of bringing succor to the wounded. The name of this gentleman was Jean Henri Dunant; he was Swiss, and he later described his experience in the classic *Un Souvenir de Solferino.*

Inspired by the work of Miss Nightingale in the Crimea, he then decided to devote his life to the prevention of a repetition of the needless horrors of Solferino. He traveled from country to country explaining his scheme to all responsible persons who could help him further it. In France, Napoleon III lent a willing ear, not knowing how badly he himself would need the services of the Red Cross but a few years later. Dunant's idea was to establish bands of volunteer helpers who would seek out and treat the wounded of the battlefield without regard to nationality and in complete neutrality under the protection of all the armed forces. Further, this establishment should be sanctioned by convention and respected by all belligerents. Dunant addressed international congresses, and finally M. Gustave Moynier, president of the Society of Public Utility of Geneva, Switzerland, convened a congress in October, 1863, of thirty-six representatives from fourteen different countries for the purpose of studying M. Dunant's proposal. At this meeting the fundamental principles of the Red Cross were established, and plans were laid for organizing Red Cross societies in various countries with organization and powers to render aid to wounded soldiers and other victims of war. The congress adjourned, and work progressed to secure for the movement the necessary international legal status and to devise an acceptable emblem that would be recognized everywhere.

Even before it could be further organized, the young organization was put to a test. A short but bloody war broke out in the winter of 1863-1864 between tiny Denmark and Bismarck's newly organized Prussia. The Danish armaments were hopelessly outmoded, and the war was one long debacle for the Danes. However, it did offer the first opportunity for trying out the Red Cross, and when the Federal Council of Switzerland in August, 1864, convoked an international diplomatic conference, practical experience was available for the organization of what came to be known as the *Geneva Convention of 1864.* Dunant's original principles were established: the wounded must be respected, military hospitals must be considered neutral, and all persons, equipment, and buildings under the jurisdiction of the institution were to be marked with a red cross on a white background (the reverse of the Swiss flag).

In spite of some infractions, with many more accusations of infractions and few abuses, these original principles have been accepted and respected by almost all nations. At a conference held in The Hague in 1899, the principles were extended to sea warfare also, and at conventions held in 1906 and 1907, the Geneva and Hague conventions were revised. Curiously, Turkey, by special arrangement, has substituted for the red cross the crescent; and Iran, the lion and the rising sun. Thus, out of the Geneva Convention came the International Red Cross Committee, which is the coordinating agency of all the national Red Cross committees. Its purpose is to establish Red Cross committees in countries in which they do not exist, to act as a liaison between the various committees, and to endeavor to have the Geneva Convention accepted by all civilized countries and to ensure that it is observed. In time of war it establishes international agencies for the assistance of war prisoners and other victims of war, and in recent years it has added plans for relief during national disasters such as floods and earthquakes. Thus the international committee acts in any matter that is beyond the scope of the national committees. In 1912 the international committee instituted the Florence Nightingale medal to be given to nurses who had especially distinguished themselves.

The national Red Cross societies are the component parts of the International Red Cross. They were originally formed purely for war service, but, as we shall see, their scope has been greatly widened. To be ac-

cepted by the International Red Cross, a national society must be recognized as an auxiliary to the army of its country by its government, which, in turn, must have subscribed to the Geneva Convention. It must accept the emblem of the red cross (with the exceptions noted above) and the organization must be open to all citizens of the country regardless of sex, politics, or religion. It must also cooperate in all required respects with the international organization, which, in return, will recognize only one national Red Cross society in each sovereign state. Within each country a national Red Cross society is autonomous and free to develop its own ideas.

It may thus be seen that the Red Cross has an important official standing. In war it becomes indispensable, and it has assumed so many peacetime activities that it is rapidly becoming one of the most important social agencies of the state; yet it is entirely independent and supported by voluntary contributions.

Functions

During war, then, the National Red Cross Society assists but does not replace the regular army medical service (which, however, also uses the emblem of the Red Cross in accordance with the Geneva Convention). It mobilizes nurses, nurses' aides, and volunteer helpers and sets up ambulance services, hospitals, hospital ships, canteens, libraries for the soldiers, entertainments, occupational therapy, and many other activities. It renders aid to war refugees and prisoners of war and may assist groups of citizens in devastated countries for instance, by feeding children. When the war is over, the Red Cross becomes active in the identification and return of prisoners of war, resettlement of refugees, fighting postwar epidemics, reorganization for the next war, and relieving suffering arising from the war. It will see that disabled men get the best treatment and will train them by establishing orthopedic and other special clinics and by establishing trade schools. It may extend direct aid to widows and orphans of soldiers, or it may undertake to house permanently disabled men, as the British Red Cross does in The Star and Garter at Richmond, England.

These, then, are some of the principal activities of the Red Cross in connection with war. It is easily seen how many of these tasks concern nurses or might depend entirely on professional nurses. Nurses, therefore, formed an important part of the organization, and any properly qualified nurse in good professional standing was encouraged to join the Red Cross reserve. Until 1947 the Red Cross assumed responsibility for recruiting nurses for the military forces, which depended on the Red Cross in time of war.

The American Red Cross

The Red Cross has been discussed as an international institution. The American Red Cross, however, has its own interesting history.

The Red Cross was organized in many European countries. Clara Barton went abroad and spent years studying the organization in various countries; she established close contact with Miss Nightingale, who later followed American developments with warm interest. Miss Barton's studies were very practical—during the Franco-Prussian War from 1870 to 1871 she actually accompanied one of the Red Cross ambulances into the field. She came back firmly convinced that America must have a Red Cross society that would adhere to the Geneva Convention. The result of her efforts was the incorporation in 1881 in the District of Columbia of an American Association of the Red Cross, with Miss Barton as president. Ratification by the United States was accomplished in 1882.

The young organization was first put to the test in the yellow fever epidemic in Florida in 1888 and in the Johnstown flood in 1889. For the epidemic Miss Barton sup-

Clara Barton

plied around 30 volunteer nurses, mostly from New Orleans; they were supposed to be immunized to yellow fever, having had the disease. There was friction with the local board of health, and not without justification, for some of the volunteers were without previous experience in nursing. In the relief of the Johnstown disaster, Red Cross units came out from Philadelphia and worked under the direction of physicians.

During these years Miss Barton and others interested in the cause worked hard to develop the American Red Cross. An organization evolved with local committees and sections for the purpose of selecting and training volunteer nurses so that in time of war they could be promptly mobilized and placed in active service. The American National Red Cross was established on a firmer basis in 1893, again with Miss Barton as president. The New York branch opened a hospital for the training of Red Cross nurses. The course was planned to take two years and three months, after which the nurse graduated as a Red Cross sister. This organization adhered to the Geneva Convention, and while on service the nurses devoted their full time to their work; they received no salary but were given the best maintenance obtainable. Gradually the Red Cross School of Nursing failed because in the meantime the general education of nurses was advancing so fast that the purpose of the school was better fulfilled by some of the new, modern training schools, which developed in connection with the larger hospitals.

Toward the end of the century, trouble was brewing in the Caribbean, and the war with Spain was approaching. The Red Cross was enlisting nurses for war service, and in March, 1898, the Cuban Relief Committee chartered the S.S. *State of Texas* as a Red Cross relief ship to sail under the Red Cross flag. Miss Barton was to meet the ship in Florida. In the meantime war was declared, and the *Texas* sailed with an American convoy to be of aid to American soldiers.

Up until that time the American Red Cross had had no official standing, but its work became increasingly important. A special committee was set up to supply nurses, and in New York Mr. William Wardwell organized the American National Red Cross Relief Committee. Now the Red Cross obtained government sanction as the proper and sole representative of the international committee in the United States. Its position was thus official.

The Red Cross nurses went to the war in Cuba under the direction of Miss Barton and nursed under her in American hospitals. However, the amount of nursing work increased beyond all expectations, and it became necessary to send for reinforcements. Before these could arrive, the entire staff, including Dr. Lesser, the staff surgeon, came down with yellow fever and, to make matters worse, the hoped-for reinforcements failed to arrive. At the same time, the army organized its own regular nursing service; Dr. Anita Newcomb McGee was placed in charge directly under the surgeon general.

After World War I the Red Cross nurses were called on in much reorganization work and in the fight against the epidemics and the pandemic of influenza that swept the war-torn world. The enlarged scope of the Red Cross was then generally appreciated; it participated in disaster relief and also in public health projects in areas in which local resources proved to be insufficient. This was accomplished particularly through the Delano Red Cross Nursing Service, established by the will of Miss Jane A. Delano, and has provided nursing service for several undeveloped and inaccessible regions.

However, disaster relief remains one of the chief peacetime tasks of the Red Cross Nursing Service, and since World War I there has not been a disaster of any magnitude in which that organization has not taken an important part in the rescue work.

Other activities of the Red Cross were developed about this time. Although instruction in home hygiene and care of the sick had been conducted by the Red Cross branch in the District of Columbia as early as 1908, these programs were not promoted nationally until 1913. The same year a book on home hygiene and care of the sick was issued by the Red Cross.

Public health nursing was first proposed as a Red Cross program by Lillian D. Wald as early as 1908. It was financed mainly by Jacob H. Schiff, an officer of the New York branch. It was first confined to rural nursing but by 1913 extended to towns having populations as large as 25,000. This activity of the Red Cross was known as Town and Country Nursing Service. In 1915 the first plan for training nurses' aides was proposed. Although it was put into operation that year, it did not really develop fully until World War I. Miss Delano was, in 1917, appointed head of the new department of nursing. All phases of nursing service were included in this department— home hygiene and care of the sick, dietetics, public health nursing in rural areas and small towns, disaster nursing, and instruction of nurses' aides.

Miss Delano was succeeded by Clara D. Noyes, who had been her assistant since 1916. Miss Noyes was known internationally as well as nationally. She was twice elected first vice-president of the International Council of Nurses.

The basic international policies under which the Red Cross was first organized have permeated the national programs in all countries recognizing the Red Cross. The American Red Cross Nursing Services assist in various nursing activities all over the world. This organization cooperates with the director of the Nursing Bureau of the League of Red Cross Societies. It shares knowledge and resources with Red Cross societies of other countries, including provision for visitors to study in the United States.

The American Red Cross method of teaching instructors has been adapted to the needs of many countries and is being used in more than twenty Red Cross societies. The opportunities for nursing service and nursing education under the banner of the Red Cross are a challenge to all nurses interested in working toward one world for nursing.

The Red Cross Nursing Service no longer assumes responsibility for recruiting nurses for the army or navy. Legislation in 1947 established a permanent nurse corps for the armed forces, including the maintenance of nurse reserves. Since then, local Red Cross chapters have enrolled nurses for community services, including local and national disasters.

Since 1945 Red Cross home nursing instruction has become part of the curriculum in many secondary schools. At first instructors for these courses were nurses, but since 1948 the Red Cross has authorized for this task not only nurses but also teachers and others with teacher-training experience, who complete the instructor's course given by the Red Cross. In 1947 the new blood program was established by the Red Cross, and in 1948 an intensive training program

was begun for volunteer registered nurses. By 1956 more than 60,000 registered nurses had been trained in some phase of blood collection activity.

The various services that have developed within the Red Cross since World War II are provided to communities through approximately 3,700 Red Cross chapters throughout the nation. Each of these local chapters is an administrative unit of the Red Cross, operating within the limits of a charter granted by the national organization. A volunteer board of directors and volunteer committees direct the work of the chapter. One of the important committees in every community is the Nursing Services Committee. This committee is responsible for planning and carrying through the nursing programs within the Red Cross, in accordance with community needs and demands. The nursing programs within the Red Cross are planned in close cooperation with recognized health groups such as the National League for Nursing, the American Nurses' Association, the Children's Bureau, and the United States Public Health Service.

Contemporary programs of the Red Cross Nursing Service are planned to meet the present-day needs of American communities and include disaster nursing, home nursing (including mother and baby care), the instruction of volunteer nurses' aides, enrollment of graduate nurses in local chapters in community service, the blood program nursing, and educational and technical assistance to nurses in Red Cross societies in other countries. Some fine educational materials in the form of bulletins describing the work of the Red Cross nurse, to be used in the recruiting of graduate nurses for these activities, have been prepared.

AMERICAN MEDICAL PIONEERS

During the early nineteenth century a physiologist became well known because of his studies of gastric digestion and gastric motility, which formed the basis for all later work on the physiology of gastric digestion. He was William Beaumont (1785-1853).

On the morning of June 6, 1822, an accident happened on the little Island of Mackinac, north of Michigan, which was destined to bring fame to one man and a great increase of knowledge to the world. A young voyageur, Alexis St. Martin, happened to be in the way of a shotgun that accidentally went off 2 feet from his body. The entire charge, including his clothing, entered his left side. At first the wound was thought to be fatal, but under the care of a regimental surgeon stationed at the fort the lad recovered. However, a fistula, or opening from the stomach to the surface of the body, remained. The surgeon, Dr. Beaumont, seized this opportunity for study of gastric function and attached the boy to his household for the next few years. He performed a series of experiments that have become fundamental in our knowledge of that organ, and Beaumont's name is now known to every young medical student. His studies were performed under primitive conditions, and the brilliant results are due to Beaumont's ability for research and not to his equipment. Alexis was an unworthy fellow who repeatedly left him, and at last Beaumont failed to recover him. In 1839 Beaumont was stationed in St. Louis. Later, because of a difference with his superiors, he retired from the army and entered private practice there, where his fame and ability soon made him the leading doctor of St. Louis.

Best known of all American doctors of the period was Benjamin Rush (1755-1813). He has been referred to as the "American Sydenham." His influence in furthering the clinical method in America continued long after his death; his descendants are still practicing medicine in Philadelphia.

Perhaps the greatest medical advance made in America during this period was the use of ether for surgical anesthesia. For this

Sir William Osler

great boon to medicine we are indebted to a Boston dentist named William T. G. Morton (1819-1868). Through careful research, Morton chose ether as the drug for his purpose. He demonstrated his discovery to the Boston surgeons, and it was soon broadcast all over the world. Along with the work of Pasteur and of Lister it made possible the great advance of modern surgery. It is a curious and sordid fact that Morton, instead of granting his gift magnanimously to the world as most medical benefactors did, tried to exploit it by patent rights. This soon involved him in litigation, which broke him bodily and financially; instead of reaping the laurels of fame, his last years were spent in ignominious misery.

A historical figure in American medicine during the late nineteenth and early twentieth centuries, one whose influence is still felt today, was Sir William Osler (1849-1919). His activities were shared by three countries—Canada, the United States, and Great Britain. He combined with a thorough training in pathology outstanding clinical abilities, both as a teacher and as a diagnostician. Thus he came to be one of the founders of Johns Hopkins Medical

School in Baltimore, and it was here he achieved his greatest fame.

The last years of his life were tragic. All through his life he had given of himself freely for the advancement of knowledge and love of mankind. For himself he had but one thing, a son, and that son was sacrificed in World War I. When Osler received the telegram from the war office, his spirit died within him, and his body survived but a few years. No more direct impression of the futility and bestiality of war could be given than that conveyed by the description of this father's grief for his son.

In 1898 Pierre Curie and his wife, Marie, isolated radium, now used in the treatment of certain types of cancer. In 1910 Paul Ehrlich discovered a cure for syphilis in the form of arsphenamine. Large sums were being appropriated, particularly in America, for scientific investigation. In 1901 John D. Rockefeller endowed the Rockefeller Institute for Medical Research. Simon Flexner, an outstanding scientist, was director. He gathered about him outstanding scientists in medical and allied fields; many discoveries have come from the Institute.

In 1908 the Carnegie Foundation announced a study of medical schools in the United States and Canada; on the basis of this report medical schools began to be graded in 1910 and have been graded ever since.

SOCIAL SETTING

Medical science was confronted by a host of problems. More than 100 years ago Louis Pasteur emphasized the importance of the numerical method in medicine, but few doctors properly appreciated the necessity of suitable application of statistical methods in determining effective treatment and in evaluating data. Tuberculosis, although its incidence was receding, was still a formidable enemy and required much preventive work and improvement of treatment during its early stages. Venereal disease, especially syphilis, was yet to be conquered; in this

field, however, notable beginnings had been made by the discovery of the spirochete and the Wassermann reaction (1906), by further development of the specific drugs salvarsan and its derivatives, by the use of heavy metals, and by the general recognition of venereal disease as a public health problem. Maternal mortality was still too high for the country as a whole. Further advances in surgical technic were expected. (In this connection, however, we may remember that at a congress in England in 1872, just before Lister's work was generally appreciated, the opinion was expressed that surgery had then almost reached the limits of its achievement.) The greatest advances in the near future were expected in increased knowledge of the endocrine glands and of the vitamins, in the control of cancer, in mental illness, and in preventive medicine.

During the late eighteenth and nineteenth centuries scientific progress in all phases of diagnosis and treatment of disease had been very great. This increased knowledge had resulted in the beginning of specialization in all health activities. Increased knowledge meant the need for more and better equipment in doctors' offices, in clinics, and in hospitals. All these changes were beginning to increase the cost of medical care. As the community became educated in health matters and as confidence was created in hospitals, doctors, and nurses, increasing demands were being made on the health program of the entire United States. As health and disease became matters of public concern, we find that communities began to make plans for assuming certain responsibilities in these areas. This was observed particularly in countries in which socialism was advancing. Chancellor Bismarck was instrumental in working out a plan of compulsory insurance against illness in Germany in 1883. The German example of providing social insurance made quite an impression on other European countries. Compulsory health insurance for those of low incomes was adopted in Austria in 1888. Other countries in Europe adopting some type of compulsory health insurance or subsidizing voluntary societies were Sweden in 1891, Denmark in 1892, Belgium in 1894, Italy in 1898, and Switzerland in 1912. In Russia in 1918 a People's Commissariat of Public Health was established, and in line with other developments in the communist state almost complete state medicine developed. All these developments and their underlying social philosophies naturally were studied by and had some influence on other countries. England, although probably more individualistic politically than some of the continental countries, had become highly industrialized during the nineteenth century, and even the poorer classes were becoming better educated. In 1911 a National Insurance Act was adopted by the English Parliament. In England the state as well as employers and employees contributed to the cost. Patients had a free choice of doctors, and what has become known as the panel system developed.

5 • Nursing education and nursing service

The continuous changing and upgrading of nursing education is the cornerstone for the delivery of health services to all Americans.

The care demanded by all, not as a privilege but as a right, can only be accomplished by advances in nursing education. These changes and advances began before the turn of the century and continue constantly but now at an accelerated rate. As it has in the past, nursing will continue to meet its challenges.

In the early nineteenth century a new era began in hospital construction and in medicine, which laid the foundation and emphasized the need for a trained group of nurses to meet the growing complexities of medicine and to staff the growing number of hospitals. One of the important hospitals of this period was the Massachusetts General Hospital. It was established in 1810 as the result of a letter circulated by fifty-six men of Boston who believed that Boston, too, should have a hospital for the poor. The movement was backed by leading Boston doctors and in 1821 resulted in the opening of the Massachusetts General Hospital. Ever since its opening, it has maintained standards often far ahead of its time. The deplorable conditions of nursing that developed in many of the hospitals at this time never existed here. Another hospital that led in nursing reforms was the Johns Hopkins in Baltimore, built in 1889.

Many other communities built large hospitals because, with the growing industrialization, cities needed a place in which to house the sick. In America as in Europe, the process was largely a result of urban development occasioned by the growth of the Industrial Age. The main purpose of the hospital in the nineteenth century was to serve as a dormitory or a place of sojourn for the sick. It served incidentally as a convenient place for the practical training of doctors and later of nurses. The events of the Civil War particularly emphasized the urgent need in the United States for adequate hospital facilites and for trained personnel.

EARLY EDUCATIONAL EFFORTS

The first attempt at a regularly organized school of nursing was made in 1839 by the Nurse Society of Philadelphia under Dr. Joseph Warrington. It was inspired by the work of Elizabeth Fry in England. The instruction was elementary; there were regular courses, with lectures and demonstrations using a mannequin. After a stated period and evidence of proficiency the nurses received a Certificate of Approbation. Dr. Warrington taught nursing students at the Philadelphia Dispensary together with medical students. The nurses were called "pupils," and in 1849 they were housed in a home of their own.

Another Philadelphia attempt was the

school of nursing established in connection with the Women's Hospital in Philadelphia in 1861. The course was supposed to last for six months and was designed to appeal to the better type of young women to "train a superior class of nurses." Lectures were given in medical and surgical nursing, materia medica, and dietetics. These nurses received a diploma at the successful termination of the course.

Another aspiration to form a nursing school was frustrated by the Civil War. Dr. Elizabeth Blackwell had closely studied Florence Nightingale's ideas and wanted to establish a school for nurses in connection with the New York Infirmary for Women. This school did not materialize.

The realization of the need for nursing reforms remained, but ideas were slow in maturing. The agitation that had been going on in England and the schools that were opened following the leadership of Miss Nightingale had become known in America. American reformers, inspired by visits to England and the continent, began investigating conditions at home. Attention was also paid to the struggling efforts to establish schools of nursing. The cause was not without the support of the medical profession, for in 1869 the American Medical Association accepted a report from its committee assigned to the training of nurses. The chairman was an outstanding Philadelphia surgeon, Dr. Samuel Gross. The committee appreciated the importance of adequate training for nurses and recommended that schools of nursing be established in connection with hospitals all over the United States.

All the more important schools have their history, but because of limited space a detailed description cannot be included here.

Three early schools

In 1873 three important schools appeared, almost simultaneously. All of them were destined to influence the development of modern nursing. These schools were orga-nized more or less in accordance with Miss Nightingale's ideas. Some of these ideas later tended to be forgotten. The main principle was that the school must be considered primarily an educational institution, not a source of cheap labor. The earliest schools of nursing in America were created independently of hospitals by boards or committees with power and freedom to develop the school. However, mainly because of lack of endowment, the schools were early absorbed into the hospitals with which they were connected. Therefore the history of nursing in America is inextricably bound up with the growth and development of hospitals; most of the schools were created and conducted by hospitals to serve their needs, and the education of the nurse became a by-product of her service to the hospital.

As schools of nursing developed rapidly during the years that followed, many hospitals, especially the smaller ones, discovered that a school of nursing under the guise of "practical experience" could be made a valuable source of free, or almost free, labor. Consequently formal instruction was often neglected, and it was not until the modern reform movements became effective that this principle again became firmly established. Now it is increasingly realized that Miss Nightingale was right when she said that the education of nurses, like that of doctors, is a public duty and emphasized that a school of nursing must be endowed or supported by public funds—it cannot be self-supporting and remain a good school.

The second principle was that the school of nursing must be administratively independent although closely connected with the hospital. The head of the school, whether she is called "matron" as in England or "director" as in America, should be a nurse, responsible only to the hospital or school of nursing board. This point has been highly disputed. Another school of thought would have the director of nursing responsible to the hospital superinten-

Earlier custodial jobs

In earlier times custodial jobs such as stoking the stove were part of the hospital nurse's regular duties.

dent for the nursing care and—under a separate budget—the instruction of nurses. Only through an independent connection with the hospital can the education of nurses be ensured, free of interference by interests that may disrupt orderly planning of the course.

It was generally thought advisable that student nurses live in a nurses' home. Hours of work were often irregular, and discipline, of necessity, was strict. This arrangement was, however, not always considered necessary during preclinical courses or postgraduate work.

The importance of the head nurse, or the "sister" as she is called in England, was also an integral part of Miss Nightingale's scheme. She is a professional nurse responsible for the administration of a ward or a division and for the teaching of the student nurses that come under her charge. Much of the clinical instruction is thus her responsibility.

The young schools that came into exis-

tence could not fill all these requirements—in fact many modern schools are still striving to solve these problems—but they were ideals toward which they could aim, and during the next few years notable progress was made.

Bellevue Hospital School of Nursing

When American women interested in the Sanitary Commission no longer had to worry about the war, they turned their interests to domestic institutions of charity. They formed the New York State Charities Aid Association under which the Bellevue Hospital Visiting Committee operated, directed by Louisa Lee Schuyler. Reference has been made to the shocking revelations of that committee, and it was realized that improvement of the nursing was one of the essential requirements for hospital reform. From the start the committee met the resistance of most of those in authority, but that did not stop it. It publicly appealed for funds; Dr. Gill Wylie, who had been an intern in the hospital and who was sympathetic to the reform movement, was sent abroad to learn what he could directly from Miss Nightingale and from the schools that she had helped to organize. Consequently the plan for organization of the school of nursing at Bellevue followed closely Miss Nightingale's principles; in America the system became known as the "Bellevue system."

There was some difficulty in finding someone to take charge of the new school. Public announcements were made, in response to which Sister Helen of the Order of the Holy Cross offered her services. She was accepted, and the school was established May 1, 1873.

Sister Helen (Miss Bowden), a member of the Sisterhood of All Saints, had been trained at the University College Hospital in London, when nursing there was in the hands of the Order of the Holy Cross. Later she had extensive experience in workhouse infirmaries, in epidemics, and during the war between France and Germany in 1870-1871. At the time of her application she was in residence at the Community House in Baltimore. Therefore she brought to Bellevue Hospital thorough training, and although she was not a Nightingale nurse, she was fully conversant with the principles of that school. She carried out these principles successfully until the school was well established in 1876, when she went to South Africa to take part in pioneer nursing there. She was a strict, austere woman with a good understanding of human nature and of politicians, for whom she was always fully a match.

Under her direction the pupil nurses were housed in a building rented for the purpose. Although many of the old nurses applied for acceptance, they were refused; an attempt was made to recruit young girls from above the servant class to make nursing attractive as a career. Their training was planned but included no regular classwork or lectures. In the beginning only a few

Linda Richards

wards were placed at the disposal of the new school for instructional purposes. This proved to be so successful that more were soon added. Although the school did publish a *Manual of Nursing* in 1876, the formal instruction left much to be desired.

In 1874, Miss Linda Richards, America's first "trained nurse," came from Boston to become night superintendent. She instituted the system of keeping written records and orders, which has since become a requirement in all nursing schools. After a while uniforms were introduced; the nurses were reluctant to wear them until someone had the idea of encouraging one of the pupil nurses from a very good family to wear one. Then a general clamor for uniforms arose. It was readily gratified.

Thus the school, founded through the efforts of Louisa Lee Schuyler, flourished and became a leading school of nursing. It has had many brilliant alumnae, notably Jane A. Delano, Isabel Hampton, and Lavinia L. Dock. In 1967 the diploma program was closed, and the school became an integral part of the Department of Nursing of Hunter College of the City University of New York.

New England Hospital for Women and Children

The New England Hospital for Women and Children attempted to form a school in 1861 but was not successful until it was reformed in 1872. Dr. Marie Zakrzewska, who studied in Berlin but took her medical degree in Cleveland, Ohio, urged that a school of nursing be established in the New England Hospital. A charter for a training school for nurses was included in the hospital charter of 1863. She personally took active part in the training of nurses, but it remained on a rather informal basis until the hospital was rebuilt in 1872 and placed under the charge of Dr. Susan Dimock who, like most good American doctors of the time, had been trained in Europe. She had been to Kaiserswerth, and when the reorganized school opened in 1872, it largely followed the pattern of Kaiserswerth. The course lasted one year and included both practical instruction and lectures. The school achieved its greatest fame because an alumna became one of the leaders of nursing in the following generation.

Miss Linda Richards began her nursing career in the Boston City Hospital. Eager for training and advancement, she entered the first class of the New England Hospital and graduated one year later. After graduation she worked for a while as night superintendent at the Bellevue Hospital; she later returned to Boston and took over the school at the Massachusetts General Hospital. When this school was well organized, she resigned to study English methods of nursing. During this period she became personally acquainted with Miss Nightingale. On her return she began a remarkable career reorganizing the nursing services of hospitals throughout the country; in 1885 she was called to Japan where she organized and led the first Japanese school of nursing at Kyoto for five years. Back in the United States she took up the organization of mental hospitals and spent the remainder of her long and remarkable career moving from one mental hospital to another, improving their nursing services. She has left a record of her experiences in her *Reminiscences*, published by Whitcomb and Barrows.

The nursing instruction at the New England Hospital as described by Miss Richards was largely practical, hours were long, and time off was limited to an afternoon every two weeks. There were no night nurses. Very sick patients could interfere seriously with the nurses' sleep, for their rooms were between wards. In this early school there was little formal teaching and there were no textbooks. Some bedside instruction was provided by women interns.

As we note from the general tenor of such descriptions, which practically applied to other Boston hospitals as well, they were a far cry from the medieval conditions at Bellevue and many other places. Nursing was to a certain extent systematized, and a measure of cleanliness and acceptable care was extended to the patients. There was still plenty of room for reform, however.

Perhaps even better conditions existed at the Massachusetts General Hospital. In fact, by the standards of those times, a nursing reform was not urgently needed; both governors and medical staff prided themselves on the care that their patients received. Nevertheless, the spirit of nursing reform that the Civil War had engendered extended to Boston where the Women's Educational Union appointed a committee to look into the opportunities that nursing could offer women as a career. It is of interest to recognize the appearance of professional aspiration, for on the committee were ladies of the best families of Boston. Their goals were not hospital reforms, but opportunities for career women. Purely on the strength of the social and intellectual standing of the women on this committee, the hospital trustees and doctors accepted the experimental establishment of a school of nursing in the Massachusetts General Hospital. It was opened on November 1, 1873; six student nurses enrolled. The equipment was elementary, but there was an organized attempt at formal instruction closely supervised by the members of the committee. Certain innovations were actually tried. This school pioneered the "preliminary course" in America.

In spite of all this the young school had difficulties getting started. The early superintendents seemed to lack vision and were unable to break with old ways. Long hours and menial tasks interfered with the training of the students. Proper leadership was needed. Miss Richards, then in New York, was selected. She accepted and within a year conditions were much improved; classes were organized and the proper emphasis was placed on the training. The more menial tasks were gradually relegated to attendants, and the doctors began to recognize the advantage of having properly trained nurses. After a year's trial under Miss Richards' guidance, the school was accepted by the hospital and it has ever since maintained the highest standards and traditions. This feat was all the more remarkable when comparing Miss Richards' professional training with minimum requirements today. After some preliminary work at Boston City Hospital she had received such formal training as was possible in the first class of the New England Hospital; her "postgraduate" experience was limited to what she had been able to learn as night superintendent at the newly reorganized Bellevue. She herself realized that she still had much to learn, and after two and one-half years she resigned to visit England and Miss Nightingale and to study the work that was being done overseas.

Connecticut School

Among the three early schools of nursing, the Connecticut School was the first to receive its charter, but for some time it admitted no students. In 1872 the New Haven Hospital appointed a committee to investigate the feasibility of organizing a training school for nurses. In their study they heavily relied on the report of Dr. Wylie, which had just become available. They were remarkably farseeing in adopting one of Miss Nightingale's principal ideas: they did not want the hospital to start a school, but they wanted a school organized independent of the hospital, which then would serve as a field for the practical training. By such an arrangement they made it difficult for the hospital to use the nurses as cheap labor. After extensive advertising for potential students they finally were able to open on October 1, 1873.

The training school was an immediate success; the number of students rapidly increased, and soon the school was a source of superintendents for other hospitals. In 1879 it published the *New Haven Manual of Nursing*, a textbook created by the committee consisting of both nurses and doctors; it was a comprehensive text and soon found wide acceptance among nursing schools, which by then were being organized throughout the country. The New Haven school has retained its position of leadership. Later, when it became endowed and obtained university affiliation, it made another important contribution to nursing.

DEVELOPMENT OF NURSING EDUCATION

The period that followed was one of quiet progress in nursing education. The early development of many movements that later were to become important, including the Red Cross, army nursing, and some of the functions of public health nursing, will be discussed later.

There was also a steady growth of nursing schools. The growth was closely associated with development of modern surgery and medicine, which occurred very rapidly as the result of Pasteur's and Lister's work and the advances in bacteriological knowledge. When it became evident that so much new work could be done if hospital facilities were available, hospitals grew rapidly

Nurses of Sacred Heart Hospital in Yankton, S.D., marching in a community parade about 1880

(Reprinted from Doctors of the old West by Robert F. Karolevitz, Seattle, Wash., 1967, Superior Publishing Co.; courtesy Sacred Heart Hospital, Yankton, S.D.)

in number and size all over the country. Their function changed. Instead of being refuges of the destitute, hospitals became the natural work setting for surgeons and physicians. Facilities had to be created and organized to accommodate all socioeconomic classes. Part of the original function of the hospital was assumed by the infirmary. With the increase in both quality and quantity of hospital work, the demand for trained nursing care accelerated. Nursing developed largely as an inevitable consequence of these circumstances. It was fortunate that within its membership the necessary leaders existed to carry nursing through this formative period.

As early as 1909 there were already 1,105 hospital-based diploma schools of nursing (Jensen). A developing dilectic force in nursing led to the establishment of the first collegiate school of nursing at the University of Minnesota in that year.

The improvement in educational standards occurred in several areas. Originally one year had been considered sufficient for the training of a nurse; that was Miss Nightingale's idea, and it was the accepted period of training in the early schools. It was probably sufficient for the needs of the times. Most of the academics of a modern nurse's education are necessitated by developments in medical knowledge and public health, which require practical application, since the first schools were opened. As more knowledge and skill became necessary, the course was extended. At first it was done by adding a few months for special work. Soon, however, it became necessary to reorganize the courses completely, and courses were planned for two and eventually for three years. The full three-year course was, however, not generally accepted until well into the present century.

The problem was not merely one of

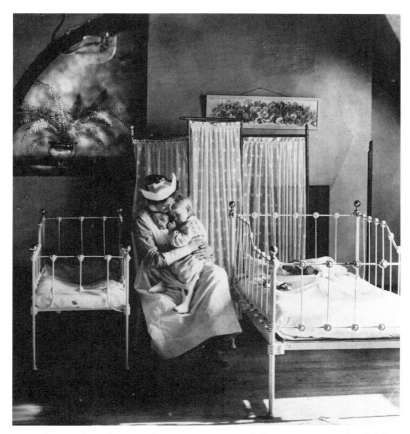

Children's ward in the Northwestern Hospital for Women and Children in Minneapolis about 1880

(Reprinted from Doctors of the old West by Robert F. Karolevitz, Seattle, Wash., 1967, Superior Publishing Co.; courtesy Minnesota Historical Society, St. Paul, Minn.)

lengthening the course but also one of practical understanding. The nurse needs to be told that she must not touch the instruments on the operating table but must understand why she should not touch them; she must understand why it is dangerous, and not just unpleasant, to have a diphtheria patient or a tuberculous patient cough into her face. She can administer a dietary or drug treatment far better if she knows something about the physiology and pathology of the diseased organs and about the action of the drugs. The nurse's role in the structure of health care is filled much better if she understands rather than simply follows directions. To the modern reader

this sounds like a statement of the obvious, and yet it was not at all accepted outside of nursing circles. For example, nurses were often not privileged to know the contents of medications and therefore were required to dispense them by number.

As nursing has evolved, a continued struggle has existed against the attitude of "overtraining" nurses. It was thought that education elevated the nurse beyond her essential task and wasted time on unnecessary knowledge. This attitude among members of the medical profession and society has been the chief obstacle. The struggle for progress was strengthened rather than weakened by this attitude. A nurse is as efficient as her education and understanding; she is not necessarily "good" because of her education but a good education is important.

The demand increased for promised lectures actually being delivered, lecture courses being split up and lengthened, and new subjects being added to the curriculum. In the beginning student nurses attended lectures for medical students; later, lectures were prepared especially for them. Instructors were better selected. It was learned that not all nursing lectures were best given by doctors but that prepared instructors, themselves nurses, were preferable in providing much of the student's education. It was found essential to add courses that were not strictly technical but dealt with ethical and professional problems and attitudes. In some respects, the preparation of nurses evolved with a broader base in the social and behavioral sciences than is required of medical students. This period was very much concerned with the germination and growth of this new thought.

Because of these advances, it became necessary to provide the proper equipment. The early student nurses often slept in rooms between the wards where they were readily available for emergencies in the night; some were housed in special buildings. The facilities for instruction were inadequate, and the requirements for equipment were simple: a few mannequins and models of limbs on which to learn how to apply bandages, a skeleton, a blackboard, and a few books. As standards were elevated, demands rose with them, and gradually beds, ward equipment, laboratories, and up-to-date libraries became essential if schools were to meet even minimum standards.

In 1896 the maximum hours of theory in the few good schools of nursing were 105. The standard course included 38 hours practical nursing, 36 hours anatomy and physiology, 4 to 6 hours gynecological nursing, 4 hours obstetrical nursing, 1 hour each

in eye, ear, nose, and throat, and 2 hours in hygiene. When one compares this with the course suggested in *A Curriculum Guide For Schools of Nursing* and with the course being taught in good schools today, some measure of the progress made in nursing education in over eighty years may be appreciated.

The Curriculum Committee of The National League of Nursing Education made an outstanding and tangible achievement in the compilation of *A Curriculum Guide For Schools of Nursing*. It was originally titled *A Standard Curriculum For Schools of Nursing*, published in 1917. This publication offered concrete suggestions on how standards in schools could be improved; included outlines for courses, mainly in the theoretical subjects; and outlined the classwork for the three-year course.

In 1927 a revision was published under the title *A Curriculum For Schools of Nursing*, embodying the advances in nursing education since the first edition and emphasizing courses in public health, prevention of disease, and sociology, which began to be included in the basic course in the 1920s. The third edition was published in 1937 under the name *A Curriculum Guide For Schools of Nursing*. This revision contained two important changes:

1. It no longer laid down inflexible rules. Recognizing the varying conditions of different schools, it called itself a "curriculum guide" rather than a "curriculum."
2. To counteract the charge that the many classes would render the nurses' course too theoretical, it was proposed to move the instruction back into the wards as "ward teaching."

The suggestion was taken and effort was made to expand this practical form of teaching. It may be beneficial in part but brings with it many problems of cost, safety, and privacy to the consumer of health care.

As schools of nursing developed toward the end of the century under the leadership

Nursing education lamp

of ambitious and farseeing women, it was natural that these leaders should strive toward the highest standards for their young profession. They were favored by an ever-increasing demand for well-qualified nurses and an ever-increasing number of tasks that nurses could do if they were properly prepared. All this called for increased basic education in nursing. There remained the duties of making beds, giving bed baths to convalescent patients, and many tasks of hospital housekeeping, which required some training for their expert performance. The issue then became whether all nurses should receive the highest possible professional education or to what extent they could relegate simpler tasks to less trained attendants, marking the establishment of various levels of nursing education.

It was soon realized that nurses wishing to prepare for administrative and teaching positions must have certain experiences not offered in the organized courses to train themselves for such tasks. These principles evolved fairly promptly and have in the course of time obtained general acceptance, but the major problem still remains: how far should the nurse's basic preparation go? The question is to some extent answered by its economic aspects: there must be a certain proportion between the expense involved in obtaining an education and the financial reward that can be anticipated.

The American Society of Superintendents of Training Schools soon realized that there were three ways of establishing university standards for nurses: (1) they had to establish leadership, (2) they had to improve the student body by raising entrance requirements, and (3) they had to improve the quality of the schools by endowments and through recognition by the universities. It was not enough to establish the schools in university hospitals. This had already been done repeatedly without any appreciable effect on the course offered in nursing.

The first step was taken about 1894 when the University of Texas established its school of nursing as a regular division of its medical department. However, its leadership proved inadequate, and the requirements of this school did not meet the general requirements for university students. The plan was frustrated, and the effort has only historical interest now.

TEACHERS COLLEGE, COLUMBIA UNIVERSITY

The first effort of enduring value was the establishment of a course in hospital economics at Teachers College, Columbia University, in 1899. In 1898 Mrs. Robb had read a paper before the American Society of Superintendents of Training Schools, recommending that a committee be appointed to study how special instruction could be provided for nurses who wished to prepare themselves for advanced positions. The committee was appointed with Mrs. Robb as its chairman. After having surveyed the field, it approached Dr. James S. Russell, dean of Teachers College, Columbia University, in New York, with its plans. As a result the college was opened to qualified nurses who could attend all courses that they required. Courses specifically for nurses had to be organized and maintained by the Society.

In retrospect, this was a tremendous advance. Here was a group, which thirty years before had had little if any professional education or standing, now actually transformed into a group qualified by general and special education to aspire to university degrees. With the opening in 1899 of the course in hospital economics, the revolution was practically complete. The work of the following generations consisted merely of extending the advantages thus gained and of building on a firmly established foundation.

Although only two students registered for the new course, the superintendents went to work with great enthusiasm; they gave freely and often gratuitously of their time and efforts to make the course successful. Gradually more nurses registered.

In 1907 Miss Nutting became the first professor of nursing in a university. She established "a new department of household administration which included the division of hospital economics."* Under her guidance the department rapidly developed and achieved international fame, attracting students from abroad who later were to lead nursing developments in their own countries. The first actual head of a training school for nurses in Denmark was a graduate of the New York Presbyterian Hospital and had studied at Teachers College, Columbia University. One of the most important activities of the new department was to establish the Henry Street Settlement to develop public health nursing. To accomplish its task, money was necessary. The department was fortunate in receiving an endowment of $200,000 from Mrs. Helen Hartley Jenkins. In 1925 Miss Isabel M. Stewart, who had been Miss Nutting's assistant since 1909, became head of the department.

The purpose of this department was to offer thorough and advanced courses for nurses destined to become heads of nursing schools and who were to seek other advanced positions in teaching and hospital administration. Until the fall of 1964 it offered short refresher courses for persons who had some experience in the field. It has succeeded eminently in these tasks and remains a leading institution of its kind in the country and perhaps in the world. In the course of time, other colleges and universities have established postgraduate courses of varying scope, many of them modeled after that of Teachers College, Columbia University.

CURRICULUM ORGANIZATION

Another step in advancing nursing education was the gradual improvement of entrance requirements.

While it became known that higher entrance requirements would result in better nurses, it also became clear that a graduate course could best be undertaken if it were preceded by a preliminary course given in the classroom. This was originally a Scotch plan that had been tried in Boston and was reintroduced into this country by Miss Nutting at Johns Hopkins Hospital in 1901. It was so successful that by 1912 there were 114 schools in the United States giving preliminary courses. These varied in time from a few lecture courses to a regular six-month course. Some included physical and social sciences and practical work, either on mannequins or in the wards themselves, so that when the students entered the wards, they felt confident enough to adjust quickly to hospital routine. Sometimes the preliminary course was given at a college that was not an integral part of the school of nursing. In some countries, notably in Finland, this led to a central school for these preliminary courses, after which the students were transferred to their separate schools. The system of preliminary courses greatly increased the efficiency of the program as a whole. The principle objection to it has been its cost. Although expensive at first sight, the gain in efficiency was considerable.

EDUCATION OF THE PUBLIC HEALTH NURSE

Special training was required for the nurse who was to do community nursing. Special knowledge was required to practice this type of preventive nursing. The skill necessary to make a bed or care for the physical needs of a patient is different from the

---

*Roberts, Mary May: American nursing: history and interpretation, New York, 1954, The Macmillan Co.

skill necessary to detect a child with measles in the classroom or to understand the epidemiological aspects of tuberculosis contact in a private home. This was soon realized, and a question remained about the preparation that this type of nurse should have.

Many views were advanced from different countries and each prevailed to some extent. Some strongly favored complete specialization for all tasks, even those which require a simple technique. Basic education in nursing was not considered necessary. It was argued that, to do district midwifery only, it was not necessary to have had a full course in nursing. Midwives in many countries are not nurses; they are trained not only to see that nature takes the normal course but also to know and recognize complications and to prevent those which can be prevented. Other similar arrangements have been made when tasks are big enough to occupy persons full time but special and simple enough to be done without extensive training other than that immediately pertaining to the job. This principle is just now gaining acceptance in the United States.

Most tasks in preventive medicine were not simple. It was generally accepted that the majority of them required some knowledge of anatomy, physiology, hygiene, or pathology, such as was included in the modern nursing course. On the other hand, it was accepted that with the growing importance of public health, almost every nurse would at some time encounter some problems of public health. It was thus deemed advisable to include some public health instruction in the undergraduate course. This was done either by affiliation with a visiting nurses' association or through a district nursing service maintained by the hospital. Because the emphasis was mainly on hospital training, most of these arrangements were not very satisfactory until the importance of public health was recognized by the teaching staff of the hospital and until the curriculum of the schools had devel-

oped to a point where such a course could be integrated into the curriculum. The first undergraduate courses in this field were given in Boston.

As the scope of public health nursing expanded, it became more evident that student contact with the field was not enough. Undergraduate courses became inadequate for learning all that was necessary. In 1914 Miss Nutting offered the first postgraduate course in public health nursing at Teachers College in affiliation with the Henry Street Settlement. This was successful, and soon the city of Boston began the special training of public health nursing that soon developed into an eight-month course at Simmons College. Later other centers, mostly university schools, developed public health courses. Now public health (community) nursing is an integral part of all higher education curricula for nurses. Public health nursing increased in scope and so have opportunities in the field.

All this made it more obvious that schools preparing nurses to practice in the community must be more closely affiliated with educational institutions. In 1908, mainly through the efforts of Dr. Richard Olding Beard, the School of Nursing at the University of Minnesota became part of that university. Particularly since World War I, studies and surveys were conducted to determine the position schools of nursing should have in the educational structure of this country from the viewpoints of both administration and financial support. The first major study, published in 1923, is called *Report of the Committee for the Study of Nursing Education* made under the direction of Josephine Goldmark. As a result of it, the Rockefeller Foundation endowed the School of Nursing at Yale University.

Continuing interest in the study of nursing education was shown by the Committee on the Grading of Nursing Schools, which began under the direction of May Ayers Burgess in 1925. One report of this committee, *Nursing Schools Today and Tomor-*

row, published in 1934, set the blueprint for the organization of the diploma school.

EARLY LEADERS

The early leaders were consistent in their wish to improve the educational program in schools of nursing because of their feeling that the professional nurse could not fulfill her responsibilities to the patient and the community until she was really prepared to do so. Two names stand out in connection with almost every development of professional nursing. Isabel Hampton Robb was the product of the nineteenth century but was farsighted enough to envision the possibilities and tireless enough to try to improve educational facilities. Her name is linked with almost every type of nursing organization, every plan, and every activity at the turn of the century. One of her outstanding students at the Johns Hopkins Hospital was Mary Adelaide Nutting. Miss Nutting complemented Mrs. Robb in many ways and lived long enough to carry out many of the plans and programs that had been the dreams of her teacher.

Every good school has its leaders during the period of organization, growth, and change. The nursing profession also has its leaders. Among them and perhaps the most outstanding were Isabel Hampton Robb, Lavinia L. Dock, Mary Eliza Mahoney, Mary Sewell Gardner, Annie W. Goodrich, and Isabel Maitland Stewart.*

Isabel Hampton Robb (1860-1910)

Miss Isabel Adams Hampton was born in Canada in 1860 and began her career as a schoolteacher. This, however, did not satisfy her, and she applied for nurse's training at Bellevue, from which she was graduated in 1883. In 1886, following two years of work in Italy, she became superintendent of nurses

---

*For information about Mary Adelaide Nutting and Lillian Wald, see the previous edition of this book: Griffin and Griffin, ed. 7, 1973.

Isabel Hampton Robb

at the five-year-old Illinois Training School for Nurses. During her three years of office in Chicago she introduced two important reforms. She began a graduated course of clinical experience and classwork, so that nurses advanced step by step, and she arranged for affiliation of her students with other hospitals that possessed advantages, especially in private nursing, not obtainable at Cook County Hospital. When the school of nursing at Johns Hopkins opened in 1889, she was made its "principal" (a term then used for the first time in this connection). Her chief contributions here were in better organization of the work so that the student nurse's day could be limited to twelve hours, including two hours off for recreation. Both the hospital and Miss Hampton earned the highest reputation. She was made chairman of the nursing section of the Congress of Hospitals and Dispensaries that was held at Chicago in 1893. She read a paper on nursing at the meeting. When, at the subsequent meeting, the Society of Superintendents was formed, she was one of the leading organizers and became the first president. The next year she married Dr. Hunter Robb and resigned from active administrative work. Her interest in nursing continued as is evidenced by the two texts that she wrote at this time (*Nursing, Its Principles and Practice for Hospital and Private Use* and *Nursing Ethics*) and by her further organizational activities.

In 1896 she became the first president of the newly formed Nurses Associated Alumnae of the United States and Canada; as such she was active in the system of offering the services of that association in the Spanish-American War. Her next important activity was the role she played in establishing university affiliation for nursing education and postgraduate courses. At first, courses were offered in hospital economics in the Department of Science. Officially the Department of Nursing and Health began some eleven years later in 1910 at Teachers College, Columbia University. After the turn of the century she again came into prominence as one of the founders and original stockholders of *The American Journal of Nursing*. Her authority and prestige did much to bring the young journal through its first difficult years. When she died in 1910 in a street accident at the relatively early age of 50, in her short career of less than 30 years in nursing she had done more for American nursing than any other person. It will be noted from studying the subsequent pages that there was no important nursing enterprise during the years when she was active in which she did not take a leading part.

Lavinia L. Dock (1858-1956)

A leading nurse educator at the turn of the century was Lavinia L. Dock. While the number of hospital schools of nursing was proliferating, she was concerned that these training schools were seemingly being opened with little thought given to the use of educational principles and even less to standards for curriculum development. Along with Isabel Adams Hampton, she was

Lavinia L. Dock

(Copyright July, 1975, American Journal of Nursing Co.; reprinted from American Journal of Nursing, vol. 75, No. 7.)

at what was then the best American school —Johns Hopkins Hospital Training School for Nurses in Baltimore.

Although most nursing leaders at that time did not seriously question male dominance in the health field or the oppression that male dominance and its long-term effects had on women, Lavinia Dock spoke out boldly on the issue. She warned her colleagues that male dominance was a major problem confronting the nursing profession. Developments that were destined to ensure male dominance in 1903 did not escape her attention or her public expression of concern. She urged nursing leaders to think of the covert and often unsuspected power with which aggressive medical men and hospital administrators threatened nurses both personally and professionally. She resented the professional injustices and indignities that nurses suffered and reminded them that their continuing acceptance of such abuse made them neither friends nor benefactors of nursing or of women. She urged nurses to organize so as to be an effective force in speaking out on various public issues that were of concern to women in general. In spite of her efforts, male dominance continued, nursing leaders ignored her warnings, and in the second decade of the twentieth century nurses actually became nonvoting members of the American Hospital Association (Transactions, 1913).

She was the first secretary of the National League for Nursing and a founder of the American Nurses' Association. Assistant to the Director of Nursing at the Johns Hopkins Hospital in Baltimore, later Superintendent of the Illinois Training School and staff member of the Henry Street Settlement in New York, Miss Dock worked with Mrs. Bedford-Fenwick and Miss Isabel Hampton (Mrs. Hampton Robb) on generating early plans for an International Council of Nursing. As the *American Journal of Nursing* was founded in 1900, she appropriately was designated to deal with all foreign correspondence.

Mary Eliza Mahoney (1845-1926)

The first professional black nurse in the United States entered the New England Hospital for Women and Children in 1878 and completed the 16-month course in 1879. Miss Mahoney had a good record at the school, and after graduation did private nursing mainly in Boston and its suburbs. She gave the address of welcome at the first conference of the National Association of Colored Graduate Nurses in 1909. She died in the New England Hospital in January, 1926, at 81 years of age. After her death the Mary Mahoney medal was established by the National Association of Colored Graduate

Nurses and was first presented in 1936 to a member of the organization making an outstanding contribution to nursing. Throughout her more than forty years of professional activity, Miss Mahoney gave devoted service to her patients and the nursing profession and did much to further intergroup relationships so that the nonwhite nurse could become a vital part of the community.

Mary Sewell Gardner (1871-1961)

Probably one of the most outstanding nurses in the history of public health nursing is Mary Sewell Gardner. She was born in 1871 in Massachusetts and graduated cum laude in 1905 from the Newport Hospital Training School for Nurses. Soon after her graduation, she became the director of the Providence District Nursing Association, Rhode Island, a post she held until her retirement in 1931.

She is probably best known for her influence on the development of the National Organization for Public Health Nursing. She was one of the nursing leaders who helped to initiate the National Organization for Public Health Nursing in Chicago in 1912. Miss Lillian Wald was the first president, and Miss Gardner was the first secretary. In 1931 she was made honorary president of the organization, which she had done so much to develop.

Miss Gardner was instrumental in the transactions that resulted in the taking over of the *Cleveland Visiting Nurses' Quarterly* when it was offered to the National Organization for Public Health Nursing as an official journal, and as the *Public Health Nurse* it became the monthly magazine of this new public health organization.

Miss Gardner was also responsible for helping to develop public health nursing services in the American Red Cross. In 1912 she was given leave of absence from the Providence District Nursing Association for a year and became temporary director of the Town and Country Nursing Service, the Public Health Nursing Service in the Red

Cross. After World War I she visited many European countries as special adviser to the nursing service work being done by the American Red Cross.

Miss Gardner described three phases of development in- school health. At first, it was thought sufficient for the health officer to conduct periodic "inspections" of school children, thereby to discover those who obviously needed medical care. This method was found to be inefficient and was supplemented by periodic examinations of the individual children to discover defects not immediately apparent, such as defective vision, poor teeth, or heart murmurs—a great step forward. It did not, however, provide health services in the area of prevention. Emphasis is now placed on this phase, utilizing health teaching and immunizations against preventable communicable diseases.

Miss Gardner is well known for many articles published in the *Public Health Nurse, The American Journal of Nursing,* and numerous other magazines. However, in nursing literature she is best known for her book, *Public Health Nursing,* first published in 1916, which has become a classic. A second revision of this book was published in 1924 and was translated into French, Chinese, Spanish, and Japanese. A third and last edition of this book was published in 1936. For the lay reader she wrote *So Live We* in 1942, and in 1946 *Catherine Kent* was published, which contained many autobiographical experiences.

Annie W. Goodrich (1876-1955)

Annie Warburton Goodrich graduated from the New York Hospital Training School for Nurses in 1892. She was one of the pioneer leaders who actively helped nursing to develop from an apprenticeship to a profession. She was an outstanding and inspired nurse educator. Her first important position was as superintendent of nurses at the New York Post-Graduate Hospital, a position she held for seven years. Then she was superintendent of nurses at St. Luke's

Hospital in New York and then superintendent of nurses at the New York Hospital. She left the New York Hospital in 1907 to become superintendent of Bellevue and Allied Training Schools for Nurses. In 1910 she resigned to become state inspector of nurse training schools in New York. In 1914 she went to Teachers College as assistant professor.

All during these years she had worked with other leaders in nursing organizations, both national and international, to develop the nursing profession. She was president of the International Council of Nurses from 1912 to 1915. She had always been interested in public health and in 1916 became director of the Visiting Nurse Service of the Henry Street Settlement. During these years of great developments in nursing, Miss Nutting, Miss Wald, and Miss Goodrich were often referred to as "the great trio." All three were associated with every great idea and movement of the young profession.

In 1918 she was given leave of absence from Henry Street Settlement to make a survey of the military hospitals with the Nursing Department of the United States Army. When the Army School of Nursing was organized in 1918, she was appointed dean. At the same time, she was instrumental in developing the Vassar Training Camp Program as a part of the war effort.

After the war she returned to Henry Street Settlement and continued her activities in nursing education. She was particularly interested in the Goldmark study, "Nursing and Nursing Education in the United States." In 1923 she was appointed dean of the new school of nursing at Yale University, endowed by the Rockefeller Foundation, a position that she held until 1934. Miss Goodrich received many honors and was one of the outstanding nurse educators of this century.

Isabel Maitland Stewart (1878-1963)

The influence of Miss Stewart as an educator, writer, organization worker, and important figure in international nursing affairs for over forty years was not recognized until recently. She took her basic training at the Winnipeg General Hospital Training School and, being attracted by an article written by Miss Nutting in *The American Journal of Nursing,* entered the course in hospital economics at Teachers College, Columbia University, in 1908. She was the first nurse to receive a master's degree from Columbia University. She remained at Teachers College for the rest of her professional career, holding the positions of assistant instructor, assistant professor, and finally in 1925 succeeding Miss Nutting as the Henry Hartley Foundation Professor of Nursing. Miss Stewart was keenly aware of the new concepts in the field of general education and always tried to evaluate new developments in relation to the specialized field of nursing. She was very active in the Education Committee of the National League of Nursing Education. While she was chairman, the curriculum committee first published the original guide to curriculum upgrading in 1917, with revisions published in 1927 and 1937 under her guidance.

She served as chairman of the Vassar Training Camp Program during World War I and wrote a pamphlet for general circulation on this and on other wartime activities. In July, 1940, when the National Nursing Council for National Defense was organized, mainly as the result of Miss Stewart's suggestions, one of the important committees appointed was that on educational policies and resources with Miss Stewart as chairman. She was interested in international affairs and was very active in the Committee on Education of the International Council of Nurses. She prepared a pamphlet called *The Educational Program of the School of Nursing,* which was translated into English, Spanish, German, and French by the Nursing Bureau of the League of Red Cross Societies. In 1950 she finished a study of postgraduate education in nursing for the international council. As author and editor she is well known to nurses all over the world for her books *Education of Nurses* and *A Short History of Nursing,* which she coauthored with Lavinia Dock.

In 1916 she became the first editor of the Department of Nursing Education of *The American Journal of Nursing.* She participated in the founding of the Association of Collegiate Schools of Nursing and in the early developments of the National League of Nursing Education, the International Council of Nurses, and the Florence Nightingale International Foundation.

ORGANIZATIONAL DEVELOPMENT

With improved hospitals, medical practice, education (physicians, nurses, and all health personnel), and more effective health teaching throughout the community, the welfare of the group has emerged as a definite concept. Modern health care is interested in protecting every individual from the hazards of life, particularly diseases, by scientific knowledge. To do this, the health of the individual becomes the concern of many groups in the society. Sanitary legislation, city and state public health agencies, and the organization and support of many private health organizations, particularly in the fields of tuberculosis, cancer, heart disease, and mental illness, have been developed. In some countries health care is being socialized. Other countries, such as the United States, have public and private enterprises working together to control disease and to provide the best care possible for every individual: national health insurance is being discussed.

Organizational developments and specialization were evident in the professionalization of nursing. Nursing education has become established in universities, and the profession has become more visible through its publications.

Nursing service

Until the time of Florence Nightingale, nursing as a profession had not been sufficiently developed to make worthwhile differentiation between nursing services within and those outside the hospital. She, however, developed the nursing school, with resultant better nursing in the hospital, the opening of hospital careers, and the consequent organization of nursing service and nursing education. Nursing service in those early hospitals which sponsored schools of nursing improved with the quality of students admitted.

Not all sick people go to the hospital; in fact, for many centuries none but the poor went to the hospitals, and even the improvements that followed Miss Nightingale's reforms still left a great void of nursing service outside the hospital among both the rich and the poor.

In "private nursing" the patient bears the entire cost of the nursing. If he cannot do so, the cost is borne partly or entirely by the community either in the form of governmental support funds or private endowment. This latter form of nursing was at first called visiting nursing. Later, as the emphasis changed, it was called public health nursing.

A hundred years ago people who were ill had nurses in their homes. These nurses were women often with vast practical experience but without formal training because none existed at that time. Naturally, as young women received such training and acquired special skill in attending the sick and carrying out doctors' orders, which were becoming ever more technical in nature, people who could pay for their services would demand them, and nurses trained in hospitals would go into private homes. There was nothing striking or dramatic about such a development, and it left no historical landmark. In the early days of many schools, student nurses did private duty in both hospital and home. The hospital usually collected the fee.

About the turn of the century, emphasis on prevention of disease began to emerge as a principle underlying all health care, including nursing service. In many instances the reason disease cannot be prevented is

not always poverty but often lack of knowledge of the simplest rules of health. The difference in cost between simple, clean, and healthy living and squalor is not as great as one would think. And so it became impressed on these young professional nurses, as they worked in the slums or in the wilderness, that if people knew a little more, much suffering could be alleviated.

This was a period of changing social outlook. The duty of the state to improve and to protect the health of the citizens who cannot do so themselves was just beginning to be emphasized. Furthermore to do so is good business, for it is ultimately the state that stands to lose through sickness and premature death of its citizens. It is less expensive to prevent an obstetrical complication than to have the mother of a family a chronic invalid for years; to have a child properly fitted with glasses than to spend money on his education, which he partly misses because he cannot see; to have a tuberculous patient isolated than to lose years of work from others who have become contaminated because the patient was allowed to go about his business when he should have been in a sanatorium; or to treat and to cure early syphilis rather than to have the loss and expense later of keeping the patient for years in a mental hospital or to have him die prematurely from syphilitic heart disease. The age of "rugged individualism" was giving way to a sense of social responsibility.

Thus the obligation of the community was readily recognized once it was pointed out, but who was to bear the expense? Charity (for "free" preventive medicine is a form of charity) to a large extent had been borne by private organizations. The visiting nurses' societies were private enterprises; the Rockefeller Foundation was promoting public health, and so was the Red Cross. Concurrently, local communities were establishing health departments. Problems vary so much from one area to another that prevention of disease is often best handled locally by municipalities or state governments. The United States Public Health Service was developing quickly, and there were many health problems that definitely were nationwide, such as harbor quarantine and maintenance of food and drug standards in interstate commerce. Later, the prevention of spread of certain infectious diseases, such as leprosy and syphilis, was deemed to be a federal problem. All these arguments had something in their favor, and all types of agencies sponsored health services so that private organizations, municipal and state governments, and the federal government all needed nurses. Often they collaborate; sometimes they act independently of each other.

Private duty nursing

Hospitals a half century ago could retain the private duty nurse on their payroll and collect the fee for services rendered. It was satisfactory to the nurse because it provided her with security and occupation between private cases. As private nursing grew, this arrangement was found to be unsatisfactory. A system of nursing through "registers" or employment offices developed. A percentage of the nurse's wage was retained as a commission. Sometimes such registers provided not only private cases but also permanent appointments, and some of them are still doing well in this respect. Registers for private nursing, however, sometimes fell into unscrupulous hands, and the nurses were exploited. Therefore they often placed the register in the hands of someone whom they cooperatively employed or with their professional organization. These methods reduce the cost to a minimum and are extensively used now.

Another aspect of private nursing that had become a serious problem was the cost to the individual patient. As the nurse's education and skill became more complex, she expected increased remuneration. With the introduction of the eight-hour day, twenty-four hours of private nursing became expensive. Three attempts were made to overcome this difficulty: "hourly nursing," admission to private hospitals in which nursing service could be obtained from general duty nurses, and insurance. This leaves only the more serious cases still requiring full-time special-duty nursing.

In hourly nursing the nurse, like the doctor, goes from patient to patient in their own homes, carrying out the procedures that require extensive nursing skill and leaving the simpler tasks to an attendant or member of the family. The most common practice today is admission to private hospitals. As well as the nursing service, it offers many other advantages such as the services of laboratories, diet kitchen, and resident physicians. Insurance plans to pay for the rising cost of nursing are also gaining ground, especially in the form of group insurance, which lowers the overhead cost. In historical perspective, private nursing was at its height in the "roaring twenties." In the subsequent depression many private duty nurses fell into dire need.

Today the concept is all but extinct and has little or no appeal for the young graduate, even though the vestigial group has a fairly solid organization.

Development of visiting nursing

It is important that the American nurse understand the development of nursing in the community, for although the first organized attempts at visiting nursing began quite early in this country, the movement was slow to gain momentum, and many influences can be traced back to English beginnings.

In 1842 an early Philadelphia institution established a Nurse Society for the purpose of supplying nurses alternately to indigent sick and to those who could pay for them. This service was similar to what we now call visiting nursing. Then in 1877 the Women's Branch of the New York City Mission established a nursing service for the

Visiting nurse

The visiting nurse, forerunner of today's community nurse practitioner. (Courtesy Bettmann Archive, New York, N.Y.)

sick poor by graduate nurses. However, their effectiveness may have been somewhat hampered by the expectation that, as nurses, they must also promote and promulgate the church. For example, the Ethical Society of New York placed four nurses in New York Dispensaries for the purpose of spreading the gospel of healthful living.

During this period visiting nursing in England had passed through its initial stages, had been under scrutiny, and now was developed into a valuable social service. With such an example before them it is not surprising that various American communities established similar societies. During the middle 1880s visiting nurses' associations developed in Buffalo, Boston, and Philadelphia. Although the first of these were started under the auspices of the Presbyterian church,

all of them soon became independent organizations established solely for the purpose of maintaining visiting nurses. These societies, inspired partly by those in England and partly by those in New York, have survived to become some of the leading organizations of this type in our day. The example was soon followed by New Bedford, Chicago, and Kansas City.

The settlement

A new development occurred in the year 1893 that was to have an enormous influence on work among the poor, for much of public health and social service actually dates back to the first American settlement. The "settlement" was not a new idea. For years English philanthropists had gone to live among the poor, but this was the first time that an American nurse brought her special training to the task. Miss Lillian D. Wald and her friend, Miss Mary Brewster, settled on Henry Street, one of the poorest neighborhoods in the metropolis, to give their lives to improving the conditions of the poor. Their scope extended far beyond nursing the sick; it even extended beyond preventing disease; they aimed at eradicating, as far as it was in their power, those causes that were responsible for poverty and misery. That, in its essence, is social service. The experiment was so successful that Miss Wald became an accepted authority on all subjects in that area and the place itself, Henry Street Settlement, has become the clinical setting for training and experience for students in social work from Columbia University and other educational institutions.

The social aims, however, were not pursued to the neglect of nursing or preventive medicine. All of them are considered important, and the institution itself has become the prototype of others of its kind across the country. Among the first to follow were the nurses' settlements in Richmond, Virginia (1900), San Francisco, California (1900), and Orange, New Jersey (1903).

School nursing

School nursing has become one of the most important public health functions. In the nineteenth century, when compulsory schooling became general, it was necessary to pass certain health measures that eventually became centered in the periodic health inspection of premises and pupils. In 1872 in the school of Wild Street, Drury Lane, London, a desire arose to have a nurse look into the method of feeding the schoolchildren. A request was made to the Queen's Nurses, and Miss Amy Hughes, then their superintendent, decided to look into the matter herself. Her investigation revealed much unnecessary suffering among schoolchildren, and she began at once to place Queen's Nurses in London schools. However, the London school board was slow to see the value of this service, and eventually it became necessary for the London County Council itself to appoint a staff of municipal school nurses. This did not happen until 1904. By then, Liverpool already had an eleven-year-old school nursing service financed by voluntary subscription. By 1902 when Miss Wald visited in England, school nursing there had reached such a high level of development that on her return to the United States she was inspired to fight for instituting a similar service in the New York schools.

In those days children were barred from school if the teacher found reason to do so, but no effort was made to see that such exclusion was medically necessary or that the children excluded received proper care. Miss Wald was able to convince the authorities of the inefficiency of this method. In 1903 she was permitted to place a nurse experimentally in each of the four schools showing the highest incidence of exclusions. The nurses' work was so successful that in the experimental schools the exclusion fell some 90%. Such a result naturally led to the employment of school nurses throughout

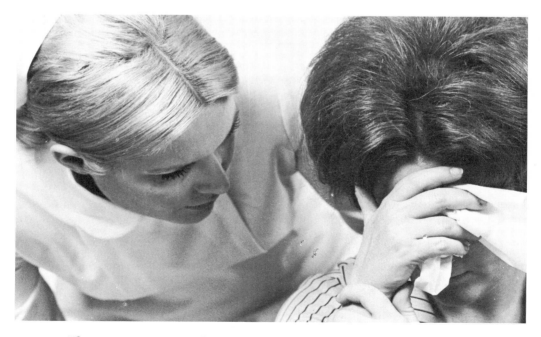

The nurse strives to understand the problems of the depressed patient

(From Mereness, Dorothy A., and Taylor, Cecelia M.: Essentials of psychiatric nursing, ed. 9, St. Louis, 1974, The C. V. Mosby Co.)

New York and other large cities, Los Angeles following suit as early as 1904. Today the school nurse is an integral part of the educational team. The nurse supplements the work of the doctor, and she is capable of providing health care in many areas. She can follow cases during treatment until recovery and can make necessary contacts and readjustments within the home and community. This provides the doctor with time to do that work which is outside the scope of nursing. It is the pattern of the health service of private and special schools as well as colleges and universities to have their own health service.

Demands for nursing services are constantly increasing, and specialization has entered the wide field of nursing. Opportunities in nursing are greater today than ever before and seem to be increasing constantly. Not only is there a need for many more nurses than are now available, but also many nurses are needed in such clinical specialties as medical-surgical nursing, maternal and child nursing, psychiatric nursing, rehabilitative nursing, and community or public health nursing. In addition, there are such specialized fields as the military, government health field research, the Peace Corps, and international organizations like the World Health Organization, which require nurses who can function as supervisors or educators.

Traditionally nurses have worked in hospitals or other institutions, in private homes, or with the military in giving care to patients. As the field of health services developed, expanded, and became specialized, variations and job combinations extended far beyond the relatively simple nursing situations of fifty years ago.

Nurse clinician

One of the more recent developments in nursing was that of the nurse clinician or clinical specialist. This functional role evolved on a more or less equal basis with that of the teacher and supervisor, requiring postgraduate educational preparation usu-

ally on the master's level or beyond. Until federal cutbacks of 1975, education at this level was financially available to most qualified applicants because of large numbers of scholarships, fellowships, and educational grants and loans. An extensive list of these is available from the Committee on Careers, a joint ANA-NLN committee.

Anesthesia

Since the 1880s nurses have been administering anesthetics in America, and postgraduate instruction of nurses in anesthesiology was instituted about the same time. The first schools for teaching this specialty for nurses, however, were not organized until about 1910.

Many states by law allow the administration of anesthetic by nurses. A case in the Supreme Court of California in 1946 decided that administration of anesthetics by a nurse was not contrary to the Medical Practice Act of that state. In no other state has the legality of nurse anesthetists been tested. As in other specialties in nursing, there is a great need for nurse anesthetists, not only in civilian but also in military hospitals. The professional organization of this group is the American Association of Nurse Anesthetists. Membership in this association is open to all qualified nurse anesthetists.

Industrial nursing

Industrial nursing, which had its origin at the end of the last century when some manufacturers employed nurses to visit sick employees, was stimulated by the war effort. The usefulness of nurses within industrial plants was discovered and by World War I the employment of nurses in industry was quite general. The nursing profession found itself closely tied to the economic cycle as industry turned to production of war material. When unemployment followed in the postwar period, industrial nursing shared in the retrenchment, and only in the last few years before World War II did industry again make a great demand on nursing. However, the rising demand for better working conditions and early health care measures regenerated industrial nursing as a field of practice. In April, 1942, the American Association of Industrial Nursing was organized from a nucleus of several industrial nurses' clubs, which had existed for several years to stimulate interest in the special problems of the industrial nurse and to provide a means for the discussion of these problems.

Industrial nursing has expanded, as has industrial medicine, from first aid stations to a complicated practice of industrial health.

This field has been given great impetus since World War II. It is estimated that there are over 10,000 industrial nurses in this country. The industrial nurse needs technical skill to deal with diagnostic and treatment situations. She must come in close contact with all workers and their health problems. Knowledge of the health problems of the worker and his family combined with a knowledge of community resources helps industry to maintain health and individual productivity on as high a level as possible.

Requirements in this field are that the

Josephine Catherine Chatter Wood

Early midwife Josephine Catherine Chatter Wood, known as "Aunt Jody" to hundreds of pioneer families in Utah whose children she helped deliver. Like country doctors, midwives served wide areas of the western frontier. Few had special training; most got by on experience, common sense, and intuition. (From Doctors of the old West by Robert F. Karolevitz, Seattle, Wash., 1967, Superior Publishing Co.; courtesy Utah State Historical Society, Salt Lake City, Utah.)

person be a registered nurse with a foundation for nursing in modern health care. Current state registration is necessary. In industrial work the nurse must like people, be able to work effectively on the health team, and be able to work well with patients' families. Industrial nursing is extremely varied; for example, the industrial nurse may work in an industrial hospital or in an industry in which the services are comparable to those in outpatient departments.

Nurse-midwifery

The first school for nurse-midwifery in the United States was opened in 1932 by the Association for the Promotion and Standardization of Midwifery, Inc., in cooperation with the Maternity Center of New York.

In 1935 the Lobenstein Midwifery Clinic was consolidated with the Maternity Center Association. During the first twenty years this school graduated 231 nurse-midwives, but with the growing recognition of the place of this professional worker, the demand for graduates has always far exceeded the supply.

At present several universities offer courses in nurse-midwifery. The one at the Johns Hopkins University School of Medicine and the one under the Faculty of Medicine of Columbia University have been developed in cooperation with the Maternity Center Association of New York. A third program is part of the facilities of the Yale Medical Center. Numerous other schools are now preparing graduates for the practice of

A

Frontier nurses

A, Half a century ago, nurse-midwives in Kentucky's Frontier Nursing Service negotiated this rocky stream bed on horseback. Today they drive a jeep to reach an isolated patient. **B,** Today's graduates of the Frontier School of Midwifery and Family Nursing deliver health care to the elderly as well as the childbearing family. (Courtesy Frontier Nursing Service, Wendover, Ky.)

B
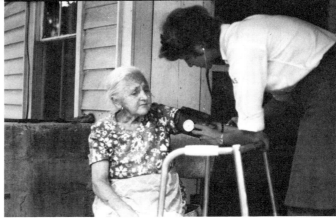

nurse-midwifery. Among these are Frontier Nursing Service in Lexington, Kentucky, and Santa Fe, New Mexico. Historically, practice of this specialty has been in rural areas where there was inadequate prenatal care. A fascinating account of the development of the Frontier Nursing Service is found in *Nurse on Horseback* by Mary Breckinridge, founder of the service.

Nursing in the federal government

Nursing in the federal services has become extremely varied. Nurses are employed in many branches of the federal government, all the positions being classified by the United States Civil Service Commission except those in the Navy Nurse Corps and, since January, 1946, in the Veterans Administration. Through the years, positions in these agencies have followed the general lines of specialization existing elsewhere in the wide field of nursing and range from general duty or staff nursing to top administrative positions.

Army Nurse Corps. The Army Nurse Corps is the oldest of all the women's military services and is made up entirely of registered nurses representing all fields of nursing. It was first established by Florence Nightingale during the Crimean War (1854).

The Army-Navy Nurses Act of 1947 granted to nurses permanent commission status in the United States Army. An Army Nurse Corps section was established in the Officer Reserve Corps. Colonel Florence A. Blanchfield was the first woman to receive permanent commissioned rank of colonel. Not only the variety of service but also the security found in the military nursing fields may be attractive: personnel policies; complete hospital, medical, surgical, and dental care when needed; limited health services for dependents; generous retirement benefits after twenty years of service; substantial allowance for initial purchase of officer's uniform; and, of course, pay increases for all grades, depending on length of service.

In addition to such positions as head

Army Nurse Corps insignia

nurse, chief of nursing service, instructor, general duty nurse, and supervisor, many specialized positions such as an army health nurse, chief of nursing personnel, and nurse education coordinator exist. Specialists are needed in various fields and are given instruction by the army; for example, in operating room technique and management, in anesthesiology, in neuropsychiatric nursing, and in nursing and hospital administration. Through the army's information and education program, army nurses may enroll in extension and other collegiate courses at reduced rates.

Army nurses may serve in America or in any of the foreign stations in which the United States Army functions. Applicants must be registered professional nurses, citizens of the United States, physically and professionally qualified, and graduates of schools acceptable to the Surgeon General. Married nurses are accepted for reserve appointments or extended active duty if they do not have dependent children under 18 years of age. Applicants must pass a physical examination conducted at an army or air force medical center or by a civilian physician at no expense to the government. For appointment as a second lieutenant, the nurse must be a high school graduate, have graduated from a basic nursing program, and meet citizenship and physical qualifications and moral requirements specified. As a first lieutenant the young nurse must meet the above requirements, be registered in the United States or United States territory, and have fifteen semester hours in an accredited college or university, and three years' professional experience. A nurse currently certified by the American Association of Nurse Anesthetists with three years' professional experience in anesthesiology or experience within twenty-four months prior to the appointment may also be appointed as first lieutenant. For appointment as a captain the basic requirements for first lieutenant are needed plus a bachelor's degree from an accredited college or university, with the major field in nursing and seven years' experience including two years' teaching, supervising, or administration; or a master's degree from an accredited college or university, with the major field in nursing, allied medical science, or personnel field, and six years' experience, including two years' supervision or administration; or current certification by the American Association of Nurse Anesthetists and seven years of anesthesia practice, terminating not more than twenty-four months prior to the appointment. As members of the various branches of the military, nurses are provided with immunizations, regular health supervision, and hospitalization when necessary.

Navy Nurse Corps. The Navy Nurse Corps was established in 1908, but it was not until 1920 that the first navy nurses were assigned to serve aboard a hospital ship. This first assignment was on the U.S.S. *Relief.* In 1922 J. Beatrice Bowman was appointed to succeed Mrs. Higbee. During 1920 the Navy Nurse Corps was reduced, in keeping with the total program of disarmament. Educational programs in dietetics, laboratory technique, anesthesia, and tuberculosis nursing were instituted. Salaries gradually increased, gratuity for uniforms was provided, and legislation was passed providing for retirement with pay for members incurring physical disability in the line of duty.

Today, navy nurses serve in the United States and abroad. Nurses in this military branch have an opportunity to practice all phases of nursing care for men and women of the navy and marine corps and their families. All initial appointments are made by the Nurse Corps, United States Naval Reserve. The basic qualifications for commission are that the individuals be graduates of NLN-accredited schools of nursing whose educational and professional standards are approved by the Surgeon General, United States Navy; currently registered at least in one state or the District of Columbia; applicants with baccalaureate preparation in nursing are preferred. They may be a native-born or naturalized citizen of the United States. The maximum age for becoming commissioned is 35, either single or married, but with no dependents under the age of 18 years; and they should be physically qualified by the standards set up for naval officers. Appointments are made in grades of ensign through lieutenant, senior grade, depending on professional experience and academic qualifications.

The functions of the navy nurse are to give bedside care to patients, to instruct hospital corpsmen, and to help in the management and supervision of wards and clinics. In addition to the officers the men and women of the armed forces and the families of the armed forces are also given care. As in the army, there is an extensive in-service educational program in all navy hospitals. Members of the Nurse Corps may be assigned to attend educational programs in colleges and universities. All nurses are encouraged to continue their education.

In keeping with the development of educational programs, both in civilian and in military groups, the navy nurse postwar educational program was established in 1946. Navy nurses were assigned to schools for training in physiotherapy, anesthesiology, occupational therapy, dietetics, and ward administration. In 1947 the army nurse act established the nurse corps as a permanent staff corps of the United States Navy. Captain DeWitt became the first director of the permanent corps.

The Korean emergency of 1950 necessi-

Navy Nurse Corps insignia

tated a recall of reserve nurses to help care for casualties of the conflict. In 1955 continued education for the navy nurse was stimulated by Public Law 20, called The Career Incentive Act, which provided incentives in increased pay and allowances. Later in the same year an educational program was instituted that allowed a limited number of hospital corps Waves to enroll in approved collegiate schools of nursing with the expenses borne by the navy. On the satisfactory completion of this program these students are commissioned ensigns in the Navy Nurse Corps Reserve.

During 1957 and 1958 educational programs were continued, and increases in salary and promotions resulted. In 1957 the Navy Nurse Corps Cadet Program permitted qualified students in approved collegiate schools of nursing to enlist during their final year in the school of nursing. Educational expenses were paid by the navy, and on graduation from the school of nursing the nurses were commissioned as ensigns in the Navy Nurse Corps Reserve.

In May of 1958 the nurse corps proudly celebrated its golden anniversary, having established for itself, as other branches of the military had, an honored place in the military history of America.

Air Force Nurse Corps. Until 1949 army medical personnel had been assigned to duty with the air force. Since that date, however, the Air Force Medical Service has become an entity distinct from the Army Medical Service. Since World War I, air force medicine had been concerned with such problems as lack of oxygen at high altitude, the forces and strains to which the human being is subjected because of great rates of speed, quick changes in temperature, and other areas now included in aviation medicine.

The United States Air Force Medical Service is composed of five groups of medical personnel: medical, medical service, dental, women's medical specialist corps (dietitians, physiotherapists, and occupational therapists), and the Air Force Nurse Corps, which includes both flight nurses and air force nurses serving on the ground in air force hospitals. Until recently there was also a group of veterinary personnel.

During World War II official air evacuation was begun in 1942 when an Air Ambulance Battalion was organized at Fort Benning, Georgia. This was moved to Beaumont Field, Kentucky, later in the year, and training for flight nurses in air evacuation squadrons began. Flight teams consisting of one flight medical technician and one flight nurse were organized. The Flight Nurse School is now located at the Gunter branch of the Aviation School of Medicine, Gunter Air Force Base, Montgomery, Alabama.

Nurses entering the Air Force Nurse Corps today must be graduates of an NLN-accredited nursing school acceptable to the Surgeon General, United States Air Force; have active registration in any state, territory, or the District of Columbia, and be physically and professionally qualified. Applicants with baccalaureate education in nursing are given preference. The maximum age for commission to second lieutenant is 30, to first lieutenant is 35, and to captain is 39. Applicants may be either single or married and must be citizens of the United States with high moral standards. Appointments are made from second lieutenant to major, depending on professional experience and educational preparation. The minimum tour of active duty is two years. Training programs and in-service education are an important part of the program.

The course of study includes such subjects as aviation physiology, psychology, nursing procedures for in-flight care of patients, and the newest development in therapeutics. The course is difficult, but responsibilities as a flight nurse are great. Satisfactory completion of the course entitles the nurse to wear silver wings with an "N" superimposed on them.

In addition to bedside nursing and the instruction and supervision of nonprofessional workers, a nurse may be assigned to many specific duties such as that of head nurse, supervisor, chief nurse, or administrative director. She may also go into one of the specialized fields—operating room supervision, nurse anesthetist, psychiatric nursing, or flight nursing. Personnel policies make it possible for both regular air force and reserve nurses to become eligible for retirement benefits. Regular air force nurses may retire after twenty years; retirement pay is determined by length of service and grade held. Reserve air force nurses may apply for retirement benefits after the age of 60 years, having completed twenty years of satisfactory active and/or reserve service. A number of regular and reserve air force personnel nurses were given university education leading to a degree, during which time they received full pay and allowances. Other educational opportunities were made available through the United States Armed Forces Institute and the United States Air Force Extension Institute.

Aerospace nursing. A relatively new specialty developing within the Air Force Nurse Corps is aerospace nursing. An intensive fifty-two–week course was initiated in 1965 at Patrick Air Force Base, Cape Kennedy, to equip nurses to function as part of the Bioastronautic Operational Support Unit. BOSU is engaged in intensive research on the effects of all forms of stress on healthy human beings. This research reveals new knowledge that can be applied here on earth as well as in space. Nurses working in BOSU are concerned not only with the care

Space program

One of the most exciting fields in modern life, the space program, presents new opportunities for the nurse and her special skills.

of the astronauts but also with the preparation for disaster on the test range.

Nursing service in the Veterans Administration. The history of the present nursing service of the Veterans Administration has a multiple origin, originating principally from developments after World War I.

On May 1, 1922, as the result of an executive order signed by the President, 46 hospitals of the United States Public Health Service were transferred to the jurisdiction of the Veterans' Bureau. This resulted in the transfer to the Veterans' Bureau of 12,069 World War I veterans and 10,251 hospital personnel, including 1,420 professional nurses. Also, 755 commissioned medical officers in the Public Health Service were detailed to the Veterans' Bureau. All personnel other than physicians were converted to civil service status. Thus for the first time a superintendent of nurses and an assistant superintendent were assigned to the Veterans' Bureau in Washington, D.C.

The passage of Public Law 293 by the Seventy-ninth Congress, January 3, 1946, raised the status of the nursing service immeasurably. Shortly before this the Civil Service Commission had changed the classification of nurses from subprofessional to professional. While this was a step forward, Public Law 293 removed them from civil service, making them members of the Department of Medicine and Surgery of the Veterans Administration, along with doctors and dentists. Salaries were made commensurate with their professional qualifications, regardless of duties performed. Many highly qualified nurses were attracted to the new department. The Veterans Administration has been a leader among the federal nursing services in utilizing male nurses.

The Veterans Administration is the third largest federal agency, serving some 28 million veterans. The nursing service is the largest service of its kind in the United States and offers unusual career opportunities to nurses with varied professional interests. Following the war in Vietnam, an extensive modernization of facilities, personnel, and services was instituted. Professional nurses staff hospitals, clinics, and nursing homes for veterans of all wars.

In 1972 the number of inpatients totaled 855,000, and the outpatient service facilities extended to over 8 million.

Peace Corps and VISTA. The Peace Corps presents that great opportunity for "people to help people" directly in providing economic, social, or educational assistance. The cause of peace is thus advanced through mutual understanding, through personal love and affection, and by sharing.

The corps came into being on March 1, 1961, under the overall governmental umbrella of ACTION, when President Kennedy issued an executive order establishing the corps on a provisional basis. Congress established the Peace Corps permanently on September 21, 1961. Objectives defined by the act for the Peace Corps are to promote world peace and friendship by making available to interested countries Americans who will do the following: (1) help the people of these countries meet their needs for trained manpower, (2) help promote a better understanding of the American people on the part of the peoples served, and (3) help promote a better understanding of other peoples on the part of the American people.

Registered nurses are in demand by the Peace Corps, and any registered nurse or student nurse in her last year of nursing school, regardless of age, who is a United States citizen may apply for service as a Peace Corps volunteer. Volunteers must be in excellent physical and mental health. After intensive Peace Corps training designed to prepare volunteers for effective service overseas, a nurse will be sent to any one of twenty countries in Latin America, Africa, the Near East, southeast Asia, or southwest Asia.

Under the ACTION program also exists a national component called VISTA (Volunteers in Service to America). This program focuses on work in the inner city, alleviating poverty and disadvantages of all kinds.

Nursing in the United States Indian Service. The Office of Indian Affairs has had a nursing service for a long time. However, in 1924 with the appointment of Elinor Gregg as supervisor of nurses for the Bureau of Indian Affairs, many important and lasting improvements were made; she laid the foundation for the modern program of health work with the American Indian in the states, including Alaska. Nurses are assigned to hospitals on Indian reservations and to other medical stations. Those in field positions must be public health nurses. In Alaska a physician along with two to six nurses is employed in each of the government hospitals; in addition, public health nurses do rural nursing. Medical care for the Indian is now under the United States Public Health Service of the Department of Health, Education, and Welfare.

Nursing in the Children's Bureau. The nursing division of the Children's Bureau greatly expanded as the federal government through grants-in-aid began to assist states in planning and implementing programs for handicapped children as well as maternal and infant welfare services. The Children's Bureau was first proposed by Lillian Wald, a public health nurse. Public health nursing consultants were employed by the bureau, especially after the Sheppard-Towner Act in 1921. The passage of the Social Security Act in 1935 served as a renewed stimulus to the improvement of maternal and child health services provided for in the act. The Children's Bureau was to administer three types of services: (1) maternal and child health services, (2) services for crippled children, and (3) child welfare services. During the same year a unit of public health nursing was set up and a director, Naomi Deutsch, was appointed.

Nursing in the Department of Health, Education, and Welfare. Under the Department of Health, Education, and Welfare a nurse may work in one of the public health service hospitals serving seamen, personnel of the United States Coast Guard, officers of the Coast and Geodetic Survey, federal employees injured at work, and public health officers. The nurse may also work with American Indians in one of about fifty Indian hospitals and clinics scattered throughout the states. In 1956 responsibility for the health of the Indian was placed in the Department of Health, Education, and Welfare.

In 1953 the National Clinical Center opened in Bethesda, Maryland, as part of the National Institutes of Health of the United States Public Health Service. The National Institutes of Health include separate institutes concerned with cardiovascular disease, cancer, mental health, arthritis, gastrointestinal and metabolic diseases, neurological diseases, allergy and infectious diseases, child health and development, and dental health. Currently more than 1,400 research projects are in progress at the National Clinical Center. Each year four sessions of planned practice in providing nursing care are offered through the Clinical Electives Program for Nursing Students. Selected senior students in basic baccalaureate nursing programs are given an in-depth exposure to, and opportunity for, providing continuity of nursing care in the research-oriented setting. It is intended that this experience supplement what the students learn in their respective nursing education programs. In the large 511-bed hospital, research and clinical care of patients are closely integrated. The nurse is a member not only of the patient care team but also of the research team.

Members of the U.S. Public Health Service do valuable work in the field of public health nursing by participating in studies, working on health teams in various control programs, working on migrant health as well as on other special projects, and, when qualified, by serving as nurse consultants.

The U.S. Public Health Service has expanded its overseas program since World War II. These nurses serve in many areas of Latin America, Africa, the Near East, and the Far East. In the United States Public Health Service a graduate nurse, male or female, may enter either by appointment to its commissioned corps as a regular or reserve officer or through federal civil service employment.

Associations

Professional societies can be developed in two ways. Someone can decide that it would be well for the members of a certain group to be organized for the purpose of controlling conditions of training, or work, and of compensation and of controlling new knowledge concerning the group. On the other hand, persons who have lived closely together during a period of training and education may wish to meet or at least keep in touch with each other when they scatter after graduation. This sentiment is the primary cause for the organization of alumni associations. Both of these purposes can be found in the organizations of the young nursing profession.

Alumni associations

As nursing schools developed, the alumni formed associations; the first were those of Bellevue (1889), Illinois Training School (1891), and Johns Hopkins (1892). It may be more than a coincidence that these were the very schools with which Miss Hampton had been connected, for, as noted earlier, she became their first president when they were consolidated into a national association. These associations must not be looked on as primarily social in purpose. In a few years these groups had joined together to become the Nurses' Associated Alumnae of the United States and Canada. The purpose was enlarged and became national in scope to embrace the general betterment of the profession. This occurred especially because the advancement of educational standards was being sponsored by the American Society of Superintendents of Training Schools, which also was active in organizing the Associated Alumnae. When the scope became broader incorporation became necessary. For legal reasons Canadian nurses then had to organize a separate society, which, however, continued to cooperate cordially with the sister society south of the border. The aims and purposes of the two societies remained similar.

With the development of the society as a national organization, it naturally became organized into city, county, and state societies and affiliated with similar groups in other countries into international association.

American Nurses' Association

The function of a professional organization in general is to protect the members and the public it serves. Specifically, this is done by formulating and imposing a code of ethics on its members and assuring the public of the proficiency of its members by testing their ability before allowing them to practice. The employment of educational standards and the licensing of professional nurses developed early and are controlled by the profession. The professional organization is pledged to safeguard its members from unfair competition, to guarantee conditions of employment, and to ensure fair remuneration.

It is not possible for professionals to form organizations until certain basic concepts have been accepted by the members. It is not strange to learn that the earliest American nurses' association known is the Philomena Society formed in New York in 1886. Only its name is known, for it disbanded after a year, leaving no records. Professional nursing organizations did not develop until almost ten years later when it became clear that the small local groups and alumnae associations which had begun to organize in the late eighties and early nineties and were collectively labeled as the Alumnae Association no longer fit its name. Not primarily an alumnae association any longer, the association made a new departure under the name of American Nurses' Association in 1911. As such it has continued to grow and is largely responsible for the reforms that developed during the years that followed. In December, 1962, its membership was 168,912. When it was organized in 1897 the purposes of this association were to (1) establish and maintain a code of ethics, (2) elevate the standards of nursing education, and (3) promote the usefulness and honor, the financial and other interests of the nursing profession (ANA, 1941). Throughout the years the association has continued its work. Its program has been altered and shaped by the continuous changes that have taken place in nursing as the profession has developed.

The years 1964 through 1973 were ones

of ferment and turmoil for nursing. All over the country courageous nurses banded together for the first time in history to act as a cohesive social force in a battle to win improved working conditions and increased economic security.

The first major victory, which received national attention from the public, was won by over 3,500 nurses employed in the New York City Department of Hospitals. Negotiations begun in May, 1965, were concluded one year later, just five days before the nurses' resignations would have become effective. National news was also made by nurses who resigned, or threatened to resign, in Chicago, San Francisco, and Los Angeles. It was not just in the giant metropolises that these actions occurred, however. The ANA Economic Security Unit reported over 140 "situations" all over the country in the first six months of 1966.

The public's support was behind nursing when they learned that the resignations, "slow downs," and "strikes" were not only over salaries but also because of hospital conditions that made adequate patient care impossible. Major contractual concessions included establishment of committees to examine nursing and non-nursing duties and released time and reimbursement for attending professional meetings and workshops.

The most significant gain, however, has been substantial salary increases across the country. At the biennial convention of the American Nurses' Association in 1966 the House of Delegates adopted a resolution calling for a minimum base salary of $6,500. In a nationwide press conference about this salary goal, Jo Eleanor Elliot, ANA President, said, "If quality care is to be assured to all persons, salaries of nurses must be more attractive. Today's salaries discourage the recruitment of qualified young people. We know, too, that many married nurses with young children cannot afford to practice their profession; the salaries they can earn are not enough to compensate them for costs of child care. Substantial increases in salaries are required to regain the services of many nurses."

The American Nurses' Association has continued to help the individual nurse. Uniform licensing laws in the states have been developed to protect both the nurse and the public. Today professional nurses of every state have to be registered.

The International Unit of the American Nurses' Association supports the International Council of Nurses and the specialized agencies of the United Nations in promotion of better understanding among nurses of all countries. The activities of this unit center about exchange programs for graduate nurses endorsed by the International Council of Nurses. Nurses from other countries come to the United States for observation, study, and experience, and nurses from this country go abroad for similar experiences.

The membership in the American Nurses' Association is open to all graduate nurses registered in the state, who join through their local district or who join directly with the State Nurses' Association if the state is not districted.

The platform of the American Nurses' Association, adopted at the biennial convention in Chicago in 1948, emphasized the expanding role of the American nurse in world affairs, increased participation of the nurse in national affairs, and provided for the rapid expansion in nursing service to meet the health needs of the American people.

National League for Nursing

Another nurses' society was organized in order that nurses could work more efficiently. When, in 1893, Chicago decided to celebrate the March of Civilization toward the West with a World's Fair, a Women's Building was in the plans. One exhibit in this building was to be sponsored by British nurses under the direction of Mrs. Bedford-Fenwick. Recognizing the difficulties that the British nurses had surmounted when organizing their society, Mrs. Fenwick suggested that a place be provided where American nurses could meet and get acquainted. She visited Miss Hampton, and as a result the superintendents of eighteen training schools for nurses met and formed a section under the chairmanship of Miss Hampton. As might be expected, the heterogeneous nature of nursing education was then revealed. Although most schools had been patterned from the Kaiserswerth or Miss Nightingale's ideas, the whole program was still so young that the various courses could not be compared, so much had they been shaped by local circumstances. If a profession were to be created, certain standards had to be universally accepted, and new departures had to be watched and controlled.

For this purpose plans were made toward forming a permanent organization, and in January, 1894, the American Society of Superintendents of Training Schools came into being. In the beginning, membership was limited to the heads of the larger schools, but it gradually became apparent that it would be for the good of the profession to include the smaller schools also. Later it was decided to extend the membership to others interested in nursing education even though they were not heads of schools. It is this society that has sponsored the reforms in nursing education that have gradually evolved. The work has particularly been along the lines of (1) higher minimum entrance requirements to attract top students into nursing, (2) improvement of living and working conditions, and (3) increased opportunities for postgraduate and specialized training. In 1952 the National League of Nursing Education, in conjunction with the National Organization of Public Health Nurses and American Association for Collegiate Schools of Nursing, joined to become the National League for Nursing.

National Organization for Public Health Nursing. The appearance of a new group of nurses with different interests—the public health nurses—demanded some form of organization. This did not happen, however, until 1911 when a joint committee was appointed by the two national nurses' organizations, the American Nurses' Association and the American Society of Superintendents of Training Schools, for the purpose of standardizing nurses' services outside the hospital. The chairman of the committee was Lillian D. Wald and the secretary was Mary S. Gardner. After thorough consideration, the decision was made to form a new organization that could answer the needs of nurses in public health. The committee invited all the 800 agencies that they knew to be engaged in public health nursing activities to send delegates to the forthcoming meeting of the two established nursing organizations in Chicago in June, 1912. At the meeting the interest was great and a most heated discussion continued for two days. One of the difficulties was to find a suitable name for the new organization. Finally at noon on June 7, the National Organization for Public Health Nursing was unanimously voted into existence, with Lillian D. Wald as its first president. The discussion during the proceedings must have been lively from Miss Gardner's description of the "hot morning of June seventh."

The purpose of the new society was to standardize public health nursing activities on a high level and coordinate all efforts in the field. Although primarily a nurses' organization, membership was not restricted to registered nurses but included all whose work was concerned with this field. The organization was ready to cooperate with all other groups having mutual interests. It grew quickly, and almost ideally served its purpose; its growth reflected the growth of public health nursing in America. With the establishment of the American Public Health Association, public health nurses joined with professionals in other health disciplines, and the National Organization of Public Health Nursing dissolved.

SUMMARY

In a dynamic society any fundamental function such as nursing must also change if it is to meet the needs of society. Nursing functions today range from uncomplicated activities (those dealing mainly with personal hygiene or assisting with and carrying out relatively simple procedures) to complex ones demanding not only expert skill, judgment, and technical experience but also knowledge in such fields as sociology, psychology, social work, and other health, social, and welfare areas. The very nature of nursing and the wide range of functions from the relatively simple to the complex have resulted in the need for more than one level of nursing skills.

The educational programs for preparing nurses today are changing to meet the changing demands made on the profession. Conditions are progressing so rapidly that changes may be made in a program during a student's own experience in school. In such areas as mental health, maternal-child health, cancer care and treatment, intensive care, cardiac care nursing in various community agencies, and such administrative positions as those with state and national nursing organizations, there is ever-growing specialization, resulting in a large variety of job opportunities.

There was a traditional attitude against married nurses, and particularly against any students getting married during World War II. This attitude has changed dramatically, as has the situation: the number of married women in nursing as well as in other occupations has increased to the point that there is no longer any distinction in many statistical reports. Until recently all professional nurses except a few in public health nursing lived highly institutionalized lives and even after graduation continued to live in nurses' residences, with little opportunity or wish for outside activities. It is becoming more and more important for nurses to take an active part in community activities, in addition to belonging to professional organizations. They are active in legal and political as well as civic and volunteer programs and activities.

In some areas the demand for nurses still outruns the supply. In rural United States a shortage still remains. In some areas there is an oversupply of nurses prepared at one level and a shortage of those prepared at another level. Graduates of vocational (LPN) programs as well as two- and three-year programs far outnumber graduates of baccalaureate and higher degree programs; they often assume greater responsibility than that for which they are really prepared because someone must perform the tasks. Increasing demands from hospitals and expanding community health services as well as international programs for better-prepared nurses have all contributed to this situation. Opportunities in nursing will continue to diversify and expand.

Since World War II new hospitals were built in many communities and old hospitals increased their facilities. It was not uncommon to find that many institutions were not able to expand as rapidly as needed because of the lack of qualified nurses and other health personnel. Many agencies, both civilian and military, annually reported shortages.

Keeping current with new developments has brought about the need for continuing education for all workers in the health field. The cost of nursing service has made it necessary to evaluate the kind of practitioner needed at each level of health care delivery. Changes in demographic data also require changes in the number and type of nurses needed.

The establishment of the first school of nursing by Florence Nightingale at St. Thomas's Hospital in England in 1860 was a turning point. Until that time few people believed that nurses—that is, females—should have or even needed any training, much less formal education. Once the idea of education was introduced, however, it spread rapidly. Nursing was swept along

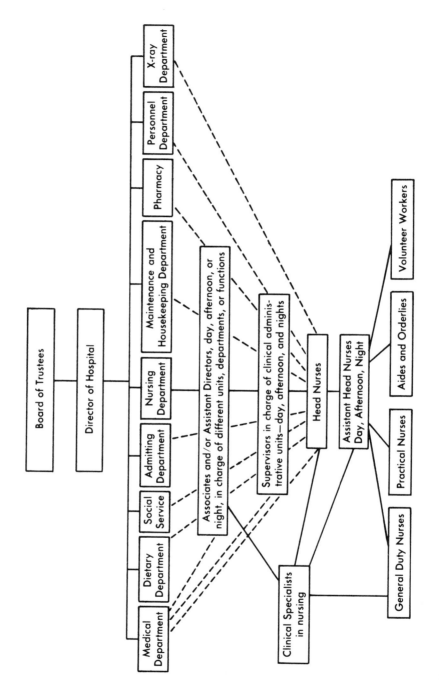

Nursing service in the organization of a hospital.

with the general feminist movement both in terms of education of women and professional status. In the mid-nineteenth century a number of colleges for women were founded in the United States and shortly thereafter were accepted into universities (Case Western Reserve in Cleveland in 1887 and Tulane in New Orleans in 1888). Other universities opened their doors to women soon thereafter. As nurses received more education and developed increased specialization, they were beginning to develop their independent role, they were no longer content to accept the menial tasks that physicians relegated to them. They attempted to develop an equal status and autonomy of function through the establishment of programs within the college and university setting, the first of these being at the University of Minnesota in 1909.

According to a recent study conducted by the Bureau of Health Manpower's Division of Nursing, most nurse graduates are not only employed six months after licensure but are also employed by the type of employer who was their first preference. In a survey conducted by the Research Division of the National League for Nursing in 1973, only 3% of more than 6,000 nurses participating in the survey responded that they were currently unemployed and looking for a new position. The overwhelming majority of new nurses, approximately 81%, were employed in either public or private hospitals. This certainly indicates that although greater emphasis is being placed on prevention and care outside hospital settings, most nurses are still employed in the traditional institutional setting. This is particularly true with diploma graduates, of whom 87% were hospital employed.

6 · Nursing during World War I

The declaration of war made by Germany against Russia on August 1, 1914, eventually became a global war involving thirty-two nations. Twenty-eight of them, known as the Allies and the Associated Powers, included Great Britain, France, Russia, Italy, and the United States. They opposed a coalition known as the Central Powers, which included Germany, Austria-Hungary, Turkey, and Bulgaria. It was originally a local European conflict between Austria-Hungary and Serbia, but the ultimate precipitating factor was the assassination of Archduke Francis Ferdinand of Austria-Hungary by a Serb nationalist. The conflicts were complex and deeply rooted in the European history of the previous century, involving political and economic policies within and among the nations of Europe and the increasing emergence of Germany as a great world power.

The idea of political democracy had spread after the French Revolution and the Napoleonic era. Ethnic, political, and linguistic ideas were becoming increasingly important to groups trying to achieve separate identities by establishing independent nationalities. This movement was in conflict with the existing geographic boundaries.

One by one, European nations had won independence: the Netherlands in 1831, Italy in 1861, and Germany in 1871. A number of areas remained where the problem of nationalism was unresolved, and tensions continued both within the regions and between European nations. Alsace-Lorraine between Germany and France and the Tyrol region between Austria-Hungary and Italy serve as examples.

Revolts occurred in the region controlled by the Austria-Hungarian government, with a simultaneous drive on the part of various kingdoms for separate identity and a strong nationalistic Slav movement advocating cultural and political union of all Slavic peoples. The latter was supported by Russia, not only because of ethnic consanguinity but also because any force that might weaken Austria-Hungary would also aid Russia in its long-range ambition to control the seaports within countries bordering the Mediterranean Sea and thereby facilitate Russian trade.

As well as political conflicts, economic conflicts were significant. The Industrial Revolution, which took place in Great Britain at the end of the eighteenth century, in France about 1830, and Germany about 1870, created a marked increase in the manufacturing capacity of each country and a subsequent need for foreign markets to absorb their products. At the same time, natural resources and raw materials were in demand and imperialism (acquiring colonies for economic exploitation) began to run rampant.

Political, social, and economic tensions increased to such an extent that no domestic or foreign measures were possible to avert an all-out war. Attempts at worldwide disarmament and high-level international conferences were unsuccessful, since each nation considered itself in danger against others and prepared for war and for self-defense. Alliances with other powers were sought in the event that war did break out. The battles that took place on first one front and then another occupied the energies of people everywhere. Nursing the sick and wounded was like the proverbial putting a finger in the dike. Nurses in Europe were occupied with their own problems and were virtually cut off from developments in nursing occurring in the Americas.

THE UNITED STATES ENTERS THE WAR

The United States entered the war in April, 1917, for the second great Allied offensive. German attempts to drive Great Britain to surrender because of destruction by submarine of its shipping of food and other supplies had failed. Fresh manpower from the United States included nurses who served on the battlefield caring for men of the Allied armies. American doctors and nurses served on a much more limited basis than their British and French counterparts.

At the outbreak of World War I in 1914, the American navy had no hospitals in Europe. Some navy nurses were temporarily enlisted to serve in France with the American Red Cross. In 1916 the United States Naval Reserve Force was created, including a provision for reserve nurses. The total number was small. By 1917 regular and reserve force nurses totaled only 466. Nurses began to be sent to the navy's base hospitals in England, Ireland, Scotland, and France. During this same year, schools of nursing were established by the navy nurses at St. Croix and St. Thomas in the Virgin Islands, and one of these nurses was assigned to the Richmond Insane and Leper Asylum as a supervisor.

By 1918 the total number of navy nurses had increased to 1,386. It was not until 1918 that the base pay was increased to $60 per month.

No record is available to document nursing activities during the great battles at sea, which involved large and magnificent ships.

The Army School of Nursing was established in 1918 to relieve the exceedingly serious shortage of nurses. Miss Annie W. Goodrich was the first dean. This school of nursing served as a major source for career army nurses until it was closed in 1931 as an economy measure.

In 1901 the Army Reorganization Act established the Nurse Corps (female) as a permanent corps of the medical department. The first Chief of the Corps was Miss Dita H. Kinney. Military rank was not given to members of the Corps until 1920 when 21,480 Army nurses had served in World War I. Women of the Army Nurse Corps were granted temporary commissions in the Army of the United States in June 1944. It was not until after the Corps became a part of the regular army in 1947 that its members were granted actual commissioned rank. In 1955, under Public Law 294, passed by the Eighty-fourth Congress, male nurses were authorized commissions in the U.S. Army Reserve and appointed to the Army Nurse Corps. More than ten years later the Eighty-ninth Congress passed Public Law 89-609, which authorized male nurses to receive commissions in the regular army (Engleman and Joy).

Nursing owes much to all branches of the service for the continuous upgrading of nursing care.

THE AMERICAN RED CROSS

It was fortunate that Jane Delano was head of nursing in the American Red Cross when the United States entered World War I. She was an experienced nurse administrator and former superintendent of the Army Nurse Corps. The nursing service of the Red

Cross immediately became a recognized reserve of the Army Nurse Corps.

In addition to recruiting army nurses, the Red Cross Nursing Service staffed many American Red Cross installations overseas and recruited nurses for the Navy Nurse Corps and for the United States Public Health Service.

The Red Cross recruited a total of over 20,000 professional nurses during World War I. This was about four fifths of the total number of professional nurses who served in the World War. During this same period the Red Cross recruited and trained over 2,000 nurses' aides. Of these, about 250 were sent overseas.

The increased importance of home-nursing instruction was evident as the war continued and was emphasized during the influenza epidemic of 1918 and 1919.

During and immediately after World War I it became clear that the Red Cross could be an instrument of the greatest social service also in peace. The president of the War Council of the American Red Cross, H. P. Davison, therefore proposed in 1919 that a "league" of Red Cross societies be formed for the general relief of suffering humanity, the prevention of disease, and the improvement of health—a greatly expanded program. The league is ruled by a board of governors, one from each component society. The secretariat of the league was originally in Geneva but was transferred to Paris in 1922 with the international committee. By thus enlarging and extending its purpose, the Red Cross now found it easy to extend into South America, which had previously considered Red Cross activities occupied chiefly in war relief. The establishment of the league resulted within a few years in the accession of twenty-three new societies and a great increase in its membership.

To encourage international cooperation and to exchange experiences, the league has sponsored world international and regional international congresses, and museums have been established for collections of Red Cross material in order that technical improvements in one geographic area can be readily made available to other societies.

The local chapters of the Red Cross are primarily responsible for disaster relief. Each chapter is organized with a group of volunteers ready to respond to any call. Dressings and other relief material are stored in readily accessible places. The various chapters are coordinated to meet an emergency of any magnitude, even on a national scale, such as the great earthquakes in Nicaragua and Italy. Some of the volunteers are laypersons with varying amounts of training in first aid; others are trained nurses and doctors.

Work in public health has been conducted as an educational campaign, more specifically in maternal and child welfare. Close cooperation has been established with other international societies with related purposes, such as The International Union Against Tuberculosis and societies for better working conditions of seamen. It is noted that much of this work is of a social service nature.

NURSING AND THE LEAGUE OF RED CROSS SOCIETIES

Of greatest interest for our purpose is the work of the league in the field of nursing. Under its auspices an international nursing center was established in London in 1920 with a graduate nurse as its head. The chief purposes in the field of nursing were to encourage the highest standards of nurses' training—particularly in Third World nations (in some nations this is done by actually sponsoring schools of nursing) by emphasizing for specially trained nurses the opportunities in public health and the prevention of illness—and to improve international relations by offering postgraduate courses to nurses from various nations. This last was done at Bedford College for Women and at the College of Nursing in London. The British Red Cross provided the league with a house in London for the students. By acting as a stimulus and coordinating the field of nursing with all its other activities, the

League of Red Cross Societies has tremendously furthered the cause of nursing and has helped to increase the opportunities in the field.

Finally it must be mentioned that by establishing the Junior Red Cross, the league has strengthened itself by extending its activities to boys and girls who, thus trained in first aid and relief, have become a valuable recruiting ground for the organization.

VASSAR TRAINING CAMP PROGRAM

In answer to an appeal for college women to assist in the war, Vassar College offered its facilities for the training of college women in the summer of 1918. A twelve-week preclinical course in the basic sciences and elementary nursing was offered as part of a two-year course in nursing for college women. When the summer courses had been satisfactorily completed, students were assigned to selected general hospitals as regular students for the remainder of the nurse program. In all, 430 young women from 115 colleges and universities, representing 41 states, enrolled for the Vassar Training Camp Program. These young women were from many professional fields and created a great interest in nursing in colleges and universities throughout the country.

VETERANS ADMINISTRATION NURSING

Changes in warfare equipment and tactics through the years brought with them changes in the kind of health care and facilities that were required to fulfill the federal government's obligation under the Soldiers and Sailors Civil Relief Act of 1912. The actual quantity of services and manpower required increased markedly as the United States' involvement in war became more global in nature during World Wars I and II.

The invention and use of aircraft in war, chemical warfare, brainwashing techniques, and atomic weapons resulted in new problems. Amputations, neurological dysfunction,

psychiatric breakdown under stress, and results of exposure to radioactivity serve as examples. At the same time that Americans were viewing health care more as a right than a privilege, veterans were beginning to feel perhaps even more strongly about the issue. After having given of their very life blood for their country, they felt entitled to enjoy a maximum state of health.

The immediate search for new treatment approaches were sought as one result. This prompted large research efforts. Veterans hospitals became major medical complexes emphasizing teaching of all types of health personnel and research. Employment in veterans hospitals required the dedication of male and female nurses with the stamina to continue in settings where patient progress is often slow and discouraging. In some situations, essentially no positive movement is perceptible, nor can it ever be expected. Yet each patient remains a human being deserving of every opportunity for all the professional care that nurses can give.

SUMMARY

At the end of World War I, Julia Stimson, the first woman major in the United States Army, was superintendent of the Nurse Corps. She headed the corps from 1920 to 1937, when she was succeeded by Colonel Julia O. Flikke. Major Stimson felt strongly that because nurses were part of the army organization, they should hold rank. This was further emphasized by conditions in the British army in which nurses did have military rank. The defect was remedied in 1920 when the superintendent of the corps was created a major, and all nurses below her were given appropriate rank.

Shortly after the Armistice, Jane Delano went to Europe for a tour of inspection of nursing in military hospitals. While there she contracted an ear infection and died of mastoiditis in France in 1919. She was succeeded in her work with the Red Cross by Clara D. Noyes, who had acted as her assistant for several years. In 1929 the League of

Red Cross Societies, an international organization, was created to continue the work of the Red Cross in peacetime.

Casualties among land forces during World War I amounted to a total of about 37 million. In addition, deaths among the civilian population of Europe caused indirectly by the war were estimated at approximately 10 million. President Woodrow Wilson, in peace negotiations and the creation of the League of Nations, hoped to establish a basis for a just and lasting peace so that this war would be "a war to end wars." Such was not to be, as evidenced by the second world conflict that began about twenty years later.

7 • The Great Depression

Wars have always accelerated the need for nurses and emphasized the necessity of better nursing service, and in nursing, the years between World Wars I and II were anything but quiet. The type of nursing education prevalent before World War I was no longer adequate to meet the demands placed on it. Increased specialization in nursing service developed rapidly, and the need for a better basic nursing education as well as for the development of postgraduate education was evident. The years between wars were characterized by study and research.

Business cycles, the fairly regular recurrence of alternately prosperous and depressed economic conditions, affect the health of the general public as individuals shift their priorities, demand better health care, or are prompted to take better care of their health through subsidized programs. Such factors affect the supply of manpower in health, including nursing. There have been at least seven or eight major business cycles in the United States since 1865. Minor cycles are usually referred to as recessions and represent interruptions in the expansion phase of a major cycle. These minor cycles or recessions usually have a duration of only two to four years.

Major cycles such as that of the Great Depression of the 1930s create a profound upheaval within a society. "Business cycle" as a term refers to the economy of a single country or of a closely interrelated area such

as western Europe. Because of increasing economic interdependence, however, business cycles are beginning to assume an international character. So it was that the crisis of 1929 in the United States, which initiated the Great Depression, was followed by the worldwide depression of the 1930s.

As president of the United States, Franklin Delano Roosevelt designed and implemented a program referred to as the New Deal. He pledged himself to "a new deal for the American people." This program consisted of two parts. The first included temporary measures that were expected to provide relief and counteract the effects of the widespread economic depression. The second was comprised of more permanent measures designed to rehabilitate and stabilize the economy of the United States to prevent a recurrence of similar severe economic crashes.

Among the temporary measures that were adopted was the Emergency Bank Relief Act passed in 1933 to prevent the breakdown of the national banking system. In the same year the Federal Emergency Relief Administration was established to allocate relief funds for distribution to the needy of the nation; this distribution was accomplished at the state level and was a program in which many nurses participated. Other programs in which there was some participation by nursing included the Civilian Conservation Corps, designed to employ young people in reforestation and soil conservation, and the

Federal Civil Works Administration, which created jobs for the unemployed. Many nurses worked in government-supported health care.

The New Deal was attacked by conservatives as destructive of private enterprise, including the American system of private health care. Scholars later set forth the theory, now generally accepted, that the New Deal did introduce into the United States an attitude justifying governmental regulation of goods and services to whatever extent necessary to maintain minimum needs of public welfare.

COMMITTEE ON GRADING OF NURSING SCHOOLS

In 1920 standards in the best schools of nursing had been high, but the greatly increased demands for nursing students during and after World War I had forced many schools to relax their entrance requirements to attract more students. Thus many less desirable applicants were admitted to the schools, resulting in such heterogeneous educational standards that before anything serious could be undertaken, the current state of affairs had to be recorded and analyzed. Then recommendations could be made for standardization and improvements.

The trend was to place even greater emphasis on public health and preventive medicine. This happened to be the exact field in which the Rockefeller Foundation was much interested. It became possible for the foundation to finance the Committee for the Study of Nursing Education, which was organized in 1918 as a result of a meeting called by the foundation and attended by about fifty persons, including doctors, nurses, and others interested in public health. The committee was headed by Professor C. E. A. Winslow of Yale University, but most of the work was done by its secretary, Josephine Goldmark, who by her previous training in social research was especially well fitted for the task. Sometimes the committee has been called after her—the "Goldmark committee." Originally the task of the

committee was to study educational requirements for public health nursing. However, by 1920 it had become clear that this problem was so inextricably tangled with other aspects of nurses' preparation that the inquiry was extended to encompass the entire field of nursing education. Accordingly the investigation proceeded along wider lines; twenty-three hospital schools of nursing, representative of all types and localities, were carefully analyzed, as well as all nursing activities, with emphasis on public health nursing.

The entire investigation resulted in the publication in 1923 of *Nursing and Nursing Education in the United States*. The following three important points were brought out by the investigation:

1. There was widespread neglect of the field of public health.
2. Many schools were deficient in technical facilities for the teaching of nurses and had instructors inadequately prepared for their tasks. The course was unstandardized, especially in the relationship of theory to practice.
3. It was general practice for the chief nurse of the hospital also to be the head of the school of nursing. The cause of nursing would be better served by having these two duties vested in separate persons.

Nursing's experience with deteriorating standards of education was not unique. At the beginning of the century the training of medical students in America had been very poor. Thousands were poorly trained for even the simplest medical responsibilities; yet they were graduates of "accredited" schools. The American Medical Association about 1910 investigated all medical schools and graded them A, B, and C. The results of this grading were astounding. A prospective medical student realized that if he graduated from a grade B or grade C school, it would lower his professional standing. As a result, poor medical schools either improved to meet acceptable standards or discontinued the course.

The plan was so successful that in 1925 nurses decided to sponsor a committee on the grading of nursing schools. Its scope was somewhat wider than was suggested by its name, for besides grading schools the committee was also to study in detail the work of nurses and to define the duties belonging within the scope of nursing. It was also to study the supply of nurses and the demands for nursing services, including the problems for public health nursing. In other words, the committee was to carry further the task that had been started by the Rockefeller committee. The grading committee, however, was only in part financed by outside sources; among themselves the nurses raised $115,000 over a five-year period. The chairman was Dr. William Darrach, but Dr. May Ayres Burgess, a trained educator and statistician, was actually in charge of the work.

The committee was naturally comprised of representatives of the three national nursing associations—the National League of Nursing Education, the American Nurses' Association, and the National Organization for Public Health Nursing—and also representatives from the American Medical Association, the American Hospital Association, and the American Public Health Association. Besides these there were representatives of the general public and educators. Miss Mary M. Roberts, editor of *The American Journal of Nursing*, placed the columns of this nursing publication at the disposal of the committee.

The committee worked for about seven years finding facts that were published in three reports. The first, a preliminary report, was *Nurses, Patients, and Pocketbooks*, which appeared in 1928. In 1934 *An Activity Analysis of Nursing*, a partial report comprising the studies of Ethel Johns and Blanche Pfefferkorn, was published. The final report, *Nursing Schools Today and Tomorrow*, was completed about a year later and goes into great detail concerning all the problems involved.

The grading of nursing schools, which was the original purpose of the committee, was not carried out by this committee. In the beginning it was thought that without personal visits to each school by the grading committee, a fair grading would not be feasible, and such a system would be too expensive. Later questionnaires were sent out to the schools and, after a study of these, each school was shown how it stood in relation to other schools. In 1932 a second survey of the schools proceeded along similar lines. The first questionnaire brought to light a great many facts—some of them new even to the trustees of the nursing schools—concerning requirements, equipment, and costs. The result was that many smaller schools decided their effort was not worth the cost and the schools were discontinued. Others realized their defects and had them remedied, with the gratifying results revealed in the second survey.

Although the immediate results may not have been as striking as they would have been by grading schools as the medical schools had been graded, this analysis had a profound effect upon the schools during the next ten years, and reforms of various kinds were greatly supported by it. The actual grading of schools was later started by the accrediting committee. It was recommended that courses in nursing schools should be on a college level, entrance requirements for schools of nursing and for colleges should be similar, close cooperation between the schools should be encouraged, and they should advance along similar but not identical lines, lest nurses' preparation be frozen; there were still many problems to be solved by experiments. It was also pointed out that improved standards of instruction would lead to improved and greater opportunities for the graduate.

In a practical way the survey inquired minutely into what actual nursing was in the eyes of those who could form an opinion on the question, such as hospital administrators, nurses, doctors, and patients. It also studied working conditions, including working hours, remuneration, and opportunities for advancement.

The practical results were the elimination of inferior schools and a temporary decrease in the number of students admitted, with nine tenths of the schools admitting only high school graduates. The decrease in the number of students led to more graduate nurses being employed in the hospitals. The instruction passed into better qualified hands. Also, the entire course gradually was fitted to the students' needs rather than to the hospitals' requirements.

In this whole reform movement the American Nurses' Association and the National League of Nursing Education worked closely together. To further improve this coordination the NLNE began to serve as the educational department of the NLN in 1932.

The Committee on the Grading of Nursing Schools did not actually grade schools as medical schools had been graded into A, B, and C schools. Too much material had to be studied and evaluated because of the great variety of standards and working conditions found in schools in the United States. However, this study did lead eventually to the accrediting of nursing schools undertaken as a function of the National League of Nursing.

The aims that were formulated by the accrediting committee were stated as follows:

1. To stimulate through accrediting practices the general improvement of nursing education and nursing practice in the United States.
2. To help those responsible for the administration of schools of nursing to improve their schools.
3. To give public recognition to schools that voluntarily seek and are deemed worthy of professional accreditation.
4. To publish a list of accredited schools for the purpose of guidance to prospective students in their choice of schools of nursing and to aid secondary schools and colleges in their guidance programs.
5. To serve as a guide to state accrediting agencies in further defining their standards for recognition of schools and to promote interstate relationships in professional registering of nurses.
6. To make available to institution administrators, students or graduate nurses advanced standing information that will help in evaluating credentials.
7. To provide information which may be made available to lay and professional groups for the purpose of developing an understanding of the ideals, objectives, and needs of nursing education.[*]

The accrediting committee worked hard on standards for the evaluation of nursing schools. The school, as a whole, was to be judged, and the list of accredited schools would be those that had satisfactorily met the criteria set up by the committee. The accrediting committee would visit schools at their request and examine them. The individual school would pay the cost of such evaluation, and the individual school must apply to the committee for accreditation.

The committee then made several recommendations, some pertaining to public health nursing. It was recommended that public health nurses needed a sound basic hospital training of about two and one-third years, plus an eight months' course in public health nursing. Although the number of nurses had increased from about 83,000 in 1910 to over 149,000 in 1920 shortages were still apparent in certain areas. This committee pointed out that the old apprenticeship type of training was outmoded in preparing nurses. The committee also recommended that the training of attendants should be developed further. The requirement of a grammer school education and a training program of about eight months in a good hospital was suggested.

Other recommendations concerned the general education of nurses. The current tendency to lower requirements should be discontinued and efforts made to raise the general standards of nursing education to the level of the best schools. Instructors and other officers of schools of nursing should receive special training to prepare them for their tasks. The development of university associations working in conjunction with schools of nursing should be strengthened,

---

[*]Editorial: Field work of the accrediting committee begins, American Journal of Nursing 38:461-462, April, 1958.

and schools should be given adequate financial backing. It was further suggested that "subsidiary nurses" be trained for eight or nine months to carry out nonnursing tasks in institutions and to take charge of patients who do not need skilled nursing care. This meant the introduction of a group of subsidiary workers with a certain elementary training. Within the past few years this group has increased in number and, together with attendants and orderlies, pages, clerks, and secretaries, has been added to ward personnel to do work formerly done by nurses, while nurses now perform those duties requiring special skill and technique.

The recommendations of this committee have profoundly affected the education of nurses in America. They immediately led to the endowment of the Yale School of Nursing by the Rockefeller Foundation (p. 95). Their indirect effects extended much further, and there are few schools of nursing throughout the country that are not better for its efforts.

GROWTH OF UNIVERSITY PROGRAMS IN NURSING

A greater interest in nursing was developed by the community during and after World War I. Professional nurses began to work more closely with educational institutions in solving common problems in education. All these activities needed financial support, and endowments from private funds and grants from public sources began to be available.

Traditionally nursing had offered three main fields of endeavor: hospital nursing (including teaching and administration), public health nursing, and private duty nursing. After World War I, nursing in each of the first two areas developed and created a tremendous need for nurses with advanced preparation for special jobs in hospitals, health agencies, schools, and industries. To meet the great need for specialization, many courses were worked out, mainly in connection with colleges and universities, to give special preparation.

It is necessary to follow the further development of some of the movements that had started before the war, notably the establishment of schools of nursing within universities. Following the success of Dr. Richard Beard's Minnesota experiment, other schools adopted the idea, and by the year 1920 there were 180 nursing schools with academic standing. By 1938 there were forty-five universities sponsoring complete courses in nursing. They did not all follow the same pattern, and they did not all endeavor to serve the same purpose. So vast had the field of nursing become that many schools could afford to emphasize certain aspects thereof only to the neglect of others. Often the schools at the same time achieved the endowment that had been envisioned by Miss Nightingale as a necessity, without which the best work could not be done unless funds were contributed by the university. Some of these endowed schools resulted, but they are also the logical consequences of the movement being discussed here.

During the years that followed, many schools of nursing were reorganized on a university basis; some courses were four years and some were five in length. At the end of the course students received both a baccalaureate degree and a diploma in nursing.

The outstanding attempt at an endowed university school admitting only students with a college degree was the Yale University School of Nursing, which in its organization followed many of the recommendations made by the Committee for the Study of Nursing Education. Its endowment was granted by the Rockefeller Foundation. In this school the balance between the needs of the hospital and the needs of the students was struck entirely in favor of the students. All theoretical and practical work was planned to fit their requirements. Patients allotted to each student were assigned on this basis, and the case method was worked out in nursing. The staff, too, was chosen for its teaching ability. Annie W. Goodrich was the first dean of this school.

The experiment proved eminently successful, and in 1929 the school was established on a permanent basis with a large foundation grant. The Rockefeller Foundation was particularly interested because this school was in keeping with the trend of placing an increasing emphasis on the public health aspects of nursing. However, because of changing needs in nurse education, the corporation of Yale University in 1956 voted to discontinue the basic program and to concentrate on graduate nurse education.

The School of Nursing of Western Reserve University came into prominence in the early 1920s; it was made financially independent by the Frances Payne Bolton Foundation. Since then other endowed nursing schools have been established along the same general lines, placing emphasis on education and public health. Some have been established abroad, such as the School of Nursing at Toronto University, Canada.

The development of some form of association between nursing schools and colleges or universities continued. This relationship varied from a loose nonacademic tie, in which the school was called a university school merely because the supporting hospital was attached to a medical school, to the establishment of the nursing school as a professional school meeting academic standards set up by the college or university. This situation in university schools of nursing and the variety of standards were studied for several years before the establishment of The Association of Collegiate Schools of Nursing. A first conference held at Teachers College, Columbia University, in January, 1933, was formed of 21 institutions whose representatives agreed to formulate standards and to set up machinery for the permanent organization, which took place in 1935. The objectives of the association as stated in the constitution were:

1. To develop nursing education on a professional and collegiate level.
2. To promote and strengthen relationships between schools of nursing and institutions of higher education.
3. To promote study and experimentation in nursing service and nursing education.

Membership in the association was restricted to schools or departments on a collegiate and professional level or part of the system of higher education. It provided for two classes of membership:

1. Active membership shall be open to an accredited school of nursing definitely established as a constituent part of an accredited college or university which offers a combined academic and basic professional program leading to a baccalaureate degree. The organization of the school shall accord with that of other professional schools in the university or college.
2. Associate membership shall be open to an accredited school of nursing whose professional curriculum meets the standards set by the ACSN, provided that the school (a) is definitely established as a constituent part of an accredited college or university or one of the divisions thereof or (b) maintains a close educational and organizational relationship with an accredited college or university or one of the divisions thereof which makes its resources and facilities available to the school of nursing.

DELANO RED CROSS NURSING SERVICE

Cooperation between the American Red Cross and public health nurses did not stop with World War I. When it was over, thousands of nurses, freed from war service, thronged to participate in the rapidly expanding public health activities. The task of the cooperating societies was twofold: organization of the field and an endeavor to fill the posts with properly qualified nurses, which in many cases meant that the nurses had to be prepared in this field before they could be appointed. One thing was in their favor: the trend of the times was to give to worthy causes so that financing was relatively easy. The Red Cross could finance scholarships through which nurses could properly prepare themselves. Generally the county was considered the unit suitable for such a project. Child welfare, tuberculosis prevention, and other similar endeavors have prospered under the joint auspices, often in co-operation with special national associations such as the National Tuberculosis Association.

One practical expression of cooperation is the Delano Red Cross Nursing Service established by a bequest from the will of Jane Delano. It provides one or more public health nurses to go into regions in which such work would otherwise not be financially possible. Under its provisions nurses have gone into the mountains of North Carolina, the cold of Alaska, and the islands off the coast of Maine.

The cooperation became international in scope when the Red Cross sponsored public health efforts in war-torn Europe, especially child welfare, and still more so when the above-mentioned courses were established in London under the international auspices of the League of Red Cross Societies. This effort was far more than technical in scope. It demonstrated such association of young persons from all countries could perhaps lay a foundation for eventual world peace.

SUMMARY

The period between World Wars I and II is considered by many people as an armistice. However, in the United States the wish of the people to do away with warlike activities as soon after any war as possible was observed in, among other things, the reduction of nurses in the army and navy corps during the 1920s and 1930s.

These were important years for nursing. During this period, nurses became aware that they were a potent social power. Nursing was being recognized as something far more comprehensive than taking care of the sick. An equal emphasis was to be placed on the prevention of illness. From their inauspi-cious beginning, visiting nurses developed the still expanding field of public health nursing.

While realizing their importance, nurses became critical of themselves. It was not enough to have established high aims and standards—the time had now come to formulate and enforce them.

All surveys that were made during this period pointed to the fact that the nursing profession was aware it needed to change to meet, on the one hand, demands being made by the community for quality nursing service and, on the other hand, demands being made by prospective students for a better professional course. A monograph, *Nursing as a Profession*, prepared by Dr. Esther Lucile Brown under the auspices of the Russell Sage Foundation, published in 1936 and revised in 1940, focused attention on some of the problems, such as the control of nursing education. In 1936 the National League of Nursing Education published a manual, *Essentials of a Good School of Nursing*. In the same year, in cooperation with the Division on Nursing of the Council of the American Hospital Association and a committee of the league, a manual called *Essentials of Good Hospital Nursing Service* was published. These publications pointed out that due to the nature of each, the major goals of nursing schools vary from those of nursing services and these differences must be planned for in the organizations and programs of each.

One handicap in carrying out some of these programs in nursing education was lack of trained personnel. The league tried to help schools and nurses all over the country. In 1933 it published a manual, *The Nursing School Faculty: Duties, Qualifications and Preparation of Its Members*.

References for unit two

American National Red Cross: The American Red Cross: a brief story, Washington, D.C., 1951, American National Red Cross.

Baker, Nina Brown: Cyclone in calico, the story of Mary Ann Bickerdyke, Boston, 1952, Little, Brown & Co.

Barton, William E.: The life of Clara Barton—founder of the American Red Cross (2 vols.), Boston, 1922, Houghton Mifflin Co.

Berry, Elizabeth J.: Hope Docks in Guiana, American Journal of Nursing 66:2238-2242, Oct., 1966.

Blanchfield, Florence A., and Standlee, Mary W.: Organized nursing and the army in three wars. Unpublished manuscript on file, Historical Division, Office of the Surgeon General of the Army, Washington, D.C.

Brockett, L. P., and Vaughan, Mary C.: Women's work in the Civil War: a record of heroism, patriotism and patience, Rochester, N.Y., 1867, R. H. Curran.

Chayer, Mary Ella: School Nursing, New York, 1937, G. P. Putnam's Sons.

Christy, Teresa E.: Portrait of a leader: Lavinia Lloyd Dock, Nursing Outlook 17:72-75, June, 1969.

Christy, Teresa E.: Portrait of a leader: M. Adelaide Nutting, Nursing Outlook 17:20-24, Jan., 1969.

Christy, Teresa E.: Portrait of a leader: Isabel Hampton Robb, Nursing Outlook 17:26-29, March, 1969.

Christy, Teresa E.: Portrait of a leader: Isabel M. Stewart, Nursing Outlook 17:44-48, Oct., 1969.

DeBarberey, Helen: Elizabeth Seton, New York, 1931, The Macmillan Co.

Dock, Lavinia L., and others: History of American Red Cross nursing, New York, 1922, The Macmillan Co.

Dubos, Rene J.: Louis Pasteur: Free lance of science, Boston, 1950, Little, Brown & Co.

Dulles, Foster R.: The American Red Cross: a history, New York, 1950, Harper & Brothers.

Epler, Percy H.: The life of Clara Barton, New York, 1919, The Macmillan Co.

Engelman, Rose C., and Joy, Robert J. T.: Two hundred years of military medicine, Fort Detrick, Md., 1975, The Historical Unit, U.S. Army Medical Department.

Evaluation of employment opportunities for newly licensed nurses, Pub. No. (HRA) 75-12, Bethesda, Md., 1975, U.S. Department of Health, Education, and Welfare, Public Health Service.

Gladwin, Mary E.: The Red Cross and Jane Arminda Delano, Philadelphia, 1931, W. B. Saunders Co.

Greenbie, Marjorie Barstow: Lincoln's daughters of mercy, New York, 1944, G. P. Putnam's Sons.

Gumpert, Martin: The story of the Red Cross, New York, 1938, Oxford Press.

Jensen, Deborah M.: History and trends of professional nursing, St. Louis, 1959, The C. V. Mosby Co.

Kernodle, Portia B.: The Red Cross nurse in action, 1882-1948, New York, 1949, Harper & Brothers.

Livermore, Mary A.: My story of the war, a woman's narrative of four years' experience as a nurse in the Union Army, Hartford, Conn., 1888, A. D. Worthington Co.

Marshall, Helen E.: Dorothea Dix, Chapel Hill, 1937, University of North Carolina Press.

Nursing and the League of Nations, American Journal of Nursing 31:1283-1284, Nov., 1931.

Nutting, Mary Adelaide: History of nursing (in collaboration with Lavinia L. Dock), vols. 1 and 2, New York and London, 1907; vols. 3 and 4, 1912.

Pickett, Sarah Elizabeth: The American National Red Cross, New York, 1924, Century Co.

Roberts, Mary M.: American nursing: history and interpretation, New York, 1954, The Macmillan Co.

The American National Red Cross: Jane A. Delano: a biography, ARC 781, Washington, D.C., 1952.

The A.N.A. and you, New York, 1941, American Nurses' Association, p. 2.

Tiffany, Francis: Life of Dorothea Lynde Dix, Boston, 1890, Houghton Mifflin Co.

Transactions of the American Hospital Association, p. 91, 1913.

Vreeland, Ellynne M.: Fifty Years of Nursing in the Federal Government Nursing Services, American Journal of Nursing 50:626, Oct., 1950.

Wald, Lillian D.: Windows on Henry Street, Boston, 1934, Little, Brown & Co.

Williams, Blanche Colton: Clara Barton, daughter of destiny, Philadelphia, 1941, J. B. Lippincott Co.

UNIT THREE
Contemporary nursing

8 • Nursing during World War II

Immediately prior to World War II, curriculums in schools of nursing were being readjusted to meet the modern situation. More emphasis was placed on the social sciences. The preventive and social aspects were integrated in the clinical programs, as were mental hygiene and health teaching. More community experiences were recommended for all students. All these changes brought up the question of cost. A study made jointly by a committee of the league and the American Nurses' Association resulted in a pamphlet, *Administrative Cost Analysis for Nursing Service and Nursing Education,* published in 1940. The accrediting program of the league was progressing, and collegiate programs were increasing in number.

In 1941 the first list of schools accredited by the National League of Nursing Education was published. The war slowed down the work of the committee but did not entirely stop it; however, because of lack of finances and lack of personnel, the program moved rather slowly during the war years.

More money, although not nearly enough, was being made available for nursing education from private endowments and from public sources. This, then, was the situation at the beginning of World War II.

NATIONAL NURSING COUNCIL

The United States was not actively engaged in World War II until the end of 1941. However, by the middle of 1940 the Nursing Council of National Defense (forerunner of the National Nursing Council for War Service, Inc.) was organized by the six national nursing organizations. Julia C. Stimson was president, and Alma Scott was secretary. These six national nursing organizations were the American Nurses' Association, the National League of Nursing Education, the Association of Collegiate Schools of Nursing, the National Organization for Public Health Nursing, the American Red Cross Nursing Service, and the National Association of Colored Graduate Nurses. One of the main purposes of this council was to serve as a coordinating agency made up of representatives from professional nursing organizations and later representatives from hospital and medical groups and the general public. The major activities that began at once included the recruitment of student nurses and the classification of all graduate nurses in the country as to their availability for military service. Under the direction of the Nursing Division, Procurement and Assignment Service, War Manpower Commission, considerations of whether the nurses were essential on the home front were made. The council cooperated with the American Red Cross in recruiting nurses for the Army and Navy Nurse Corps.

INVENTORY OF NURSES

The national inventory of nursing personnel showed that there were about 100,000 nurses under 40 years of age and unmarried who were potential recruits for the Red Cross Nursing Service, first reserve. This national survey also revealed an acute shortage of nurses. In July, 1941, through the efforts of the National Nursing Council and the Committee on Educational Policies and Resources and with the cooperation of the U.S. Public Health Service, under the sponsorship of Representative Frances Payne Bolton of Ohio, Public Law 146 was passed by Congress (1943). This provided for the first government funds for the education of nurses for national defense, and under the terms of the act 1,000 graduate nurses were given postgraduate preparation and 2,500 nonpracticing nurses were given refresher courses. Over 200 basic schools of nursing were given financial assistance, which enabled them to increase their facilities and their enrollment. During 1942 the council worked in cooperation with the armed forces trying to meet the demand. Recruitment was stimulated by advertising, and schools were helped in adopting an accelerated program. State and local councils were given assistance in recruiting graduate and student nurses. During this period the council's main financial support came from the Kellogg Foundation. The Milbank Memorial Foundation also helped, as did the professional nursing organizations.

Early in 1942 the plan that eventually produced the United States Cadet Nurse Corps was discussed, and in July the bill that has become known as the Bolton Act became a law. The main purpose of this act was to prepare nurses in adequate numbers for the armed forces, government and civilian hospitals, health services, and war industries through appropriations to institutions qualified to give such preparation. The program was carried out by a newly created Department of Nursing Education in the U.S. Public Health Service, with Miss Lucille Petry as chief director, responsible to Surgeon General Parran.

According to *United States Cadet Nurse Corps, 1943-1948:* "The nurses of this coun-

try—and those who worked with them in planning, organizing, and directing their voluntary mobilization in World War II—may well be proud that the unprecedented needs for nursing services both in the war theaters and at home were met. Contributing in a major way to this achievement was the United States Cadet Nurse Corps."

FINANCING OF NURSING EDUCATION

The participation of the federal government and the financing of nursing education culminated in the Cadet Nurse Corps. This participation was made possible by the Bolton Act (sponsored by Mrs. Frances Payne Bolton, congresswoman from Ohio who had been interested for years in nursing education), which was passed in July, 1942. However, a great deal of planning and work had been done prior to that. The need for more nurses had been apparent long before Pearl Harbor. In early 1940 nursing organizations, government agencies, hospital administrators, and interested people in the community were beginning to think and to plan toward alleviating the nurse shortage. The needs of the country had been defined as follows:

1. To step up recruitment of student nurses.
2. To educate further and better prepare graduate nurses.
3. To induce professional, inactive nurses to return to service and if necessary to take refresher courses.
4. To train and use voluntary nurse aides under professional supervision.*

The first national inventory of nurses was taken in 1941, directed by Pearl McIver of the U.S. Public Health Service and largely financed by that agency. The cost of the survey was $100,000, of which the American Red Cross contributed $5,000 and the Health

---

*United States Cadet Nurse Corps, 1943-1948, Washington, D.C., 1950, Federal Security Agency, U.S. Public Health Service, Government Printing Office, p. 4.

and Medical Committee $10,000. This inventory showed that in 1941 there were 289,286 registered nurses in the United States. Of these 171,055 were actively practicing nursing.

LOCAL NURSING COUNCILS

The National Nursing Council for War Service, Inc., stimulated the organization of local nursing councils for war service. District and state nursing associations assumed leadership of these local councils and provided a channel for better distribution of professional nurses and auxiliary help for military and civilian nursing needs. Through these councils the needs and resources of communities all over the country were studied, in many instances for the first time. A great deal of help was given to the local groups by the National League of Nursing Education and by the Nursing Division of the U.S. Public Health Service. The National Council had given attention to the training and use of practical nurses and to the training of nurses' aides. Working with the Red Cross Nursing Service, more than 200,000 nurses' aides were recruited and trained all over the country. As the war went on, the National Nursing Council for War Service, Inc., had representatives from the six national nursing organizations already mentioned and in addition included representatives from the Council of Federal Nurse Services; the Division of Nursing Education, the U.S. Public Health Services; the Nursing Division, Procurement and Assignment Service, War Manpower Commission; the Subcommittee on Nursing, Health and Medical Committee; the International Council of Nurses; the American Hospital Association; and members-at-large. All during the war the national council provided a way of integrating and coordinating the programs of organized nursing and of fulfilling the war needs, both civilian and military.

In 1943 when the federal nursing programs were established, the national council members voted to keep the council incorporated and active for the duration of the war and six months thereafter. Soon after V-J Day the Kellogg Foundation guaranteed to finance the national council programs through the middle of 1946. The name was changed to the National Nursing Council.

RECRUITMENT

In the period immediately before the outbreak of war there had been discussion among nursing leaders and the Surgeon General of the advisability of having either an army school of nursing or a summer training camp for nurses similar to the Vassar Training Camp of World War I. Neither of these ideas seemed to be completely satisfactory, although in the summer of 1941, Bryn Mawr College contributed its campus and facilities to this project, in cooperation with the Red Cross. However, only thirty students instead of an anticipated 200 registered for the course, probably because this country was not yet at war and so there was not the interest.

In the summer of 1941 some American nurses went overseas with the American Red Cross–Harvard Field Hospital Unit. This unit was intended primarily to function in England as a research center in communicable disease; when fully staffed, it included sixty-three nurses. In crossing to England five nurses and a housemother were lost because of German submarine activity. The bombing of England had increased during 1941, and many of these American nurses worked in British hospitals and air raid shelters.

The Red Cross, in cooperation with the Office of Civilian Defense, developed a program for training volunteer nurses' aides. This program was actually carried out by Red Cross chapters all over the country and greatly relieved the pressure in civilian hospitals. During World War II the Red Cross certified almost all of the more than 77,000 nurses who served with the armed forces.

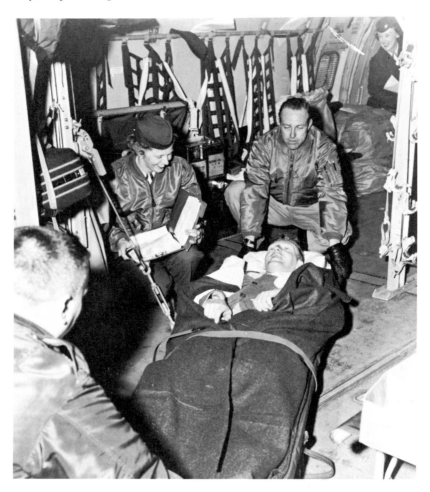

Members of the Air Force Nurse Corps "on duty."

(Courtesy U.S. Air Force; from Morison, Luella J.: Steppingstones to professional nursing, ed. 4, St. Louis, 1965, The C. V. Mosby Co.)

The need for extending the nurses' aide program during World War II was evident. The Red Cross Volunteer Special Service, in cooperation with the Office of Civilian Defense, recruited and trained more than 200,000 nurses' aides. This training course supplied the country with a large group of nurses' aides who gave invaluable service in relieving the shortages in hospitals and health programs that resulted from the large numbers of nurses serving in the armed forces.

Instruction was given in two home-nursing programs: the Home Care of the Sick, and Mother and Baby Care. Many of the teaching techniques that were being used successfully in industry to teach skills safely and quickly were used in this instruction.

The nursing service of the Red Cross during World War II also recruited nurses to serve in the blood collection centers, which had been established to recruit blood donors to meet both military and civilian needs.

NAVY AND ARMY NURSE CORPS

With the outbreak of World War II, members of the Navy Nurse Corps found themselves in the center of initial activity. When the Japanese attacked and took Guam in December, 1941, five nurses were taken prisoners. Just about one year later they were returned to the United States aboard the exchange ship *Gripsholm*. At Manila eleven nurses were captured in 1942 and were held as prisoners of war for thirty-seven months.

By July, 1942, a total of 1,778 nurses were on duty with the navy; 827 were United States Navy, and 951 were United States Naval Reserve. In that year legislation was passed giving navy nurses relative rank, from ensign through lieutenant commander. The base pay for an ensign was increased from $90 to $150 a month. Sue Dauser was superintendent of the Navy Nurse Corps at that time and took the oath as its first captain, as well as the first woman captain of the American navy.

Early in 1944 student nurses under the cadet program reported to naval hospitals to begin a six months' practice period during their senior year. By 1945 the Navy Nurse Corps had increased to over 11,000, including both regular and reserve corps members on active duty. In the United States they served in 40 naval hospitals, 176 dispensaries, and 6 hospital corps schools. They served aboard 12 hospital ships and at land base establishments in many foreign countries.

In 1944 the destroyer U.S.S. *Higbee* was launched. This was the first combat ship to be named for a woman of the service.

When the surrender was signed aboard the U.S.S. *Missouri,* navy nurses were stationed aboard three hospital ships of the Third Fleet, waiting to go ashore to Allied prisoners and to help evacuate them from Japan.

In line with other military developments, training for the air evacuation of casualties became increasingly important, and the first naval school for the instruction of nurses in the air evaluation of casualties was opened.

Instruction and developments during World War II were rapid and followed developments in general naval science, as indicated by the overall military training plans and programs.

All during the war basic training or indoctrination courses were given to nurses in the army and navy. Education in various nursing specialties, particularly in such areas as psychiatric nursing, was provided. It was not until April, 1947, through Public Law 36, that a permanent nurse corps for the army and navy was established by the government. This act removed the need for the Red Cross to maintain a roster of reserve nurses for the army and navy.

At times nurses resented entering the armed forces through the Red Cross because they did not understand the reason. The Surgeon General's office had stated repeatedly that it did not want to assume the responsibility for recruiting nurses. The situation was clarified a great deal in 1942 when the Surgeon General's office made an announcement that the Red Cross was the official recruiting agency of the Army Nurse Corps. The Navy Nurse Corps did not work so closely with the Red Cross as the Army Nurse Corps did, and by the end of 1946 the Navy Nurse Corps had taken over the processing of its own applicants. In spite of all these activities, the number of nurses in actual service was less than the number needed. Although in the spring of 1944 the goal of 40,000 nurses for the army had been reached, the Surgeon General was already requesting 10,000 more. The critical situation on the battlefields was acknowledged by the leaders of this country as never before, and in January, 1945, when the president gave his annual message to Congress, he requested a draft of nurses. Three days later a draft bill was introduced in the House of Representatives. The nursing organizations at once took a position in favor of a national service act for all men and women, not only for nurses. The bill was discussed for three months, during which time the Red Cross nursing organizations and others made a supreme effort to recruit an adequate number of nurses. Fortunately the war in Europe came to an end, and in May, two weeks after V-E Day, action on the bill was dropped.

IMPACT ON MILITARY NURSING

Nursing in World War II differed from nursing in any other war, as did all war activities. Tremendous advances in medical science and the widespread activities of a large variety of fighting men presented a challenge and a great responsibility to the Army and Navy Nurse Corps. In World War II the army and navy nurses served in every part of the world. World War II has often been described as a total war, and for that reason the nurse had to be trained under combat conditions and had to know how to adapt her techniques to meet changing situations. The medical department worked as a team so successfully that 97% of all casualties were saved, and the death rate from diseases was reduced to one twentieth of what it had been in World War I. In 1944 full military recognition was given to the nurses of World War II, and they became a permanent part of the regular military force. Colonel Julia O. Flikke, superintendent of the Army Nurse Corps from 1937 to 1942, was the first woman to be a colonel in the United States Army. In 1942 she was succeeded by Colonel Florence A. Blanchfield. Training for all military nursing personnel was the responsibility of the Office of the Surgeon General. Direction of the Navy Nurse Corps was under the chief of the Bureau of Medicine and Surgery.

The Seventy-eighth Congress passed legislation in 1943 which provided for the appointment of female physicians and surgeons in the medical corps of the Army and the Navy until the end of World War II and six months thereafter. Dr. Margaret D. Draighill was the first woman to be commissioned in the Army Medical Corps. Commissioned as a major, she was assigned the responsibility of medical care for the newly formed Women's Auxiliary Army Corps (WAAC, later called WAC).

POSTWAR DEVELOPMENTS

World War II stimulated many new advances in medicine and nursing. Psychiatry and neurology came into their own as modern specialty areas; physiological research related to the design of protective clothing and individual equipment was important, as soldiers were exposed to extreme climatic conditions. Examples of research in this area include a definition of water requirements in the heat, development of cold weather clothing, description of processes such as acclimatization and physical conditioning, and the relationship between physical anthropometry to the human engineering of vehicles. Penicillin, discovered and developed by British scientists before World War II, was first used in military campaigns by the Allies in North Africa in 1943. Atomic research that led to the development of the atomic bomb carried with it responsibilities for safety of the population residing and working in the secret atomic research sites. DDT, first synthetized in 1870, was studied by the U.S. Department of Agriculture in 1942, and field-tested by the medical department in Naples in 1943, where it stopped a typhus epidemic. The following year army malaria control teams introduced DDT to control mosquitoes in the Pacific, and it has been utilized as the primary insecticide for malaria control since that time.

The opportunity to study wounded men, rather than to continue hypothesis based on the use of animal subjects, led to many developments in the understanding of blood replacement, study of shock, and the process of resuscitation. It was learned that infectious and serum hepatitis were two different entities, and gamma globulin was discovered to be useful in providing passive immunity against viral hepatitis.

Many men returning from battle with

hopes of leading normal productive lives stimulated prosthetic research development, education, and rehabilitation.

Dietitians, physical therapists, and occupational therapists were part of the Women Medical Specialist Corps and were authorized regular army commissions in 1947. But it was not until 1955 that men in these fields were authorized reserve commissions and the name of the corps was changed to Army Medical Specialist Corps. In 1966 Public Law 89-609 permitted male dietitians and physical and occupational therapists to be commissioned in the regular army.

In 1949 a program was begun that provided forty-eight weeks of instruction at the practical nurse level for enlisted personnel at Walter Reed Medical Center. It became the Medical Specialists Advanced Corps and prepared graduates for state licensure as practical nurses.

The Korean War from 1950 to 1953 prompted studies on frostbite. Through epidemiological data it was possible to make a direct correlation between cold injury and ambient temperature, effect of the specific protective clothing, and interaction of various psychosocial factors, as well as the value of specific weather observations in tactile planning and prevention. Both military and civilian cold weather living was made safer and more functional as a result of these efforts. By the end of the Korean War in 1953 helicopters had been developed as a major means of evacuating large numbers of casualties and became widely used as ambulances and rescue vehicles both in the civilian world and later in the Vietnam War.

Medical care of dependents of military personnel has required an enormous number of health care professionals, many of them nurses. The Dependents' Medical Care Program, commonly referred to as Medicare, was enacted in 1956 to provide inpatient and outpatient services in civilian medical facilities. This Medicare program was amended and expanded in 1966 in the form of Civilian Health and Medical Program of the Uniformed Services (CHAMPUS).

A new generation of army hospitals was started in 1960 with the opening of Walson Army Hospital at Fort Dix, New Jersey. Ten more new hospitals were dedicated in the next five years: Munson at Fort Leavenworth, Kansas; Kimbrough at Fort George G. Mead, Maryland; Dunham at Carlisle Barracks, Pennsylvania; Kirk at Aberdeen, Maryland; McDonald at Fort Eustas, Virginia; Kenner at Fort Lee, Virginia; Noble at Fort McClellan, Alabama; McAffee at White Sands, New Mexico; Darnall at Fort Hood, Texas; and General Leonard Wood at Fort Leonard Wood, Missouri.

Restrictions on the promotion of Army Medical Specialists Corps and Army Nurse Corps officers were removed in 1967. Subsequently, the same criteria for promotion and retirement would apply to these corps as did to other corps of the Army. In 1968 Congress changed the Army Medical Service (which had received that name only eighteen years before) back to the Army Medical Department, a designation it had held for 132 years previously.

Colonel Anna Mae V. Hays, Chief of the Army Nurse Corps, was nominated for the grade of Brigadier General in 1970. She was promoted to that grade and became the first woman general in the United States Army. In July, 1975, the Army Medical Department observed its bicentennial anniversary of the beginning of health care for the American soldier.

SUMMARY

During World War II, nursing in every branch of the armed forces matured, and the army, the navy, and the air force found that nurses were proving themselves in the medical and health areas of their respective military programs.

Recruitment of the necessary numbers of nurses was a significant problem. With men overseas in battle, special programs were set up to train nurses, supported by Federal funds and the Red Cross. The problem was especially acute because time was of the essence and there were many other fields recruiting women.

The war did stimulate the upward mobility of women; for the first time, top ranks were achieved by at least a few women in the armed services. The wars after World War II required nursing personnel in hospital evacuation sites, behind battle lines, on ships and aircraft carrying casualties back to the States, and then in Veteran's Hospitals providing care to the mentally and physically disabled. This period was indeed the beginning of contemporary nursing.

9 · Increased support from government

War always produces major changes in various aspects of people's lives, interests, and priorities; thus changes in the area of health have occurred. Armies have introduced fatal diseases into populations that lacked resistance; war and stress of battle have created varying social and emotional problems for all whose lives were touched by the events. The community's interest in matters of health is accelerated by war; even when the acute war need is past, interest in all matters of health is higher than it was at the beginning of the war.

Since World War II the fields of public health and psychiatric–mental health have expanded in many directions. Many communities have increased the scope and size of existing health facilities or have built additional ones, aided by funds from both voluntary and governmental sources.

Most middle-class Americans are covered by some form of health insurance, either to pay possible hospitalization expenses or to provide for payment of other medical expenses. Mass media bombard us with information and misinformation about health and illness. All these factors contribute to an increase in utilization of existing health facilities and a public demand for quality care.

MAJOR TRENDS AFFECTING HEALTH CARE

Among major factors influencing health care and the provisions of health services are the following:

1. *New knowledge.* A surge of new knowledge has occurred within the health sciences concerning people and health problems. Diagnosis and treatment have undergone revolutionary changes due to new developments in drugs and equipment and new research findings in psychosocial aspects of health care. Communicable disease control and better child welfare programs have greatly reduced the incidence of contagious diseases. Such conditions as smallpox, diphtheria, and typhoid fever have been almost eliminated in many communities.

Technological developments refine the quality of care that can be provided but make the administration of that care far more complex. Renal dialysis and heart-lung machines, monitoring devices, closed-circuit television, computers, and radioactive isotopes are only a sampling of the complex equipment used. Knowledge and management of these machines demands vigorous scientific training of responsible health personnel.

2. *A basic change in attitude toward health.* A basic attitudinal change has stemmed from the philosophy set forth by the World Health Organization that health is more than the absence of disease; that it is a state of physical, psychological and social well being; and that it is a right, not a privilege, to which all individuals are entitled. Modern mass media have increased public awareness of various diseases and

143

health problems, even though that awareness is sometimes inaccurate.

When a society views health as a right rather than a privilege, it assumes an obligation to provide service to its members, regardless of their ability to pay for it. The British Health Service is an early example. In the United States, Medicare and Medicaid provide financial access to this right for older citizens and others deemed financially eligible. These and many other forms of health insurance are now operational; they not only make better care more available and accessible to the particular citizens for whom they are designed, but also indirectly benefit all people.

An informed demand for health care means that many people now receive direct health supervision on a regular basis. Almost all industrial plants have nurses educated to provide such service among an entire work force. In larger cities, children are registered at clinics for well-child supervision shortly after birth. Children's health is monitored from the time they enter elementary school until they graduate from high school. Most colleges now have a health service staffed with a medical officer and at least one nurse. Federal programs now ensure retired workers and the unemployed the financial ability to continue to receive competent health supervision.

Three major issues still currently under discussion are the health maintenance organizations (HMO's), national health insurance, and nursing home care. These will be discussed later in this chapter.

3. *Health care personnel supply and distribution.* The effects of President Truman's commission to study the health needs of the nation are still being felt. Much of this report dealt with health personnel: physicians, dentists, nurses, and various allied health professionals. It emphasized the concept of the health care team led by physicians and nurses, augmented with assistants and technicians. Increased specialization in medicine has created a need for workers trained in

areas closely allied to the various specialties. Expansion of preventive, psychiatric, and rehabilitative services has demanded auxiliary workers in these fields. Additional schools of practical nursing have been established and supported by federal funds.

One of the great difficulties in providing adequate care for everyone in the United States is that health workers and health facilities are located in urban centers. Better distribution of institutions and personnel is a problem now being studied by medical, health, and nursing organizations—state, regional, and federal. A system is emerging to deliver health care to underserved populations according to their particular needs. New means are evolving for bringing client, patient, and health personnel together. Rural health teams serve as an example of the cooperative system of health care delivery in which nurses play a more active part in coordinating efforts and skills of various health professionals. These nurses will specialize, and at the same time continue to reflect the needs of the general population that they serve. In this development the nurse now is challenged with much more independent practice and responsibility.

4. *Decreased hospitalization.* Incidence of disease has undergone vast change, and the emphasis has shifted to home care or early discharge from the hospital when hospitalization is necessary. Follow-up care is provided in clinics or by community health nurses. Long-term illness is managed through outpatient and extended care facilities.

5. *Population trends.* Between 1900 and 1952 the nation's population doubled. Following World War II, great impetus was given to the family planning movement. Prior to this time, contraceptive techniques had been available to only a selected segment of the population. Society desired to limit the rate of population growth and many parents chose to space their children. These factors spurred the development of more effective contraceptive techniques and access to information about them until in 1973

population growth was reduced to zero. This reversal of the population explosion, due in part to the continued emancipation of women, has resulted in closing of schools, shifting the focus of clinical facilities to take care of the older age group, and difficulty of nursing students in obtaining clinical obstetric and pediatric experiences.

Increased longevity has changed the face of the health care delivery system. Statistics indicate that the number of persons 65 years of age or more had increased from 3 to 11.5 million between 1900 and 1952, and by 1960 reached 15.5 million. Hospital admissions in 1966 totalled more than 29 million. In addition, there were more than 100 million visits to outpatient and emergency departments.

Changes in morbidity and mortality patterns mean that today's nurse needs a different type of preparation from that needed fifty or even twenty-five years ago. Heart disease, cancer, and kidney disease rank high as causes of death. Chronic problems associated with the increased incidence of degenerative diseases are more frequent. Alcoholism, drug addiction, mental illness, and child abuse are just some of contemporary society's problems that nurses are called on to help prevent and treat.

Prevention and better treatment are gradually replacing custodial care of the mentally ill. However, lack of finances, well-prepared personnel and adequate institutions are making this change a very slow process. There has been a significant reduction in maternal and infant mortality, as well as an improvement in diagnosis and treatment of many heretofore incurable conditions. Chemotherapy has revolutionized the treatment of many severe illnesses. These trends all demonstrate the dynamic state of health care and the internal and external pressures on nursing and other health services.

6. *Continued emancipation of women.* Not only are more women entering the labor force, but opportunities for employment in service occupations are also increasing. The predominantly female occupation of nursing no longer has the first claim on young women it previously enjoyed. According to Bureau of Labor Statistics of the Department of Labor, the total number of health workers needed to meet the demands increased, yet the percentage of eligible young women electing nursing as a career declined from 7% in the 1950s to 5% in the 1960s.

7. *Growth of junior and community colleges.* The tremendous growth of junior and community colleges followed a population explosion after World War II and the demand of youth for a college education. By 1970 nursing programs within these institutions had increased 445%. Besides nursing, many other health careers established educational programs under the aegis of the junior/community college. The number of categories of both professional and technical health workers categorized by the Department of Health, Education, and Welfare has greatly increased.

• • •

In its report of July, 1975, the NLN Committee on Perspectives noted that of 450 million episodes of illness or injury during 1972, Americans totalled 4 billion disability days. Of these 4 billion days, 3 billion were spent in noninstitutional settings. The total death rate has remained about the same over the past several decades. The number of inpatient health care facilities has increased to 35,000, including 7,000 hospitals and 22,000 nursing care homes. Inpatient care facilities contain a total of 3 million beds and employ 4 million personnel. The number of acute-care beds has increased by about 210,000, a total of about 850,000 in the past decade. At the same time, the number of unoccupied acute-care beds has risen from 178,000 to 228,000 (a 28% increase). The lowest admission rate is among children while the highest rate is among the elderly.

New medical techniques and drugs have helped to shorten the average patient's stay in the hospital from eighteen days to less than a week. Skilled nursing care is now needed in the community as well as in the hospital. Cost of hospitalization as well as an emphasis on maintaining persons in the environment that is familar to them has stimulated the development of a major shift in the mode of health care delivery.

All the changes in the patterns of illness and health care have created the need for not only a different kind of education but also a different type of hospital structure. For example, instead of hospitals for communicable diseases, more facilities are needed for out-patient services, extended care of mentally and physically handicapped, and chronic custodial care.

Hospitals may be classified in two general ways—first by type of service offered and second by ownership or control. In 1951 the American Medical Association found that nongovernment or private hospitals comprised nearly 70% of the hospitals in this country and government hospitals, 30%. Church and religious groups have from pioneer days controlled and administered many of our hospitals. This is reflected by the national hospital organizations—the American Hospital Association, and the American Protestant Hospital Association. The modern hospital is a diagnostic, therapeutic, preventive, rehabilitative, and educational institution as well as one carrying on the traditional functions of providing health facilities and services. With medical progress, specialization within the hospital has revolutionized hospital administration and structure.

HEALTH MAINTENANCE ORGANIZATIONS (HMO's)

One stimulus to the establishment of prepaid comprehensive health care organizations was Health Maintenance Organizations legislation. This legislation (Public Law 93-22, Title XIII, Public Health Ser-

vice Act) is a means of delivering health care to individuals and families by a program of assistance from the federal government. Health maintenance organizations have been in existence for more than forty years, providing comprehensive health care services on a prepaid, capitation basis and emphasizing primary care, preventive services, and efficient operation. In 1971 the Department of Health, Education, and Welfare initiated a limited plan in support of developing HMO's. By 1973 federal seed money and technical assistance were provided for the development of twenty HMO's, which enrolled more than 75,000 persons. Numerous other HMO's were in operation by that time, and although many provided less comprehensive services, they served an estimated 5 million persons. By fiscal year 1975 the proposed budget for HMO's was $60 million.

NATIONAL HEALTH INSURANCE

There are those who believe our health care system at the present time is essentially sound; there are others who believe that our health care system has failed to produce health services efficiently or to distribute them appropriately, that the only solution is a national health insurance plan. Numerous variations of a national health insurance program have been proposed that differ in their protective capacity, cost, and distribution. A national health insurance plan could mandate a total reorganization of the present health care system or only moderately alter it, depending on the ultimate outcome of negotiation, planning, and political exchanges. It will undoubtedly proceed in incremental steps, through compromise, and come forth as a hybrid that will fit best with our tradition. Developments must go on concurrently to bring about the desired effects: (1) structural change must be introduced to alter the organization and remuneration of health care services delivery and (2) a means must be instituted for monitoring professional performance and performance of the health care system that processes patients from admission to discharge. Both are absolutely essential and each depends on the other.

National health insurance has been an issue discussed by both the Ninety-third and Ninety-fourth Congresses. The American Medical Association originally supported voluntary participation in the purchase of private insurance, then later moved in the direction of a more liberal, compulsory system. The United States appears closer to finally enacting legislation to provide national health insurance after decades of debate over the issue.

In February, 1974, the Board of Directors of the National League for Nursing approved a statement of NLN's *Goals for a National Health Insurance Program*. In so doing, the League went on record in support of a program to "restructure the delivery of services" and "provide equal insurance benefits to all citizens." To reform the system, nursing must identify where to direct its efforts and must project forward by defining new nursing roles in health assessment and maintenance, coordination of health services, care of the chronically disabled, primary care, and home care. The "progressive development of curricula" as well as additional federal support of such education is being stressed.

In 1974 the Subcommittee on Long-Term Care and the Senate Special Committee on Aging released a report that served as an introduction to nursing home care in the United States and was followed by nine supporting documents subsequently released. Both the legislative and executive branches of the federal government became involved in the nursing home reform after widely publicized investigation of nursing home abuses. The introductory report pointed out that Medicaid pays about 60% of nursing home costs and Medicare another 7%. This means that $2 out of every $3 in nursing home payments is public revenue (taxes). In 1975 there were more nursing home beds

in the United States than general and surgical hospital beds. Medicaid paid out more for nursing home care than for surgical and general hospitals. Between 1960 and 1970 the number of nursing home facilities grew by 140%, the number of beds by 232%, and the number of patients by 10% (NLN P.A. Rep. No. 2).

At the biennial convention in May, 1975, members of the National League for Nursing unanimously passed two resolutions addressing this issue: (1) that the National League for Nursing encourage and emphasize gerontological nursing in all basic nursing education programs as well as encouraging graduate specialization in gerontological nursing for leadership in service, education, and research; and (2) that the National League for Nursing board of directors identify, develop, and implement that organization's unique role in improving nursing home care, and give a status report at the next biennial convention (NLN P.A. Rep. No. 2).

FINANCING OF NURSING EDUCATION

One great stumbling block in the development of collegiate programs in nursing has been finances. The traditional pattern was that students through an apprenticeship or internship gave service to the hospital and thus paid for their education. In many diploma schools, tuition is usually very low or in some cases nonexistent, and additional education costs are minimal.

As nursing education moves from the hospital-controlled schools into colleges or universities, students must assume more financial responsibility for their education. In the United States, state and city colleges provide less expensive education than do private institutions. Many scholarships, loan funds, and fellowships exist for students of nursing.

Leaders in the health-related occupations and professions believe that education should be the responsibility of the educa-

Table 1. Admissions, graduations, and enrollments in schools of nursing—R.N. by type of program and NLN accreditation as of January 1, 1975

| Type of program and accreditation status | No. of programs Oct. 16, 1973- Oct. 15, 1974 | | No. of students | | | | | | | |
| | | | Admissions Aug. 1, 1973- July 31, 1974 | | Graduations Aug. 1, 1973- July 31, 1974 | | Fall admissions Aug. 1, 1974- Dec. 31, 1974 | | Enrollments Oct. 15, 1974 | |
	No.	%	No.	%	No.	%	No.	%	No.	%
Baccalaureate										
Accredited	239		27,538		15,956		24,399		82,961	
Not accredited	77		5,134		1,093		4,614		11,970	
Total	316	22.3	32,672	30.2	17,049	25.2	29,013	30.4	94,931	38.8
Associate degree										
Accredited	236		25,163		16,484		21,627		44,576	
Not accredited	368		23,432		12,815		21,247		40,876	
Total	604	42.7	48,595	44.9	29,299	43.3	42,874	45.0	85,462	35.0
Diploma										
Accredited	430		24,835		19,631		21,614		59,021	
Not accredited	65		2,108		1,649		1,888		5,062	
Total	495	35.0	26,943	24.9	21,280	31.5	23,502	24.6	64,083	26.2
Grand total	1,415†	100.0	108,210	100.0	67,628	100.0	95,389	100.0	244,486	100.0

*From State approved schools of nursing—R.N., 1975, ed. 33, New York, 1975, National League for Nursing.

†Includes 43 programs that closed between October 16, 1973, and October 15, 1974, but admitted 44 and graduated 1,504 students.

tional institutions of the country, both public and private, and that preparation for nursing should be considered as education rather than as work experience. They believe that these programs should be administered and controlled by educational institutions, that money from public and private sources should be available for all nursing education—for the development of instructional facilities as well as research (Table 1). The question may be asked, "Who should pay for the nursing education? The student? The patient? Educational institutions? The public?" The public pays a large share of the bill for preparing workers for other professions: should it not also be prepared to pay for the education of nurses?

Many schools of nursing reported that they lack qualified faculty. In 1956 the Professional Nurse Traineeship Program under Title II of the Health Amendment Act (Public Law 911) provided funds to graduate nurses for advanced preparation in teaching, administration, and supervision. This program, administered by the Division of Nursing Resources of the U.S. Public Health Service, was designed to help relieve the shortage of well-prepared nurses in these three important areas. Later R.N.'s were granted eligibility for traineeships. In 1975 Congress added a section relative to advanced nurse training. This refers to development of nurses with primary care skills.

In a statement released in June, 1964, Surgeon General Luther Terry reported that over 24,000 registered nurses had studied under this program. Of these, 10,000 nurses pursued full-time academic study at colleges and universities to prepare for teaching or administration or both, and 14,000 nurses took intensive short-term courses to improve and update their skills. Dr. Terry said, "The training of nurses is a national concern because nurses now require more knowledge than ever before, to be able to use the ad-

Table 2. Admissions and graduations[*]

	Academic year 1968-1969	Academic year 1973-1974	Increase (+) Decrease (−)
Admissions			
Baccalaureate	15,983	32,672	104.4%+
Associate Degree	18,907	48,595	157.0%+
Diploma	29,267	26,943	8.0%−
Total	64,157	108,210	68.7%+
Graduations			
Baccalaureate	8,381	17,049	103.4%+
Associate Degree	8,701	29,299	236.7%+
Diploma	25,114	21,280	15.3%−
Total	42,196	67,628	60.3%+

*Nursing enrollment reported on the rise (News). Copyright October, 1975, American Journal of Nursing Co.; reprinted from American Journal of Nursing, October, vol. 75, No. 10.

vanced techniques which modern medical science makes possible."

Each trainee received tuition and fees, transportation to the institution and to and from field practice centers, and an allowance for living expenses and for legal dependents. In 1969 the stipend allowances were radically revised. Baccalaureate and higher degree programs protested this action and in 1974 this program was phased out entirely.

A similar program under Title I of Public Law 911, providing funds to graduate nurses preparing for staff level positions in public health nursing, was also phased out. Education is invariably expensive.

While the number of nursing schools increased by only 2.7% in the United States between 1969 and 1974, graduations and enrollments (Table 2) in all R.N. programs went up about 60%. The number of diploma programs as well as their enrollments continue to decrease, but baccalaureate and associated degree enrollment figures have more than doubled.

Nurse Training Act

In 1964 Public Law 88-591 was passed by Congress and signed into law. It became known as the Nurse Training Act of 1964. Its purpose was to increase the supply of well-prepared nurses in the United States

through a program of federal assistance to schools of nursing and students of nursing. The major points of the law consisted of the traineeship program, project grants for improvement in nurse training, nursing student loan program, payments to diploma schools of nursing, and construction grants to schools of nursing. It was a giant step in giving nursing education a broader financial base for operation to provide better patient care.

The original act was to be instituted for five years, but from the evaluation report submitted in the spring of 1968, there was every indication that it would be renewed and expanded. Expansion of the act included a system of institutional grants and scholarships to schools of nursing. The Nurse Training Act amendments were signed into law on August 16, 1968, and continued through fiscal 1971.

Of great interest to junior colleges was the change in accreditation requirements incorporated into the 1968 act. Under the new amendments the present system of program accreditation is augmented with accreditation of the institution as a whole by a regional accrediting body—a state agency or other accrediting body.

The commissioner of education is directed by the act to publish a list of recognized accrediting bodies and of state agencies that he determines to be reliable judges of the quality of training. This expanded definition of "accreditation" will make it possible for some 500 previously excluded schools of nursing to participate in the benefits of the Nursing Training Act. The new law made the act's provisions available to all accredited schools, whether they have program accreditation of nurse training or regional accreditation of the institution as a whole.

On November 18, 1971, President Nixon signed the Nurse Training Act of 1971 (Public Law 92-158). This act continued with modifications. Major features of the new act include extension and amendment of student assistance; grant and contract authorities for special projects for improvement in nursing training; start-up grants for new nurse training programs, and capitation grants to encourage expansion of enrollment and preparation of nurse specialists.

The act authorized assistance to schools in the form of construction grants, loan guarantees and interest subsidies for construction, financial distress grants, and capitation grants; it also authorized assistance to schools and other institutions for special project grants and contracts to strengthen education programs, and for start-up grants for new nurse training programs. Assistance to students was authorized in the form of traineeships, loans, and scholarships. There was also provision for grants and contracts to recruit potential nursing students.

The general provisions affecting implementation of the legislation include the following:

1. Increase in the membership of the National Advisory Council on Nurse Training from 16 to 19. Three of the appointed members will be full-time students enrolled in schools of nursing; they will be appointed for one-year terms and will be eligible for reappointment to the council.
2. Prohibition against discrimination by schools on the basis of sex. The secretary may not make a grant, loan guarantee, or interest subsidy, or enter into a contract unless the school of nursing furnishes assurances that it will not discriminate on the basis of sex in the admission of individuals to its training programs.
3. No change in definition of schools of nursing. Diploma, associate degree, and collegiate (baccalaureate and higher degree) schools of nursing are defined as programs of nursing education, but only if they are accredited.
4. No change in definition of "accredited." A program of nurse education is accredited if the program is accredited, or if the institution in which the program is located is accredited by recognized bodies or state agencies approved for such purpose by the commissioner of education; or if there is reasonable assurance of accreditation.

The increase in the number of nurses has been almost double that of the population increase in the past decade. There is still a decided shortage at the baccalaureate, masters, and doctoral level, especially to fill positions as nurse practitioners, teachers, and researchers. Even the modest proposed goal of 300 nurses/100,000 population in 1960 reached only 282/100,000 by 1970.

More than $6 million in contracts has been awarded by the Department of Health, Education, and Welfare to train registered nurses for new and expanded responsibilities as nurse practitioners, since the Nurse Training Act of 1971 authorized such training.

In making these awards, the Division of Nursing director, Jessie M. Scott, said, "By preparing nurses in all areas of practice for expanded roles in the primary care and teaching of patients, we can reduce gaps in medical services and bring quality health care to greater numbers of people. In these contracts we are focusing on improving care both in hospitals and out in the community, for entire families as well as individual patients."

The type of training includes the following:

1. Pediatric nurse practitioner
2. Pediatric and maternal nurse practitioner
3. Nurse midwife
4. Medical nurse practitioner
5. Family nurse practitioner

Involvement by government

In 1971 the Secretary of the Department of Health, Education, and Welfare acknowledged the expanding role of the professional nurse in a report entitled *Extending the Scope of Nursing Practice.* The combined effort of nurses at all levels in every part of the United States, in conjunction with many interested health groups, has affected a significant turn of events with regard to Nursing Training authorizations in 1975. Following a presidential veto of the Nurse Training, Health Revenue Sharing, and Health Services Act of 1976 (S. 66), the Senate overrode President Ford's veto by a vote of 67 to 15. A week later the House of Representatives also overrode the veto. This legislation provided for construction monies, institutional support in the form of capitation, financial distress, special projects, advanced training nurse practitioner programs, and start-up grants as well as student assistance in the forms of traineeships, student loans, and scholarships. The funding was for the years 1976-1978. The first veto overridden in 1975, this served as evidence of solidarity in terms of political support for health services and education. The veto override may have been a major turning point in nursing history in terms of national legislative matters.

Regional programs

As a result of the passage in 1974 of the National Health Planning Resources Development Act, the Health Systems Agency (HSA) governing groups assume responsibility for developing and carrying out short-term and long-term health care plans in various parts of the United States. Nurses are gradually becoming members of Health Systems Agency governing boards in the United States. In Tennessee there is nurse representation on each of six HSAs within the state. State nurses' associations, state health departments, and health care providers are still in the process of delineating the composition and qualifications for member-

ship as well as which state government group will become the state agency provided for in the bill.

The Western Interstate Commission for Higher Education was granted $233,621 by HEW to improve the care provided by nurses in rural areas of Idaho, Wyoming, and Montana (N.O. **23**:544, 1975).

As with all trends, there has been a swing of the pendulum in the United States Department of Health, Education, and Welfare: first a consolidation of departments, that is, health, education and welfare, took place, followed by a decentralization, producing a regionalization of the various institutes within the division where the Department of Health, Education, and Welfare is located. Until the recentralization of the National Institutes of Health (NIH) in 1972, the Division of Nursing had fifty-five staff personnel. A centralization then took place, which pulled people back into the Washington central office. With the new decentralization currently in progress there has been a return to the concept of regionalization, but the number of staff in the Division has been cut to thirty-five to cover the original ten regions.

SUMMARY

Rapid change strains society's existing institutions and professions, particularly in such traditional institutions as the hospital and such traditional professions as nursing and medicine. No longer are old methods of treatment adequate, and no longer are old methods of educating doctors and nurses satisfactory to meet the demands placed on these workers by society. The distribution of health care facilities and personnel continues to change to meet these changing needs. National and state professional organizations are constantly studying the activities of their members and striving to adjust their educational standards so that health care professionals will be able to function more effectively in contemporary society.

10 • Change in educational patterns

Modern nursing has evolved from the religious, militaristic, and social backgrounds described earlier. Because of the Nightingale type of preparation in the United States, nursing education developed within the hospital. Much of this education, until the last quarter of the nineteenth century, was based on the apprenticeship system; the student worked in the hospital and by doing more work than was necessary for her nursing education, paid for her room and board and part of her instruction. A similar system exists in relatively few schools of nursing today. A majority of nursing schools have worked out a type of affiliation with an educational institution in which the student's program is based on her educational needs. To meet the requirements set by the state and the accreditation standards established by the National League for Nursing, hospital schools have carefully worked out educational programs in conjunction with educational institutions.

The first schools of nursing in the United States were organized on "the Nightingale system." When the schools first tried to become independent under the support of committees of women, the economic problem of supporting them became too great. Therefore the pattern in America was for hospitals to support and control schools of nursing. When a hospital sponsors a good school of nursing, however, it finds that funds must be set aside for this purpose. Although nursing schools originally developed as educational institutions, they were supported or administered not by educational institutions, but by hospitals, whose main focus of interest and concern must always be the care of the patients. It was within this setting that the diploma programs, the oldest form of nursing education in the United States, developed. Baccalaureate programs, in which a student enrolls as a regular college student and earns a college degree as well as being eligible to sit for licensure examinations, were the second form of educational program to develop in nursing.

The entry of nursing into the framework of higher education is relatively recent. The first collegiate school of nursing was established at the University of Minnesota in 1909 with a three-year curriculum; graduates were awarded a diploma but no degree. In 1916 the University of Cincinnati and Teachers College, Columbia University (in conjunction with the Presbyterian Hospital School of Nursing), established five-year programs leading to a baccalaureate degree in nursing. These consisted of two years of college and three in a hospital. This pattern was followed by colleges establishing nursing programs until the end of World War II. There have been extensive changes in the curriculums of these schools since then.

BROWN REPORT AND IMPORTANT FINDINGS

The National Nursing Council for War Service, Inc., initiated a domestic postwar planning group, which in 1944 developed into the National Nursing Planning Committee. This committee was composed of presidents, executive secretaries, and other representatives of national nursing organizations. It outlined objectives and defined areas in which programs for study should be developed. The results of its deliberations are to be found in "A Comprehensive Program for a Nationwide Action in the Field of Nursing" (A.J.N. Sept., 1945). In general the areas for study and action were (1) the improvement of nursing services; (2) the total program of nursing education, practical as well as professional; (3) the distribution of nursing services; (4) the study of standards and the improvement of public relations; and (5) general information about nursing.

Because members of the National Nursing Planning Committee believed that a comprehensive study of nursing education was indicated, they did not abruptly terminate their activities at the end of World War II. They requested and received financial support for the study from the Carnegie Corporation of New York. Dr. Esther Lucile Brown, director of the Department of Studies in Professions of the Russell Sage Foundation, served as the director of the study. This study was published in 1948 and is known either as the Brown Report or *Nursing for the Future*. Dr. Brown approached the problem from the standpoint of provisions made for nursing and health needs of society. Future nursing education programs could be worked out only in consideration of meeting these needs. Few reports have had such a tumultuous reception as the Brown Report. Nurses, hospital administrators, and doctors have been loud in their approval or disapproval of it. The report was made and from the findings, programs and plans for the future were studied and implemented.

The Brown Report recommended that the term "professional" when applied to nurses should be used only for those who studied in schools designated as "accredited profes-

sional" schools. The education, financial support, and legislation for the training of practical nurses were discussed and recommended. This report also pointed out the following: (1) schools of nursing should be nationally classified and accredited; (2) faculty standards, such as those formulated by the Association of Collegiate Schools of Nursing, should be accepted in all schools; and (3) nursing courses as given in the hospital school should be both shortened and improved, particularly as schools of nursing were developing in connection with teaching resources of colleges and universities. It pointed out that nurses could no longer function adequately in the face of increasing demands made on them unless they become an integral part of health teams or of allied professional groups, such as physicians, health officers, social workers, and teachers. The report also pointed out that nursing education needs financial support from both private and public sources. It recommended that state and regional planning for nursing service and nursing education should be started immediately so that plans for the future could be worked out on the basis of need.

Two major changes suggested by Dr. Brown's recommendations were that schools of nursing should have affiliation with universities and should have separate school budgets. Some of the schools of nursing in this country were still hospital schools, and of these, some had very little if any affiliation with educational institutions so that far-reaching changes were indicated. Dr. Brown pointed out that the inadequacy of nursing service in most hospitals existed because nurses were poorly trained in schools of nursing that were inadequate in terms of academic base. There was a great deal of criticism about this report by nurses, particularly of the recommendation that professional nurses be college trained and that two-year courses in collegiate nursing be established to relieve the shortage of nurses. Many registered nurses feared that if these recommendations were carried out, they may be demoted to the status of a practical nurse.

One important and constructive outcome of this report has been that nurses, doctors, hospital administrators, and the lay public began to study the whole issue of nursing service and nursing education more throughly. To stimulate thinking about the situation, the National Nursing Council sponsored three regional conferences in 1948 in connection with the study. The results were published in a book, *1000 Think Together*. Bringing together nurses, doctors, hospital administrators, and interested lay people was most constructive. Group dynamics techniques were used in these meetings, and for many in the nursing field this was their first experience with this method of conducting conferences.

The National Nursing Council, which stimulated the study *Nursing for the Future,* later changed its name to National Committee for the Improvement of Nursing Service.

THE ROCKEFELLER FOUNDATION —THE COMMONWEALTH FUND

The influence of the Rockefeller Foundation has been somewhat different in that it supported largely educational efforts and was even more international in scope than the Red Cross. The foundation supported schools of nursing that emphasized the health aspects of nurses' education. Yale and Toronto Universities serve as examples of institutions where projects were supported by the Rockefeller Foundation as a part of an international plan. It was active in furthering education in public health in Brazil, China, Czechoslovakia, and France, to mention but a few countries. Following World War II it supplied traveling fellowships for the exchange of public health nurses and supported the work of the Nightingale Foundation. The Rockefeller Institution stands out among great institutions interested in public health.

The Commonwealth Fund has done simi-

lar work. Its activities are also to some extent international in scope. Most outstanding is the work done to further the health of children in Austria following World War I. In the United States, promotion of child welfare has been foremost among its activities. Rural health conditions is another interest. In 1934 the Commonwealth Fund helped to finance a survey of rural health by the National Association for Public Health.

NATIONAL COMMISSION FOR THE STUDY OF NURSING AND NURSING EDUCATION

The most recent study of nursing and nursing education can be traced directly to the final document of the Surgeon General's Consultant Group on Nursing, *Toward Quality in Nursing—Needs and Goals.* Shortly after this report appeared, the two major organizations in nursing—the American Nurses' Association and the National League for Nursing—appropriated funds and established a joint committee to study ways for conducting and financing such a national inquiry.

In April of 1966 W. Allen Wallis, president of the University of Rochester, agreed to head such a study if adequate financing could be obtained. That same fall the board of directors of the American Nurses' Foundation voted to grant up to $50,000 to help launch the study. The Avalon Foundation and the Kellogg Foundation gave $100,000 each to support the investigation. Coincidentally, an anonymous benefactor contributed the sum of $300,000 to ensure the undertaking. In January of 1967 the National Commission for the Study of Nursing and Nursing Education was officially formed.

Although the commission was a direct outgrowth of the keen interest of the ANA and NLN, it was set up as an independent agency and functioned as a self-directing group, with the power to plan and conduct its investigations as necessary. At the first formal meeting of the commission in August of 1967, a director, Jerome P. Lysaught, and an associate director, Charles H. Russell, were appointed to conduct the planning and actual operation of the inquiry. A headquarters was established in Rochester, New York, through the cooperation of the University, and a small staff was acquired to develop the research proposal. In addition to the director, Dr. Jerome P. Lysaught, the staff was comprised of Ms. Sydney Ann Sutherland, assistant to the director; Ms. Maryann E. Pierleoni, staff associate; Dr. Natalie S. Pavlovich, staff associate; and two secretaries, Ms. Gilda M. Orioli, and Ms. Ann C. Murphy.

The primary objective of the investigation asked: How can we improve the delivery of health care to the American people, particularly through the analysis and improvement of nursing and nursing education?

Following are the recommendations:

1. The federal Division of Nursing, the National Center for Health Services Research and Development, other governmental agencies, and private foundations appropriate grant funds or research contracts to investigate the impact of nursing practice on the quality, effectiveness, and economy of health care.

2. The same agencies and foundations appropriate research funds and research contracts for basic and applied research into the nursing curriculum, articulation of educational systems, instructional methodologies, and facilities design so that the most functional, effective, and economic approaches are taken in the education and development of future nurses.

3. Each state have, or create, a master planning committee that will take nursing education under its purview, such committees to include representatives of nursing, education, other health professions, and the public, to recommend specific guidelines, means for implementation, and deadlines to ensure that nursing education is positioned in the mainstream of American educational patterns.

4. Federal, regional, state and local governments adopt measures for the increased support of nursing research and education. Priority should be given to construction grants, institutional grants, advanced traineeships, and research grants and contracts. Further, we recommend that private funds and foundations support nursing research and educational

innovations where such activities are not publicly aided. We believe that a useful guide for the beginnings of such a financial aid program would be in the amounts and distribution of funds authorized by Congress for fiscal 1970, with proportional increases from other public and private agencies.

5. A national Joint Practice Commission, with state counterpart committees, be established between Medicine and Nursing to discuss and make recommendations concerning the congruent roles of the physician and the nurse in providing quality health care, with particular attention to: the rise of the nurse clinician; the introduction of the physician's assistant; the increased activity of other professions and para-professions in areas long assumed to be the concern solely of the physician and/or the nurse.

6. Two essentially related, but differing, career patterns be developed for nursing practice:
   a. One career pattern (episodic) would emphasize nursing practice that is essentially curative and restorative, generally acute or chronic in nature, and most frequently provided in the setting of the hospital and inpatient facility.
   b. The second career pattern (distributive) would emphasize the nursing practice that is designed essentially for health maintenance and disease prevention, generally continuous in nature, seldom acute, and most frequently operative in the community or in newly developing institutional settings.

7. Continued study to be given to the use of technology, organizational practices, and specialized personnel (e.g., ward clerks and unit managers) that can release nurses from nonnursing functions while maintaining nursing control over the delivery of nursing care.

8. No less than three regional or inter-institutional committees be funded for the study and development of the nursing curriculum (similar to previous national studies in the biological, physical, and social sciences) in order to develop objectives, universals, alternatives, and sequences for nursing instruction. These committees should specify appropriate levels of general and specialized learning for the different types of educational institutions, and should be particularly concerned with the articulation of programs between the two collegiate levels.

9. The Congress continue and expand such programs as the Health Manpower Act to provide educational loans to nurses pursuing

graduate programs with provision for part or whole forgiveness based on subsequent years of teaching.

10. Federal and state funds should be provided to institutions for nursing education:
    a. For financial support proportional to the number of students enrolled, such moneys to be used to defray expenses of operation and expansion, and to provide salary increments for qualified faculty;
    b. For the building and construction of facilities including laboratories and classrooms.
11. Federal, state and private funds be utilized to implement continuing education programs on either a state-wide or broader basis (as suggested by the current inter-state compacts for higher education) in order to develop short courses, seminars, or other educational experiences. In the face of changing health roles and functions, a greater measure of continuing education programs should be planned and conducted by inter-disciplinary teams.
12. Health management and nursing administration seek to reduce turnover, increase retention, and induce a return to practice by nurses through:
    a. Building on current improvements in starting salaries to create a strong reward system by developing schedules of substantially increasing salary levels for nurses who remain in clinical practice.
    b. Establishing conditions, through organizational and staffing practices, that will give nurses an opportunity to provide optimum care to their patients, including individual planning and implementation of the care plan.
    c. Adopting personnel policies that provide for planned orientation and in-service education courses, flexible employment policies respecting part-time work, scheduling, maternity leaves, assistance for continuing and graduate education to qualify for advancement, and leaves for educational purposes.
13. Both professional organizations and educational institutions in nursing increase counseling services and recruitment efforts directed at mature females seeking initial entries into nursing programs. These efforts should include overtures to both high school graduates and college graduates from the liberal arts and sciences.
14. A single license be retained for registered nurses. Differences in levels of nursing should be recognized through: (a) designation of master clinicians by approved bodies for such purposes, presumably the Academy of Nursing; (b) state licensing standards for health service units; (c) qualifications regarding personnel specified in accreditation standards for health service units; (d) institutional personnel policies respecting appointments, grades or ranks, and qualifications for promotion.
15. The national nursing organizations, particularly the American Nurses' Association and the National League for Nursing, press forward in their current study of functions, structures, methods for representation, and inter-relationships in order to determine: a) areas of overlap or duplication; b) areas of unmet needs; and c) areas or functions that could be transferred from one organization to another in the light of changing conditions.*

The original commission was altered somewhat to respond to new and continued activities. Regional associates were appointed by the director and charged with the responsibility of serving as consultants to the various regions of the United States, to assist in planning to implement the recommendations. The following were regional associates:

Myrtle Aydelotte
    Director, Department of Nursing Service
    The University of Iowa
    Iowa City, Iowa
Virginia Z. Barham
    Nursing Consultant
    The Permanente Medical Groupe
    Oakland, Calif.
Luther Christman
    Dean, Rush College of Nursing and Allied
        Health Sciences
    Rush-Presbyterian-St. Luke's Medical Center
    Chicago, Ill.
Grace L. Deloughery
    Dean, Inter-Collegiate Center of Nursing
        Education
    Spokane, Wash.

---

*An abstract for action: report of the National Commission for the Study of Nursing and Nursing Education. Jerome P. Lysaught, editor. Copyright 1970 by McGraw-Hill Book Co. Originally published in the American Journal of Nursing **70:** 286-294, 1970.

Maryann E. Pierleoni
  Nurse Practitioner
  Overland Park, Kan.
Charles H. Russell
  Dean of Instruction
  Mattatuck Community College
  Waterbury, Conn.

To help ensure the implementation of the recommendations, Dr. Lysaught received an additional grant from the Kellogg Foundation totaling $215,948. The sum of $90,948 was support of commission activities through September 30, 1973, when the national commission concluded its work, and for the support of related activities in nine designated target states being utilized as demonstration laboratories for implementation efforts.

The National Commission for the Study of Nursing and Nursing Education and the impact it had on the thinking of nurses and others will perhaps go down in the history of nursing as one of the major catalysts to the increasing professionalization of nursing in our day.

JUNIOR AND COMMUNITY COLLEGES

The junior and community colleges evolved over the last half century into the most dynamic force in higher education today. Some of the early colleges limited their role to providing the first two years of a baccalaureate program. The original plan has been altered by the social forces of population and the demand for college opportunity for all youth. Thus, although the original concept of liberal arts and general education courses for transfer purposes is still a part of the junior college, most of the institutions now emphasize studies that prepare men and women to take jobs immediately in industry, government service, and service occupations, such as hotel management. The basic change in philosophy is dramatized by the growth of junior colleges. Over 300 junior colleges have been established since 1952, when there were 597; to date there are well over 1,000.

Mildred Montag

The first programs in nursing within the framework of community colleges followed the publication of Dr. Mildred Montag's doctoral thesis, *Education of Nursing Technicians,* 1951. Montag's study proposed a new type of worker, a nursing technician, and a new type of education consisting of two years in junior or community college.

In 1952 a national research project was started to determine the feasibility of developing this new type of nursing education. The project, the Cooperative Research Project in Junior and Community College Education for Nursing, was under the direction of Dr. Montag. One purpose of the project was to develop and test this new type of program preparing young men and women for those functions commonly associated with the registered nurse. The concept had mushroomed before schools that were included in the five-year project had been geographically determined.

The curriculum is generally offered in a two-year academic period, in accordance with college policy and regulations of the various state licensing agencies. The Surgeon General's report, *Toward Quality in Nursing—Needs and Goals,* anticipated a 445% increase in the number of graduates from associate degree programs by 1970, which was reached.

The characteristics of associate degree nursing programs are described in a set of *Guiding Principles for the Establishment of Programs in Nursing in Junior and Community Colleges* as follows:

1. It is desirable that only junior colleges that are accredited by the appropriate regional educational associations establish associate degree programs in nursing.
2. The junior college assumes the same responsibility for the nursing program as it does for other programs; that is, it has complete control of the program and is wholly responsible for its quality.
3. The structure and organization of the junior college are such as to make possible the effective performance of its total function and to permit inclusion of nursing education as part of that function.
4. The administrative leadership in the junior college fosters a democratic environment throughout the entire institution, providing opportunities for the faculty and students of the nursing department to participate in the affairs and life of the college in the same way as do members of other departments.
5. The junior college provides competent leadership for the nursing program, selecting a qualified nurse educator as head of the nursing department and a qualified faculty in nursing.
6. The administration of the junior college takes the initiative in the organization of such lay advisory committees as may be deemed essential to assist the nursing department to achieve a quality program.
7. The junior college provides appropriate resources and facilities for the nursing program.
8. When a junior college makes arrangements with a hospital or other cooperating agencies

for the use of facilities in which the college provides instruction for its students, there is an established formal relationship.
  a. This relationship is entered into only after the groups involved have thoroughly studied and reached agreement on the ways in which the facilities are to be used and the conditions governing their use.
  b. This relationship is clearly defined in a written statement approved by the appropriate boards of control.
  c. The junior college sees to it that the policies established and the mutual obligations specified in the formal agreement are implemented.
9. The junior college assumes full financial responsibility for providing a quality educational program in nursing and has the financial resources to meet such commitments.
  a. The student in nursing is not expected to bear any greater portion of the direct and indirect cost of the program than is required of any other student in the junior college.
  b. The junior college has a sound budgetary procedure for its nursing program as well as for all other programs.
  c. There is opportunity for the nursing faculty and administrative staff to participate with others in the preparation of the budget and in other financial matters.*

The first technical nursing program was opened at Orange County Community College, Middletown, New York, twenty-five years ago. In 1976 there were approximately 818 associate degree nursing programs listed in *The World Almanac.* This number includes only programs that responded to a request for information, are accredited by the National League for Nursing, and have an enrollment of at least 200 students and 30 faculty. This points up only that there has been a fantastic proliferation of the associate degree nursing program in a relatively short period of time.

In her report of the four-state, five-year Kellogg project to develop associate degree

---

*Committee of the National League for Nursing and the American Association of Junior Colleges: Guiding principles for junior colleges participating in nursing education, New York, 1961, National League for Nursing.

nursing education, Anderson predicted that the shortage of qualified faculty for these programs will increase rapidly. White, in her study, found that the teacher in an associate degree nursing program needed graduate preparation in nursing as well as general education beyond that being offered in most masters programs in nursing. It seems relevant to extrapolate from Hoexter's statement that "no matter what may be its material resources and programs, a college or university cannot rise above the level of the quality of its faculty," nor can a community college.

Qualifications for associate degree nursing educators require additional exploration so that obstacles to the educators' securing sufficient preparation for their task may be better understood. It may be that existing graduate programs are not adequately developed for this population, and consequently nurses with masters preparation tend to gravitate to other educational or service settings.

In small communities the faculty is often drawn from a group of married women whose personal and family obligations along with the inavailability of graduate offerings make it impossible for them to continue their professional education. The magnitude and scope of the problem, however, obviously demands rigorous scientific investigation and planning.

CONTINUING EDUCATION

In its *Standards for Nursing Education,* the American Nurse's Association states that "the primary goal of continuing education in nursing is to assure continued competence of nursing personnel in the delivery of health care to all people. Continuing education also includes goals related to personal and professional development." The ANA assumed responsibility for assisting the state nurses' associations for planning and initiating continuing education programs, developing guidelines for approval of continuing education offerings, and a system by which to evaluate the effect of continuing educa-

tion on nursing practice as well as a national system of recording continuing education and consultation services. An example is given of a typical Critical Care Course programed for a typical four- to six-week period and consuming considerable classroom time. If the course is offered twice a year to a group of twenty nurses, one can calculate the following costs:

> Nurse Time = 100 classroom hours × hourly rate + fringe benefits × the number of learners (using a rate of $5.00 + 10% fringe benefits for the nurses participating and $6.00 + 10% fringe benefits for the instructors) will cost a total of $11,000.00 in payroll for the nurses in addition to $2,320.00 in payroll cost for instructors. This is equivalent to 2,000 patient care hours lost.[*]

This kind of expenditure does not include planning time, overhead costs, materials, and various other expenditures. Assuming that it is possible to incorporate an evaluation that shows an increase in nursing knowledge and skill, the expenditure of $13,320 and 2,000 lost patient care hours is somewhat overwhelming. Many questions could be asked, but the most obvious is whether this is in fact the best way to improve accountability.

State nurses' associations have responsibility to develop specific criteria for the approval of education programs consistent with national standards and guidelines and to determine the number of credit hours that will be required in the individual states.

The goal of continuing education in nursing is to update knowledge and facilitate application of that knowledge in the provision of nursing care. To achieve this goal requires use of the best available educational techniques, while keeping cost to a minimum.

Local programs with the coordination of the district nurse's association, other organi-

---

[*]del Bueno, Dorothy: Accountability: words and action Inservice Education, Washington State Journal of Nursing, p. 8, summer, 1975.

zations and institutions, as well as private and local resources are to be provided at the state level.

While the American Nurse's Association has published *Standards on Continuing Education*, so has the National League for Nursing. In November, 1975, the board of directors of the National League for Nursing approved a statement in support of a "gradual and carefully planned implementation of a continuing education requirement for renewal for nursing licensure." Goals that the National League for Nursing identified follow: (1) to continue to develop accreditation criteria and to evaluate continuing education offerings sponsored by nursing schools and nursing service agencies, (2) to plan, conduct, and evaluate continuing education programs for NLN membership, (3) to provide consultation in continuing education, (4) to develop testing or other measuring devices for evaluation of continuing education, and (5) to collaborate, coordinate, and plan with other appropriate health professional groups for the continuing education of nursing personnel. The National League for Nursing recognizes the continuing education unit (CEU) as the standard measurement for continuing education offerings and follows the guidelines developed by the National Task Force of the Continuing Education Unit (1974).

The CEU is a nationally recognized standard measurement for noncredit continuing education programs in any field and is defined as ten contact hours of participation in an organized continuing education experience under responsible sponsorship, capable direction, and qualified instruction. The CEU was developed by the national task force on the continuing education unit of the National University Extension Association to reduce confusion and facilitate communication between and among people, institutions, and employers, from one area of the country to another and from one period to another. They have their parallel in formal academic settings in terms of units of measurement called credits.

Late in 1975 Illinois joined six other states requiring continuing education as continued proof of nurse's competence. The other states are Florida, California, Minnesota, New Mexico, Oregon, and New Hampshire.

Because of the explosion of knowledge and new techniques in medicine and health care, mandatory continuing education for the health care worker has gained support from the national organizations, federal government, and many state nurses' associations.

The Special Committee on Continuing Education of the New York State Student Nurses' Association approved the following recommendations for New York State in the fall of 1971:

a. That New York State Student Nurses' Association sponsor legislation in the 1973 legislative session to require participation in continuing education approved by the professional association as a condition for re-registration of the license to practice as a registered professional nurse.

b. That the effective date of the above legislative proposal be 1975 in preparation for the 1977 biennial registration period.

c. That the Board of Directors establish at the earliest possible date, a permanent body within the Association to be known as the Committee to Approve Continuing Education Programs. This body is charged with the ongoing responsibility for establishing requirements for mandatory continuing education, and for approving continuing education programs and experiences applicable toward such requirements.

d. That the Board of Directors adopt in principle, the Committee's protocol for use in interpreting the essence of the Association's proposal for mandatory continuing education and that this protocol be referred to the permanent Committee to Approve Continuing Education Programs.

e. That the Committee be authorized to present its proposals for review and recommendation to the nurses in attendance at the 1972 New York State Student Nurses' Association Convention and at other NYSSNA programs prior to and during the 1973 legislative session.

f. That the life of the Committee be extended

in order that it may address itself to the task of proposing a system for certification of nursing practitioners through the professional association.

Mandatory continuing education is in the process of being signed into law in many states. California, an early state to do so, experienced great difficulties in implementing the requirement. More care has subsequently been given to planning prior to the development of such rules and regulations. As an example of legislative action, parts of the Assembly Bill No. 449 of the California legislature, approved by the Governor November 15, 1971, filed with the Secretary of State November 18, 1971, reads as follows:

Chapter 1.5. Continuing Education

900. In its concern for the health of the people of California, the Legislature intends to establish in this chapter a framework for the continuing education of those persons licensed in the healing arts who are subject to this chapter. It is the purpose of this chapter to provide a system for assuring that such healing arts professionals are fully informed of current technical knowledge in their professions, thereby providing to the citizens of California the best possible health services. It is the intent of the Legislature that the Council on Continuing Education for Health Occupations established by this chapter assume primary responsibility for the implementation of all statutory continuing education requirements for those health professions licensed in California which are subject to this chapter.

901. There is established in the Department of Consumer Affairs, to be transferred to the Department of Health whenever the healing arts licensing agencies are transferred to the Department of Health in accordance with the Governor's Reorganization Plan No. 1 of 1970, a Council on Continuing Education for Health Occupations, consisting of the director or his designee, who shall serve as chairman of the council, and four additional members, appointed by the director, as follows:

(a) One administrator of a licensed hospital.

(b) One registered nurse.

(c) One licensed vocational nurse.

(d) One public member.

902. The council shall be appointed and begin its meetings by July 1, 1972.

903. The Council on Continuing Education for the Health Occupations, by regulation, shall establish standards for the continuing education in each of the fields covered by this chapter which will assure reasonable currency of knowledge as a basis for safe practice by licensees in each such field. The standards shall be established in a manner to assure that a variety of alternatives is available to licensees to comply with the continuing education requirements for renewal of licenses and taking cognizance of specialized areas of practice. Such alternatives include, but are not limited to, academic studies, inservice education, institutes, seminars, lectures, conferences, workshops, extension studies, and home-study programs. The council may organize committees from its membership to formulate proposed standards in each occupational field, and shall, in addition, invite and consider recommendations from each of the affected licensing agencies or boards concerning such standards. The occupations subject to this chapter are those of licensed vocational nurse and registered nurse.

Many questions must be addressed by state boards of nursing as they plan to move rationally toward mandatory continuing education for nurses. Some questions are:

- How many hours will be required?
- Will retroactivity be considered?
- Will clinical experience substitute or count?
- What fiscal restraints will there be?
- What is the employer's responsibility for freeing individuals to attend continuing education offerings?
- Who will determine approval of continuing education presentations?
- Will there be "cross-approval" between and among disciplines and states?
- What will be required of individuals who maintain double licensure, that is, R.N.'s who are certified registered nurse anesthetists?
- Can educational television be utilized?
- How can programs be offered to nurses who work varying shifts?

A controversial issue currently under discussion is related to the accreditation of continuing education programs. A national accreditation board, under the auspices of the American Nurses' Association, has been selected to develop the accreditation procedure. However, at its regular meeting in November, 1975, The American Association of Colleges of Nursing (formerly the American Association for Collegiate Schools of Nursing) went on record in opposition to this move and took the position that the National League for Nursing should review continuing education programs within the framework of its routine accreditation procedure within those schools of nursing conducting continuing education programs.

MINORITY EDUCATION

Nursing has been traditionally a female, white profession. Both these characteristics are changing. Nurses, like people in other roles, are only worthwhile models if they feel worthwhile to themselves. This applies particularly to those groups which are in a minority and have traditionally had less opportunity to enter and be successful in the field of nursing. Before being anything else, the nurse must be a person with self-respect, assured of worth, and above all must feel that not an unreasonable price was paid for the position in terms of personal drive and aspirations. As practitioners, nurses must be models to the next generation of aspirants. Nursing must be satisfying to the self. This can happen only when the nursing role is defined in such a way as to accommodate both (1) the affiliative and nurturant aspects, which prompt individuals to enter the field, and (2) the aggressive and egocentric impulses, which are within all individuals in greater or lesser degrees.

Men in our society are discovering and utilizing their nurturant capabilities and inclinations while women are discovering their new freedom in the world of careers; men and women who enter the profession of nursing must also find a place that is comfortable between the two aspects of human behavior—both the nurturant and the aggressive, egocentric.

According to the 1958 to 1960 U.S. census figures, there were 440,355 nurses in the United States. Of this total, men nurses comprised 1%; this made them the smallest subprofessional group in the health field in the United States. The history of men in nursing extends back through the history of the Christian Era. It reached its height during the time of the Crusades when European manhood was personified in various military religious orders whose essential work was nursing and hospital administration. Their many hospitals and holdings dotted the countryside of Europe. Some remnants of these orders still remain, but for the most part, the role of men in modern nursing in the United States began about 1888 when the first school of nursing for men was established at Bellevue Hospital in New York City. It was named the Mills School, after Ogden Mills who had endowed the school. Except for the war years, the school was in operation for some time. Many other schools of nursing for men developed, but only recently have men been admitted into regular schools of nursing in any large numbers. The percentage of men in nursing schools, particularly in the associate degree programs, is much higher than the 1% of nursing practitioners from this group would indicate.

In 1972 the percentage of men admitted to nursing programs was nearly double that of 1969. The number of men in R.N. programs increased from 3.5% to 6%, and the number of men in practical nurse programs increased from 4.4% to 5.3%. The South and West had a somewhat higher percentage than that of the Northeast and Midwest (Johnson, 1974).

There are regional and state variations in the number of men and minority students admitted to R.N. and L.P.N.-L.V.N. schools of nursing. There are, for example, more black students admitted in the South and more of the Hispanic background in certain

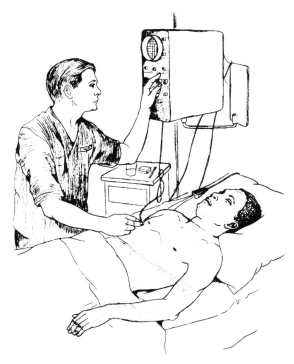

Men in nursing

Nursing is becoming an increasingly popular occupation for men as it expands in scope,
especially in the associate degree programs.

southern and western states. In 1971-1972
the national summary was as follows*:

	Percent of all admissions
Men	5.7
Black	11.6
Spanish-speaking	3.0
American Indian/Oriental	1.3
Total	21.6

The sex and race stereotyping of various
occupations is gradually breaking down.
The number of men entering nursing has increased by 236% in a six-year period (Health
Res. News, 1975). Likewise, the number of
blacks listing nursing as their career choice
rose 294% between 1966 and 1972.

The need to prepare nurses from among

*Johnson, Walter L.: Admission of men and
ethnic minorities to schools of nursing 1971-1972,
Nursing Outlook **22**:49, Jan., 1974.

minority groups stimulated the development of special projects in part or fully
funded by federal monies. Capitation grants
and other grants supporting nursing education required evidence that efforts were being directed toward encouraging enrollment
of minority students and employment of
minority faculty. The Western Council on
Higher Education for Nursing, a branch of
the Western Interstate Commission on
Higher Education (WICHE), as a part of
their overall program, developed workshops
to assist schools of nursing to deal with the
problem of recruitment, teaching and retention of minority students, faculty, and the
provision of nursing care to minority groups.
Discussion included the identification of so-
cial-cultural-physical characteristics of various minorities that must be addressed in providing nursing care. WICHE was awarded
a special federal grant in 1975 to support

its efforts in the area of nursing education for minorities. Ms. Marie Branch, a long-time advocate of minority groups, was named head of the project.

Care for the poor nonwhite segment of our population through the years has been provided mainly by white professionals. This was true also with nursing. Cultural barriers that nurses experienced were often not recognized and if recognized were not dealt with. Nursing care to members of minority groups consequently was not optimal. This situation was addressed at the same time when that of many other issues related to minorities—in the areas of education, employment, housing, and not being able to obtain their goals as all other American citizens—created a restlessness among minority groups, which resulted in public demonstrations and a state of affairs referred to by some as a revolution.

During the 1960s a number of federal laws were passed to protect the basic rights of minorities. It was during the same decade also that there evolved a greater acceptance of the fact that problems of minorities and civil rights problems could not be resolved quickly and easily, and that there were no simple solutions. There evolved also a greater realization that such complex problems would take a great amount of energy and thought for resolution. It would require a change in attitude, provision of new opportunities, and action on the part of professional organizations. Schools of nursing were encouraged to address problems encountered by minority students, including those of loneliness due to separation from ethnic, social, and cultural supports. Tutorial assistance or remedial work along with a great deal of individual counseling and support must be provided to minority students to assist them in meeting the demands of educational programs.

Historically, schools that were predominantly black were almost alone in offering educational opportunities in nursing to black students. In other baccalaureate programs and in graduate schools, relatively few were admitted or were able to complete the course of study. One of the most perplexing and continued problems in nursing is that of increasing the resource of baccalaureate-prepared students from minority groups. It was in 1963 that the Surgeon General's Consultant Group on Nursing began to outline the number of minority nurses needed to meet the current health needs of minority peoples. A systematic effort was then put forth to support education for minority students in nursing.

Originally, the minority movement was stimulated in large part by blacks. However, it was necessary to identify that minorities were of various sociocultural origin, including Spanish-Americans, Puerto Ricans, Mexicans, Cubans, American Indians, and Orientals. These groups maintained that learning to serve the black population was not relevant to them in their preparation to serve their own people. Special efforts were also made by the American Nurses' Association, the National League for Nursing, and the National Student Nurses' Association to recruit minority students into nursing. The Division of Nursing of the Department of Health, Education, and Welfare funded numerous special project grants to recruit minorities into nursing during that period. At the present time more than 80% of all R.N. programs in the United States report that they have no black enrollment. Fewer schools of nursing report having Spanish-American students. Again, the largest number are enrolled in practical nursing programs. There is no question that the number of minority admissions, enrollments, and graduations is continuing to increase. Their acceptance in all types of nursing programs is becoming much easier and more satisfactory. ANA took the position that preparing minority group nurses should not be reverse discrimination but should ensure that all members of our society can enter the nursing profession and advance according to their abilities.

In 1972 the American Nurses' Association House of Delegates passed an Affirmative Action resolution and began to develop a program to address the inequities in nursing. The American Nurses' Association, through the Affirmative Action program, began to work toward full opportunity and equal justice for all members of the profession.

In 1971 there were 15,633 black students admitted to state-approved nursing programs. The majority of these (8,545) were admitted to practical-vocational nursing programs. The next highest number attended associate degree programs. Still fewer were students in three-year diploma programs. At the same time that associate degree programs were increasing in number, there was also a significant increase in the number of minority students admitted to associate degree programs. There was a marked increase between 1968 and 1972 in the number of black students admitted to baccalaureate programs. Perhaps this is in part due to increased efforts on the part of federal and state governments to provide financial assistance to minority students.

Approximately three times as many blacks graduated from practical nursing programs in 1971-1972 than did from associate degree programs and ten times more than did from diploma or baccalaureate programs. For the ten-year period between 1962 and 1972, admissions of blacks to practical nursing programs have been consistently high and admissions to diploma programs consistently low (Lenburg).

To indicate the progress made in minority education assisted financially in 1975, the first ten nurses, were named fellows under the American Nurses' Association Registered Nurse Fellowship Program for Ethnic-Racial Minorities (A.J.N. **75**:1413, 1975). These nurses will receive up to $7,500 annually for a maximum of three years of study in doctoral programs. The purpose of the fellowship program is to prepare minority nurse-researchers. Seven of the ten are Afro-American, one is Asian-American, and two are Spanish surnamed. They will be studying at Emory University, New York University, University of Nebraska at Lincoln, Northwestern University, University of North Carolina, St. Louis University, Fordham University, University of Arizona, University of Texas, and University of Wisconsin at Madison (A.J.N. **75**:1413, 1975).

CAREER MOBILITY— LADDER CONCEPT AND OPEN CURRICULUM

Statistics* indicate that there are 1,374 nursing programs in the United States. Of these, 430 are diploma–three-year hospital programs, 618 are associate degree programs, and 326 are baccalaureate programs.

Admissions to nursing programs in 1974-1975 are as follows:

> 24,322 in diploma programs
> 50,491 in associate degree programs
> 34,495 in baccalaureate programs

Enrollments and growth rates are as follows:

Student enrollment		Growth rate
In diploma programs	60,880	0.95
In associate degree programs	88,852	1.04
In baccalaureate programs	101,084	1.06
Total	250,816	

Currently there are 258 baccalaureate nursing programs and 69 masters degree programs in nursing that are accredited by the National League for Nursing; 9 schools offer doctoral programs in nursing.

There has been a shift in recent years to an emphasis on vocational education. This seems to have resulted from the difficulty that graduates of universities and colleges experience in finding positions in the field which they studied. This trend toward vocational education is opposite from what is being experienced in nursing in which the

*State Approved Schools of Nursing—R.N. 1975, ed. 33, New York, 1975, National League for Nursing.

emphasis is on professionalism and college or university education. A recently installed college president states that liberal arts colleges must integrate the curriculum with career education. The distinction was made between career education and vocational education: "Career education from our institution's point of view is not only professional preparation but also inspires an attitude toward work and our commitment to work in this society" (Winona Daily News). There have been questions about whether the Puritan work habit has finally been abandoned and whether people still want to work, whether there is a need for more meaningful jobs and whether young people have become alienated from the traditional work environment. In recent years some authors have even put forth the idea that our society is so affluent that not all people need to work and that many could live in comfort supported by those who have become addicted to work.

Different from the old notion that nurses must be totally unselfish and concerned with only the preservation of life and institutions, it is now recognized that it is not selfish to work to maintain oneself and one's family, or to put away reserves, and/or to plan for retirement. On the other hand, these activities may be totally unselfish, since the pursuit of work and profit are efforts directed toward freeing oneself from economic dependence on others.

Attitude toward work is significant. The question has been raised what it would be like to spend an entire week inserting a small sphere into a series of holes spaced widely apart with equipment that is poorly designed. As work, it would be terrible; as pleasure, it is called golf. Ways need to be found to make work pleasureable. The routine tasks that cannot be eliminated from nursing or from any other job must be utilized to provide satisfaction to the individual nurse. This is in part accomplished through satisfying relationships with patients-clients, but the importance of equita-

ble salary and fringe benefits cannot be minimized.

At the same time, to carry out the increased number and variety of nursing activities, more personnel are needed to help at the less technical level. The practical nurse and the nurses' aide, the ward clerk, the unit manager, and the messenger have been added to the nursing team. Until quite recently there was some resistance to the practical nurse. At first the practical nurse was an untrained person who, because of her aptitude for nursing and her interest in it, became a useful person in the hospital and community. As the duties given to the practical nurse increased, it became apparent that a formal course of education must be worked out and that this group should be licensed. The National Association for Practical Nurse Education was established in 1941 and consisted of individuals who trained practical nurses. By 1949 State Board Test Pool examinations were administered to practical nurses seeking licensure to practice.

After World War II the number of approved schools of practical nursing has increased nationally. Most of these have developed in the vocational department of the local board of education. Many programs were developed through use of funds from federal as well as from state sources. All this instruction in approved schools for practical nursing is under the direction of professional nurses. Today all states have some type of licensure.

The "ladder concept" in nursing has grown with the continued development and expansion of both the licensed practical nurse and associate degree nursing programs.

There has been a growing demand for career mobility opportunities in nursing. R.N.'s who have graduated from an associate degree or diploma school program have applied increasing pressure to receive recognition for previous learning of theory and clinical nursing skills. Career mobility opportunities have proliferated during the past three or four years. Nurses are pressing for admission to programs that give credit to their previous education and experience. The traditional pattern of nursing education is being challenged. The open curriculum constitutes a new approach to nursing education for which administrators and planners must prepare. Great impetus has been given this idea because in many areas promotion in the hospital setting is based on the achievement of a bachelor of science degree.

In some fields, graduates found that receiving a baccalaureate degree in 1975 was of little help in landing jobs. At the same time, however, hospitals and agencies were unable to fill the positions with nurses holding baccalaureate degrees. Consequently many young people are seeking admission to nursing programs. Lawsuits have developed in some areas of the country, including the University of Washington and the University of Wisconsin at Oshkosh, because students feel that it is unfair to spend several years preparing for the nursing major and having no guarantee of admission to the professional component of the program. The student's concern is real and deserves careful consideration. On the other hand, there have been projections of filling the job market by 1980 if professional nursing programs continue to graduate nurses at the current rate. The question remains whether opening the doors to all who apply to nursing programs is the answer when, in the end, jobs would be already filled. Like graduates in other areas, then, these nurses would find their degree to be of little help in obtaining a position. A solution does not appear to be immediately forthcoming.

The increase in basic nursing education programs manifested in the middle and late 1960s has seemingly reached its peak in the middle 1970s. In 1974 the number of programs producing R.N.'s was 1,372 (Table 3); this is one less than in 1973. Diploma programs continue to decline in number while associate and baccalaureate programs are still growing; the losses and additions essentially balance one another out. Practical nursing programs, which also grew significantly in number for many years, are now increasing at a much slower rate from 1,306 in 1973 to 1,315 in 1974.

Along with the decline in rate of growth of programs there is a decline in the admissions growth rate for all types of programs (Table 4).

The number of graduates from baccalaureate programs who were registered nurses is increasing (Table 5).

With the increasing demand from R.N.'s for upward mobility, the number of baccalaureate programs adapting to the need will undoubtedly continue to increase.

The number of nurses graduating from masters programs in nursing increased from 2,446 in 1972-1973 to 2,643 in 1973-1974. Enrolled in masters programs were 6,783 students in 1973 and 7,924 in 1974 (Johnson, 1975).

With the clamor for admission to nursing

Table 3. Number of programs which prepared for beginning practice in nursing as of October 15, for the years 1970 through 1974*

Academic year	Associate degree	Diploma	Baccalaureate	Total basic R.N. programs	Practical or vocational	Grand total
1970	444	641	270	1,355	1,253	2,608
1971	491	587	285	1,363	1,291	2,654
1972	541	543	293	1,377	1,310	2,687
1973	574	494	305	1,373	1,306	2,679
1974	598	461	313	1,372	1,315	2,687

*Johnson, Walter L.: Educational preparation for nursing—1974. Copyright September, 1975, American Journal of Nursing Co.; reprinted from Nursing Outlook, vol. 23, No. 9.

Table 4. Number of fall admissions and growth rates*

Fall admissions August 1 through July 31	Associate degree		Diploma		Baccalaureate		Total basic R.N. programs		Practical or vocational		Grand total	
	Number admitted	Growth rate	Number admitted	Growth rate	Number admitted	Growth rate	Number admitted	Growth rate	Number admitted	Growth rate	Number admitted	Growth rate
1970	26,483	1.25	27,817	1.01	16,993	1.13	71,293	1.12	33,731	1.05	105,024	1.09
1971	32,871	1.24	28,479	1.02	22,463	1.32	83,813	1.17	38,249	1.13	122,062	1.16
1972	37,366	1.14	28,422	1.00	26,627	1.18	92,415	1.10	38,075	1.00	130,490	1.07
1973	43,032	1.15	26,059	0.92	27,837	1.05	96,928	1.05	38,568	1.01	135,496	1.04
1974	42,874	0.99	23,502	0.90	29,013	1.04	95,389	0.98	40,098	1.04	135,487	1.00

*Johnson, Walter L.: Educational preparation for nursing—1974. Copyright September, 1975, American Journal of Nursing Co.; reprinted from Nursing Outlook, vol. 23, No. 9.

Table 5. Graduations and annual growth rates, registered nurses in baccalaureate programs*

Academic year August 1 through July 31	Number graduated	Growth rate
1970-1971	2,214	0.92
1971-1972	2,337	1.06
1972-1973	2,681	1.15
1973-1974	3,003	1.12

*Johnson, Walter L.: Educational preparation for nursing—1974. Copyright September, 1975, American Journal of Nursing Co.; reprinted from Nursing Outlook, vol. 23, No. 9.

programs, there is an overwhelming shortage of nurses qualified to teach the students. It would seem that the increasing number of graduate-prepared nurses would have an impact on the great need for teachers, clinical specialists, researchers, and administrators; however, the data is somewhat spurious in that some of the increase in enrollment is attributable to nurses pursuing part-time study. The minimum requirement of a masters degree in nursing for all instructors of nursing is not yet a reality in many NLN-accredited schools of nursing. This is particularly true in certain parts of the country and a typical problem in the more rural areas. While some universities are seeking the support and funding for doctoral programs to prepare nurses at that level, others are losing the battle with their state legislatures to continue ongoing funding for existing programs, not to mention an increase in enrollment or to begin new masters programs.

Though the National Commission for the Study of Nursing and Nursing Education, in its recommendations, outlined the need for an increased number of graduate-prepared nurses, more nursing research, and return of the best prepared nurse practitioners to the bedside, the reality is that those who are prepared with graduate degrees remain so few that they are needed in the areas of teaching and administration.

Developing a professional curriculum that

can be completed within four academic to five calendar years is a problem. In 1961 Rogers pointed out that preparation for professional practice required "substantial knowledge in the liberal arts, the biological, physical, and social sciences, and nursing theory." The curriculum needed to be planned and taught by a knowledgeable nursing faculty whose qualifications were comparable to those of any other faculty in the institution.

Many colleges, some very prestigious, are once more giving blanket credit to both diploma and associate degree graduates, promising a bachelor of science degree with no upper division major in nursing but courses "that will enhance the basic education of the new graduate." The new baccalaureate program is generally about two years in length.

The American Nurses' Association published a statement on graduate education in 1969. This statement reflects the position that the core knowledge needed in graduate education is that of science and practice of nursing, regardless of what roles or functions nurses perform. The nurse pursuing advanced education specializes in a clinical area, chooses an area of role development, develops and tests nursing theories, advances knowledge in the field of nursing through systematic observation and experimentation, relates basic science theories to the development of knowledge in both the clinical and functional areas of nursing, identifies and implements the leadership role in the provision of health care services, and collaborates with others in the provision of health care.

In 1953 Bridgman observed that the growing interest of colleges and universities in providing nursing education has not always been accompanied by a thorough study of the nature of the responsibilities assumed. Graduate programs have accepted students with baccalaureate degrees from fields other than nursing. A real problem exists in the fact that the National League

for Nursing, as the accrediting agency, looks with a scrutinizing eye on these "special" programs and does not readily grant accreditation to them. As a result, many nurses graduate from programs that they believe will lead them to job opportunities but find that they do not qualify in the manner they had anticipated. The frustration and hostility that is theirs is no credit to the nursing profession or to the institutions sponsoring the educational programs.

The practice became so widespread that the Board of Directors of the National League for Nursing in 1970 and 1971 issued the following two statements:

A statement of concern about degree programs for nursing students that have no major in nursing[*]

The National League for Nursing notes with concern the growth in the number of collegiate programs that have no major in nursing but are designed to appeal specifically to potential and enrolled nursing students and registered nurses. Publicity about these programs leads students to believe that they offer preparation for advanced positions in nursing or provide the base needed for further education in nursing when this is not the case.

The programs in question lead to associate or baccalaureate degrees in such fields as applied science, biology, education, health science, occupational therapy, psychology, and sociology. Large blocks of credit are promised the student for nursing education obtained outside the college. The collegiate programs may provide the student with increased knowledge in the specified area of the major, but they do not offer additional preparation in nursing.

The National League for Nursing believes the misguidance of the students occurs because of publicity about these programs which:
1. Implies that a major in another field is the equal of the major in nursing as preparation for nursing practice—when it is not.
2. Implies that they are acceptable as a base for further education in nursing—when they are not.
3. Implies that they lead to advancement in employment—which in many instances they do not.

[*]Statement approved by the Board of Directors, National League for Nursing, Oct., 1971.

4. Implies that because only graduates of NLN-accredited nursing programs are awarded credit, the degree programs are therefore approved by NLN—which they are not.

All too frequently it is only after a considerable investment of time and money that students in these programs discover how limited the programs are as preparation for nursing practice and a career in nursing. The National League for Nursing therefore believes that colleges that offer these special degree programs have an obligation to interpret them accurately in all promotional and descriptive materials.

The open curriculum in nursing education*

An open curriculum in nursing education is a system which takes into account the different purposes of the various types of programs but recognizes common areas of achievement. Such a system permits student mobility in the light of ability, changing career goals, and changing aspirations. It also requires clear delineation of the achievement expectations of nursing programs, from practical nursing through graduate education. It recognizes the possibility of mobility from other health related fields. It is an interrelated system of achievement in nursing education with open doors rather than quantitative serial steps.

The National League for Nursing believes that:
1. Individuals who wish to change career goals should have the opportunity to do so.
2. Educational opportunities should be provided for those who are interested in upward mobility without lowering standards.
3. In any type of nursing program opportunity should be provided to validate previous education and experience.
4. Sound educational plans must be developed to avoid unsound projects and programs.
5. More effective guidance is urgently needed at all stages of student development.
6. If projects and endeavors in this area are to be successful, nursing must accept the above concept of the open curriculum.

The concept has several names—ladder, lattice, open curriculum, career mobility, upward mobility, and articulation. The recent nursing literature is filled with references and articles referring to the concept. It is truly one of the most discussed issues in nursing at the present time.

---

*Statement approved by the Board of Directors, National League for Nursing, Feb., 1970.

The concept is exemplified by the Regents External Degree of the University of the States of New York. The first candidates for the nursing program were admitted in September, 1973. The school of nursing has now received NLN accreditation.

Requirements for the associate in applied science in nursing degree include the cognitive and clinical aspects of the nursing sciences and general education. The widely accepted college proficiency examinations in the nursing sciences provide a useful point of departure.

In California the career ladder concept is extended:

The people of the State of California do enact as follows:

Section 1. In its concern for the quality and availability of health care services in California, the Legislature finds that a number of factors prevent the full utilization of the service capabilities of nursing personnel, as well as preventing full career development for nurses. First, the ability of a licensed vocational nurse has been hampered because responsibility for licensing these two occupations was divided between two licensing boards. Second, basic differences in the content and duration of various training programs for registered nurses prevent development of a nursing "career ladder," and is particularly discouraging to minorities who wish to become registered nurses. Third, the legal status of nurses performing certain procedures or acting in certain roles is ambiguous at this time, despite the demonstrated competence of many nurses to perform them. Fourth, the lack of any legal standards for nurses aides prevents them from receiving credit for their knowledge and skill in attempting to advance to a licensed category of nursing, as well as failing to provide adequate standards for public protection. Fifth, the full development of career opportunities and service utilization of psychiatric technicians is limited because they are licensed by the same licensing board as licensed vocational nurses.

It is the purpose of the Legislature in enacting this act that:

(a) Responsibility for licensing vocational and registered nurses be combined under one licensing board, with a view of nursing education as a continuous process for training nurses to perform at successively higher levels of responsibility.

(b) Training programs for registered nurses are encouraged to offer courses enabling students to become licensed as vocational nurses after the first year of training, to give vocational nurses maximum opportunity for advancing to the registered nursing field.

(c) Licensing requirements for categories of nurses should not include graduation from an educational program if the courses required for graduation do not relate to the capability of graduates to perform as nurses.

(d) Nursing education programs offering a baccalaureate degree are encouraged to offer licensure-related courses first, as lower division courses, so that registered nurses who are graduated from other types of nursing programs can transfer to these schools for advanced training without loss of credit.

(e) The licensing board for nursing personnel should develop a standard equivalency test for licensure as a vocational nurse, and for licensure as a registered nurse, to eliminate the problems that have occurred by delegating this function to schools. The parts of these tests should relate to the educational qualifications for licensure, so that an individual should not have to take courses for licensure if he demonstrates his proficiency by passing that part, or parts, of the equivalency examination.

(f) The state should issue a state associate of science degree to every nurse who is a graduate of a diploma nursing education program and does not already possess a degree. This associate degree will be equivalent to associate degrees issued by community colleges to nursing graduates for purposes of matriculating to schools offering a baccalaureate in nursing and shall be accepted by all universities and colleges in California with a nursing program.

(g) Responsibility for licensing psychiatric technicians should be separated from the agency licensing nurses, and phased into an appropriate licensing body.

(h) Training programs for nurses aides should be certified to allow graduates to achieve recognition for their capabilities in advancing to higher levels of nursing.*

In 1967 Hoexter demonstrated in her study using the faculty members from twenty-nine generic baccalaureate programs that faculty members in nursing are not acculturated to the academic community. However, as nurses become better educated and join the ranks of college and university

faculty, they are expected to maintain the same standard as that of other faculty with whom they work. Nursing has traditionally been more task oriented than theory oriented so that pressures to publish and conduct research, and other expectations imposed on all faculty in academe, are having an impact on nursing.

These expectations serve as a stimulus in moving toward true professionalization and making the profession in fact an academic endeavor. It is eliminating some of the mystique of scholarly publishing, although for many nurses publishing is not an enjoyable experience. It is serving the purpose of disseminating knowledge that nurses gain through experience and learning. The following generations can then build on that learning, and a positive change may be brought about in health care. It is those nurses who are in the forefront in academic institutions who are the gatekeepers of ideas that must be shared through conferences, discussions, and publications.

The need for cooperation between nursing service and education has been stated many times. The actual carrying out of collaboration remains a problem. Changing human behavior may be effected through workshops, but change does not take place in institutional structure. Improper utilization of nurses and ritualistic practices continue in many areas.

The cost of nursing education has concerned hospitals and other agencies as well as schools of nursing. Schools of education have long paid for placement of student teachers with preceptors for practice teaching. A large part of physician education has been borne by the student, another part by large university hospitals, and a smaller part by the federal government. Nursing education is only a small fraction of that cost, but the patient or third party (insurance companies) is increasingly alarmed about the matter as hospital and health care costs continue to rise.

The National League for Nursing, re-

*California legislature Assembly Bill No. 1495, amended in assembly April 27, 1972.

sponding to increasing concerns about collaboration, coordination, and cooperation between nursing service and nursing education, sponsored a series of regional conferences focusing on the education and utilization of graduates from associate degree, baccalaureate, diploma, and practical nursing programs. Additional conferences are planned to consider the roles of graduates from masters and doctoral programs. The East Coast Regional Conference was held in New York during October, 1975; the Southern Regional Conference was held in Atlanta in January, 1976; the Midwestern Regional Conference was held in Chicago in March, 1976; and the Western Regional Conference was held in Denver in May, 1976. Sponsors of the conferences were the Council of Associate Degree Programs, the Council of Baccalaureate and Higher Degree Programs, the Council of Diploma Programs, the Council of Practical Nursing Programs, the Council of Home Health Agencies and Community Health Services, and the Council of Hospital and Related Institutional Nursing Services.

Regional workshops are being sponsored by the American Nurses' Association Commission on Nursing Education during 1975-1976. Their purpose is to explore the implications and plan for the implementation of the standards for nursing education that were recently published by the ANA Commission on Nursing Education. It is the responsibility of this commission to set forth the major goals of basic, graduate, and continuing education programs for nurses. These workshops are part of the commission's ongoing efforts toward meeting those goals.

The image of nurses in the military is changing significantly. Brigadier General Claire Garrecht, Chief of the Air Force Nurse Corps; Brigadier General Madelyn Parks, Chief of the Army Nurse Corps; and Admiral Maxine Conder, Chief of the Navy Nurse Corps, refer to their military careers as satisfying and challenging.

Considering that the armed forces exist because of a role in war and preparing for war, the image of the nurse in military service has been one of "toughness," but that image is now obsolete. Even though the United States is not involved in actual duties related directly to war, there are responsibilities for coordinating health care teams and being leaders as well as opportunities for education to improve nursing skills and to add new skills. Both civilian and military nurses work in the same clinical areas, including specialization in pediatrics, family nursing, critical care, rehabilitation, and medical-surgical nursing. In addition, military nurses may be responsible for training of enlisted health personnel, serving in field medical units during combat, and working with hospital designers to ensure that facilities are properly planned and equipped. They may specialize in aerospace or undersea problems, occupational health hazards in special areas such as shipyards or air bases, and may staff flying hospital wards. Navy nurses are likely to spend some time aboard ship.

Between 30% and 40% of all military nurses are married (Arnold)—a major shift from the past.

The first Nurse Practitioner Program was developed in 1965 by Dr. Henry K. Silver and Dr. Loretta Ford in Denver, Colorado. Their definition of nurse practitioners follows:

Nurse practitioners are registered nurses who have an expanded role in level of responsibility in the provision of primary health care. Nurse practitioners have the competence to provide a broad range of direct primary health care services: they are prepared to assess health status; perform physical examinations; initiate and provide plans of care, counseling, and anticipatory guidance; make decisions and assume responsibility for management and follow-up care; refer patients and coordinate services appropriately; and help to achieve continuity of care for patients. Nurse practitioners have acquired advanced knowledge and clinical skill in nursing through successful completion of a formal program of study which was developed jointly by Nursing and Medicine, meet guidelines established by the two professions, and there continues to be a collaborative effort between them. The care provided by nurse practitioners combines selected services of registered nurses as well as those traditionally provided by physicians; the latter services are conducted under the direction and review of physicians. Nurse practitioners function as associates and colleagues of physicians and work collaboratively and interdependently with them and other health personnel.*

A similar definition is published in *The National Register.*

Nurse practitioner programs are of three types:

1. Continuing education program. These are about 120 in number with only 20% requiring a baccalaureate degree for entry. Successful completion entitles the nurse to a certificate.

2. Expanded role programs leading to a baccalaureate degree. Many nurses completing a certificate seek the baccalaureate degree thereafter. Although one might be led to believe these nurses seek knowledge and skill, status and opportunity may be motives not to be dismissed completely. Nurses with a baccalaureate degree should be prepared for primary care on graduation. Until these primary care skills are included in all baccalaureate programs, some graduates will need an internship prior to entering a practitioner program at the graduate level.

3. Expanded role programs leading to a graduate degree. Among these are faculty who serve as role models to students at the baccalaureate level.

The development of these practitioner roles has resulted in more nursing participation in a wider variety of kinds as well as quality of health care, national health policy formulation, and enjoyment of newly founded colleague relationships. There is increasingly less concern about role development, maybe due to more confidence in the

role and comfort with the function. Probably about 90% of graduates from nurse practitioner programs are in active practice, seeming to indicate more satisfaction and job longevity, thus making a greater impact on health care in the long run.

Nurse practitioner programs are an expensive educational endeavor and can best be accomplished in institutions of higher learning. They require appropriate and sufficient quantity of patient and/or clinical material as well as interdependent and independent faculty modeling.

It has not yet been calculated how many nurse practitioners are needed to meet health care needs as currently defined in the United States. Studies conducted by Silver and McAtee indicate that 90% to 95% of consumers believe that care they receive from nurse practitioners is as good as that received from physicians. Nurse practitioners are also well spoken of by those who have worked with them and allow them to function up to their potential.

The question of whether efforts of nurse practitioners save money and time remains unanswered. Data is still limited. This provides a challenge that nursing must address.

The nurse practitioner versus the physician assistant role remains an issue. Nursing and medicine must work together to resolve that issue. It is considered, however, that the potential of nurse practitioner has barely been tapped.

There has been a great increase in the number of doctorates earned by nurses over the past twenty years. In 1958 only six nurses earned Ed.D. degrees and five earned Ph.D. degrees, paralleling the establishment of predoctoral fellowships and nursing science programs by the U.S. Public Health Service. Initially the increase was largely in the number of Ed.D. degrees earned, but by 1961 an increase in the number of Ph.D. degrees earned was evident. The general trend has been toward an increase in the number of Ph.D.'s earned as compared with Ed.D.'s. Such data can be

---

*Report of Dr. Henry K. Silver and Dr. Patricia Rooney McAtee at the NLN Council of Baccalaureate and Higher Degree Programs, March 18, 1976, Houston, Texas.

obtained from the *Directory of Nurses With Earned Doctorates,* published by the American Nurses' Foundation. The first edition of this document was published by the American Nurses' Foundation in 1969 and listed 504 qualifying individuals. A 1970 supplement included 83 additional names. By 1972 a total of 786 nurses held earned doctorates (Vian). The number continues to increase. The proportion of men who hold earned doctorates compared to the total number of men in the field of nursing is larger than the proportion of women who hold earned doctorates compared to the total number of women in the field.

A 1973 survey of nurses with doctoral degrees (Nurs. Res. 24:340-351, 1975) indicated that about half of all nurses with doctorates reported their major field of study to be education. The study showed that the majority of these nurses considered themselves still in the field of nursing even though their doctoral study frequently took them into other fields. Their work responsibilities were reported as being largely administrative. This study, conducted by the American Nurses' Foundation, raised some questions as to how nurses who are qualified to conduct research will continue to pursue research related to nursing when their responsibilities develop into being largely administrative. A further question is how research efforts of nurses with doctorates will affect the future quality of health care.

There are currently 1,300 R.N.'s in the United States who hold earned doctorates.* Twelve universities currently offer doctoral degrees in nursing:

New England	1
Mid-Atlantic states	4
Midwest	3
South	2
West	2

---

*Material presented by Helen Nahm at the NLN Council of Baccalaureate and Higher Degree Program, March 17, 1976, Houston, Texas.

Seven universities offer nurse scientist programs:

New England	1
Mid-Atlantic	2
Midwest States	2
West	2

The first year in which the first nurse earned a doctoral degree was 1927. At the present time 0.1% of all R.N.'s now hold doctoral degrees. Of these, 85% earned the doctoral degree since 1960. Of these, 80% are now working in academic institutions, as full or associate professors. Others are in governmental agencies and/or hold positions in clinical research and other areas that affect health care.

The question remains whether the nurse with an earned doctorate must be able to teach expertly, practice expertly, as well as conduct research. The need for more nurses conducting research has been a cry that cannot be dismissed, but the question remains whether one individual is realistically able to be an expert in all areas. Perhaps the problem is that nurses have not been able to become comfortable with being expert in one area and are expecting too much of themselves and each other. The fact is still very evident that female faculty in academic settings with degrees and experience equivalent to those of men, hold lower rank than do their male faculty counterparts. There still remains a discrepancy in salaries at all ranks and in all kinds of academic settings, public and private; this situation is improving slowly.

The Western Interstate Commission for Higher Education was established in 1951 to expand opportunities in higher education in thirteen western states. It currently is implementing forty-three programs in the areas of higher education, health, mental health, corrections, and management information systems in postsecondary education. The Western Interstate Council on Higher Education for Nursing (WICHEN) is made up of nurse leaders from the thirteen constituent member states. WICHEN recommends policies relating to education and research in nursing and provides for the exchange of ideas and experiences through workshops, conferences, and continuing education offerings.

In March, 1975, the Western Interstate Commission for Higher Education initiated a nationwide project to identify and develop new ways of analyzing nursing manpower needs and to promote use of this information in the determination of policy at state, regional, and national levels.

The title of the project is Analysis and Planning For Improved Distribution Of Nursing Personnel and Services. The projected length of the program is eighteen months and it is funded by the Division of Nursing, Bureau of Health Resources Development, Department of Health, Education, and Welfare. Personnel directing the project include Miss Jo Eleanor Elliot, Director of Nursing Programs at WICHEN. The project goals are to develop tools that can be used to analyze nursing skills and manpower distribution, to explore ways of alleviating uneven distribution of nursing services, and to make available nationally those techniques in training and planning for nursing manpower resources requirements.

It may be well that doctoral degrees in nursing are slow in becoming reality. As nurses obtain advanced degrees, they seem naturally to be called on to fill administrative positions and provide leadership for those with less educational preparation. With a nonnursing doctorate, the nurse learns and her behavior is reinforced by the cultural norms and specific behaviors of those in that field: the innate differences between others and the nurse exploring a new field become somewhat neutralized, and the nurse attains a level of rationality, independence, aggression, and outward orientation that later serves her well in future situations.

As a group, nurses sometimes prematurely step out of the handmaiden role to display ostentatiously new-found independence. The new assertiveness may take on an air of superciliousness and improper outward orientation. Actions are often not perceived as caring ones, and independent thinking comes on strong and monolithically. Until the nursing profession has gained further maturity and lost some of its idealism, it may be best that we continue to learn from other communities of professionals what is acceptable, responsible, and the best utilization of latent creativity that exists within us. We must continue to remember our past, but, be aware of our present in order that we may move ahead in our efforts toward true and meaningful professionalization.

Nursing texts and reference

When instruction for nurses became organized and particularly when the first schools modeled on the Nightingale plan were started, books became a necessity. Miss Nightingale's *Notes on Nursing, What It Is and What It Is Not,* appeared and became the textbook not only for nurses at St. Thomas's School for Nursing but also for other schools, both in England and in America, and was translated into foreign languages. Many of the early schools of nursing used medical texts. In this country the first manual for nurses, the *New Haven Manual of Nursing,* was published by the Connecticut Training School in 1879. Other schools, including Bellevue, worked out manuals for nursing. They were what we would now call books in nursing arts. As nursing became organized, as leaders became more sure of nursing needs, and as more leaders appeared, they became articulate in print. One of the early books to obtain wide circulation, believed to be the first nursing text in America, was *Textbook of Nursing* written by a nurse, Clara Weeks Shaw, and published in 1885. It was a standard nursing text for many years. Another early text, written by

Diane Kimber in 1893 particularly for nurses, concerned the fields of anatomy and physiology. Succeeding editions of that book have continued to be published, and it is now known as Kimber and Gray's *Anatomy and Physiology*. Other well-known texts were Lavinia Dock's *Materia Medica,* Mary Reed's *Bacteriology* and Harriet Camp's *Ethics.* Isabel Hampton Robb wrote two texts, *Nursing Ethics* and *Nursing, Its Principles and Practice for Hospital and Private Use.* These were all written at the turn of the century.

Before World War I, books on clinical subjects written particularly for nurses began to appear. These were usually written by doctors, occasionally by a nurse in collaboration with a doctor. Few were written by nurses alone.

Since World War I a more dynamic approach to nursing texts and reference books has taken place. One of the early books giving the new look to texts for nurses was Bertha Harmer's *Principles and Practice of Nursing,* which appeared in 1923. *Facts About Nursing,* a statistical summary, published annually by the ANA, began in 1935 as the *Yearbook on Nursing.* Both NLN and ANA publish bulletins and books from time to time on subjects that are of special interest.

The first issue of the *International Nursing Index* (INI) was published in 1966. It is sponsored jointly by the American Nurses' Association and the National League for Nursing and published by the American Journal of Nursing Company in cooperation with the National Library of Medicine. It is available as a quarterly cumulative in paperback and an annual clothbound volume. The development of the *International Nursing Index* has rendered it possible for nursing to make its literature accessible to others in the field. Since then, in nursing as in all other fields, the amount of literature available is tremendous, with an increasing amount being written by nurses.

CONTEMPORARY NURSING LEADERS

From among so many, it is difficult to single out those nurses who, in fact, made the most significant contribution to nursing in recent years. Special recognition is given here to a few whose contribution has already had and/or will have major implications on the future of nursing and health care throughout the world.

Faye G. Abdellah

Faye G. Abdellah was one of the first two women to receive the commission of admiral in the U.S. Public Health Service and became its chief nurse officer.

Dr. Abdellah graduated as an R.N. in 1942 from Fitkin Memorial Hospital School of Nursing, New Jersey. She received her B.S., M.A., and Ed.D. degrees from Columbia University, New York. In 1967 she received an L.L.D. degree from Case Western Reserve University in Cleveland.

Dr. Abdellah began her career as a nurse researcher for the federal government in New York City. She served on the faculty of Yale University School of Nursing and was a research fellow and member of the faculty at Teachers College, Columbia University, from 1948 to 1949. From 1949 to 1959 she was chief of the Nursing Education Bureau, Division of Nursing Resources, U.S. Public Health Service, Department of Health, Education, and Welfare, Washington, D.C., and was a senior consultant in nursing research from 1959 to 1962. Dr. Abdellah was a consultant for the Western Interstate Commission for Higher Education and a recipient of the Federal Nursing Service award, 1964. She is a fellow of the American Psychological Association and a member of the American Nurses' Association and the National League for Nursing.

Dr. Abdellah is the author of many articles in the field of nursing and is recognized as one of the ablest researchers in the nation. She wrote *Patient-Centered Ap-*

proaches to Nursing, published in 1960, and (with Eugene Levine) *Better Patient Care Through Nursing Research*, published in 1965. She also was director of health education of the Child Education Foundation, New York.

Pearl Parvin Coulter

Formerly dean of the University of Arizona College of Nursing, Tucson, Pearl Coulter received her A.B. degree in 1926 and her M.S. degree in 1927 from the University of Denver. She attended the University of Colorado School of Nursing in 1935 and received a certificate in public health nursing from George Peabody College, Nashville, Tennessee, in 1936.

Ms. Coulter was educational director of public health nursing at the Nashville Health Department from 1939 to 1941. Her teaching experience includes the positions of instructor, assistant professor, and associate professor at Peabody College, associate professor of nursing at the University of Wisconsin School of Nursing, associate professor at the University of Colorado School of Nursing, and later professor at the same school.

A board member and later elected president of the Arizona State Board of Nursing in 1964, Ms. Coulter also served as president of the Colorado State Nurses' Association and was a board member of the American Journal of Nursing Company and the National League for Nursing.

Ms. Coulter received the Public Health Nurse of the Year award from the American Nurses' Association in 1962 and was chairman of the Mary Roberts Scholarship Committee.

She has written many journal articles and is the author of *The Winds of Change, A Progress Report on Regional Cooperation in Collegiate Nursing Education in the West*, published in 1962, and *The Nurse in the Public Health Program*, published in 1954.

Ruth B. Freeman

Ruth Freeman was president of the National League for Nursing from 1955 to 1959. She graduated from the Mount Sinai Hospital School of Nursing, New York, and received her M.A. and Ed.D. degrees from New York University, New York. Dr. Freeman was professor of public health administration, School of Hygiene and Public Health, Johns Hopkins University, Baltimore, from 1950 to 1962. She was a member of the World Health Organization's expert advisory panel on nursing and a member of the White House Conference on Children and Youth from 1959 to 1960. She served as a consultant on nursing for the medical and natural sciences program of the Rockefeller Foundation. Dr. Freeman was national administrator of the American National Red Cross Nursing Services and consultant to the National Security Resources Board.

Among the many awards she received are the National League for Nursing Mary Adelaide Nutting Award, Pearl McIver Public Health Nurse award, and annual nursing award of the Department of Nurse Education, New York University.

Lulu Wolf Hassenplug

Lulu Hassenplug is professor and dean emeritus of the School of Nursing, University of California at Los Angeles.

She is a graduate of the Army School of Nursing, Washington, D.C., and received her bachelor's degree from Teachers College, Columbia University, New York, and her master's degree in public health from Johns Hopkins University, Baltimore.

The *Los Angeles Times* in 1958 named her Los Angeles Woman of the Year in Education. She has received many awards, among which are the National League for Nursing Mary Adelaide Nutting award in 1965 for her constructive devotion and contribution to the development of nursing as a professional discipline within the system of higher education in America. The University of New Mexico and Bucknell University have awarded her honorary doctor of science degrees.

Governor Reagan of California appointed her for a four-year term (1971-1975) to the Advisory Committee on Physician's Assistant Programs of the California Medical Board. As part of the Nursing Advisory Committee of the National Institute of Mental Health, she served as a civilian nursing consultant. Ms. Hassenplug served as a member of the Surgeon General's Consultant Group on Nursing, whose report was the basis for the Nurse Training Act of 1964 granting federal aid to nursing education.

Ms. Hassenplug has held the teaching positions of professor of nursing, Vanderbilt University, Nashville, Tennessee; associate professor, Medical College of Virginia; educational director, Jewish Hospital School of Nursing, Philadelphia, and instructor in nursing, the Piedmont Hospital, Atlanta.

Inez Haynes

Inez Haynes was general director of the National League for Nursing for ten years. She holds the United States Legion of Merit and the Distinguished Service award of the University of Minnesota.

Having begun her army career in 1932 as second lieutenant, she served as operating room nurse in Texas and the Philippine Islands. She advanced to administrative and supervisory positions with the army in the United States, Europe, and the Far East. In 1959 she was chief of the Army Nurse Corps, holding the rank of colonel, which was the highest rank for a nurse to achieve at that time.

Ms. Haynes received her nursing degree at Scott and White Memorial Hospital School of Nursing in Texas and her bachelor's degree from the University of Minnesota.

She was a member of the board of directors of the National Council of Homemaker Services, the Nursing Advisory Committee of the United States Department of Defense,

and the executive committees of the National Health Council and the National Assembly for Social Policy and Development. She was active in the American National Council for Health Education of the Public, Pilots International, the Council of Federal Nursing Services, and Sigma Theta Tau. Ms. Haynes was vice-president of the Citizens Committee for the World Health Organization.

Lucile Petry Leone

Lucile Petry Leone held the position of chief nurse officer and assistant to the Surgeon General of the U.S. Public Health Service in 1949. She was the first woman in the United States to hold the rank of brigadier general.

In 1927 Ms. Leone graduated from the Johns Hopkins School of Nursing. She has held teaching positions at many universities, including the University of Minnesota, Texas Woman's University, the New York Hospital School of Nursing, where she was dean, and Yale University School of Nursing.

Ms. Leone was director of nursing education of the U.S. Public Health Service, administering the Cadet Nurse Corps program, and was a consultant for the U.S. Public Health Service on nursing problems of enrollments at schools of nursing. She was a technical expert on nursing in Geneva in 1948 at the second assembly of the World Health Organization. She was also the chairman of the Joint Committee on Unification of Accreditation Activities.

In 1966 the U.S. Public Health Service established a Lucile Petry Leone award for the contribution she has made to nursing and nursing education through her leadership.

R. Louise McManus

Louise McManus has been active in nursing for more than forty-five years and is recognized as the designer of the first national testing service for the nursing profession, which is considered the second largest educational testing program in the country.

Having graduated from the nursing school at Massachusetts General Hospital, Boston, she earned her B.S., M.A., and Ph.D. degrees at Columbia University, New York.

Dr. McManus advocated experimentation with a two-year academic nursing program in junior and community colleges and arranged for establishment of a national cooperative research project at Teachers College, Columbia University, to assist in developing programs in nursing in community and junior colleges to test the quality of the programs. She also helped to establish the Institute of Research and Service in Nursing Education at Teachers College, which serves as a training center for research workers in nursing, as well as being an agency for research.

From 1949 to 1953 Dr. McManus was honorary consultant to the Bureau of Medicine and Surgery of the United States Navy and served as an adviser to the Surgeon General in the National Advisory Health Council. She also served on the Defense Advisory Committee on Women in the Services and was consultant in nursing at the Walter Reed Army Institute of Research in Washington, D.C., in 1956.

Dr. McManus was chairman of the Nursing Council of the Florence Nightingale International Foundation and served as director of the Department of Nursing Education at Teachers College, Columbia University. Before going to Teachers College, she was director of nurses at Waterbury Hospital School of Nursing, Waterbury, Conn.

She also has written many articles for nursing journals, in addition to being the author of *The Effect of Experience on Nursing Achievement* and coauthor of *The Hospital Head Nurse*.

Mildred L. Montag

Mildred Montag was professor of nursing education at Teachers College, Columbia University, for twenty years from 1952 to 1972. She received her A.B. degree from Hamline University, St. Paul, Minnesota, her B.S. and M.A. degrees from the University of Minnesota, Minneapolis, and her Ed.D. degree from Teachers College, Columbia University, New York.

Dr. Montag held the position of instructor of nursing arts at Lincoln General Hospital School of Nursing, Lincoln, Nebraska, at the University of Minnesota School of Nursing, and at St. Luke's Hospital School of Nursing, New York. She was director of the School of Nursing, Adelphi College, Garden City, New York, staff nurse at the Henry Street Visiting Nurse Service, New York, and assistant director of the Nurse Testing Division, Psychological Corporation, New York. She became a member of the faculty of the Division of Nursing Education, Teachers College, Columbia University, in 1950. From 1952-1957 she was director of the Cooperative Research Project in Junior and Community College Education for Nursing.

Among the many awards she received are the Outstanding Achievement award of the University of Minnesota; Distinguished Alumni award, Hamline University; Linda Richards award, National League for Nursing; Achievement award, School of General Studies, Brooklyn College, New York; and Ella Goldthwaite award, University of Texas, School of Nursing.

Two honorary degrees have been conferred on Dr. Montag—the degree of doctor of laws from the University of Bridgeport, Connecticut, and the degree of doctor of humanities from Adelphi University, Garden City, New York.

Dr. Montag has written many books and articles; they include *Fundamentals in Nursing Care, Education of Nursing Technicians, Community College Education for Nursing,* and *Pharmacology and Therapeutics.*

Helen Nahm

Helen Nahm has retired as dean of the School of Nursing, University of California at San Francisco.

Dr. Nahm received her masters and doctoral degrees from the University of Minnesota and is a graduate of the University of Missouri School of Nursing.

Dr. Nahm was awarded the National League for Nursing Mary Adelaide Nutting award in 1967 for outstanding leadership and achievement in nursing. She was also cited specifically for her efforts in creating a national accrediting service for schools of nursing.

Dr. Nahm has served on the Commission on Nursing Education of the American Nurses' Association. She is also a member of the American Psychological Association. She has received many citations, among which are a Citation of Merit from the University of Missouri and a Distinguished Service award from the University of Minnesota.

Dr. Nahm served on the Board of Directors of the National League for Nursing from 1959 to 1967 and was second vice-president from 1959 to 1963. She was the first director of the National Nursing Accrediting Service, which became a program of NLN on its founding in 1952. For four years Dr. Nahm was director of the Division of Nursing Education of the NLN. She has been a contributor to numerous important publications.

Martha E. Rogers

Martha Rogers is presently professor and head of the Division of Nurse Education, New York University, New York.

Dr. Rogers received her doctoral degree in 1954 from Johns Hopkins University, Baltimore; she was graduated from the Knoxville General Hospital School of Nursing, Knoxville, Tennessee, in 1936, and received her B.S. degree from George Peabody College, Nashville, Tennessee, in 1937, her M.A. degree from Teachers College, Columbia University, New York, in 1945, and her M.P.H. degree from Teachers College, Columbia University, in 1952.

Dr. Rogers is a member of the National League for Nursing's Commission on Historical Source Materials in Nursing and was president of the New York State League for Nursing.

Dr. Rogers has received many awards, among which are an award from New York University in 1965 for her outstanding contribution to nursing and an award for inspiring leadership in intergroup dynamics.

Dr. Rogers has been executive director of the Visiting Nurse Service, Phoenix, Arizona, secretary of the Arizona State League for Nursing, assistant educational director and assistant supervisor of the Visiting Nurse Association, Hartford, Connecticut, and staff nurse and rural public health nurse at Children's Fund of Michigan. She was a research assistant at Johns Hopkins University from 1953 to 1954.

Dr. Rogers is the author of numerous articles and books, including *Educational Revolution in Nursing* and *Reveille in Nursing*.

Jessie M. Scott

Jessie Scott now holds the positions of assistant surgeon general and director of the Division of Nursing, National Institutes of Health, Bethesda, Maryland. She was one of the first two women to receive the commission of admiral in the U.S. Public Health Service.

Ms. Scott received her nursing diploma from Wilkes-Barre General Hospital School of Nursing, Pennsylvania, in 1936, her B.S. in education from the University of Pennsylvania, and her M.A. degree from Teachers College, Columbia University, New York, in 1949. Her years of nursing experience have been in many specialty areas.

Since coming to the Public Health Service in 1955, Ms. Scott has been with the Division of Nursing continuously, acting as consultant to many states and conducting surveys defining their nursing needs. She conducted many workshops to teach hospital staffs how to curtail the loss of professional nurse time.

Ms. Scott was assigned to India to counsel on problems of nursing shortages and education and to promote improved utilization

Jessie M. Scott

of nursing personnel. She helped plan for a national survey of nursing needs and resources. Ms. Scott also was the only nurse on a five-member team from the Public Health Service and the American Hospital Association that made an on-site study of the organization of services for the chronically ill in England and Scotland in 1961. She also was a member of a team that studied health needs and services in Liberia.

Ms. Scott was assistant executive secretary of the Pennsylvania Nurses' Association for six years. She taught at Jefferson Medical College Hospital, Philadelphia, St. Luke's Hospital, New York, and the University of Pennsylvania. She was educational director at Mt. Sinai Hospital, Philadelphia, and has been a visiting lecturer at graduate seminars.

Ms. Scott is a member of the American Nurses' Association, the National League for Nursing, and the American Public Health Association and is active on many U.S. Public Health Service committees, including the Committee on Career Development for Nursing.

Judith G. Whitaker

Judith Whitaker was executive director of the American Nurses' Association for ten years, from 1959 to 1969. She increased the membership of the ANA during her tenure as executive director and more than doubled its staff and operating budget. She extended its activities and functions on behalf of nursing in the public interest.

Ms. Whitaker visited and worked with constituent associations and served on national and international commissions dealing with all aspects of nursing.

She received her nursing degree from Nebraska Methodist Hospital School of Nursing, Omaha, Nebraska, and received her M.A. and B.S. degrees from Columbia University, New York.

11 • Nursing at the international level

All women in international society have had to deal with the problem of male dominance, but nurses have had special problems. Physicians continue to heatedly argue that nursing oversteps its bounds and is going too far in building a profession controlled by women. Being predominantly women, the nursing profession has not been allowed to make progress rapidly because of its position in a professional world that is still dominated by men.

Women achieved the right to vote at the turn of the century, but did not achieve the political status that should have gone hand in hand with the franchise. It was a result of the effort of radical feminists who endured beatings, hunger strikes, and gross embarrassment that women obtained their right to vote but because of the influence of a large majority of conservative women who went about their daily work, very little else was achieved. Women remained relatively powerless even until today and have depended largely on the decisions made by men in the political and economic arena.

It is of interest to realize that professional women were among the conservatives, nurses being no exception, who thwarted their own educational and professional development. As a matter of fact, much to their own detriment, nurses were perhaps among the most conservative of all. Except for the rare individual, they were nonfeminists. Early leaders in nursing identified with movements such as development of hospitals rather than seeking to change the social order which would have led to the liberation of both nursing education and practice. As a result, nursing education was absorbed into the whole of hospital management. The economic value of utilizing women allowed hospitals to grow and prosper at the expense of the nurse. Not politically or economically equal with physicians, they were expected to provide efficient care for the sick although frequently not even consulted when plans for building hospitals were drafted. Not uncommon are commentaries such as the discovery that such essentials as utility room sinks were eliminated from the architectural plan.

The Economic Welfare Committee of the International Council of Nurses (ICN) was established in 1947. Its primary responsibility was to secure information about (1) professional recognition that has been granted to nurses and other aspects of professional and economic welfare and (2) economic conditions of nurses throughout the world in regard to salaries, pensions, and working conditions. The replies of twenty-one countries to a questionnaire were presented at the International Council of Nurses' conference in Brazil in 1952. The questionnaire concerned the problems to which the Economic Welfare Committee had addressed itself. Information from the replies to the questionnaire was presented in a report. This report should be revised, corrected, and brought up to date during the next quadrennial period, and the work of the committee should be continued through the appointment of an economic correspondent in each country.

Because of the great difference in professional status, working conditions, general economic conditions, and many other aspects peculiar to each country, much work remains to be done, but a first step has been taken to study economic conditions under which professional nurses work all over the world.

Professional nurses are finding their places as world citizens not only through the International Council of Nurses but also through such international organizations as the World Health Organization in which they are cooperating with doctors and other health workers to improve the level of health for all people.

The international movement toward emancipation of women stimulated an increasing professionalization of nursing around the world. This in turn became an international development advancing first nursing, then the larger sphere of feminism, and ultimately that of internationalism and good fellowship among peoples of the world.

INTERNATIONAL COUNCIL OF NURSES

Determined to become a nurse, Ethel Gordon Manson (later Mrs. Bedford-Fenwick) negotiated with the matron of Children's Hospital in Nottingham, England, and Manchester Royal Infirmary in Manchester for an experience that required more than a year. She served as a "paying probationer" to learn what she could about the care of the sick. Her motivation and vision during the period of 1878 to 1899 evolved into the founding of the ICN in 1900. It was through her many experiences, reflections, overtime and motivation that a great idea for an international forum for nurses was conceived by this remarkable woman.

The *Nursing Record* was frequently used by Mrs. Bedford-Fenwick to express her views as she became increasingly active in the suffragist movement. One column in 1899 expressed her support for increased education for girls. Later she reported on women's suffrage demonstrations and the speeches that accompanied them. She advised women not to pay taxes as long as they did not have the right to vote on how it would be spent and who should spend it.

History

When Mrs. Bedford-Fenwick was later asked about where she had gotten the idea for the ICN, she reported on her invitation to sit on the Women's Committee of the British Royal Commission and to act as president of the British Royal Section at the World's Fair in Chicago in 1893. In those days matrons of hospitals were usually not known to one another but it was on this occasion that she became acquainted with Miss Isabel Hampton (Mrs. Isabel Hampton Robb). On that occasion, Mrs. Robb invited her to visit the Johns Hopkins Hospital in Baltimore where she was the superintendent of the nurse training school; Miss Lavinia Dock was assistant superintendent. Mrs. Bedford-Fenwick spent several productive days there and she believed that this was indeed the beginning of the International Nursing Movement. Regardless how one interprets the sequence of events, the outcome is fact, for on July 1, 1899, Mrs. Bedford-Fenwick spoke at a meeting of the Matron's Council in London and proposed steps toward organizing an international council of nurses. The group agreed unanimously and began to work on a constitution. Its Preamble later read:

We, nurses of all nations, sincerely believing that the best good of our Profession will be advanced by greater unity of thought, sympathy and purpose, do hereby band ourselves in a confederation of workers to further the efficient care of the sick and to secure the honour and the interest of the Nursing Profession.

The simplicity with which the preamble is written is deceiving in terms of the tremendous vision and foresight which those words reflect. At the meeting of the Matrons Council in London, Mrs. Bedford-Fenwick expressed her belief that nurses must be united and that organization within the profession depends on the individual and collective work of nurses in the provision of care. The best care can only be given if nurses are well prepared to assume those duties for which they are responsible, including the lives of persons entrusted to them. She strongly encouraged reforms in the nursing education system and ultimate control over the nursing profession by nurses. She contended that the work of nursing is a humanitarian effort in all parts of the world and should recruit women everywhere without distinction of social, economic, or cultural factors. Nursing, she maintained, is the same the world over and the need for progress requires the work of all nurses. The central theme for which the ICN stands is self-government of nurses in their professional association.

The aims of the ICN are to increase the educational level of nurses, to increase professional ethics, to more adequately meet societal needs, and to raise the civic spirit of its members. The goal is not only to increase the professional level of nurses but also to help each develop more fully as a human being and citizen; this in turn is expected to enable the nurse to apply more knowledge and skill in the increasingly complex situations in which modern society demands her services. Mrs. Bedford-Fenwick had a glimmer of vision that "training of nurses in hospitals was not adequate without some more comprehensive control over curricula by state authority." This leads one to envision a future development of state boards of nursing to endorse nursing education programs, which did indeed happen. She urged that the nursing profession of every country work toward enactment of legislation and regulations relative to the ed-

ucation of nurses and protection of the public. State examinations and public registration were proposed along with the need for applying proper penalties for nonenforcement. Even at this early stage of development, the ICN at the Congress held in Buffalo, New York, in 1901 passed a resolution reporting that nurses had a role to develop in the prevention of illness as well as in the restoration of health.

In striving for improvement of international health standards, the International Council of Nurses does not stand alone. The World Health Organization (WHO), the League of Red Cross Societies, and the International Health Board of the Rockefeller Foundation have similar and supplementary aims. The total enterprise of advancing public health by international cooperation continues to make marvelous progress even when world politics are not conducive.

Through the ICN the nursing profession's link with WHO has been represented at the latter's recent meetings. Many American nurses have gone to different countries under the auspices of WHO. They have helped teach school nursing, midwifery, and dispensary work, and they have taught people of underdeveloped areas to purify water, to improve nutrition, and to grow vegetables and fruits.

Nurses of various nationalities are employed by WHO and are engaged in nursing projects in many countries. The WHO publication, *Guide for National Studies of Nursing Resources,* is used by WHO advisers. The assistance that WHO gives in countries varies a great deal. Sometimes it helps to establish good basic schools, or it assists in curriculum planning or the development of regional seminars and workshops. Sometimes nurses study and observe in fields of nursing education, clinical supervision, administration, public health nursing, and midwifery. WHO has been helpful in translating nursing texts and other literature into Spanish, particularly for use in Latin America. WHO is interested in building up professional nursing in different countries capable of participating in health and nursing activities and in providing leadership in those countries. The standards of the profession set up by the ICN are promoted in these activities.

To understand the development of professional nursing at the international level, one needs to understand some history relative to the development of nursing in those nations which were prominent in the establishment of the ICN. Much has been discussed about the development of nursing in the United States so that comments here will be limited to other member nations.

One nation important in the development of nursing at the international level was Great Britain. Three strong national elements in Great Britain—English, Scotch, and Irish—did not always lend themselves to a perfect blend. Certain national characteristics of each led to a question whether each should have a separate council or be combined into one. The largest group of nurses in Great Britain at that time was Queen Victoria's Jubilee Institute. Ireland had the Irish Nurses Association, but the Scotch were not yet well organized. English nurses were divided politically into two parties, the Reactionaries and the Progressives, neither having much to do with the other. To solve the problem, a Provisional Committee was established that represented seven separate societies and was charged with the task of serving as an intermediary between Great Britain and the ICN until unity in numbers became sufficient to consider establishing a national council.

The German Nurses' Association had been formed by nurses called Free Sisters. Like their English and American counterparts, these nurses led a secular life following their training period. This group acknowledged the good work done by nurses under the auspices of religious orders but claimed the right to an individual and professional life without constraints placed on them by religious communities.

The United States, Great Britain, and Germany were the earliest to establish national organizations of any major significance. Their total number was approximately 8,000, which provided a solid base for the beginning the ICN.

FLORENCE NIGHTINGALE INTERNATIONAL FOUNDATION

In reflecting on Mrs. Bedford-Fenwick's call for the improvement of education for the "trained nurse" in 1899, one may see profound and far-reaching activities by the ICN to improve the education of nurses. In 1909 an International Standing Committee on Education was created. The vision and action of these early leaders led to the development of educational standards for nurses and ultimately to the establishment of a very active Education Division in the ICN. While these nurses were working very hard on educational matters, a growing interest was stirring among nurses to honor Florence Nightingale through the establishment of an appropriate international memorial to be used in the area of education. This memorial was first proposed in 1912 at the ICN Congress in Cologne, Germany, but plans came to a halt with the eruption of World War I.

After the war international courses for nurses in administration and public health were offered through the League of Red Cross Societies (LORCS). There was a great demand for these courses, which were offered by Bedford College and the College of Nursing in London. It was known that the League of Red Cross Societies was planning to discontinue offering the courses. This prompted the recommendation that the proposed memorial to Florence Nightingale be utilized for the purpose of offering these courses, since they were educational and international in nature. The idea was presented in 1931, and the issue that had been discussed since 1912 was settled. The memorial was established as an independently endowed international foundation for postbasic nursing education.

The inaugural ceremonies of the Florence Nightingale International Foundation (FNIF) were held in London in July, 1934. It remained a separate body managed by a board of directors comprised of members of ICN and the League of Red Cross Societies. Interest in closer relationships between FNIF and the ICN continued, but it was not until 1949 that the FNIF asked to be incorporated within the ICN. Approval was granted and the new organization became the International Council of Nurses, with which is associated the Florence Nightingale International Foundation. The latter resumed the responsibility of long-range planning of educational programs.

From its inception in 1912, FNIF assumed responsibility for its overall educational activities and finally became the Education Division of ICN in 1957. Although this seems to have been an extremely slow development, both groups assisted the profession significantly through their formulation of educational programs in legislative documents.

Two international conferences on legislation have been held. The first was in Poland in 1970 and the second in Colombia in 1974. Both were supported by funds from FNIF, whose funds have also been utilized in the development of many educational publications that are of international interest and concern. Documents developed by ICN are published in the languages of its member nations. The ICN assumed responsibility for the Displaced Persons (Nurses) Professional Register from the International Labour Organization in 1950 after having worked closely with that organization following World War II. As the International Refugee Organization discontinued its work, the register that contained the names of more than 4,000 displaced nurses and all relevant correspondence was turned over to the ICN. Moreover, the ICN was one of the first nongovernmental organizations to be granted an official relationship with WHO, which was established in 1948. The ICN is recognized on the register as a con-

sultant to the Economic and Social Council of the United Nations and maintains an increasing number of alliances with many organizations as well.

DEVELOPMENT OF THE CODE OF ETHICS

The subject of ethics in the profession was at first limited largely to teaching ethics as a subject. A standing committee, The Ethics of Nursing Committee, was established in 1933 (1) to study the method of teaching ethics in schools of nursing, (2) to survey any work undertaken by a national organization relative to ethics, and (3) to collect problems that were viewed as ethical in nature. It was from this point that the International Code of Nursing Ethics evolved. The American Nurses' Association as well as a few other member organizations had already developed such a code when, after a long delay in part due to World War II, an International Code of Nursing Ethics was presented for approval and accepted in 1953 at a meeting of the Grand Council in Sao Paulo, Brazil.

International Code of Nursing Ethics°

Professional nurses minister to the sick, assume responsibility for creating a physical, social and spiritual environment which will be conducive to recovery, and stress the prevention of illness and promotion of health by teaching and example. They render health service to the individual, the family, and the community, and coordinate their services with members of other health professions.

Service to mankind is the primary function of nurses and the reason for the existence of the nursing profession. Need for nursing service is universal. Professional nursing service is therefore unrestricted by considerations of nationality, race, creed, color, politics, or social status.

Inherent in the code is the fundamental concept that the nurse believes in the essential freedoms of mankind and in the preservation of human life. It is important that all nurses be aware of the Red Cross principles and of their

°Adopted by the International Council of Nurses, July, 1953; printed in American Journal of Nursing **53**:1070, Sept., 1953.

right and obligations under the terms of the Geneva Convention of 1949.

The profession recognizes that an international code cannot cover in detail all the activities and relationships of nurses, some of which are conditioned by personal philosophies and beliefs.

1. The fundamental responsibility of the nurse is threefold: to conserve life, to alleviate suffering, and to promote health.
2. The nurse must maintain at all times the highest standards of nursing care and of professional conduct.
3. The nurse must not only be well prepared to practice but must maintain her knowledge and skill at a consistently high level.
4. The religious beliefs of a patient must be respected.
5. Nurses hold in confidence all personal information entrusted to them.
6. A nurse recognizes not only the responsibilities but the limitations of her or his professional functions; recommends or gives medical treatment without medical orders only in emergencies and reports such action to a physician at the earliest possible moment.
7. The nurse is under an obligation to carry out the physician's orders intelligently and loyally and to refuse to participate in unethical procedures.
8. The nurse sustains confidence in the physician and other members of the health team; incompetence or unethical conduct of associates should be exposed, but only to the proper authority.
9. A nurse is entitled to just remuneration and accepts only such compensation as the contract, actual or implied, provides.
10. Nurses do not permit their names to be used in connection with the advertisement of products or with any other forms of self-advertisement.
11. The nurse cooperates with and maintains harmonious relationships with members of other professions and with her or his nursing colleagues.
12. The nurse in private life adheres to standards of personal ethics which reflect credit upon the profession.
13. In personal conduct nurses should not knowingly disregard the accepted patterns of behavior of the community in which they live and work.
14. A nurse should participate and share responsibility with other citizens and other health professions in promoting efforts to meet the health needs of the public—local, state, national, and international.

Several themes are noted in this first code. The major focus remained on nurses rather than on nursing or nursing service. The dependent role and perhaps subservience of the profession is certainly reflected in the document. The nurse was expected to recognize not only responsibilities but also limitations of the professional nurse's functions and strict adherence to the carrying out of the physician's orders intelligently and loyally. The nurse was to give medical treatment without medical orders only in emergencies, reporting such action to the physician at the earliest possible moment.

The code was revised slightly in 1965 at the Grand Council meetings in Frankfurt, Germany. The title was then changed to the Code of Ethics as Applied to Nursing. It was not until 1973 at the meeting of the Council of National Representatives in Mexico City that any drastic change took place which expanded the role of the nurse and eliminated the pervasive element of dependence and loyalty. The statement that best serves to characterize a change in focus is "the nurse's primary responsiblity is to those people who require nursing care." The title of the code was changed to Code for Nurses/Ethical Concepts Applied to Nursing. The profession by now had matured significantly so that statements were positive in nature and emphasized to an amazing degree the independence and responsibility that members of the nursing profession were expected to exhibit.

Code for Nurses—Ethical Concepts Applied to Nursing (adopted 1973)

The fundamental responsibility of the nurse is fourfold: to promote health, to prevent illness, to restore health, and to alleviate suffering.

The need for nursing is universal. Inherent in nursing is respect for life, dignity and rights of man. It is unrestricted by considerations of nationality, race, creed, colour, age, sex, politics or social status.

Nurses render health services to the individual, the family and the community and coordinate their services with those of related groups.

Nurses and people

The nurse's primary responsibility is to those people who require nursing care.

The nurse, in providing care, promotes an environment in which the values, customs and spiritual beliefs of the individual are respected.

The nurse holds in confidence personal information and uses judgment in sharing this information.

Nurses and practice

The nurse carries personal responsibility for nursing practice and for maintaining competence by continual learning.

The nurse maintains the highest standards of nursing care possible within the reality of a specific situation.

The nurse uses judgement in relation to individual competence when accepting and delegating responsibilities.

The nurse when acting in a professional capacity should at all times maintain standards of personal conduct which reflect credit upon the profession.

Nurses and society

The nurse shares with other citizens the responsibility for initiating and supporting action to meet the health and social needs of the public.

Nurses and co-workers

The nurse sustains a cooperative relationship with co-workers in nursing and other fields.

The nurse takes appropriate action to safeguard the individual when his care is endangered by a co-worker or any other person.

Nurses and the profession

The nurse plays the major role in determining and implementing desirable standards of nursing practice and nursing education.

The nurse is active in developing a core of professional knowledge.

The nurse, acting through the professional organization, participates in establishing and maintaining equitable social and economic working conditions in nursing.°

With the implementation of a new constitution in 1965 also came a transfer of headquarters from London to Geneva. Certain internal organizational changes also occurred at that time. The Grand Council was replaced by an elected board of directors. The number of standing committees was reduced from eleven to two, and the functions of the Professional Services Committee were expanded. The ICN promoted an outreach program during the 1960s under the watchword "unity" in an effort to strengthen relationships between the ICN and member associations. Field visits were made by ICN staff to promote the leadership role of the ICN throughout the world.

The Professional Services Committee, which was expanded during the reorganization, must necessarily be given credit for preparing the Statement of the Developing Role of the Nurse and the Code For Nurses. This was an enormous task to undertake in that both documents must necessarily be broad enough to apply to all nursing situations in all countries. It was also necessary to identify nursing as an autonomous profession having its own identity and conscience, being an integral part of and having a collaborative role in the total health care delivery system. During the second term (1969-1973), the committee was chaired by Ingrid Hämelin. First a study of auxiliary nursing personnel was made to obtain data on the number, education, role and status of various levels of auxiliary nursing personnel in the various nations. Second, the committee concerned itself with the qualifications, responsibilities, and rights of these personnel in the international context. Two documents evolved—the *Special International Instrument on the Status of Nursing Personnel* and the *International Standard Classification of Occupations*—which were submitted to the appropriate component of the United Nations.

The present Professional Services Committee, elected in Mexico in 1973, is comprised of seven members drawn from five continents (North America, South America, Europe, Asia, and Africa), and includes specialists in the areas of education, administration, and clinical practice. Its activities, according to ICN regulations, may be very broad and are covered by the

---

°International Nursing Review **21**:104, May/Aug., 1974.

statement "To study problems and to make recommendations in relation to nursing practice: practice and the social and economic welfare of nurses." It is the only remaining standing committee at this time.

Studies relating to the working conditions of nurses were conducted as early as 1927 in collaboration with international organizations dealing with labor issues. There was not always agreement about the amount of collaboration that was professional and appropriate; concern was expressed that nurses should not become suspected of inappropriate political activities. The International Labour Organization and WHO were the two major bodies with which the ICN worked to improve not only the work and life of nursing personel but also the status of nursing relative to the improvement of nursing service. The basic premise was that the socioeconomic status of nurses should reflect the important role of nursing in the provision of health care. These discussions have continued to be a theme throughout the history of the ICN, and records reflect many references to the "proper education of the nurse" and "professional ethics" of nurses.

INTERNATIONAL DEFINITION OF NURSING

The development of an internationally acceptable definition of "nurse" remained somewhat of a problem. The confusion was earlier evidenced by the fact that other terms such as "specialty nursing" and "general nursing"—for example, general nurse or mental nurse—were used at the Congress in Montreal in 1929. The issue was undertaken and brought forth considerable discussion. In the proceedings of the Congress the term "trained nurse" is defined as "a nurse who during her period of training has received instruction and experience in at least four of the main branches of learning, including medical and children's nursing, and who is prepared on graduation to enter the general practice of nursing and to un-

dertake the fundamental duties and responsibilities which are common to nurses in all the main fields of nursing including private nursing, hospital and visiting nursing."

Subsequent years saw rapid growth and changes within the profession due to many changes occurring in the world. In 1973 the definition was broadened to read "a nurse is a person who has completed a programme of basic nursing education and is qualified and authorized in his-her country to provide responsible and and competent professional service for: the promotion of health, the prevention of illness, the care of the sick and rehabilitation. Basic nursing education is a planned educational programme which provides a broad and sound foundation for the effective practice of professional nursing and a basis for post-basic education."

Future activities of the ICN will include a continued refinement of the definition of "nurse" and a discussion of the possibility for international registration of nurses. The ICN is also exploring ways in which student nurses may meet in conjunction with meetings of the international congresses.

INTERNATIONAL WOMEN'S YEAR

International Women's Year (IWY) was honored in 1975. It is of particular interest to the nursing profession, since approximately 98% of all nurses in the United States are women, being the largest single occupational group of women both in the United States and many other countries. The IWY was established by the United Nations General Assembly in 1972. The Commission on the Status of Women, comprised of women members from thirty-two countries, initiated the resolution.

The chief purpose of the IWY was to focus attention on the situation of women and ways of improving it, activating the concern for the equality of rights and opportunities that men and women experience, along with promoting action on behalf of women throughout the world. Rallies in various cities stimulated attacks from men and angry protagonists. In Frankfurt, Germany, at an IWY meeting of some 600 feminists, women were called on to strike and refuse to perform all "wifely services" for a day. In other places in the world the response was less extreme and in some cases even apathetic.

The struggle for women's rights grew out of a movement for freedom for blacks more than a century ago. A second struggle for blacks emerged, a movement for peace in Vietnam was in progress, and women again saw a parallel between their own situation and that of many people for whom they were struggling. Women's Liberation was founded as a political and social movement to redefine the feminine and masculine roles. Many nurses do not think of themselves as "women's libbers" but participate in this movement to alter their traditional life patterns. Because of the distinguished set of feminine traits ascribed to nursing, members of the profession are automatically vulnerable to discriminatory practices that are experienced by all women.

In an effort to appreciate the new freedoms that have formally been made available to women, women's groups and organizations have pressured for new laws such as the Equal Rights Amendment so that those freedoms to which women have been legally entitled can become a reality to them. Women and nurses in the United States were urged in nursing publications to provide leadership during the IWY in an effort to offer hope to women in other parts of the world (Am. Nurs., Nov. 28, 1975).

The ICN passed a resolution during the IWY, which called for "equal pay for equal work." The resolution requested the ICN member associations to urge their own governments to adopt such laws during that year if they had not yet done so. The ICN urged members to direct their efforts ". . . to changing the cultural and social values that would generate a climate in which employment discrimination against individuals, on the basis of their sex, would become unacceptable to all people."[*]

The American Nurses' Association will host the 1981 Quadrennial Congress of the ICN. It is expected that 10,000 nurses from eighty-six nations will meet in Kansas City, Missouri (Am. Nurse, Oct. 17, 1975). Concerns to be discussed include the nurses' role in safeguarding the environment, nurses' role in the care of prisoners of war, human rights in nursing, authority in nursing services, and education.

Internationally, nurses have worked hard to promote congeniality even in spite of major political differences between them. This is emphasized by the fact that the NLN was able to sponsor a Soviet-American Conference on Nursing and Health Care Delivery in August, 1976.

SIGNIFICANT DEVELOPMENTS IN SPECIFIC COUNTRIES OUTSIDE THE UNITED STATES
Canada

On the American continent the development of Canadian nursing closely resembled the development of nursing in the United States. Nursing education in a university setting was recognized as valuable and in 1919 the University of British Columbia, in cooperation with the Vancouver General Hospital, established a department of nursing. This was soon followed by similar developments in other universities. When efforts were directed at improving nursing education in the United States, criticism grew in Canada about nursing practice and training; this criticism was followed by the joint medical nursing committee under the direction of Prof. G. M. Weir of the Department of Education, University of British Columbia. Like similar committees in the United States, the committee recommended higher educational

---

[*]Editorial: The American Nurse (official ANA newspaper) p. 7, Nov. 28, 1975.

standards, higher requirements from the schools, more graduate nurses for the staffing of hospitals, 8-hour shifts, better qualified teachers, and more structured tuition charges rather than the "working for room and board" arrangement previously accepted.

A Proposed Curriculum for Schools of Nursing in Canada was presented in 1936 by a committee that included several doctors and hospital administrators. In 1940 a Supplement to the Proposed Curriculum for Schools of Nursing in Canada was prepared by the National Committee on Education of the Canadian Nurses' Association. It aimed to recruit the more capable and intellectually bright students and emphasized cultural advantages of higher education. It is of interest to note that this development occurred during the depth of an economic depression when one would have expected a less progressive spirit.

To draw a further parallel between the development of nursing in Canada and the United States, the Canadian Association of Superintendents of Training Schools was formed in 1907 with Miss Snively as its president. In 1917 the name of this organization was changed to the Canadian Association of Nursing Education. The Canadian Nurse's Association was created in 1924 and combined the Associated Alumni (which encompassed both Canadian and American nurses) and the Association of Nursing Education. Membership in the Canadian Nurses' Association is limited to those members who belong to provincial associations; both the national and provincial associations are divided into sections: nursing education, private duty, and public health nursing.

The Canadian Nurses' Association (CNA) became a member of the ICN in 1909 and is one of the largest in membership in the council.

The first *Canadian Nurse Journal* was published in 1905 and was incorporated in 1910; like its United States counterpart, it is owned and controlled by the National Nurses' Association.

An interesting development was that in 1958 the *Canadian Nurse* was first published in French. By 1967 the number of subscribers had increased to more than 80,000.

The increased demand for nursing service, which has been an international problem, has been somewhat extenuated in Canada by the relatively recent introduction of government-sponsored provincial health programs. Education in the university setting to prepare professional nurses who are competent to care for individuals and families both in their homes and in hospitals, as well as the recognition of the importance of research and postbaccalaureate study, has directed efforts toward increasing the caliber of graduate programs to produce nursing administrators, teachers, and researchers.

As in the United States, Canada has some similar concerns, as evidenced by the literature. *Canadian Hospital* in December, 1971, included an article entitled "Saskatchewan Presses for National Nursing Home Association." Likewise there is concern for drug treatment (Mackenzie and Bruce).

One of the contributions that Canadian nursing has made to nursing in the United States is that of addressing manpower distribution and concern for rural care, including crisis care. In rural areas in Canada this is often referred to as outpost nursing and may be sponsored by federal or provincial governments, religious organizations, or voluntary agencies such as the Red Cross. Although there is no clear stereotype of the outpost nurse, certain characteristics within individuals motivate them, make them self-sufficient, and sustain their energies in areas where entertainment is limited or nil and the challenges are overwhelming. Outpost stations are generally located in settlements of 200 persons or more and are remote from hospital and medical services for at least a part of the year because of weather or other conditions that cut them off from the general population (Keith).

Canada also has a Canadian Nurses' Foundation, similar in function to the American Nurses' Foundation.

Israel

Nursing in Israel (Golub) has been greatly influenced by the United States, which in turn has been influenced by Great Britain. The American version of nursing was introduced to Israel by Hadassah, the Women's Zionist Movement of America, in 1918. There was only one school of nursing in Israel for about eighteen years. Today Israel has about twenty schools of professional nursing and the curriculums are patterned after the three-year diploma programs in the United States, but with greater emphasis on public health. This is based on the premise that students have much to learn about immigrants with various backgrounds through making home visits. It is also assumed that students become more aware of social problems that have a carry-over from hospitalization of patients into their home and community. Because of the Zionist Movement and the large immigrant population, nurses must work to function in a multicultural setting. Family dynamics is stressed in their course of study, along with public health nursing. The family nurse has a role different from that of the hospital nurse in that it is related to ambulatory care, curative and preventive services for schools and clinics, making referrals to other health professionals as necessary, and care of the sick in the home. In the senior year students care for a chronically ill patient who has been discharged from the hospital. On successful completion of the three-year nursing program, students are awarded the Diploma of State Registered Nurse.

Following the completion of this program, students may continue their education in postbasic educational programs, which prepare them as graduate nurses in public health, midwifery, operating room techniques, and mental health nursing. These specialized programs are six months to one year in length; graduates then may enter those fields and aspire to higher salaries and upward mobility.

Changes are taking place in nursing education in Israel, however, and the nursing schools are changing from the traditional three-year hospital program to the college-based program, which leads to a baccalaureate degree. As the rationale goes in the United States, such university education prepares better nurses and attracts a population of students who wish to build a career that offers greater opportunities.

The Hadassah School of Nursing may be described as an upper division program, with the first two years including such subjects as chemistry, sociology, and biology. The third year is heavily concentrated with clinical work, and the fourth consists mainly of an intership in the specialty area that interests the student.

The problems with the baccalaureate degree in Israel are similar to those which occur in the United States. The questions of whether it is necessary for nurses to be college- or university-prepared or whether they are as well-prepared as hospital graduates are matters of debate.

Upward mobility, that is, obtaining a baccalaureate degree, for the hospital nurse is seen as perhaps more difficult than in the United States. At the Hadassah Hospital in Jerusalem the proportion of registered nurses to practical nurses and nurses' aides is about 60% to 40%. It seems as though there is less competition and ill feeling between the two groups than there is in the United States. As in the United States, practical nurses in Israel often function in positions of greater responsibility than those for which they are prepared.

The philosophy of nursing in Israel, as in the United States, is patient centered and stresses psychological and sociological aspects of patient care as well as the physical aspects. Nurses face essentially the same types of health problems as do those in other countries of the Western world. Cancer, heart disease, mental illness, accidents and crime are commonplace. While health care in the United States remains private, the system of health care in Israel is socialized. Hospitals contain no private rooms, there is no private duty nursing, and rooming-in for maternity care is standard practice. Out-patient care, in conjunction with hospital backup, is a major means of health care delivery. Minor surgery and many complicated treatments are now performed on an outpatient basis.

It is interesting to note that nurse practitioners in Israel have been incorporated into the kibbutz system of life. Also, it has been said that nurses command greater prestige in Israel than they do in other countries, including the United States.

In 1967 a team system (Yodfat) consisting of family doctor and nurse was put into operation in conjunction with the outpatient clinics under Kupat Holin. Kupat Holin is the workers' sick fund, which runs a network of urban and rural clinics. This sick fund provides health care to about 75% of the population. The physicians working in this system are employed on a full-time basis and are responsible for the total gamut of health care for the patients in their jurisdiction. Nurses work on the team as physician's assistants. The teamwork approach was operationalized in 1967 in the development town of Beit Shemesh, Israel.

Patients may request to see the doctor, but otherwise the nurse assumes the responsibility for the services received from the time the patient walks in. Nurses classify patients by diagnosis and refer cases as appropriate. They administer injections—mainly penicillin, iron preparations, sedatives, and gamma globulin—as well as regular vaccinations and immunizations. Nurses write prescriptions, mainly those used in the treatment of chronic illness—digitalis preparations, diuretics, penicillin for pa-

tients who have rheumatic heart disease, and ointments for patients with chronic skin conditions. Following an initial thorough examination by the physician, the nurse measures blood pressure periodically and refers hypertensive persons to the physician as appropriate. Patients with various chronic conditions receive examinations by the physician at regular intervals, although maintained in the interim by the nurse. Nurses are responsible for all dressings. They teach and encourage the patient and/or family to change dressings at home in cases of severe skin lesions and other conditions such as injuries. The nurses carry out venipuncture for diagnostic purposes, give out the results of laboratory tests together with instructions for treatment (which is decided on by the doctor), or schedule the patient for reexamination by the doctor in the light of laboratory test results. Nurses order laboratory tests that they deem to be in keeping with symptoms presented by the patient prior to the patient's examination by the physician.

Coordination with the social worker, with or without the participation of a physician, is part of the nurse's role. Home visits are made to chronically ill patients or to families whose members consistently make frequent, unnecessary calls to the clinic for some health reason. Attempts are made to discover the problems that disturb the family, instruct them about good health measures, and/or make referrals to resources able to help solve the problems. Most of the time spent by nurses is concerned with classification of patients, giving injections, writing prescriptions, and applying dressings. An evaluation of the system shows that from 1966 to 1968 the number of visits per year to the physician decreased markedly, waiting time of the patients decreased considerably, and the patients' satisfaction increased, as did the nurses' satisfaction with their own work. The nurses found a new interest in their jobs, partially due to their feelings that they were making important independent decisions. Physicians (yodfat) also were more satisfied because they were able to devote more time to those patient problems which challenged their professional training. Incidence of disease and the proportion of cases hospitalized decreased significantly. The success of this system makes it a model for a new approach in family medicine and provides a fresh look at the doctor-nurse team concept.

In a nation that has experienced rapid change and mobile populations, there is an extreme challenge for nurses. Nursing in the United States and Israel show many similarities, since both nations are comprised of culturally diverse people bringing with them different ways of living, attitudes, and ideas. Preventing illness requires the teaching of basic principles of good health in the face of these factors.

Australia

Australia is among those nations undergoing rapid sociocultural and technological change. Like the United States and Israel, Australia is a blend of people from many parts of the globe. The early immigrants from the British Isles had a significant influence on subsequent developments. Thus one might expect that early nursing in Australia had a distinctive British flavor. However, as a relatively new nation, it was able to adopt much from the pattern set by the United States.

At present, Australia is recognizing its need for professional expertise and supports a program that pays for transportation to and from an area, requiring that professionals stay for one year of practice in that area to qualify.

Communication is a significant problem because of the distance from point to point.

There is only one east-west train route; also, much education takes place by means of radio. Bush pilots are one means of getting from place to place away from the main routes. In addition, transportation between Australia and other parts of the world, including the United States, is not so common. The Australian people have learned to be quite self-sufficient within their own environment. Consequently much of what is happening is not known to the outside world.

There is a definite categorization along color lines, with the aborigines being somewhat similar to the American Indians in social position. Climate reversal within the country itself due to the vernal equinox also has its influence on the very existence of life.

The nursing profession has moved forward in preparing practitioners for the expanded role. Because much of the country is rural, there is a real need for redistribution of health manpower from the major cities to the vast underpopulated areas. Nursing in Australia is faced with a real challenge to make available to all people a minimum level of nursing care. Midwifery is a natural area for clinical nursing practice. There has been a unique situation relative to preparation of nurses not only for practice in providing physical care, but pyschosocial care as well. This has come about because of the British influence on nursing, which early distinguished mental nursing from other nursing practice.

The profession recognizes the need for communication among its members and is developing its organization and publications, which serve as communication. Efforts are being made to encourage input of new ideas from the United States and elsewhere at meetings, conferences, and exchange programs. This nation offers a challenge to any nurse who wishes to pioneer and is not overwhelmed by so much that is waiting to be done.

SUMMARY

The movement of nursing at the international level has taken place concurrently with the international movement toward an emancipation of women. International nursing has required unity and education along with a demonstration of an ability to serve the needs of humanity. Although a few women such as Mrs. Bedford-Fenwick (Ethel Gordon Manson) and Florence Nightingale have been credited with providing the real impetus for the international movement, it would never have had the power to take root nor the structure to remain and grow had it not been for many other nurses whose maturity, insight, and humanitarian spirit nurtured its development. International nursing is evidenced in general worldwide acceptance and practice within the International Code of Nursing Ethics.

The development of professional nursing in all nations has been influenced by the political, economic, and social climate of the past and present. Although a temporary block toward success, these factors have not been able to prevent sharing knowledge and experiences and the ultimate establishment of closer relationships among nurses everywhere. The rapid movement toward professionalism and the development of the modern nursing role taking place in newer nations such as Israel and Australia serve as stimuli to nurses in all countries and especially in those nations which are underdeveloped, where, relatively speaking, the breakthrough is yet only dimly in view and hardly even a call to action.

12 · Professionalism

Many articles in nursing literature, particularly in *American Journal of Nursing* and *Nursing Outlook,* discuss nursing as a profession. Many people have tried to answer the question, "What makes an occupation a profession?" Sociologists point out that professionalization of an occupation arises to protect both the worker and the public. When great responsibility and trust as well as technical knowledge are involved, practice must be limited. The professions well established for centuries were medicine, law, and the ministry. Only individuals properly qualified by training and by character were allowed to enter these professions. During the twentieth century many other occupations have become professionalized. Nursing is one of these. The selection of candidates to practice nursing is complicated. Professional nursing organizations are constantly alert to standards of education and standards for practice.

It is emphasized by scholars of history and other social sciences that professional organizations have a responsibility to their members and the public to set standards for admission, to control education, to impose a code of ethics, and to safeguard the conditions under which its members practice. The standards set by the profession benefit the public served.

Brown describes the professional nurse as follows:

In the latter half of the twentieth century the professional nurse will be one who recognizes and understands the fundamental health needs of a person, sick or well, and who knows how these needs can best be met. She will possess a body of scientific nursing knowledge which is based on and keeps pace with general scientific advancement and she will be able to apply this knowledge in meeting the nursing needs of a person and a community. . . .

She must be able to exert leadership in at least four different ways:
1. In making her unique contribution to the prevention and remedial aspects of illness
2. In improving those nursing skills already in existence and developing new nursing skills
3. In teaching and supervising other nurses and auxiliary workers.
4. In cooperating with other professions and planning for positive health of community, state, national and international levels. . . .

The professional nurse must be able to evaluate behavior and situations readily and to function intelligently and quickly in response to their variations. She must recognize physical symptoms of illness that are commonly identified with organic changes. She must also recognize the heretofore less considered manifestations of illness such as anxieties, conflict, and frustrations which have a direct influence on organic changes and are now thought to be the result of an incompatible interaction between a person and his environment. . . .

The nurse must be able to direct her actions and her verbal expressions on the basis of a sound understanding of human behavior and human relationship.[*]

The struggle to differentiate the functions and practice of the technical and profes-

---

[*]Brown, Esther Lucile: Nursing for the future, a report prepared for the National Nursing Council, New York, 1948, Russell Sage Foundation, pp. 73-74.

196

sional nurse is reflected in the number of meetings, seminars, and studies devoted to this subject.

Dr. Ruth Matheney, in a historic paper presented at a meeting of the Councils of Associated Degree Program and Baccalaureate and Higher Degree Programs at the National League for Nursing Convention in 1967, lists several functions of the technical nurse. These include the following:

1. Identifying nursing problems; for the technical nurse this includes the common, recurring problems (for example, maintenance of oxygen, nutrition, elimination; prevention of cross infection).
2. Selecting appropriate nursing action; for the technical nurse this includes listening, observing, environmental manipulation, feeding, and other nursing measures.
3. Providing continuous care for the individual's total health needs; for the technical nurse this includes referral to other members of the health team and to other health agencies.
4. Providing care to relieve pain and discomfort and promote security; for the technical nurse this means measures of physical hygiene, maintenance of body alignment, keeping channels of communication open, and avoiding adding to patient stress.
5. Adjusting nursing plans to the patient as an individual; for the technical nurse this includes recognizing and utilizing the significance of the patient as a person and a social being.
6. Helping the patient toward independence; for the technical nurse this means helping the patient to help himself when he is ready.
7. Supporting nursing personnel and family in helping the patient to do for himself that which he can; for the technical nurse this means listening, suggesting, and informal teaching with nursing personnel and patient families and referral to other members of the health team (such as the professional nurse or physician) where indicated.
8. Helping the patient to adjust to his limitations and emotional problems; for the technical nurse this means creating an environment where the patient is free to focus on feelings and reactions, and referrals to appropriate members of the health team where indicated.

Dr. Shirley Chater, director of a funded study entitled A Study of Content Differentiation Between Technical and Professional Nursing Education and Practice, concludes "that technical and professional nursing are different, and that each is dependent upon and complementary to the other. We believe that it is professional nursing particularly that requires further definition and elaboration if the status quo of nursing practice and patient care is to be bettered and not simply maintained. A most critical and immediate need is the clarification and demonstration of professional nursing practice."*

In December, 1965, the American Nurses' Association, through its committee on education, set forth the following position concerning education for the practice of nursing:

The education for all those who are licensed to practice nursing should take place in institutions of higher education.

The minimum preparation for beginning professional nursing practice at the present time should be baccalaureate degree education in nursing.

The minimum preparation for beginning technical nursing practice at the present time should be associate degree education in nursing.

The education for assistants in the health service occupations should be short, intensive, preservice programs in vocational education institutions rather than on-the-job training programs.†

After months of discussion by units across the country, the House of Delegates of the American Nurses' Association unanimously approved the work of the education committee at the San Francisco convention in May, 1966.

In May, 1965, at the biennial convention, the following resolution was adopted by the National League for Nursing membership:

The NLN in convention assembled recognizes and strongly supports the trend toward college-based programs in nursing. The NLN recommends

---

*Chater, Shirley, Wilson, Holly Skodol, and Waters, Verle H.: Differentiation between technical and professional nursing–an annotated bibliography, New York, 1972, National League for Nursing, League Exchange No. 97.
†American Nurses Association first position for nursing education, American Journal of Nursing, Dec., 1965, pp. 107-108.

community planning which will recognize the need for immediate expedition of recruitment efforts which will increase the numbers of applicants to these programs and implement the orderly movement of nursing education into institutions of higher education in such a way that the flow of nurses into the community will not be interrupted.

To forward the continuing professionalization of nursing reflected in this statement, the National League for Nursing shall sponsor a vigorous campaign of interpreting the different kinds of programs for personnel prepared to perform complementary but different functions.

The NLN strongly endorses educational planning for nursing at local, state, regional, and national levels to the end that through an orderly development a desirable balance of nursing personnel with various kinds of preparation become available to meet the nursing needs of the nation and to insure the uninterrupted flow of nurses into the community.

In 1915 Dr. Abraham Flexner read a paper before the National Conference of Charities and Correction in which he set down certain criteria that have ever since formed a basis for judging whether an occupation has attained professional status. According to his interpretation of the professions:

. . . (1) they involve essentially intellectual operations accompanied by large individual responsibility; (2) they are learned in nature, and their members are constantly resorting to the laboratory and seminar for a fresh supply of facts; (3) they are not merely academic and theoretical, however, but are definitely practical in their aims; (4) they possess a technique capable of communication through a highly specialized educational discipline; (5) they are self-organized, with activities, duties, and responsibilities which completely engage their participants and develop group consciousness; and finally (6) they are likely to be more responsive to public interest than are unorganized and isolated individuals, and they tend to become increasingly concerned with the achievement of social ends.*

In most states today licensure is required to practice nursing. Licensing is necessary for the protection of the nurses as well as

the patients, the community, and employment agencies. Until 1944 each state made up its own examinations; as a result they were quite varied. An important educational advance was made when the National League of Nursing Education (one of the organizations that became the National League for Nursing in 1952) developed, through its evaluation and guidance service, examinations that could be used by all the states. These examinations are composed by experts and are distributed to the states, where they are administered in local centers. The papers are returned to headquarters for grading and evaluation. This is known as the State Board Test Pool and is controlled by the Council of State Boards, which is under the jurisdiction of the American Nurses' Association. States are developing strong departments or divisions of licensure. The state boards automatically come within this central control, but some of the lines of authority are not clearly defined.

The rapidly expanding junior college programs have, in many instances, encouraged the state boards and nurse educators to reexamine minimum requirements and the methods in which to achieve the educational goals.

The basic purpose of all nursing education is to prepare qualified graduates to meet the current and future challenge of nursing. Basically a school of nursing must meet the requirements set up by the state board of nursing. Many nursing schools now meet the higher standards required for accreditation by the National League for Nursing. Many nursing programs in colleges are accredited along with the other college curricula by the appropriate regional accrediting board, such as the Middle-States Association of Colleges and Secondary Schools. At the present time students may learn nursing in three general types of schools: diploma, associate degree, and baccalaureate. The first two prepare for technical practice, the last for professional practice.

---

*Is social work a profession? In Proceedings of the National Conference of Charities and Correction, 1915, pp. 578-581.

The subject of accountability, which is inherent in professionalism, has received much recent discussion. Designed to make nurses more aware of their responsibility to health care consumers, it has been the subject of workshops, seminars, and studies. To translate these discussions into action means developing strategies for measuring the effectiveness of nursing care and implies more than "satisfying" the patient or client. To date, however, there is little evidence to demonstrate the therapeutic effect of nursing interventions on the health status of patients-clients.

Improving the health care that patients-clients receive often means that certain long-established rules must be changed. This can be expected to consume a long period of time. The same or related changes are also necessary if nurses are to find increased job satisfaction and remain active in their profession. Barriers to any change are often enormous and may require alteration of an entire institutional environment, especially requiring higher levels of authority to grant more autonomy of action to others working there. In some cases this has been such a discouraging process that professionals have banded together to establish a totally new facility in which they practice. Here, prospective doctor-nurse colleagues jointly develop the services that they will render, often without precedent. To allow for the development of healthy interprofessional relationships in any manner, institutional, professional, and political forces must be supportive.

A second aspect of accountability is another unknown variable—efficiency. It appears that budgets and staff are almost always inadequate in terms of projected goals. To improve accountability, considerable expenditure of funds and staff time has been allocated by health care organizations. Education and training of staff is expensive, both in terms of payroll dollars spent and, perhaps more important, of lost patient care hours.

ORGANIZATIONS AND PUBLICATIONS

In 1939 the question arose of uniting more closely the three oldest nursing organizations: the National League of Nursing Education, the National Organization for Public Health Nursing, and the American Nurses' Association. World War II both helped and hindered this movement. It was not until 1944 that definite plans for these three organizations could be considered. In 1945 the National Association of Colored Graduate Nurses, the American Association of Industrial Nurses, and the Association of Collegiate Schools of Nursing were added to the committee.

The National Nursing Council for War Service, Inc., prepared a comprehensive program for postwar nursing, which appeared in the *American Journal of Nursing*, September, 1945, under the title "A Comprehensive Program for Nationwide Action." Many doubts were revealed about the existing structures of the national nursing organizations, and it was believed that these doubts could be resolved only by a complete study. Consequently the Raymond Rich Associates were empowered to make this study, hereafter referred to as the Structure Study.

At the biennial convention in 1946 the Rich Report was studied and discussed. The study was continued during the greater part of 1946 and the spring and summer of 1947 through the national and state Structure Study committees. In September, 1947, the House of Delegates of the American Nurses' Association held a special meeting to study the Rich Report. At that session the delegates of the American Nurses' Association were given the right to express opinions and to vote on the Structure Committee as other delegates had from the beginning. At this time the average nurse showed more interest in the organization of the profession than ever before. The Rich Report actually gave the nurses and lay persons a new interest in and knowledge about nursing. They asked questions:

- Why is a new organization necessary?
- Why should all types of nursing care be organized under one head? Or should they?
- Can the industrial nurse join the staff nurses and have specialized needs in organization recognized?
- Should black nurses be given additional assistance that will be found in a large organization of all nurses, or will this cause black nurses to become a minority group without voice?

In the 1947 plan, called a tentative plan, there was to be one organization, to be known as the American Nursing Organization, with nurse members grouped into sections of interest and composing the house of delegates and the board of governors.

Every profession that functions within a dynamic society must constantly evaluate its standards, its objectives, and its performance in the light of changing circumstances. In nursing this means planning, establishing immediate and long-range goals for continued development of the profession, and improvement in the quality of health care delivered, and devising means to implement those plans. Planning and implementation require organization and leadership.

In addition, this single association was to have divisions, which were to have non-nurse, agency, and school members as well as nurse members. Only nurse members of the divisions were to be eligible for election as division representatives in the house of delegates and board of governors, but all types of members were to elect the division representatives.

This organization was not considered adequate by the National Organization for Public Health Nursing and the National League of Nursing Education, who had had great support and help from their lay members. They believed that the lay members should have equal consideration in an organization if they were to continue to take an active interest in that organization.

The question of membership in the International Council of Nurses arose. Could an organization with active lay participation still remain a member of the ICN? The ICN rules state that the member organization from any country must be of, and controlled by, nurses. After extensive study there seemed no way to have a single organization with free lay participation and continued membership in the ICN.

The solution was to create two organizations: The American Nurses' Association is the organization through which nurses will fulfill their responsibilities to define their functions, determine qualifications for practice, establish employment standards, conduct studies that will improve individual practice, and promote legislative action that will improve nursing standards and benefit nursing. The National League for Nursing provides the opportunity for nurses and allied professional personnel and the public to work together to provide the amount and kind of nursing service and education needed in this country. Without arguing the merits of one over the other, it is obvious that both the American Nurses' Association and the National League for Nursing have directed major efforts toward clarifying their roles and functions. Their current statements of purpose serve as a demonstration of these efforts.

Revised plans in 1949 provided for the establishment of two organizations. This plan was based on an effort to increase more democratic participation in the work of the organization, both by every registered graduate nurse and by the lay public interested in nursing service. The inclusion of lay members in a professional nurses' organization is a controversial subject. If a nurse believes that active lay participation is necessary to further nursing service, this nurse will believe that it should be provided for in the organization. However, there are nurses who have never worked with cooperative lay members and who fear the idea of the lay person's taking an active voting part in the organization's work.

The Structure Study was an effort of the six national nursing organizations to coordinate their work and to make it more effective in service to nurses as they tried to meet the nation's increasing demand for nursing services. The committee's assigned task was to recommend to the profession the organizational structure most favorable to the best development of nursing.

At the biennial convention in Atlantic City in 1952, nurses voted to have two national organizations: the American Nurses' Association and the National League for Nursing. Since that time, many organizational difficulties have arisen between the two structures. Perhaps the grand ideals embodied in the original concepts were too global, too complex. Perhaps the professional organization felt it had relinquished some of its vital prerogatives to a "lay" group. Thus in 1958 the ANA House of Delegates called for one national organization. This call proved to be unobtainable for a variety of reasons. However, since this action the two organizations have improved relationships noticeably and have issued joint statements clarifying their functions. A similar motion calling for one organization was presented to the ANA Convention in 1972 and was tabled immediately and almost unanimously, thus indirectly supporting and reaffirming the concept of two national nursing organizations. Two of the joint statements follow:

The American Nurses' Association and the National League for Nursing

A joint statement on purposes and functions

The American Nurses' Association and the National League for Nursing are separate organizations with a common objective—to provide the best possible nursing care for the American people.

Each organization has distinct purposes and functions.

Purposes

Through ANA, nurses work for the continuing improvement of professional practice, the economic and general welfare of nurses and the health needs of the American public.

In the NLN, nurses and friends of nursing of all races, creeds and national origins act together to provide the people of their communities with the best possible nursing services and to assure good nursing education.

Functions and services

ANA	NLN
Defines functions and promotes standards of professional nurse practice	Defines standards for organized nursing services and education
Defines qualifications for practitioners of nursing, including those in various nursing specialties.	Stimulates and assists communities, nursing services and educational institutions in achieving these standards through effective distribution, organization, administration and utilization of personnel
Promotes legislation and speaks for nurses regarding legislative action for general health and welfare programs	Promotes continual study and adjustments in nursing services and educational curricula to meet changing needs
Surveys periodically the nurse resources of the nation	Assists with or conducts community nursing surveys
Promotes the economic and general welfare of nurses and works to eliminate discrimination against minority-group nurses in job opportunities	Provides consultation, publications, cost analysis methods and data, and other services to individuals, nursing services, schools and communities
Provides professional counseling service to individual nurses and to employers in regard	

Continued.

The American Nurses' Association and the National League for Nursing—cont'd

Functions and services—cont'd

ANA	NLN
to employment opportunities and available personnel Finances studies on nursing functions Represents and serves as national spokesman for nurses with allied professional and governmental groups and with the public Implements the international exchange of nurses program and assists displaced persons who are nurses Serves as the official representative of American nurses in the International Council of Nurses Works closely with the various State Boards of Nursing in the interpretation of nurse practice acts and the facilitation of interstate licensure by endorsement.	Conducts a national student nurse recruitment program cosponsored by the ANA, the American Hospital Association, the American Medical Association Carries out and promotes studies and research related to organized nursing services and educational programs Represents nursing services and nursing education units with allied professional, governmental and international groups and with the public Accredits educational programs in nursing Offers comprehensive testing and guidance services to institutions with practical, basic or advanced nursing education programs Provides, in cooperation with state licensing authorities, examinations and related services for use in licensing professional and practical nurses

Membership

All ANA members are professional registered nurses, representing every occupational field of nursing. There are two types of members: Active and Associate (retired or inactive nurses).

NLN members are professional and practical nurses, men and women in allied professions, other people interested in good nursing, nursing service agencies—hospitals and public health —and institutions offering educational programs in nursing.

Constituent groups

The ANA is a federation of 53 constituent associations including the [50] states, the District of Columbia, Puerto Rico and the Panama Canal Zone. State Nurses Associations, in turn, usually are composed of constituent District Associations. ANA membership also is divided into district, state and national sections according to occupational specialties within nursing.

As of April, 1954, NLN counted as affiliates 45 state Leagues for Nursing, the District of Columbia, Hawaii, and Puerto Rico. Many state Leagues are organizing constituents known as local Leagues for Nursing. A Council of State Leagues for Nursing, comprised of the president or alternate of each state League, NLN's officers and the ANA's president, coordinates state programs and purposes with those of the National League for Nursing.

Operating plan

Members of state sections elect representatives to the ANA House of Delegates who, in turn, vote for the Board of Directors. ANA section executive committees are elected by section members attending the biennial conventions. Programs and policies of ANA are determined by the House of Delegates. The work of the ANA between conventions is furthered through the activities of standing and special committees and the Board of Directors. A national headquarters with an administrative staff is maintained.

Every NLN member has a voice in the organization's policies and programs. The Board of Directors is elected by direct vote of all members. Four departments represent major fields of interest in nursing service and education. A steering committee, elected by department members, guides the staff in carrying out each department's program. Each department also has a Council of its Member Agencies. Interdivisional councils and committees represent cross-sections of special interest groups.

The American Nurses' Association and the National League for Nursing—cont'd

History

ANA

ANA was organized in 1896 as the Nurses' Associated Alumnae of the United States and Canada. When the Association was incorporated in New York in 1901, it was no longer possible for Canadian nurses to be affiliated. The present name was adopted ten years later. In 1951 the National Association of Colored Graduate Nurses became integrated with ANA. A year later, in the structure reorganization of nursing groups, ANA took over some of the work (definition of functions and qualifications by individual practitioners) formerly carried by the National League of Nursing Education and the National Organization for Public Health Nursing, which were combined into NLN.

NLN

The NLN was formed in 1952 when three national nursing organizations and four national committees combined their programs and resources. National League of Nursing education (founded 1893), National Organization for Public Health Nursing (1912), Association of Collegiate Schools of Nursing (1933), Joint Committee on Practical Nurses and Auxiliary Workers in Nursing Services (1945), Joint Committee on Careers in Nursing (1948), National Committee for the Improvement of Nursing Services (1949), and National Nursing Accrediting Service (1949)

WORKING RELATIONSHIPS BETWEEN
THE AMERICAN NURSES' ASSOCIATION AND
NATIONAL LEAGUE FOR NURSING°

The American Nurses' Association and the National League for Nursing as cooperating organizations in the field of nursing have the need to examine periodically the fundamental premises on which they will work together and serve society. While they are totally different organizations in both responsibilities and structure, they are complementary in purpose and function.

The American Nurses' Association, as the professional organization, is moving to fulfill those functions of standard setting for education, practice and organized services traditionally carried by professional organizations. In the development and modification of such standards, ANA secures consultation and advice from NLN and elsewhere, but retains responsibility for deciding the final content. Normally, standards are in advance of current practice. They are authoritative, based on the expertise of the profession. ANA works through its members and its constituencies, with NLN and with a variety of organizations and governmental bodies to implement these standards.

The National League for Nursing, composed of individuals, educational institutions, and nursing service agencies, is the organization to which the profession and the public look for services to promote and to improve nursing education programs and organized nursing services. These activities of NLN include among others accreditation, consultation, and involvement of educational programs and service agencies in programs of self-improvement. In planning and conducting such services, NLN involves its appropriate membership in the development of criteria for the purpose of evaluation. Such criteria and related guides must reflect the broad standards enunciated by ANA and their goals of the profession. NLN studies the application of criteria and their implications for standards and practice for education and for organized nursing services. These findings are shared with ANA. In these ways the two organizations are complementary, each with distinctive responsibilities and both necessary in meeting society's needs for nursing service.

The needs of the profession and the needs of the public for nursing service are different in 1966 from those of 1952 when a design for function and structure of both organizations was adopted. Change in the demands upon both organizations caused each to examine its own functions and structure, and its relationship with the other. It is essential that ANA and NLN work cooperatively in areas of common concern as each builds its program in full recognition of the role of the other.

°Statement approved by ANA and NLN boards of directors, Jan., 1966.

THE AMERICAN NURSES' ASSOCIATION AND THE
NATIONAL LEAGUE FOR NURSING JOINT STATEMENT
ON COMMUNITY PLANNING FOR NURSING EDUCATION

In recognition of the many changes taking place in the health field and the need for appropriate education for nursing personnel to meet present and future requirements, both in quantity and quality of nursing services, the American Nurses' Association and the National League for Nursing believe that sound community planning for nursing education is essential and should be begun or accelerated promptly.

The overriding concern of both organizations is that the nation receive the best possible nursing care. This will require increasing numbers of nursing personnel with quality preparation to meet the changing health care needs of the community and to fill the needs of institutions and agencies providing nursing services.

Both organizations have recently taken official positions on the future of nursing education. The American Nurses' Association in December 1965 issued a position paper stating that all nursing personnel should be prepared with the general system of education. The statement advocates baccalaureate preparation as the minimum education for professional nursing practice, associate degree preparation as the minimum for technical nursing practice, and vocational school preparation for nursing assistants. The National League for Nursing in May 1965 passed a resolution advocating community planning to implement the orderly transition of nursing education into institutions of higher education in such a way that the flow of nurses into the community will not be interrupted.

As was pointed out in the Report of the Surgeon General's Consultant Group on Nursing, "If new and expanded programs of nursing education are to be established in places where they are needed and in educational settings where they will thrive, it is essential that they be intelligently planned. Such planning . . . must consider needs for cooperation among adjoining geographic areas. . . . Cooperation within and among states in the planning of nursing education programs is desirable both to prevent needless duplication of effort and as a basis for pooling of . . . resources."

Today when major changes are taking place in the type and placement of nursing education programs, it cannot be left to chance that the right number of nurses with the appropriate level of education can and will be produced.

The ANA and NLN both believe that guaranteeing the continuity and character of the nursing supply transcends the nursing profession itself. Educational, health, and welfare authorities, professional and volunteer groups in the health field and community planning bodies must plan and work cooperatively with nursing to insure an adequate nursing supply. Careful planning on the community level should precede any action to transfer or to develop new or different programs. Depending upon the social and demographic complexion of the area, planning may be undertaken for a local community, for several communities together, for a state, or for a region.

Communities are urged to base their decision as to the types of nursing education programs to be retained, revised, or newly developed taking into account:

1. What are the nursing care needs of the community? What kinds of nursing personnel are required to meet these needs?
2. What are the physical resources now available or planned in the community for educating nursing personnel? What junior and senior colleges, universities and clinical laboratory facilities are available for educational excellence?
3. Are qualified faculty available?
4. What financial resources are available which can be utilized for nursing education?
5. How can available resources be channelled into a new design of education for nursing personnel to meet the current and anticipated needs of the community?

Only through such planning and studying of the total situation is it possible to assure that nurses will be prepared in accordance with the needs of society and to assure the most effective use of available resources.

American Nurses' Association

The American Nurses' Association has continued its twofold purpose of providing better nursing service and helping the graduate nurse in every way possible. Through its programs, better personnel policies have been worked out through state and local nursing organizations, and much closer contact is developing between local and national groups.

Since 1950 the ANA has been actively sponsoring a research program. Nurses have supported this program both through voluntary subscription and through dues. The ANA now has a technical committee on studies of nursing functions and a research and statistics unit. The changing role of the professional nurse is continually being studied, and a fact-finding and research ser-

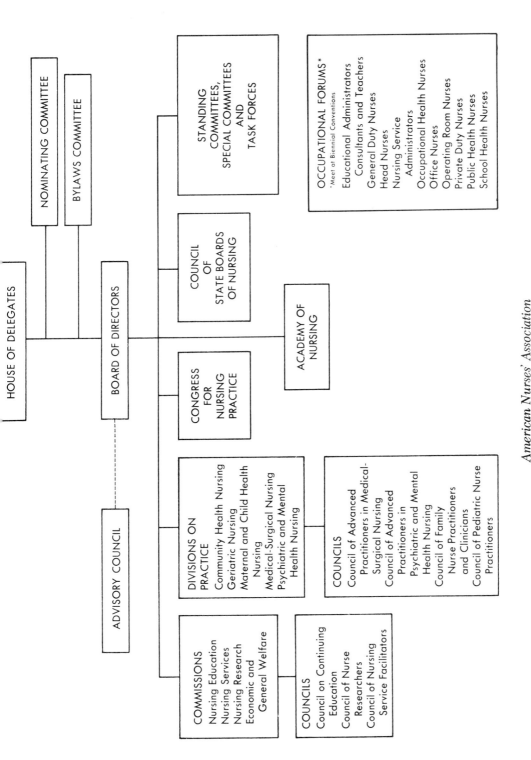

American Nurses' Association

Structural units of the ANA at the national level.

vice is available for ANA members. In addition, *Facts About Nursing* is compiled annually, and inventories of professional nurses, periodically.

The ANA special groups section was organized in 1952. Its main purpose was to bring together nurses whose occupations place them in specialized groups too small to qualify for section status. Some of the interests represented were the executive secretaries of the American Nurses' Association and district nurse associations, recruiters, military nurses, registrars, Red Cross nurses, nurses in public relations, nurse editors, nurse anesthetists, physical therapists, and occupational therapists. The second purpose for this section was to give these groups a place to discuss their problems until the groups became large enough to form new sections. The ANA bylaws provide that a new national section may be established if at least one third of the state nurses' associations have such a section.

During the 1962 convention in Detroit two new conference groups were organized: one on geriatric nursing practice with 67 nurses as members, and one on medical-surgical nursing with 144 nurses as members.

After years of study, discussion, and deliberation by the study committee on the functions of ANA, the house of delegates in San Francisco voted for sweeping organizational changes, and nursing expertise was regrouped into councils on practice and commissions.

The American Nurses' Association now has seven councils to suit the individual needs of nurses within the profession:

- Council of Advanced Practitioners in Medical-Surgical Nursing
- Council of Advanced Practitioners in Psychiatric and Mental Health Nursing
- Council on Continuing Education
- Council of Family Nurse Practitioners and Clinicians
- Council of Nurse Researchers
- Council of Nursing Service Facilitators
- Council of Pediatric Nurse Practitioners

These councils function under the structure of the ANA Division on Practice. Criteria for membership vary with the individual council. A variety of conferences and activities are carried out by each.

Most recently the Council of Advanced Practitioners in Medical-Surgical Nursing has been focusing on criteria for quality nursing practice.

The Council of Advanced Practitioners in Psychiatric and Mental Health Nursing is exploring professional development and plans for certification of the nurse in that specialty area. Many interdisciplinary activities and committees have evolved from this group.

The Council of Family Nurse Practitioners and Clinicians and the Council of Pediatric Nurse Practitioners have sponsored two joint national conferences focusing on primary care nursing. These two councils are considering a merger to form a single council of primary care providers. The Council of Nurse Researchers has been exploring federal funding for research and addressing such concerns as human rights and protection of humans as subjects.

Family nurse practitioners and pediatric nurse practitioners, although they developed roles parallel in time, continued to move within the profession separate from one another. In the fall of 1975 the Council of Family Nurse Practitioners and Clinicians joined with the Council of Pediatric Nurse Practitioners for their national conferences. This is another indication of their mutual sensitivity as it relates to maintaining the integrity and unity of the profession.

The Council of Nursing Service Facilitators, in management effectiveness institutes, has discussed such issues as the identification of nursing service costs distinct from that of other expenses.

The Council on Continuing Education developed standards for continuing education (CE) in nursing and has begun work on the transferability and recording of CE credits and a system for accrediting CE programs. (See further discussion.)

The new commissions are as follows:

- Commission on Economic and General Welfare
- Commission on Nursing Education
- Commission on Nursing Services
- Commission on Nursing Research

To encourage constant improvement for the practitioner, the new structure provides the mechanism for the recognition of excellence by the profession—an Academy of Nursing. ANA has moved forward in certifying primary care practitioners. Currently certification examinations are conducted in the following areas: maternal-gynecological, neonatal nursing, medical-surgical nursing, psychiatric and mental health nursing, community health nursing, geriatric nursing, and pediatric (ambulatory care) nursing.

In 1970 ANA had financial difficulties and made an appeal directly to its membership for extra contributions to maintain the organization until the convention in 1970, when long overdue adjustments for membership were passed by the house of delegates. In the same year the Executive Committee also contemplated moving the national headquarters out of New York City. A Search Committee was established; after it reported, the Executive Committee decided that the headquarters should be moved to Kansas City, Missouri. Kansas City, being geographically central, is more accessible from all parts of the country. This was done September 1, 1972. The Washington office was expanded, but the main part of the organization left the familiar address of 10 Columbus Circle in New York and is now at 2420 Pershing Road, Kansas City, Missouri. The library and the American Journal of Nursing Company also remained in New York City.

American Nurses' Association Professional Counseling and Placement Service, Inc.

The American Nurses' Association Professional Counseling and Placement Service, Inc., is one of the important activities ANA has developed. It is nonprofit and provides counseling and placement service without charge to ANA members. Established in 1945, this service is owned by the American Nurses' Association. Twenty-three state associations now have established counseling and placement services also. More than 120,000 nurses had their professional records on file as of December, 1972.

Counseling assists nurses to evaluate their aptitudes and skills, to learn about the types of positions for which they are best suited, and to make long-range plans. For this purpose the service keeps confidential credentials on file and will forward them to any other professional counseling and placement service office or to an employer at the request of the nurse.

Publications

Before nursing began to develop as a profession, there was little use for publications to express its needs, activities, and progress and to interpret its work to members of its own group, to other professions, and to the community. Florence Nightingale was the first nurse to contribute significantly to professional literature.

Today there are many publications in the nursing world. They can be classified as official and nonofficial organs or publications.

A magazine which is controlled, and this usually implies ownership, by the nursing organization which sponsors it, is known as the "official organ" of that association. It is the voice of the association and of the profession, or those branches of it which the association was organized to promote. Like the association itself, the publication is based upon an ideal of service to nurses and through them to the public which they serve. The primary function of a professional publication is to encourage the members to exceed their own best efforts and thus to increase their professional stature.

Professional nursing publications are not published primarily for financial profit. However, if there are earnings, they are used to extend the work of the professional group which the publication represents.[*]

[*]Editorial: What are professional nursing periodicals? American Journal of Nursing **37**:1369, December, 1937.

American Journal of Nursing. As soon as the early leaders began to meet and discuss the need for national organizations, the need for a representative nursing journal was recognized. In fact, the American Society of Superintendents of Training Schools had considered it, but because they knew their limitations, they thought this project should be delayed until the alumnae association had become a national organization and truly representative of American nurses. One of the first activities of the Associated Alumnae was to appoint a committee to investigate how a journal could be started. The first committee failed, but a second was appointed in 1899. Among its members were both Isabel Hampton Robb and Mary Adelaide Nutting; only the records of their courage can explain why these women set out on such a journalistic adventure without experience or outside financial assistance. The *Journal* was started as a joint stock company, the shares were $100.00 each, to be sold only to nurses—Linda Richards held share No. 1, Mrs. Robb No. 4, and Miss Nutting No. 6. As the *Journal* grew, it used its savings to buy back the stock, and finally in 1912 owned all the stock so that the *Journal* was then truly the property of American nurses, controlled by their association, and its official organ. Its three functions have stood the test of time and are still the same: (1) to be a continuous record of nursing events, (2) to be a means of communication between nurses, and (3) to be a means of "interpreting nursing to the public." It supports legislative efforts to regulate nursing, sponsors the cause of nursing education, and has many other functions of interest to the nursing profession. Sophie Palmer was editor-in-chief of the *Journal* from its first issue in October, 1900, until her death in 1920. Kathrine DeWitt came to assist her in 1906 and remained until her retirement in 1932. She held the position of assistant editor, editor *pro tem*, coeditor, and finally managing editor.

In 1921 Mary Roberts was appointed to succeed Miss Palmer as editor; she retained that position until her resignation in 1949, when she was appointed editor emeritus. Nell Beeby was editor from 1949 until her death in 1957. Thelma M. Schorr is the present editor. As developments in the profession demanded it, the *Journal* increased both in content and in variety of subjects discussed. Assistants were added to the staff as work increased.

During the *Journal's* early days, nurses were very much concerned about registration and the development of adequate nurse practice acts. One article by Lavinia Dock is entitled "What We May Expect of the Law." Accounts of the development of the army and navy nurse corps, nursing in the Veterans Administration, and nursing during war and disaster appear regularly in this publication, in addition to the continuous story of what nurses and their organizations are doing.

The *Journal* makes available to nurses all over the country authentic material on new and approved methods of diagnosis, therapy, and prevention, including nursing care. Circulation has grown with the increasing numbers of nurses. To help its readers, the *Journal* has a field representative on its staff who meets with nursing groups all over the country, interpreting its activities and programs. In addition, an annual index is published during January of each year. Another valuable aid is a cumulative index in six volumes, the first covering the years 1900 to 1920; the second, 1921 to 1930; the third, 1931 to 1940; the fourth, 1941 to 1950; the the fifth, 1951 to 1960; and the sixth, 1961 to 1970.

During the first half century the company published only the *Journal*. With the sudden development of *Nursing Research* in 1952, *Nursing Outlook* in 1953, the Sofia F. Palmer Library in 1953, and *International Nursing Index* in 1966, it became increasingly obvious that to manage the company's affairs there must be a full time executive director. Pearl McIver was the first person appointed to that post in 1957 and was succeeded in 1959 by Lucy D. Germain. Assuming that post in 1964 was Phillip E. Day, who continues to the present.

When the *American Journal of Nursing* celebrated its 75th birthday, it was of interest to note that subjects which were of concern to nurses at the time of its first publication were and are still concerns of modern nurses. Social and health problems, nursing specialties, legal aspects, hospital economics, and educational issues are as much a part of any table of contents today as they were in October of 1900. The *Journal* has served as a unifying force in the profession on many occasions, to mention only a few issues—the attainment of licensure for nurses throughout the nation, employment standards, ethics, women's suffrage, and ending sex discrimination. The ANA did not initially endorse the Equal Rights Amendment because of its potential threat to the protective legislation provided to women by the individual states. However, support was formalized in 1972 and a statement was made by the *Journal* following that year's ANA convention.

American Journal of Nursing Company. The American Journal of Nursing Company is a corporation with its own board of directors elected annually by the board of directors of the American Nurses' Association. It is the publishing corporation for the professional journals.

The American Journal of Nursing Company stock is wholly owned by the ANA, and the board of directors of the ANA serve as sole stockholders for the company.

The American Journal of Nursing Company continued to publish the *Journal* and added a second publication, *Nursing Research*, in 1952 and a third publication, *Nursing Outlook*, in 1953. A fourth publication, *Maternal-Child Nursing*, made its first appearance in January, 1976. This new publication seems a natural development following a significant expansion of the nursing role and primary care provided by nurses in the areas of maternity care and pediatrics.

NURSING RESEARCH. Also published by the American Journal of Nursing Company, *Nursing Research* appears four times a year. Lucille E. Notter is the present editor. First published in June, 1952, this periodical actually began before the NLN was organized as an activity of the Association of Collegiate Schools of Nursing. Early in 1952 the ACSN asked the American Journal of Nursing Company to publish a magazine that would be devoted to research in nursing. Its stated purposes were (1) to inform members of the nursing and allied professions of the results of scientific study in nursing and (2) to stimulate research in nursing. It was designed to serve nurses in all fields and branches of the profession and represents the first concerted effort for the establishment of a publication that had as its primary purpose the reporting of studies. The sponsoring organization was the Association of Collegiate Schools of Nursing; the publisher, the American Journal of Nursing Company. The editorial board consisted of twenty persons representing different branches of nursing and education and coming from different parts of the country.

To finance this project the ACSN gave $900 and the ANA, $500; individual contributions amounted to another $500. When the National League for Nursing was formed in 1952, into which the Association of Collegiate Schools of Nursing merged, it took over this new periodical. The NLN nominates members for the editorial board, and the American Journal of Nursing Company appoints them. Helen H. Bunge was the first chairman of the editorial board. Members of the editorial board are nurses, educators, or research workers in colleges, universities, or agencies interested in nursing research.

NURSING OUTLOOK. When the NLN was formed in 1952, it asked the American Journal of Nursing Company to publish its new official organ, *Nursing Outlook*. Until

1912 articles of interest to public health nurses had been presented in *The American Journal of Nursing*. Since 1909 the Cleveland Visiting Nurse's Association had been editing their own *Visiting Nurse Quarterly*. When the National Organization for Public Health Nursing was formed in 1912, the owners of the *Visiting Nurse Quarterly* gave this publication to the new organization and endowed it liberally so that it would not become an economic liability for the new organization. This periodical was a success; in 1918 the name was changed to the *Public Health Nurse,* and it was known by that title until its last issue in December, 1952. The periodical became the nucleus for *Nursing Outlook,* whose first issue was January, 1953. Hedwig Cohen was the last editor of *Public Health Nurse* and then joined the staff of NLN as associate director of public health nursing and later headed that department. On her retirement in 1969, the Hedwig Cohen Fund was established to index the articles in *Public Health Nurse. Nursing Outlook,* like the *American Journal of Nursing,* is owned and published by the American Journal of Nursing Company. The board of directors determines the overall format of the publication. NLN representatives are on the board of directors. Mildred Hall was the first editor; Mildred Gaynor was the second editor and retired in 1966. The present editor is Edith P. Lewis. The editorial staff is made up of professional nurses.

Since the NLN is interested in the development and improvement of nursing service, as well as nursing education, many articles are devoted to the two broad fields of nursing service and nursing education. As mentioned earlier, the National Organization for Public Health Nursing, the Association of Collegiate Schools of Nursing, and the NLN had non-nurse members as well as agency membership. The official publication of this new organization, *Nursing Outlook,* includes articles about nursing in relation to the community, public health in general, and public health nursing in particular.

INTERNATIONAL NURSING INDEX. The *International Nursing Index* is part of the official family of the American Journal of Nursing Company. It was first published in 1966 in cooperation with the National Library of Medicine. More than 160 nursing journals received from all over the world are indexed by subject and author.

CAPITOL COMMENTARY. Another publication that has been most helpful in keeping nurses abreast of what is happening in Washington is the *Capitol Commentary,* a small bulletin published monthly by the ANA. It summarizes Congressional actions and status of pertinent pieces of legislation that have direct impact on nursing. This publication, read by an increasing number of nurses, inherently encourages communication with nurses' local congressmen. It makes nurses aware of the ANA position on various legislation and likewise encourages them individually and collectively to make the association responsible to its constituency.

N-CAP NEWS. Nurses Coalition for Action in Politics (N-CAP) evolved from a group of nurses in Nyack, New York, who called themselves Nurses for Political Action and began in 1971. The ANA established N-CAP following the objectives set forth by Nurses For Political Action. The two groups have now merged and Nurses for Political Action has disbanded.

By 1975 there were nearly 2,000 ANA members who contributed to N-CAP. The nurses responded to a request for $2 donations with an average donation of $3.30 (Am. Nurse, Nov. 28, 1975). N-CAP is designed to make nurses more knowledgeable about the political process. Its publication, *N-CAP News,* is published monthly and contains much basic information about the workings of government, political parties, and party politics. It also encourages nurses who might otherwise feel that politics is beyond their scope to actively participate (N-CAP News, Nov., 1975).

One nurse who has become involved with N-CAP is Claudia Meier. She is a 27-year-old nurse from a rural community in Minnesota who became interested in politics while in high school, was a member of the Young Democrats Club while in college, and attended her first precinct caucus in 1972. In 1974, Ms. Meier was elected chairperson of the county Democratic Farm Labor (DFL) Party, the first woman in the history of the organization to hold that post. By holding this office, she became a member of the party committee organized to find prospective DFL candidates for public office which proves rather frustrating when in an area that usually votes Republican. Soon she was an endorsed candidate for state representative from her district on the DFL ticket and on the campaign trail. From her experiences she has been able to assist nurses who, like her, are novices in a tough political world (N-CAP News, vol. 2, No. 4).

OTHER PUBLICATIONS. Before concluding this discussion of official nursing publications, it may be interesting to know that other literature is available from the nursing organizations. For example, *The American Journal of Nursing* publishes an annual index as well as a cumulative index at the end of every ten-year period. The ANA and the NLN publish bibliographies from time to time. *Facts about Nursing*, a statistical summary published annually by the ANA, began in 1935 as the *Yearbook on Nursing*. These professional organizations also published bulletins and books from time to time on subjects of interest to nurses. Various bulletins have been published by the different organizations that came together to form the NLN. These publications are revised quite frequently.

Proceedings and statements

In 1946 the ANA adopted its first public position statement. It addressed the need for improvement in hours and living conditions so that nurses might live a more normal personal and professional life. The position brought a forty-hour work week and minimum salaries that were adequate to attract and hold qualified nurses. Greater development of collective bargaining through the professional nurses' associations was encouraged. The following year brought about the passage of the Taft-Hartley Act, which included a provision that professional employees should not be organized in the same bargaining unit with nonprofessionals unless the professional employees agreed. ANA supported this. Recent amendments to the Taft-Hartley Act address an earlier exemption of nonprofit hospitals from coverage under the Act and therefore from the obligation to bargain collectively with their employees. There is still some lack of clarity and protection for one level of employee, the "supervisor," which is not defined; it is this category of employees that is not covered under the present Taft-Hartley Act. The whole question of who is and who is not a supervisor remains a troubling one for the ANA and the National Labor Relations Board.

At the ANA Convention in 1952, Shirley Titus spoke on the economic security program and pointed out that at a time when other workers in the United States had succeeded in significantly reducing their work week, nurses were still working at least a 48-hour week. She pointed out that both organized medicine and hospitals continue to assume an active and positive role in the affairs of nursing in order that nurses and the nursing profession can continue functioning in a way that will serve their own special interests (Titus).

Not only nurses but also women in general have usually complied with systems that have kept them oppressed. This has hampered their efforts to develop their own professional organization and to improve the status of nurses while male-dominated professions have made considerably more rapid progress. Nurses have worked with physicians and administrators on joint committees, thereby expecting that they would be helped to solve nursing problems. By doing this, however, physicians and administrators were sought out for approval, remained in a position of dominance, and nurses failed to be liberated. As the largest group of female professionals, nurses placed themselves in a position that identified them with the overall development of hospitals. By doing so, they were themselves preventing the reforms necessary in the social order which might elevate the status of all women.

The apprenticeship system of educating nurses further subjected them to male authority in the hospital. Early nurse practice acts placed restrictions on the independent actions of nurses rather than making provisions for professional privileges that protected them. Nurses obtained the right to practice nursing only under the supervision of physicians after having been educated in a male dominated setting and were not given recognition as colleagues of physicians with the right to practice independently. This physician-dominated system continues into the present decade with only a few states having enacted laws that recognize nurses as independent practitioners.

With little protest, nurses accepted and lived silently with the legalized paternalism and institutionalized apprenticeship built into the laws and the educational system.

The end result of all of this has been a continuation of the low socioeconomic status of nurses. As is common in other women's occupations, nursing has been associated more with labor and domestic work than it has been with professions holding societal prestige. The economic reward for the work done by the average nurse, and even the best-educated nurses, remains low, although in some places economic security efforts on the part of organized nursing have brought about significant improvement.

The ANA house of delegates at the 1974 biennial convention passed a resolution to reaffirm its strong support of the Equal Rights Amendment and also made a resolution that the ANA encourage nurses to take all possible measures as individuals and as a group to interpret the intent of the Equal Rights Amendment and to move toward its enactment.

Salary scales according to ANA range from $3,500 at the lowest end of the nurse's aid scale up to $50,000 as a dean of some major schools of nursing in the United States (the bulk of salaries are significantly less than the $50,000 figure [Kushner]). Salaries continue to be an issue and are being dealt with at different levels by professional and/or organizational groups. With the wide range of job categories in the field of nursing, there continues to be unclear delineation of the categories. It has often been said that "A nurse is a nurse is a nurse." The nurse who is college-educated often distinguishes herself from others by considering herself "professional" while LPN's and three-year, hospital-trained RN's are labeled "technicians." These college-prepared nurses are resented by nurses with wide and varied knowledge and expertise gained through the school of experience; why should these college-prepared nurses receive high salaries "before they even learn to make a bed"? What is not understood is that "making a bed," though a technical skill, should incorporate knowledge about the patient's condition and comfort, factors that are related to the condition. It should also provide an opportunity for meaningful communication and interaction with the patient and his unique and personal situation that brought him to the point of occupying the bed and impinges on his ability to "get well."

Certification

Credentialing mechanisms serve to provide assurance of quality to the various publics that individuals, programs, or institutions serve. In nursing, accreditation of educational programs began more than fifty years ago. Licensure of individual nurses has been carried out in one or more states for about seventy-five years. Certification of nurses who have specialized in a specific area of clinical practice is a recent development.

On the international scene the ANA worked to bridge the gap for nurse refugees from Vietnam in 1975. An Advisory Committee on Vietnamese Nursing Personnel was formed by the ANA in July, 1975, and was sent in teams to refugee camps in Arkansas and California where Vietnamese nurse refugees arrived. The teams interviewed the refugees to assess their career potential in the United States in established categories of R.N., L.P.N., nurse anesthetists, nurse midwife, or nurses' aide. They also attempted to identify those who were prepared to take the NLN state pool examinations and those who would require additional study in nursing. As soon as the advisory committee determined where a refugee was to be relocated, the state and district nurses' associations were contacted and a link was made with the nearest school of nursing so that the refugee could be provided with assistance to study English, to continue her education, or to take state boards and pursue her career in a new country.

The ANA issued a position paper in 1965 that outlined the direction for systematic change in nursing education and the manner in which nursing personnel would be prepared. The position paper stated, ". . . education for those who work in nursing should take place in institutions of learning within the general system of education" (ANA, 1965).

Since that time many changes that were predicted have taken place and nursing education has been integrated within the general system of education. Professional education has become the responsibility of selected senior colleges and universities, technical education a responsibility of selected junior and community colleges, and vocational education a responsibility of selected secondary and vocational schools. The publication of *Standards for Nursing Education* by the ANA in 1975 serves as evidence that the association assumed the responsibility for shaping the educational foundation of those who practice nursing at various levels. The standards speak of major educational goals that encompass graduate education, basic education, and continuing education. The ANA assumes responsibility for formulating and publishing the standards, disseminating them, promoting their acceptance, monitoring the implementation, and evaluating the effect of implementation on the profession. The standards are to be revised as indicated by the members of the profession.

The publication of the *Standards for Nursing Education* followed the ANA's 1973 statement on *Standards of Nursing Practice.*

American Academy of Nursing

The American Academy of Nursing (AAN) was established in 1973 under the sponsorship of the ANA. Thirty-six charter members were designated by the ANA board of directors. Members are selected from among nurses who are ANA members in good standing, have five years of professional experience exclusive of educational preparation, and show evidence of outstanding contributions to nursing and potential to continue making contributions to nursing. The objectives of the Academy follow:

1. To advance new concepts in nursing and health care.
2. To identify and explore issues in health, in the professions and in society as they affect and are affected by nurses in nursing.
3. To examine the dynamics within nursing, the interrelationships among the segments within nursing, and examine the interaction among nurses as all these affect the development of the nursing profession.
4. To identify and propose resolutions to issues and problems confronting nursing and health, including alternative plans for implementation.*

The American Academy of Nursing is directed by a governing council of ten Fellows. These Fellows review candidates for admissions, make recommendations, approve statements issued in the name of the Acad-

---

*American Academy of Nursing fact sheet, June 23, 1975.

emy, authorize the release of publications, and make recommendations relative to fees charged. The ANA supported the Academy initially. Since then it has become self-supporting. New members are charged an initial membership fee of $100 in addition to a nonrefundable application fee of $10 and annual dues of $50. Fellows pay their own expenses for attending and participating in the annual meetings of the Academy. In 1975 the total number of Fellows was 125. There is a long-range plan for adding some additional Fellows in subsequent years so that by 1980 a maximum of 500 Fellows will be in the Academy.

At the American Academy of Nursing meeting in the fall of 1975, stress was placed on the need for nurses to join with consumers in improving long-term care. It was agreed that consumers, nurses, physicians, and other health care professionals must have shared control of health care, including long-term health care. The reminder was given that many people, including providers of health care, failed to recognize that ultimately decisions about health care must rest with the consumer.

National League for Nursing

In 1951 the National Committee for the Improvement of Nursing Service was enlarged to include forty members, representing education, medicine, and general citizen groups. At this time a *Newsletter* was published to keep the state nursing organizations informed and to help them organize state committees for the improvement of nursing service. Also published was the book *Nursing Schools at the Mid-Century*. When the interim classification of schools of nursing was made, schools were promised that the second study would be done within two years. However, it appeared that a temporary accreditation would be more helpful than would a second classification to schools working toward full accreditation. Funds were granted by the Rockefeller Foundation and Commonwealth Fund and the National

Foundation for Infantile Paralysis to support the program of temporary accreditation for a three-year period. This accrediting program was carried out by the National Nursing Accrediting Service, which had been organized early in 1949 under the auspices of the six national nursing organizations.

A subcommittee on the improvement of nursing service was also functioning during this period. Institutes on nursing service administration for both nursing administrators and hospital administrators were held by the National Committee for the Improvement of Nursing Service and the American Hospital Association.

In 1952 NLN was established and the structure of the six national nursing organizations changed. The work and staff of the National Committee for the Improvement of Nursing Service were absorbed into the Division of Nursing Services of the National League for Nursing.

The NLN maintains close relationships with such allied organizations as the American Association of Junior and Community Colleges, the American Hospital Association, the American Medical Association, the American Public Health Association, the National Association for Practical Nurse Education, and the National Federation of Licensed Practical Nurses. The NLN carries out its work through extensive correspondence, national and regional conferences, workshops and institutes, consultation services, staff visits to local communities, manuals and handbooks, tests and guides, printed bulletins, and leaflets. The NLN is concerned with better utilization of all nursing personnel, professional and nonprofessional; better and more extensive in-service education; and the development of teamwork among all nursing personnel, as well as with medical and nonprofessional nursing groups in the hospital and in the community.

The Assembly of Constituent Leagues for Nursing together with the Council of Home

National League for Nursing

Statement of purpose°

The National League for Nursing (NLN) is a nonprofit voluntary coalition of members that is unique in nursing. Over 15,000 individuals and more than 1,800 nursing education and service agencies provide a pioneering example of the type of social structure now considered essential in all health planning and action.

NLN's primary function is to work with health care agencies, of which nursing services are a basic component, with nursing educational institutions and with communities to improve health care services and nursing education programs needed by society through services in accreditation, consultation, testing, continuing education, research and publications.

Agency members, as well as health team and consumer members, have the opportunity to make their respective voices heard through the channels of the various councils of the League. It is these councils, supported by the work of the League's several divisions and departments, that develop and improve standards for quality nursing education and quality nursing service and guide the organization to its overall goal—meeting the health needs of the people.

Through its four education councils—the Council of Baccalaureate and Higher Degree Programs, the Council of Associate Degree Programs, the Council of Diploma Programs and the Council of Practical Nursing Programs—the National League for Nursing fosters the development and improvement of nursing education in the United States. In governmental affairs and in relationships with other health professional education organizations, NLN serves as the official representative of nursing education programs throughout the country.

The League is officially recognized as the accrediting agency for masters, baccalaureate and associate degree programs by the Council on Postsecondary Accreditation, recently formed, through a merger of the National Commission on Accrediting and the Federation of Regional Accrediting Commissions in Higher Education. NLN is also approved for accreditation of masters, baccalaureate, associate degree, diploma and practical nursing programs by the U.S. Office of Education and is recognized as the accrediting agency for practical nursing programs by the National Federation of Licensed Practical Nurses.

NLN's Council of Hospital and Related Institutional Nursing Services is a forum for nursing service directors, practitioners and administrators of hospitals and long-term care institutions to identify and discuss issues of mutual interest.

Its Council of Home Health Agencies and Community Health Services is the national spokesman for community and home health agencies to Congress, to HEW's Social Security Administration and to other appropriate government agencies. It represents those agencies which provide nursing and therapeutic services in home and community settings.

Through its 44 constituent leagues NLN has a direct channel to local and regional health programs throughout the United States. In collaboration with interested citizens in the community, governmental programs and other organizations, they identify community health problems which relate to nursing and organize community efforts to solve them. League programs involve such activities as coordinating immunization projects, setting up hypertension screenings, offering continuing education programs for health personnel, promoting consumer health education and awarding nursing scholarships and loans.

In order to foster the development and improvement of nursing education and nursing service, NLN also cooperates with individuals, organizations and other groups working toward ultimate objectives which coincide with NLN's goals. NLN maintains membership in a number of national allied health and education organizations and has established interorganization committees with other groups.

The National League for Nursing links the interest of nursing with those of the community through its membership of *individuals*, drawn from all ranks of nursing personnel, the allied professions and the community, and of *agencies* which are educational institutions and providers of nursing and other health care services.

°A statement approved by the board of directors, National League for Nursing, May, 1975.

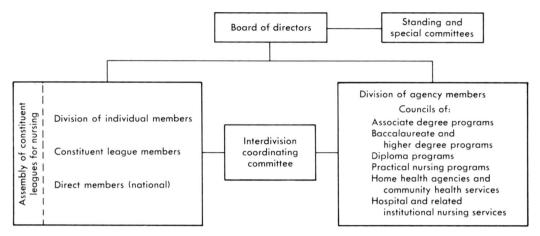

National League for Nursing

Organizational chart.

Health Agencies and Community Health Services help to meet expanding needs for nursing service in the home and community.

The league continues to have both individual and agency members. In 1971 its individual members consisted of professional and practical nurses, nurses' aides, physicians, hospital administrators, educators, social workers, therapists, and interested citizens. Agency members include hospitals and other institutions providing nursing services, public health nursing agencies, and schools and colleges offering educational programs in nursing.

Following several years of study, the NLN meeting in New York City in 1967 voted for an entirely new structure. Thus the local membership gained more flexibility, freedom, and voice.

Today one of the main functions of the NLN is the accrediting services for the various types of educational programs in nursing. They are administered and conducted through four Council units of the organization's national headquarters: the Council of Associate Degree Programs, the Council of Baccalaureate and Higher Degree Programs, the Council of Diploma Programs, and the Council of Practical Nursing Pro-

grams. The Council of Baccalaureate and Higher Degree Programs alone had a membership of 367 agencies and 4,075 individuals in 1976. These members are from institutions of higher learning only.

Marian Isaacs of Boston University was the first nurse who received the Robert Wood Johnson Foundation Award from the Institute of Medicine in 1976. This is a summer study fellowship. Nominations are made to the NLN and are granted to support students interested in studying and working on federal health policy in Washington, D.C.

Accreditation

The purposes of accrediting programs in nursing education have been stated by the NLN as follows:

1. To stimulate continuous improvement of nursing education throughout the United States and thus to promote improvement of nursing services.
2. To offer assistance to educational units in nursing in the continuous process of self-evaluation and self-improvement of their programs.
3. To describe the essential and distinctive characteristics that each type of education program should have in order to make its appropriate contribution to society.

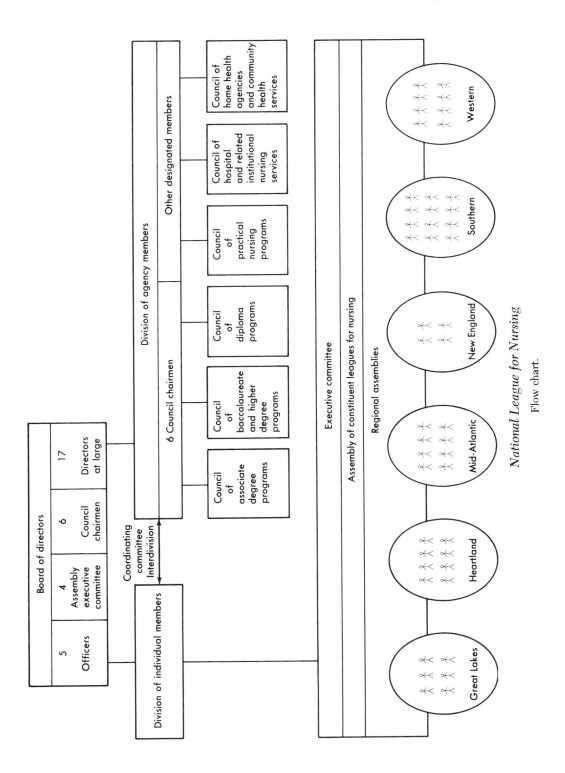

National League for Nursing
Flow chart.

4. To publish periodically lists of programs currently accredited as meeting the accepted criteria for the designated type of program.*

The lists that are published serve as guides for prospective students; in addition, they assist secondary schools, colleges, and universities in advising students in their choice of educational programs in nursing; assist employers of nurses in judging the qualifications of candidates for various types of positions; and aid interinstitutional relationships such as transfer of students and admission to graduate programs.

Accreditation is conducted under the principles adopted in 1956 for the League's total program of accrediting.

1. Accreditation in nursing is conceived as a program in which the educational units themselves play a vital part. In the process, every effort is made to involve as large a number as possible of the administrative and teaching staff of each educational unit in nursing in its own self-evaluation and thus to encourage self-development.
2. Criteria for accreditation must change as the profession itself evolves and as the society which it serves makes changing demands. The continuing development of these criteria is a responsibility of the NLN agency members. The function rests with the appropriate councils. (For associate degree programs, this is the Council of Associate Degree Programs.)
3. The individuality of institutions and their special contributions are of paramount importance. Therefore, provided that there is basic conformity to the standards generally accepted by the profession and by society as essential for the functioning of the graduate of an institution at the level and in the field for which the institution purports to train, emphasis is placed upon the evaluation of the total program and its achievement with regard to particular aspects. Furthermore, the dynamic quality of a program and the rapidity with which it is moving toward clearly defined and desirable goals are recognized. This implies that there will be flexibility in accrediting procedures.*

The NLN is recognized by the National Commission on Accrediting (under the aus-

---

* Policies and procedures of accreditation of the Department of Associate Degree Programs, NLN, New York, 1967.

pices of the Department of Health, Education, and Welfare) as the accrediting agency for baccalaureate and higher degree programs in professional nursing and as an auxiliary accrediting association at the associate degree level.

Material published by the NLN, August 6, 1965 updates data presented on August 6, 1964, to the Senate Subcommittee on Health at the hearing on HR 11083. This report states that a higher proportion of graduates (Table 6) pass state board examinations, are licensed to practice as professional nurses, and enter nursing practice. It is these nurses who graduate, are licensed, and practice that increase the manpower supply in nursing.

Data collected by the NLN in 1964 indicated that the educational preparation of the faculty teaching in accredited programs was better (as evidenced by the highest earned degrees) than that of faculty teaching in nonaccredited programs (Table 7), and a higher proportion of them entered nursing practice (Table 9).

NLN accreditation has become an important consideration of students planning to enter nursing. In 1965 (Table 8) three fourths of all professional nursing students graduated from NLN-accredited programs. Because many associate degree programs were newly established, a large proportion had not yet attained accreditation status.

Recent developments in nursing have made necessary clarification of policies related to accreditation by the NLN. With the proliferation of continuing education requirements and programs offering continuing education, the NLN Council of Baccalaureate and Higher Degree Programs and the Board of Review for Baccalaureate and Higher Degree Programs took action in 1974. It was decided that the 1972 Criteria for the Appraisal of Baccalaureate and Higher Degree Programs will be applied to continuing education programs within the context of existing nursing programs. The same is true with regard to nurse practi-

Table 6. Graduations by type of program and accreditation status, Sept. 1, 1963 to Aug. 31, 1964*

Type of program	No. of graduates from accredited programs	No. of graduates from not-accredited programs
Baccalaureate	4,445	544
Associate degree	114	1,331
Diploma	22,471	3,989
Total	27,030	5,864

*National League for Nursing, Aug. 6, 1965; data presented to the Senate Subcommittee on Health at the hearing on HR 11083.

Table 7. Accredited programs have better prepared faculty*†

Highest earned credential	Total		Accredited		Not accredited	
	No.	%	No.	%	No.	%
Highest earned credential of full-time nurse faculty employed in 195 accredited and not-accredited *baccalaureate and higher degree* programs as of Jan. 1, 1964						
Doctoral	145	4.6	130	4.8	15	4.0
Masters	2,502	80.0	2,242	81.3	260	69.9
Baccalaureate	475	15.2	381	13.8	94	25.3
Associate degree	—	—	—	—	—	—
Diploma	6	0.2	3	0.1	3	0.8
Total	3,128	100.0	2,756	100.0	372	100.0
Highest earned credential of full-time nurse faculty employed in 82 accredited and not-accredited *associate degree* programs as of Jan. 1, 1964						
Doctoral	8	1.6	2	3.5	6	1.4
Masters	336	67.8	47	81.0	289	66.0
Baccalaureate	132	26.6	9	15.5	123	28.1
Associate degree	16	3.2	—	—	16	3.6
Diploma	4	0.8	—	—	4	0.9
Total	496	100.0	58	100.0	438	100.0
Highest earned credential of full-time nurse faculty employed in 801 accredited and not-accredited *diploma programs* as of Jan. 1, 1964						
Doctoral	11	0.1	11	0.2	—	—
Masters	1,924	21.5	1,577	23.0	347	16.6
Baccalaureate	4,629	51.8	3,601	52.6	1,028	49.1
Associate degree	121	1.4	73	1.1	48	2.3
Diploma	2,254	25.2	1,584	23.1	670	32.0
Total	8,939	100.0	6,846	100.0	2,093	100.0

*National League for Nursing, Aug. 6, 1965, to update data presented on Aug. 6, 1964, to the Senate Subcommittee on Health at the hearing on HR 11083, pp. 67-69.
†The educational preparation of the faculty teaching in accredited programs is better (as evidenced by the highest earned degrees) than that of faculty teaching in nonaccredited programs.

Table 8. Graduations by type of program and accreditation status,
Sept. 1, 1963 to Aug. 31, 1964*†

Type of program	No. of graduates from accredited programs	No. of graduates from not-accredited programs
Baccalaureate	4,445	544
Associate degree	114	1,331
Diploma	22,471	3,989
Total	27,030	5,864

*National League of Nursing, Aug. 6, 1965; data presented Aug. 6, 1964 to the Senate Subcommittee on Health at the hearing on HR 11083, pp. 67-69; no additional data collected in 1965.
†Of all graduates, 77% were from NLN-accredited programs.

Table 9. A higher proportion of graduates from accredited programs enter
nursing practice*†

Type of program	Accredited		Not accredited	
	No. of candidates	% of failures	No. of candidates	% of failures
Number of candidates and percent failing state board examinations, 1961-1962				
Baccalaureate	3,127	4	664	7
Associate degree	121	6	772	21
Diploma	17,875	12	5,313	22
Number of candidates and percent failing state board examinations, 1963-1964				
Baccalaureate	3,696	6	744	19
Associate degree	144	10	1,133	25
Diploma	20,118	13	5,950	24

*National League for Nursing, Aug. 6, 1965 to update data present on Aug. 6, 1964 to the Senate Subcommittee on Health at the Hearing on HR 11083, pp. 67-69.
†A higher proportion of the graduates from accredited programs than from not-accredited programs pass state board examinations and are licensed to practice as registered nurses. It is only the graduates who are licensed and practice as registered nurses who swell the ranks of nurses to provide nursing service.

tioner programs. Any such program will be appraised for NLN accreditation purposes according to the same 1972 criteria, under the same policies and procedures, and at the same time that the institution is seeking accreditation for its baccalaureate and/or graduate program.

Nontraditional study in nursing developed in recent years and is the subject of much controversy. Nontraditional programs are defined as those in which learning experiences differ significantly from formal education in an academic area or discipline.

These include the external degree program, the extended degree program, the extended university, the open university, and the university without walls. Such nontraditional degree programs will be appraised for an NLN-accreditation according to the same criteria, policies, and procedures used for formal programs granting degrees in nursing. All programs within an institution will be reviewed and appraised at the same time.

A second major function of the NLN is helping the various constituent leagues with community planning. In 1971 the bylaws were changed once more to eliminate the division of individual members and confine this to constituent league membership for even more flexibility and ability to help.

Constituent leagues

The constituent leagues are grouped into six regional assemblies—New England, Mid-Atlantic, Great Lakes, Heartland, Southern, and Western—for comprehensive sectional planning. Representatives of the forty-four groups meet annually in regional or national assembly meetings to exchange ideas and coordinate planning toward national and local goals.

Constituent league programs are tailored to meet local needs. The leagues alert communities to nursing needs; stimulate service, education, and research programs and put together recommendations for expansion of nursing services in an area; initiate retraining courses to bring retired nurses back to work; administer nursing scholarships; sponsor continuing education workshops; and work for new health facilities or special training programs.

Publications

NLN circulates a catalog of publications each year from which publications that have been developed by the NLN staff can be ordered for a fee. Current examples include the following:

- *The Nurse Practitioner: the Current Situation and Implications for Curriculum Change*
- *Comparison of Students in Practical Nursing Programs*
- *Students in Practical Nursing Programs*
- *Students in Associate Degree Nursing Programs*
- *Directory of Career Mobility Programs in Nursing Education—1975*
- *Practical Nursing Career 1975-1976*
- *Education for Nursing: the Diploma Way—1975-1976*

NLN News is a bimonthly publication, usually consisting of about five pages, which updates the membership on action taken by various committees, legislative activities, and testimonies on current health care and nursing issues. It announces upcoming workshops and includes pictures of people and places making the news.

Testing services

After many years, nursing evolved to the point of demanding accountability. The requirement of licensure to practice nursing was discussed earlier. Licensure has been held in high esteem by the profession, and any threat to licensure is taken very personally by nurses holding the privilege to practice. In recent years the possibility of institutional licensure has stimulated nurses to rally together in support of state boards of nursing and their continued functioning in the role of licensing individual nurses. Nurses *en masse* have marched on their state capitols, either in person or by mail, thereby demonstrating a united front in support of state boards and the individual licensure system. Nurses have not been proponents of transferring licensure from the individual nurse to the employing institution.

Nursing was the first health profession to have a state board examination that is used nationwide to measure basic competence and a right to be licensed. The State Board Test Pool Examination (SBTPE) has helped to establish a minimum acceptable score and to facilitate acceptance or reciprocity of licensure from one state to another.

Although the questions on the SBTPE minimum score are achieved by a candidate writing the exam, the American principle of state's rights allows individual states to set their own standards for licensure. The SBTPE and reciprocity do facilitate interstate mobility, an integral part of the times in which we live. It is particularly important because of (1) the increasing emphasis on redistribution of health manpower under the predicted passage of national health insurance, (2) the growing search for upward career mobility, (3) the need to seek employment where the job market is open and provides opportunity, and (4) necessary relocation of spouses due to economic factors such as recession layoffs and forced early retirement.

The SBTPE was first used in 1944 by a few states. The volume of the testing service became so great that a regular department of National League of Nursing Education was created in 1946. In addition to the state board examinations, a national test for prenursing and guidance was worked out. State Board Pool tests have been used in all the states since 1950 and in the District of Columbia and several provinces in Canada.

R. Louise McManus, chairman and director of the Division of Nursing Education, Teachers College, Columbia University, was responsible for setting up the State Board Test Pool, which became a source for examinations and scoring tests for state boards throughout the country. To a certain extent this was a development of World War II when state boards of nurse examiners were being swamped with the work of testing and scoring state board tests; many graduates were being delayed because they could not obtain results from their examinations quickly enough. After two years Louise McManus had acquired a staff of thirty full-time workers in her testing service. After the war the old system of state boards was not resumed, but the National League for Nursing continued this testing service. It has become the responsibility of the Department of Evaluation Services of the NLN.

Staff workers are continually developing better techniques for testing and are closely associated with nurse educators from different parts of the United States, representing both diploma and degree programs. The Board of Nursing of every state is represented on the ANA Council of State Boards of Nursing, which sponsors the SBTPE program. The plan now worked out is that two nurse teachers in each of the major clinical areas of the basic programs spend one week

at headquarters, deciding the general scope of material and developing test questions to be included in examinations. In addition, the qualifying examinations for the graduate nurse have now also been developed. They are used by many colleges and universities for the purposes of placement and counseling of the RN student.

In 1975 the council moved toward the administration of state board exams on the same days in every state across the United States. The examination is now given only twice a year, utilizing a new examination each time. The use of new exams each time resulted from some shocking instances of cheating and breaks in security related to the administration of the examination and manipulation by candidates of the system to ensure passing.

Credentialing

At its meeting on January 4 and 5, 1976, the NLN declined an invitation from the ANA to cosponsor the study on credentialing in nursing. The NLN board's rationale was stated in the form of three concerns:

1. The design of the proposal for a study of credentialing in nursing was not perceived as one that would fulfill the stated purpose of the study. . . .
2. The role and functions of the study committee were thought to be both specific and ambiguous. The Board questioned how a research study could be carried out under the structure defined. . . . and specifically questioned why the study committee would interpret the data since this implies censorship and control over the research staff.
3. The Board further questions how a study dealing with all aspects of credentialing could be carried out in the stated time period with the proposed staffing and the present study design.*

The ANA and the NLN planned to cosponsor (Am. Nurse, April 15, 1976) the establishment of a new independent, non-

---

*Letter sent from Dorothy Jean Novello, President, National League for Nursing, Feb. 5, 1976, to Miss Rosamond C. Gabrielson, President, American Nurses' Association.

profit organization called the Commission on Graduates of Foreign Schools of Nursing. The organization is receiving some assistance also from the Department of Health, Education, and Welfare. The new program is being established to screen foreign nurse graduates who wish to practice in the United States and to provide reasonable assurance that nurses who wish to immigrate are eligible to take the state license examination in whatever state they plan to practice. All applicants for licensure in the United States are required to take and pass the State Board Test Pool Examination. There has been increasing concern about the high rate of failure among foreign trained nurses, perhaps in large part due to unfamiliarity with the English language and health care as practiced in the United States.

Specialty organizations

The varied settings in which nurses practice has influenced the development of professional organizations and groupings within organizations. This has been followed by a significant proliferation in the number and type of professional publications and journals. For professional organizations with specialized memberships, publications serve as a means of communication.

1. The American Association for Nurse Anesthetists was organized in 1931 under the leadership of Agatha Hodgins. Under this association's sponsorship, minimum standards for competent practice were established, and a program of school accreditation was begun in 1952. By 1960 there were 123 accredited schools for nursing anesthetists in the United States; the organization of this specialty group had a membership of approximately 5,000. Their official bimonthly publication is the *Journal of the American Association of Nurse Anesthetists*.

2. The American Association of Industrial Nurses (AAIN) was established in 1942. It conducts annual meetings and deals with such topics as objectives of occupational health nursing service, current trends in occupational health nursing, nursing participation in management, disease reporting, and various organizational patterns as related to occupational health nursing. Its official journal is *Occupational Health Nursing.*

3. The increasingly important specialty of nurse-midwifery had its genesis with Dr. William Shippen, Jr., son of one of the founders of the University of Pennsylvania and College of New Jersey in Princeton. The younger Dr. Shippen's lectures began with anatomy and subsequently broadened to include content in the field of midwifery as early as 1763. The first public teacher of what is currently known as midwifery, he was much maligned as a man interested in caring for a totally female population and health care situation. From his early efforts has evolved the American College of Nurse Midwifery, organized in 1955 and highly regarded as instigator of certification, legislation, and guidelines for nurse-midwifery in the United States today. Representatives of the college have participated in meeting of the International Confederation of Midwives. Their official publication is the *Bulletin of the American College of Nurse-Midwifery.*

4. The Association of Operating Room Nurses was organized in 1957 and currently has more than 4,000 members. They hold an annual national four-day congress and sponsor two-day institutes all over the country. The official journal, *AORN*, is published bimonthly.

5. The American Association of Critical Care Nurses was established in 1970. Its official bimonthly publication is *Heart & Lung*. The Association of Rehabilitation Nurses is another organization recently created. Its official publication is *ARN Journal.*

6. Special training programs to prepare pediatric nurse practitioners, funded under the Department of Health, Education, and

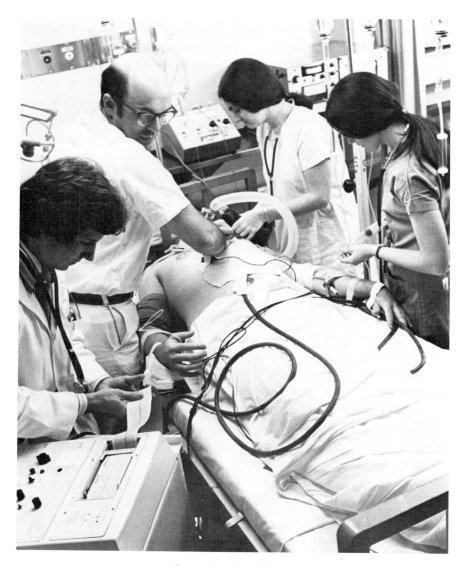

Intensive Care Unit

Intensive Care or Critical Care Units such as this one at Massachusetts General Hospital,
Boston, offer nurses the opportunity to perform at their highest potential. (Courtesy
Massachusetts General Hospital and Provandie Eastwood and Lombardi Inc., Boston.)

Welfare, U.S. Public Health Service, stimulated the organization of the specialized
group of pediatric nurse practitioners. One
outcome was the publication of a periodical
The Nurse Practitioner.

7. The Emergency Department Nurses'

Association (EDNA) concerns itself with
such issues as the roles, responsibilities, and
relationship of EDNA to emergency medical technicians and the system of prehospital
emergency care, in-service training for rural
nurses in emergency care and concepts and

skills, the alcoholic and psychiatric aspects in the emergency room, as well as positive identification of persons who enter the emergency room. The *Journal of Emergency Nursing* is an outgrowth of this group's development.

8. As specialty groups join forces to meet their specific needs, many new publications for nurses appear regularly. Other nursing publications that seek to reach a specialized audience include the following:

- *Nursing Digest*
- *Journal of Psychiatric Nursing and Mental Health Services*
- *Perspectives in Psychiatric Care*
- *Nursing Forum*
- *Nursing Research Report*
- *Nursing Update*
- *RN*
- *Nursing '77*
- *Journal of Nursing Administration*
- *Journal of Continuing Education*
- *Supervisor Nurse*

Added to these are many interdisciplinary journals reporting research conducted by nurses or publishing material that has direct implications for nursing education and service. These publications have a reading audience of nurses as well as members of various other disciplines. Included in this group are the following:

- *Respiratory Care*
- *World Health*
- *Pediatric Clinics of North America*
- *Journal of Applied Pychology*
- *American Journal of Public Health*
- *Child and Family*
- *Briefs*
- *Child Psychiatry and Human Development*
- *Comparative Group Studies*
- *Journal of School Health*

Other national organizations
National Student Nurses' Association

An interest in establishing an organization for students was stimulated by their attendance as guests at national conventions of professional nursing groups. Since 1924, students had attended conventions, exhibits, and luncheons, but it was not until 1948 that students began to have their own scheduled programs and national meetings. By 1950 the old order was changing and students began to seek a role in planning their own destiny. Student nurses met in Atlantic City, New Jersey, in June, 1952. Although 500 students were expected, twice as many arrived! A committee of students from several states and members of the ANA and NLN staffs met in New York City in December, 1952, to plan the student program for the next meeting. At the subsequent meeting in Pennsylvania, a tentative constitution and bylaws for a national organization were drawn up; NSNA was on its way. The first slate of officers was elected in 1953 at the meeting held in conjunction with the NLN convention in Cleveland. Student nurse conventions are now held in conjunction with the alternating biennial conventions of the ANA and NLN, and NSNA plans and conducts its own programs. Most of the time, attendance exceeds 4,000 members.

The National Student Nurses' Association consists of individual members in the 51 constituent associations in 49 states, the District of Columbia, and Puerto Rico. There are, in addition, about 240 district or local associations.

The purpose of the student organization as defined in the bylaws is "to aid in the preparation of student nurses for the assumption of professional responsibilities."

The organization serves as spokesman for students by taking a stand on issues of importance to nursing students. The NSNA is also a voice for students and a source of direction and information. The official publication of the organization, *Imprint,* is now being mailed to over 150,000 nursing students throughout the United States.

Imprint has recently been focusing on such current issues as minority student recruitment, the image of nursing, and PSRO's.

Student nurses take a stand

In the spring of 1975 student nurses gathered at Albany's Capitol to tell New York's Governor
Hugh Carey exactly how they felt about his proposal to stop funding the Department of
Mental Hygiene's twelve diploma programs. The New York State Nurses' Association had
asked the governor to phase out these programs in an orderly fashion and guarantee students
the opportunity to complete their education. The governor subsequently agreed that
students already enrolled would be permitted to finish the program, and those accepted into
the next freshman class would enter the program in September, 1975, but no others would be
admitted. (Reproduced with permission of the Albany Times-Union, Albany, N.Y.)

NSNA has taken official action in recent
years in support of economic security,
changes in nursing education, a broad range
of legislation, the ANA Code for Professional Nurses, and the student's right to educational experience rather than being expected to provide nursing service.

National Black Nurses' Association

The National Black Nurses' Association
grew out of a movement by black nurses
to gain more professional opportunities for
growth than those offered by the existing
ANA. The first organization for black
nurses, the National Association of Colored
Graduate Nurses (NACGN) was founded
by Martha Franklin in 1908. This was almost thirty years after the first black nurse,
Mary Eliza Mahoney, graduated from the
school of nursing at New England Hospital
for Women and Children in Boston. The
purpose of NACGN was to advance standards of education and practice for black
nurses.

Membership in the ANA was through
state associations, and because some state
associations did not allow black membership, the ANA house of delegates in 1948
voted to remove barriers to membership as
rapidly as possible. This encouraged the
dissolution of NACGN in 1958. Some states
held out a long time before removing the
color qualification for membership, the last
one being Georgia in 1961. Black nurses,

however, continued to be frustrated by the lack of integration into ANA that they were experiencing.

In 1970 at the ANA convention 200 black nurses assembled in a caucus to explore their special concerns. Paramount among the needs expressed was that as black nurses they had a special responsibility to blacks.

They organized under the tentative structure of a new Action Oriented Black Nurses' Council. A chairman and steering committee met in late 1971 and early 1972 after having received communications from many black nurses that a number of serious concerns existed. Black nurses were concerned about the lack of black leadership in ANA (in the twenty-one years since NACGN was dissolved, no president or vice-president of ANA had been black.)

At the 1972 ANA convention there were only thirty black voting delegates who were in the position of participating in ANA policy and priority setting. "Tokenism" concern for equality seemed to be persistent. Identity of the contribution made by black nurses seemed lacking. The future looked bleak from the standpoint that the number of black students graduating from RN programs was not in direct proportion to the total number graduating from RN programs.

Taking everything into consideration, it appeared that what was needed was a separate organization that did not duplicate the basic functions of the ANA but would complement them. The steering committee then followed up with initial steps for incorporating a new organization, The National Black Nurses' Association (NBNA). The purposes and objectives set forth for the NBNA follow:

1. Define and determine nursing care for black consumers by acting as their advocates.
2. Act as change agent in restructuring existing institutions and/or helping to establish institutions to suit the needs of black people.
3. Serve as the national nursing body to influence legislation and policies that affect black people and work cooperatively and collabora-

tively with other health workers to this end.
4. Conduct, analyze and publish research to increase the body of knowledge about health care and health needs of blacks.
5. Compile and maintain a national directory of black nurses to assist with the dissemination of information regarding black nurses and nursing on national and local levels by the use of all media.
6. Set standards and guidelines for quality education of black nurses on all levels by providing consultation to nursing faculties and by monitoring for proper utilization and placement of black nurses.
7. Recruit, counsel, and assist black persons interested in nursing to insure a constant procession of blacks into the field.
8. Be the vehicle for unification of black nurses of varied age groups, educational levels, and geographic location to insure continuity of our common heritage.
9. Collaborate with other black groups to compile archives relative to the historical, current, and future activities of black nurses.
10. Provide the impetus and means for black nurses to write and publish individually or collaboratively.*

The NBNA meanwhile received corporate status, and the first institute and conference was held in Cleveland in September, 1973. The program title was Emerging Roles for Black Nurses, Responsibility, Accountability and Militancy. The major outcome was that black nurses became more united in their efforts to serve in an advocacy role on behalf of blacks. Subsequent meetings were held in Miami Beach in October, 1974, and St. Louis in October, 1975. In the future NBNA may change, depending on action taken by ANA to address the issue as viewed by black nurses and by the membership of the NBNA itself.

National Joint Practice Commission

The need for collaboration between physicians and nurses has been expounded on

---

*Smith, Gloria R.: From invisibility to blackness: the story of the National Black Nurses' Association, Copyright April, 1975, American Journal of Nursing Co.; reprinted from Nursing Outlook, vol. 23, No. 4.

extensively. The quality and quantity of health care in this country depends on such collaboration. Mutual respect and cooperation is frequently lacking, however, and has been described as a "doctor-nurse game."

One author has summarized the doctor-nurse game as shown below.

The process of developing new working relationships involves personal and collective change in order that both physicians and nurses will use open and direct communications with one another.

The National Joint Practice Commission (NJPC), supported by grants from the ANA, the AMA, and the W. K. Kellogg Foundation, was established in 1972 to make recommendations that would promote congruency in the roles of nurses and physicians as they relate to health care of the American people. The commission has now had a second national conference on joint practice.

American Association of Colleges of Nursing

The American Association of Colleges of Nursing (AACN) serves as the organized voice of deans of nursing in the United States. Speaking out on legislation relating to higher education for the nursing profession and to health care delivery, this articulate, informed group of deans has had an impact on shaping, modifying, and changing legislative decisions. It has done its work through close communication and liaison with critical governmental, scientific, and professional groups. Its impact on graduate and undergraduate education, nursing research, and legislation can be documented at this time in nursing history.

The American Association of Deans of College and University Schools of Nursing grew out of an *ad hoc* committee of deans of accredited masters programs of the Council of Baccalaureate and Higher De-

---

The nurse-doctor game*

OLD RULES	NEW RULES
Medical care is more important than nursing care.	Good health care requires both good nursing care and good medical care.
The nurse can help the doctor as long as nobody knows about it, including the doctor.	The doctor and nurse are both there to help the patient and have to communicate directly and openly to do so.
The doctor knows more than the nurse.	Good doctors know more medicine than good nurses; good nurses know more nursing than good doctors.
If the doctor tells patients what to do, and they don't do it, it's the patients' fault. The doctor did his best.	If a health care plan is to be carried out, it must be worked out with the patient's needs, beliefs and capabilities in mind.
Doctors are so busy that nurses may have to take over some of the tasks.	Many doctors don't like or know much about health care. Nurses are prepared in this, like it and are usually better at it than doctors.
Good doctors rarely make mistakes and see to it that others don't either.	Everyone makes mistakes, but open communication between doctors and nurses minimizes them.*

*Thomstad, Beatrice, Cunningham, Nicholas, and Kaplan, Barbara H.: Changing the rules of the doctor-nurse game. Copyright July, 1975, American Journal of Nursing Co.; reprinted from Nursing Outlook, vol. 23, No. 7.

gree Programs of the NLN. It held the first meeting in May, 1967.

For some time the focus of the group seemed limited to concerns of deans in university medical centers. However this focus was soon expanded, but restricted to deans of educational units in nursing that offered NLN-accredited programs. It was then known as the American Association of Nursing Colleges. The bylaws of the new organization follow:

BYLAWS OF THE AMERICAN ASSOCIATION OF NURSING COLLEGES

ARTICLE I
THE CORPORATION

Section 1 *Name*
   The name of this association shall be the American Association of Nursing Colleges.
Section 2 *Purpose*
   The purpose of the Association shall be to serve the public through promotion and improvement of higher education for professional nursing.
Section 3 *Membership*
   (a) Membership in the Association shall be of two kinds, institutional and individual.
   (b) Institutional membership is available to programs in nursing leading to a baccalaureate or higher degree and located in institutionally accredited colleges and universities.
   (c) Individual membership is available to the deans or directors of the aforementioned programs.
   (d) Membership is conferred upon the payment of dues.

The organization's principal activity developed as legislative; the organization worked diligently to ensure the passage of Public Law 92-158, which includes capitation grants and other benefits to colleges of nursing and was signed into law November, 1971.

In the spring of 1973 the official name of the organization was changed from the American Association of Nursing Colleges to The American Association of Colleges of Nursing, and a Washington, D.C., office was established.

Practical nurses

Qualified practical nurses are eligible for membership in the NLN as voted at the first NLN convention in 1953. After this convention it was also voted unanimously to authorize the NLN board of directors to provide for a Department of Practical Nurse Education if advisable before the next biennial in 1955. A Council on Practical Nursing was created at the annual convention in 1957.

National Association for Practical Nurse Education and Service (NAPNES). NAPNES was organized in 1941. Membership is offered to both practical and professional nurses as well as to other persons engaged in activities to further the objectives of the association. All practical nurses are eligible for NAPNES membership if they are licensed as practical nurses or by an equivalent title in a state that provides for such licensure, or if they are graduates of an approved school of practical nursing when the state or states within which they practice or reside do not provide for licensing.

During the 1963 NLN convention the Department of Practical Nursing Programs' Council of Member Agencies met and discussed tentative criteria for evaluation of programs preparing nurses. NAPNES now serves as the accrediting audit for vocational nursing education programs. Its official publication is *The Journal of Practical Nursing.*

National Federation of Licensed Practical Nurses. The National Federation of Licensed Practical Nurses (NFLPN) is an organization for licensed practical nurses and practical nursing students. (The equivalent title "licensed vocational nurse" is used in California and Texas.) Members are enrolled in local, state, and national associations. There are 38 NFLPN constituent state associations and more than 600 division or area associations. In those states lacking constituent state associations, practical nurses and practical nursing students join the organization directly as members-at-large. The association was founded in the state of New York in 1949 and remains the only organization in the United States that is exclusively operated by practical nurses to speak and act in their own behalf.

The official publication of the NFLPN is *Nursing Care,* a monthly periodical. The national headquarters is located at 250 West 57th Street, New York, New York. Leadership of the association is provided by an executive board, which assumes responsibility for the federation's corporal and fiscal affairs; a house of delegates, which convenes annually to set policies for the organization and state presidents, who meet at conventions to make recommendations pertaining to constituent state programs and matters of mutual interest.

The purposes of the organization follow:

To provide leadership for the approximately half-million licensed practical/vocational nurses employed in the U.S. nursing field.

To foster high standards of practical nursing education, service and practice so that the best nursing care will be available to every patient.

To encourage every LP/VN to take part regularly in continuing education activities for the benefit of patient and nurse alike.

To secure recognition for an effective utilization of licensed practical/vocational nurses in every type of health facility.

To interpret the role and function of the LP/VN for the public in order to win greater understanding and appreciation of practical nursing's contribution to the nation's health care system.

To represent practical nursing at meetings with nursing and allied health organizations, legislators, government officials, health agencies and institutions, educators and other professional groups which share the common goal of improved health care.

To serve as the central source of information on what is new and changing in practical nursing education, service and practice at the local, state and national levels.°

°Facts about NFLPN, New York, March, 1974, National Federation of Licensed Practical Nurses.

RESEARCH

Research in nursing has been encouraged to identify the unique body of knowledge that is "nursing practice." Doctoral preparation in nursing is seen as one means of completing the research necessary for improvement of clinical nursing practice and nursing interventions. In support of these efforts, the Bureau of Health Manpower's Division of Nursing recently funded a two-year program to explore the nursing care process and how it affects desired outcomes for patients with medical-surgical problems as well as to assess the impact of a broad range of interventions in the light of their outcomes.

American Nurses' Foundation

The American Nurses' Foundation was established by the ANA in 1955 to support research and studies in nursing and to sponsor special projects. The foundation plans, guides, and coordinates nursing research and disseminates research findings. Supported in part by funds from the ANA, the foundation receives contributions from individuals and from other foundations. The American Nurses' Foundation publishes the *Directory of Nurses Holding Earned Doctorates.* It funds grants, usually in relatively small amounts, to support nursing research.

Council of Nurse Researchers

The Council of Nurse Researchers is comprised of nurses who have an earned masters or higher degree and are engaged in the conduct of research, in guiding students and/or registered nurses in research, or are serving as consultants in research. These nurses are invited to join the organization. It held its first meeting in Denver during the summer of 1973. Its purpose is to advance research activities, provide for the exchange of ideas, and recognize excellence in research among nurse researchers.

The Council interacts with and is accountable to the ANA Commission on Nursing Research. Functions include the planning and conducting of regular sessions for exchange of research findings at conventions, institutes, and other meetings of the ANA. It also promotes the development of necessary support systems for research in collaboration with the Commission on Nursing Research by fostering the establishment of priorities for research development, influencing sources for funding of research efforts, facilitating research both within the profession and in collaboration with other disciplines, and developing relationships with other units of the ANA as well as with related professional and community groups. The Council of Nurse Researchers provides recognition for professional achievement and excellence in nursing research.

CHANGING PRACTICE

Speaking at the ANA Council of State Boards of Nursing in May, 1975, Virginia C. Hall (a doctor of jurisprudence) referred to the inconsistency with which nurse practice acts and medical practice acts have developed in many states. She summarized findings of a survey of the legal scope of nursing practice in the medical area under nurse practice acts, which was conducted for the National Practice Commission. Of the fifty-one jurisdictions surveyed, twenty-two had amended the definition of nursing practice within the past five years. (Those states which have not amended the nurse practice act still maintain a version of the "model definition," which was adopted by the ANA several years earlier.) This definition, though vague, is perhaps useful in that until such a definition is judicially interpreted to be more restrictive, nurses practicing in the expanded role are not clearly acting outside the provisions of the law (illegally).

Practice acts and licensure

The vagueness of a definition of nursing tends to perpetuate a traditional concept of nursing care, which is more in keeping with a dependent role.

Many state boards of nursing are revising the definition of professional nursing to mean an interpersonal service of providing nursing assessment of actual and potential health needs of individuals, families or communities; providing the nursing care which is supportive to or restorative of life by such functions as skilled ministration of nursing care, supervision and teaching of nursing personnel; health teaching and counseling, case finding and referral to appropriate health resources. Evaluation of these nursing actions is an essential component of the definition of professional nursing. Professional nursing practice is further being defined to include both independent nursing functions and delegated medical functions. These may be performed in collaboration with other members of the health team or delegated by the nurse to other nursing personnel. There are also independent nursing functions that may be performed autonomously.

States that were first to plan or implement changes in the nurse practice act, including a definition of nursing and continuing education as a mandatory provision for continuing licensure, are California, Florida, Oregon, Washington, New Mexico, South Dakota, Colorado, Pennsylvania, Illinois, and New York.

In the various states (approximately thirty) that have undertaken major revisions of the nurse practice act, the nursing profession is permitted by definition to expand the role for the professional nurse in providing primary care. Primary care is considered a function of nurse practitioners who have completed a program of study leading to competence as a registered nurse. The role is then expanded to encompass taking a health history, assessing health and illness, initiating a person's entry into the health care system, supporting and maintaining persons who are ill or in danger of illness during the process of diagnosis and therapy, managing patients who are acutely or chronically ill, teaching, counseling, and supervision (ANA, July 5, 1973).

In the State of Montana, a ruling of August 28, 1975, states that physician's assistants and other professionals practicing nursing without being licensed as nurses are subject to penalties according to that state's law (Woodahl).

When the traditional definitions are revised, they are replaced either by a totally new definition or an amended definition that permits the performance of additional acts. These additional acts are usually described as acts authorized by rules and regulations of the board of nursing and/or board of medicine, those recognized as proper by nursing as a profession and in keeping with medical opinion, those which require specific education and training, and/or those which are delegated by a physician. The most appropriate amendment may be that which defines as legal those acts which are considered proper by professional nursing and medical opinion. This allows for change as the profession itself changes.

One example of a new nurse practice act is that adopted by New York State. It defines "diagnosing" and "treating" in terms of the "nursing regime" and distinguishes this from the "medical regime." One rather obvious problem with this rewritten definition is that with the expansion of the independent functions that nurses perform there is an increasing overlap with the functions that physicians perform. Yet the law specifies that acts which are newly permitted within the scope of nursing are not medical.

Another example is the new definition as adopted by the State of California. It acknowledges the existence of overlapping functions between physicians and nurses and states the legislative intent of providing "clear legal authority for this development as well as to 'permit additional sharing of functions within organized care systems which provide for collaboration between physicians and registered nurses'." In many states nurses are exempt from the medical practice act, but in several states the nurse practice act contains a statement that prohibits the practice of medicine.

Primary care

With approximately 98% of all nurses being women and about two thirds of them assuming hospital positions, there remain only a small handful to work in other areas such as the military, doctors' offices, business offices, and facilities serving rural and urban areas. Regardless of where they work, nurses are never completely their own boss. Physicians have established themselves as the legal boss; until recent years nursing did not have a legal status of its own. In addition to the physician's superior position, there are other nurse superiors and administrators to whom these nurses must be responsible.

A new breed of nurse—nurse practitioners —are increasing in number. Some are beginning independent practice.

The nurse practitioner has been described as functioning in the expanded role of the nurse and is rapidly developing because of the need for a new system of health care delivery. Another reason for the expansion is the expenditure of federal funds under the Nurse Training Act of 1971. The ANA definition of the term follows:

A nurse practitioner is a licensed professional nurse who provides direct care to individuals, families and other groups in a variety of settings including homes, institutions, offices, industry, schools and other community agencies. The service provided by the nurse practitioner is aimed at the delivery of primary, acute or chronic care which focuses on the achievement, maintenance or restoration of optimal functions in the population. The nurse practitioner engages in independent decision making about the nursing care needs of clients and collaborates with other health professionals, such as physicians, social workers and nutritionists, in making decisions about other health care needs. The nurse practitioner plans and institutes health care programs as a member of the health care team.

The acquisition of knowledge in depth and competence in skill performance in a particular field of practice enables this practitioner to:

1. Assess the physical and psychosocial health-illness status of individuals and families by health and developmental history taking and physical examinations.
2. Evaluate and interpret data in order to plan and execute appropriate nursing intervention.
3. Engage in decision making and implementation of therapeutic actions cooperatively with other members of the health care team.

This practitioner institutes and provides health care to patients within established regimens such as supervising and managing normal pregnancy and delivery, pediatric health supervision and diagnostic screening. The nurse practitioner provides counseling, health teaching and support to individuals and families.

The nurse practitioner is directly accountable and responsible to the recipient for the quality of care rendered.

For the purposes of interpreting the Nurse Training Act of 1971 the term "nurse practitioner" refers to one who has completed a program of study leading to competence as a registered nurse in an expanded role whose responsibility encompasses the following:

1. Obtaining a health history.
2. Assessing health-illness status.
3. Entering a person into the health care system.
4. Sustaining and supporting persons who are impaired, infirm, ill and during programs of diagnosis and therapy.
5. Managing a medical care regimen for acute and chronically ill patients within established standing orders.
6. Aiding in restoring persons to wellness and maximum function.
7. Teaching and counseling persons about health and illness.
8. Supervising and managing care regimens of normal pregnant women.
9. Helping parents in guidance of children with a view to their optimal physical and emotional development.
10. Counseling and supporting persons with regard to the aging process.
11. Aiding people and their survivors during the dying process.
12. Supervising assistants to nurses.

After twenty-five years in nursing, Lucille Kinlein, assistant professor at Georgetown University School of Nursing in Washington, D.C., established an independent practice in 1971 and set up her office in a residential section of College Park, Maryland. Her ultimate purpose was to provide and improve health care for persons otherwise not receiving necessary services in the present health care delivery system.

Since that time, nurses in various places —both urban and rural—have established their own practice. Some are in fact independent while others are in collaboration with physicians and other professionals.

It is not certain which was the first such enterprise; however, the Walk-In Clinic in Atlanta, Georgia (Clift), serves as an example. Patients pay $20 to the nurse practitioners for a physical examination and $2 a visit thereafter. Nurses are thus stepping in to ease the shortage of doctors and are dealing with many common ailments and routine medical procedures formerly the province of M.D.'s. Nurses give allergy shots and immunizations and deal with colds, "flu," and other minor complaints of children. They make a house call for $15 and are available for free telephone consultation around the clock. The Walk-In Clinic was initially set up by Emory University School of Nursing and emphasized health management. Health management encompasses periodic checks of patients with such chronic conditions as diabetes, hypertension, obesity, and allergies. When the patient has a written order from a physician, the nurses will give shots and medications. The nurses at this particular clinic do not prescribe or administer medications without a doctor's order. The nurses do have "standing orders" from several local physicians and make decisions about when the problems have reached the point at which they require referral to the physician. Nurse practitioners in such settings function in an area in which the roles of physician and nurse are not clearly defined and are worked out on an individual basis, requiring mutual understanding and cooperation from the nurse and the physician.

Nurse practitioners do not write prescriptions but often are supplied with prescription blanks signed by physicians, which can be completed by the nurse for certain medications used in the course of treating those conditions which they commonly encounter. Nurse practitioners are also prohibited from doing surgery in a hospital, although they may suture wounds or remove warts in their clinics. They perform routine delivery of babies and do prenatal and postnatal checkups. They order laboratory tests, take medical histories, and perform physical examinations.

The function of patient education has continued to develop as a part of the nurse's role and is no less important in the role of the nurse practitioner. Teaching diabetics the activities of daily living within the home setting, counseling regarding special diets, home care of the sick, and dealing with family problems are activities that nurses carry out in a very natural way. They are the activities for which physicians fail to find time but which have always been a part of nursing.

As independent practice and the role of the nurse practitioner continue to evolve, they cannot do so in isolation; nurses must have cooperation from and association with physicians. Some nurses pay doctors a retainer to review their patient records periodically, to be available for consultation, and to write prescriptions or standing orders. Perhaps this is one way in which the true meaning of a health team will become a reality.

Professional Standards Review Organizations

In September, 1975, the ANA recommended changes in the Medicare law designed to facilitate greater participation of nurses in planning and decision making in Professional Standards Review Organizations (PSRO). Public Law 92-603 provides

for the structure and authority for PSRO's but to date has failed to provide adequately for involvement and decision making by health professionals other than physicians. The ANA proposed that the law be amended so that registered nurses and other licensed health care practitioners would be members of PSRO's and suggested changes that would broaden participation of health professionals at all levels of the PSRO system.

Fee for service—specialization

Fee for service has been considered the direction in which nursing must go to attain its rightful place in the health care delivery system. The federal government has acquiesced to the fee-for-service system in response to the American Medical Association's strong position that this was a means of maintaining accountability. The question arises whether the fee-for-service approach is best to bring about improvement in the existing health care system. Perhaps this is where nursing must take a position if the profession is indeed serious about its concern for the health of society. If major changes are to be made in the health care system and more accountability is to be built in, perhaps nursing must take the responsibility for making the changes. The fee for nursing service may not be the answer. When physicians realize that they are losing a certain dollar value by utilizing a nurse, they will back away. It appears that the approach of the collaborative-cooperative role of nurse practitioners and physicians has been most successful when both receive salaries and are together in neighborhood centers, medical centers, or public health settings on that basis.

One area in which nurses will be able to make a significant contribution to the health care delivery system is with care outside the hospital for health maintenance of the chronically ill. Nurses can play an important part in the care of acute illness through identification and maintenance of individuals in their home setting if medical care of a different nature is not deemed necessary or when the nurse can serve on the front line with physician backup.

A second area in which nurses will be challenged to function is in the care of the aged. Geriatric care currently seems to be in a state of uncertainty. Nursing has not positively picked up the responsibility; medicine has more clearly rejected it and geriatric care is often in the hands of minimally prepared or technical people. Geriatric care has traditionally been provided for in "nursing homes." The elimination of the word "nursing" would be more appropriate in the case of many such facilities, since nursing care is not provided.

These areas provide future challenges and nursing must be willing to meet them.

Among issues concerning nurses in the 1970s are those of a family focus, drugs and alcohol along with their use and misuse, health care in transition from hospital to home, coordinating home care for the elderly, and providing quality nursing care in nursing homes. Along with these may be included a concern regarding the relationship between the new role of women and why so few American women breast-feed (Brack).

Some women within various economic groups have become disenchanted with traditional isolated care provided them in their role as women and mothers. There is an increasing interest in care provided by midwives and services provided to families under what can be termed family-centered services. Women are presently more aware and knowledgeable as well as less accepting of what happens to them during their reproductive years. This is evidenced in the proliferation of women's clinics, particularly in urban areas where gynecologic and fertility control services are made available. Home deliveries are becoming increasingly popular; if professional assistance is not available, many deliveries occur unattended. This is particularly prevalent in the western part of the country among young married or unmarried mothers. As young people become more oriented toward a recognition that childbirth is a normal process, they seem to be less concerned with institutionally provided maternity care. Although the public appears to be satisfied with the developing role of nurses in midwifery, some physicians are reluctant to accept them fully as colleagues. Until nurses demonstrate their competency and physicians recognize it, this reluctance will prevail.

Recent developments in the diagnosis, treatment and follow-up of cancer patients is placing additional demands on nurses and other members of the health care team. To increase the effectiveness with which services can be rendered to cancer patients, and because the nurse plays a unique and essential role in the implementation of these services, oncologic nursing can be developed into an expanded role for the nurse. A certain percentage of patients entering hospitals, clinics, and other facilities present oncologic problems. Whether in adult or pediatric settings, the cancer patient presents a new challenge. Radically new and different treatments require that cancer patients and their families adapt themselves and their life-styles. Because cancer is now a disease that can be treated, the diagnosis is not synonymous with death, but rather calls for an increasing awareness that emotional support is equally as important as physical treatment.

The nurse who chooses to work in this newly developing area can help the patient maintain control of his own life, understand technical language and procedures as one way of handling the anxiety of facing something unfamiliar, and share the feeling of being unjustly denied full functioning or even life itself. Providing nursing care to the cancer patient does not begin and end with chemotherapy. While radiotherapy is in progress, the nurse can provide patients with the continuity necessary to maintain cooperation and encourage recovery. The teaching of proper skin care, explanation of procedures, examination, and recording of measurements are an important part of the patients' care. It is essential to maintain the patient's independence and afford him the opportunity to remain with his family and familiar surroundings. Families require adequate support while keeping the cancer patient at home; keeping the patient at home helps alleviate the guilt families often face when patients are hospitalized. By working closely with families, educating them to possible emergency situations and how to cope with them, and being available when needed, the nurse enables the patient to enjoy his life-span to its greatest, promotes the caring relationship of the family, and offers a better quality of life itself.

Physicians who care for critically ill patients find it extremely difficult to accept responsibility for terminating support in the face of impending death. Central to the issue of discontinuing artificial means of support when the human body no longer performs the vital functions to maintain life are questions such as quality of human life and what is meaningful life. A recent legal test case, that of Karen Quinlan, was one in which the courts decided that the physician must make the ultimate decision and that the court could not direct the physician to "pull the plug." Responsible decision making calls for professional, objective, nonjudgmental action and provides no refuge for a bad conscience. The family, racked with grief and intense emotion, cannot be expected to make the decision concerning the continuation or discontinuation of life support. The recent evolvement of new belief systems and awareness and acceptance of dying as a natural human process will undoubtedly open up a wide area for nursing practice. Nurses have always shared in the experiences of birth and death, aiding the individual and family during moments of intense human relationships. Honest and caring involvement is essential; more direct responsibility in decision making relative to the dying person must take shape over time as the role of the modern nurse evolves.

Keeping people alive by use of machines such as oxygen pumps, kidney machines, and heart pacemakers are activities with which nurses of the earlier eras did not need to grapple. Along with the development of such new technologies has come a new and difficult moral and medical question. The awesome problem of how to define life is primary. It, however, goes hand in hand with the professional, legal, and moral questions with which each nurse must wrestle.

LOOK TO THE FUTURE

Somewhere in the past, it appears that nursing drifted off course and began to function as a profession ministering to the sick without evidence of concern for the teaching responsibilities and opportunities.

The Cherry Ames—Student Nurse series portrayed and perpetuated the image of nursing as a noble career almost next to sainthood and motherhood. The image continues some twenty years after that series; the public, many doctors, and even some nurses view Maggie "Hot Lips" Houlihan as portrayed in the movie M*A*S*H and even Florence Nightingale as women who dedicated themselves to subservience to find a husband, that is, doctor. And so nursing really led them only further into the blind alley in which women walk. One way in which nursing can get back on course is to be perceptive of changes within the society that provide opportunities for nurses to fill a necessary role.

This is an important time for nursing to be seen not only in a caring role but in an assertive and authoritative role as well. Nurses have become educators, researchers, writers, and public figures, while struggling to maintain their identity as nurses. There is a tendency for people to want to label them differently: when nurses are acting in an expert role, the public seems unwilling to accept them as nurses and must identify them differently.

Workshops and seminars, in conjunction with work in small groups, teach nurses to apply theory of personality, management, and politics so that they may use them in the real workaday world. An example is that of a Management Effectiveness Workshop held in Washington, D.C., in October, 1975, in which participants learned many personal and systematic approaches to solving organizational questions and problems.

There are some changes occurring in the conflict between the orientation historically related to nursing; service and obedience were associated first with the religious sponsorship, then with the military sponsorship versus that of scientific inquiry. With service and obedience comes the focus on teaching by women in academic institutions, whereas active participation in research remains predominantly the focus by men in terms of resources, time, and acceptance.

The question before nurses today is not whether service and obedience are important but rather how well-educated nurses conduct scientific inquiry and to what extent nursing faculty members are a part of the community of scholars in higher education.

One issue prevalent today is the question of whether there is in fact a discrepancy between salaries of men and women carrying out the same responsibilities and having similar educational backgrounds. This issue has been the focus of various groups such as the U.S. Equal Employment Opportunity Commission and the Women's Rights Project of the American Civil Liberties Union (ACLU). State nurses associations are concerned but in most cases do not take an official role when complaints arise, suits are filed, and arbitrations take place.

If nurses are to be successful in the future, they must be willing to look at and evaluate their position of inequality. The next necessary step is then to design and bring about public political actions aimed at improvements. Nurses can only break from the oppressive past by understanding their history. The main lesson to be learned from history is how not to repeat past errors. To identify with the women's movement today and obtain equality with men

in the health field is absolutely essential. Some progress can be seen. The ANA has identified nine cases of discrimination against women in university faculty pension plans and has brought suit. An organization called The National Organization of Women (NOW) (A.J.N., Feb., 1975) is attracting the attention of a fair number of nurses who are joining. Its current president is a housewife, Eleanor Sneal. Several chapters of nurses' NOW developed across the country, working to advance the movement of women toward social, political, economic, and professional equality.

Many questions remain to be answered relative to the future definition of what comprises a family. This has an impact on nurses not only in their professional day-to-day work but in terms of their own personal lives as well. Personal values must be adapted and each individual nurse must learn to accept these values, with or without agreement from others.

As to the future of the family, there are many current factors that are now having or will have an impact on what will be the future of the traditional family unit, the role of the family, and the identity of each family member. National economic problems and the worldwide recession could in fact reshape or revitalize the traditional family unit or, because they are cutting back on financial resources, deprive families of the vacations, camping, and evenings out which have, to some extent at least, served as a safety valve and an opportunity for "togetherness." With the large proportion of nurses being women, the change in family structure has an impact on both the nurse's own family and those with whom she works. As it is difficult for women to move into fields that were predominantly filled with men, so it is with men who are moving into nursing as a career.

In spite of what may seem to be a grim picture, there are many nurses who state that they would never leave their profession. A study in 1975 (Nurs. Outlook, Sept., 1975) revealed that 91% of newly licensed nurses surveyed were currently employed and 5% had voluntarily withdrawn from the work force to raise families or continue toward further educational goals. Only 3% were currently unemployed but looking for work. The remaining 1% did not indicate their job status.

The role of nurses will continue to change. New practitioners will function more independently and will tend to be more specialized. While in the past the care of the patient was the focus, the consumer or client will become of greater import. National health insurance will have its impact, as will the fast-moving social forces of our time. Roles and relationships of health care, personnel, their educational preparation, and the facilities utilized for delivering health services will change significantly. Problems of distribution, expenditures for health, and usage of health services will be of major concern in order that all population groups in our society will share equally in their "right to health care."

An area of deficiency is an effective system of self-evaluation and peer review in the field of nursing service. Questions are continually posed about cost effectiveness, duplication, potential gaps, and overlaps in mechanisms for providing quality assurance. Licensure and re-licensure mechanisms will be developed by states; the initiatives are likely to threaten liability, identity, and mobility of nursing as a profession. This challenges the profession to plan change following thoughtful exploration.

The options of family and career must be examined. The question is not whether to devote one's life to a family exclusively or a career exclusively, but rather how to direct energies in such a manner that both components if desired can be adequately attended to. When nurses are able to accomplish a satisfactory organization of their creative energies, personal and professional satisfaction and development will be realized. This is the challenge of every modern nurse.

References for unit three

ANF study, Nursing Research **24**:340-351, Sept.-Oct., 1975.

Are the pro's graduates of vo-tech schools? Winona Daily News, Oct. 1, 1975.

Arnold, Pam: Challenges similar for military, civilian nurses, The American Nurse, p. 7, Dec. 19, 1975.

Brack, Datha Clapper: Social forces, feminism and breastfeeding, Nursing Outlook **23**:556-561, Sept., 1975.

Brown, E. L.: A comprehensive program for a nationwide action in the field of nursing, American Journal of Nursing, Sept., 1945.

Clift, Eleanor: The new family doctor is a nurse, McCalls Magazine, p. 35, Oct., 1975.

Committee on Perspectives: Perspectives for Nursing, Pub. No. 22-1580, New York, 1975, National League for Nursing.

Council on Education shows students eyeing careers in health, Health Research News **3**:3, Oct., 1975.

Editorial—The American Nurse (official ANA newspaper), p. 4, Nov. 28, 1975.

Educational preparation for nurse practitioners and assistance to nurses, New York, 1965, American Nurse's Association.

Extending the scope of nursing practice, a report of the Secretary's Committee to Study Extended roles for nurses, Washington, D.C., 1971, Department of Health, Education, and Welfare.

First ten named by ANA in program to prepare minority group nurses as researchers (News column), American Journal of Nursing **75**:1413, Sept., 1975.

Goals for a national health insurance program, Public Affairs Report No. 3, New York, 1975, National League for Nursing.

Golub, S.: Nursing in Israel, Nursing Mirror and Midwife's Journal **136**:22-25, June 15, 1973.

ICN Congress coming to Kansas City, The American Nurse **7**: Oct. 17, 1975.

Investigations of nursing home conditions, Public Affairs Report No. 2, New York, 1975, National League for Nursing.

Job opportunities for nurses apparent (News and Reports col.) Nursing Outlook, **23**:543, Sept., 1975.

Johnson, Walter L.: Educational preparation for nursing—1974, Nursing Outlook **23**:578-582, Sept., 1975.

Keith, Catherine W.: What is outpost nursing? Canadian Nurse, pp. 41-44, Sept., 1971.

Kushner, Truchia D.: The nursing profession; condition critical, Ms. Magazine, Aug., 1973.

Lenburg, Carrie: Educational preparation for nursing—1972, Nursing Outlook **21**:586-593, Sept., 1973.

Mackenzie, K. R., and Bruce, D.: A comprehensive community drug center, Hospital and Community Psychiatry **23**:318-321, Oct., 1972.

National Task Force of the Continuing Education Unit: The continuing education unit: criteria and guidelines, Washington, D.C., 1974, National University Extension Association.

N-CAP News **2**:No. 4, Aug., 1975.

N-CAP News **2**:2, Nov., 1975.

News from here and there (column), Nursing Outlook **23**:544, Sept., 1975.

Nurses form own NOW, American Journal of Nursing **75**:200, Feb., 1975.

Nurses in the extended role are not physician's assistants, ANA's Interim Executive Committee of Council for PNP's, Kansas City, Mo., July 5, 1973, American Nurses' Association.

Report to the Senate Subcommittee on Health at the hearing on HR 11083, National League for Nursing, Aug. 6, 1965.

Saskatchewan presses for National Nurses Home Association, Canadian Hospital **48**:23, Dec., 1971.

Stimson, Julia C.: Earliest known connection of nurses with army hospitals in the United States, American Journal of Nursing **25**:15, 1925.

Stimson, Julia C.: Medical Department of the United States Army in the World War, vol. 13, part II. The Army Nurse Corps, Washington, D.C., 1927, U.S. Government Printing Office.

The American Nurse, p. 8, Nov. 28, 1975.

The ANA and NLN to co-sponsor Foreign Graduate Commission, The American Nurse **8**:1, April 15, 1976.

The HMO Act, Community health scene, No. 3, Washington, D.C., 1974, Bureau of Community

Health Services, U.S. Public Health Service, Health Services Administration.

Titus, Shirley C.: Economic facts of life for nurses, American Journal of Nursing **52**:1109-1112, Sept., 1952.

United States Cadet Nurse Corps, 1943-1948, Washington, D.C., 1950, Federal Security Agency, U.S. Public Health Service, Government Printing Office.

Vian, John: Nurse-doctorate analysis revised to include new data, Nursing Research Report, **7**:1, June, 1972.

Woodahl, Robert L., Attorney General, Opinion No. 18, vol. 36, Office of the Attorney General, Helena, Mont., Aug. 28, 1975.

Yodfat, Y.: A new method of teamwork in family medicine in Israel with the participation of nurses as physician's assistants, American Journal of Public Health, **62**:953-956, July, 1972.

Legal aspects
of the nursing profession

13 • Nursing and the law

EILEEN A. O'NEIL, J.D.

The failure to recognize the law as an overseer is our own oversight.
For the law is the very shadow of our behavior, which makes
no one really alone.

ANONYMOUS

The decision of career direction can only be formulated when respect is given for standards of education and legality of actual practice in any profession. With regard to that legality in nursing practice, a knowledge of legal aspects of nursing practice must be gained. In so doing, a study of the workings of the law is a necessary foundation for a career in nursing. In order that the law, dignity, and human rights may be upheld at all times, law becomes a two-way street in protecting not only the patient-client but the nurse-practitioner as well. Therefore that law which causes conformity to a legal standard also provides for challenge, contention, and change from the standpoint of nursing practice.

Nursing is undergoing rapid change and, as the professional role evolves, legal interventions will undoubtedly increase. As the nursing role becomes more independent, basic knowledge of legal guidelines is of paramount significance to each practicing nurse.

SOURCES AND TYPES OF LAW

The law is a system of principles that governs virtually all aspects of human conduct within a society. Laws emanate from the government, either federal, state, or local. It is therefore useful to understand the functions and interplay between the governmental branches in the formulation of law. The two sources for the establishment of legal principles are statutory and common law.

In the material that follows, types of law will be broadly described. Overall theories and legal principles of vital importance to all members of the nursing profession will follow and will be viewed as parts of law as a whole. Readers are encouraged to seek a deeper understanding of legal manifestations in the practice of nursing from more detailed sources throughout the duration of their careers.

The United States employs a tripartite system consisting of legislative, judiciary (judicial), and executive branches. The primary function of the legislative branch is the enactment of statutes, usually bills sponsored by committees whose expertise is in the area needing legislation. The legislative branch carries a responsibility to reflect changes in societal structure or attitude, either by promulgation of new law or amendment to those in existence. The judicial branch is comprised of the federal and state court systems; its essential province is interpretation of those laws issued by the legislature. The judiciary is designed to apply legislative statutes to singular case situations and, when the legislature has remained silent, define those standards of legal conduct which are cumulatively referred to as common law. A preventive principle is ingrained in the common law, known as *stare decisis* or following precedent. Adhering to previous rulings, a network of case law is established and stability in law is maintained. This "judge-made" law retains sufficient flexibility for deviation when previous judicial opinions become meaningless. In accordance with these governmental limitations on behavior, the executive branch curbs activities that violate compliance with legislative and judiciary mandates.

The Constitution of the United States describes the following hierarchy and interplay between the legislative and judicial branches. The state courts may issue opinions on conduct that are binding, unless the state or federal legislature enacts contrary guidelines by statute. Acts of Congress in the form of federal statutes prevail over contradictory legislation passed at the state level. The Supreme Court of the United States reigns in its decisions over all other governmental issuances, and functions as interpreter of the supreme law of the land, the United States Constitution.

Classifications

The entire body of law supervises the individual's interaction with others and with the government as delegate of society as a whole. *Civil law* is that group of rules which resolves disharmony between individual members of society. When an individual's rights are infringed upon, the aggrieved party has cause to seek restitution from the wrongdoer. This action forms the basis of a lawsuit.

Some forms of behavior are considered generally unacceptable; limitations on conduct and penalties for offenders are provided for the protection of society. This classification of legal sanction is *criminal law.* When a violation of these parameters occurs, the individual accused is brought before a court by the government on behalf of society.

Evidence

A person who has been accused of violating legal limitations on behavior is summoned to court. Analysis of the accused's action at the time of the wrongdoing is presented. The parties to the lawsuit present evidence to support their respective positions, either adding substance to the charge or refuting the accusation. Evidence includes that data which will enlighten the judge and jury as to the specific facts surrounding the case, provided it meets the tests of admissibility into the court.[1]

Proof of a party's contentions in court is delineated into two basic categories: tangible evidence and oral testimony. Tangible evidence includes records, objects, and documents.[2] For example, in a cause of action arising from a personal injury suffered during health care procedures, a party to the lawsuit may introduce medical records as evidence of fact.

The second type of evidence, oral testimony, is provided by a witness, who under oath is required to give account of facts surrounding the charge. A form of testimonial evidence often presented during a malpractice suit is obtained from expert witnesses, such as physicians, nurses, and other health care providers. An expert witness is one who possesses special knowledge of a particular subject matter. Testimony from these experts aids the judge and jury in determining the legal decision.[3,4]

In all types of lawsuits, evidence is necessary to substantiate facts asserted by the parties or litigants. Some communications are considered confidential by virtue of common law or statute. Refusal of a court to hear confidential communications uttered between a married couple constitutes a "privilege" between husband and wife. This "privilege" testimony by one spouse against the other forms the rationale for this exception.[5] Communications between physician and patient are "privileged" and therefore inadmissible as oral testimony. At present, medical records such as charts, physicians orders, surgical permits, and permission to treat are the only evidence considered admissible. In some cases this permission has been oral, constituting a need for oral testimony as well. This exception arises by state statute and is intended to prevent adverse testimony by one individual against another.[6]

Licensure

Health professions are regulated by means of licensing laws and practice acts, the former controlling admittance into the profession and the latter defining the scope of practice within the profession. This protection issues from the legislature, which speaks for the state and derives its authority from state policing powers, that is, those powers necessary to maintain and "promote the general welfare." Restriction of the nursing profession to individuals who possess certain credentials is an example.

The nurse licensing laws delegate this authority to control admission by creating a state board of nursing.[7] A few states have participated in an innovative motion including nonprofessionals in the provision of general public representation. Licensing boards are traditionally comprised of members involved in the field of nursing. Initially the members are nominated by professional nursing associations and appointed to the agency by the governor of the state. Three functions of the board include determination of eligibility requirements for initial licensure of professional and practical nurses, approval and supervision of educational institutions of nursing, and enforcement of restrictions through suspension, revocation, and relicensure.

Eligibility for membership into the nursing profession is determined by education and clinical training. Although curriculum requirements vary among state boards, nursing education must be obtained at board-approved schools–institutions in order that nurses may qualify for licensure. National standards appear to be evolving as a result of accreditation of state institutions by nationally recognized agencies. In some states recognition of work experience in lieu of institutional training is stated in the licensing act itself.[8]

In addition to personal qualifications such as age, United States citizenship, and good moral character, nurse licensure generally requires the applicant to pass a standard examination. This examination is either formulated entirely by the board itself, or may consist of a national board testing in whole or in part.[8] State boards may certify nurses who meet educational requirements for providing health care previously provided only by licensed physicians. Certification of the specialized practitioner is an example of the expanding legal definition of professional nursing.

A controversial alternative to professional licensure is that of institutional licensure. Under this plan, the state would license hospitals and agencies rather than individuals. In turn these hospitals and agencies would hold authority over and responsibility for the provision of health services given by skilled personnel other than physicians and dentists.[9] This type of licensing procedure is considered by professional nurses as an infringement on their capacity to act independently. This alternative, however, is advocated by the American Hospital Association and the American Medical Association.[9]

Once authority to practice nursing has been issued by the nursing board, an individual who violates a norm of professional behavior is subject to suspension or revocation of license. Violations of license include obtaining a license by fraud, immoral or illegal actions, performance of acts that may be specifically proscribed by the licensing act, and malpractice. For example, a nurse's license to practice was revoked by the Rhode Island Board of Nursing when a nurse paid visits to a patient's home without request and advised him that the physician's diagnosis was incorrect.[10] This interception caused considerable friction between the patient, his family, and his physician. Suspension and revocation procedure involve a state board administrative hearing, wherein the charges are made clear to the nurse and evidence is permissible to refute the accusation of misconduct.

SCOPE OF PRACTICE

The state has a role as guardian of the general welfare of society to ensure restrictions that nursing services are rendered only by those whose educational and experiential backgrounds are congruent with responsibility and scope of practice. State practice acts distinguish between professional and practical nursing. The Rhode Island statute[11] limits the practical nurse to performance of duties to "assist professional nursing in a team relationship" in the area of patient care. The professional nurse is, by legislation, required to possess a higher degree of knowledge in the biologic and social sciences and is therefore authorized to provide professional services such as the observation of symptoms, recording of facts, and carrying out of treatments prescribed by a licensed physician. In Washington state, on the other hand, a licensed practical nurse was administering injections according to instructions given by her physician-employer, but the court found that she was performing services outside the scope of practical nursing, since the Washington Nurse Practice Act states that administration of medications may only be done by registered nurses.[12]

Legislative distinctions between the practice of nursing and the practice of medicine are the most difficult to make. With the enhancement of education and the expansion of the role of the nurse in practice, legislatures are under an obligation to redefine the scope of practice and make that distinction. One problem is that routine services provided to patients in hospitals and other health care institutions are often outside the realm of nursing practice as defined by state statute. Particularly in the areas of emergency care and special care units, nurses perform duties involving diagnosis, treatment, and prescription which are spelled out in medical practice acts as the responsibility of licensed physicians. Physicians often issue standing orders that delegate medical functions to the nurse and provide a guideline to the nurse for use in diagnostic and therapeutic judgments. Over and above the fact that statutes governing nursing practice are outmoded, standing orders by physicians are still beyond the relegated responsibility for treatment and administration of medication.[13]

The present controversy over the scope of professional nursing is, in part, perpetuated by antiquated legislative limitations. In 1971 a special committee appointed by the Secretary of Health, Education, and Welfare announced that it perceived no need to legally redefine the nursing role. In that same year, however, Idaho perceived the need to amend its Nurse Practice Act so it would include diagnosis and treatment jointly defined by medical and nursing boards.[14]

PROFESSIONAL ORGANIZATIONS

The genesis and development of professional organizations has been discussed. In the context of the law these organizations provide legislative input, aid in expanding the statutory limitations on the practice of nursing, and serve as a resource for the practicing nurse in keeping current with changes in the legal aspects of health care services.

Membership statistics reveal that less than half of the entire force of full- or part-time practitioners belong to any professional nursing organization.[15] These organizations, particularly the American Nurses' Association and the National League for Nursing, are a powerful force in gaining legislation. Statements and guidelines issued by professional organizations have been used as a model for redefining nurse practice acts.[16] The boundaries of nursing practice should be determined by the profession itself rather than arising through dictate, default, or emergency.

Publications of professional organizations are an excellent resource for keeping current with legal aspects of nursing. Being constantly in touch with law as it evolves is necessary to the modern nurse in practice.

CONTRACTS

The professional nurse, in the course of providing health care, is engaged in a variety of relationships, some of which are affected by the principles of contract law. A contract is a set of binding and enforceable promises between individuals or groups to do, or not to do, certain activities. Promises, of course, are uttered often; the law is concerned only with those agreements which need reinforcement to keep society relatively harmonious. Contract law is a component of civil law. Therefore, in the event that a contractual promise is broken, an individual may have a cause of action against the person who has failed in the obligation.

In this area of contract law the court's attention focuses on the positions the parties to an agreement hold to one another and the content of their actions and words. Generally parties to a contract intend to avoid the need of court intervention and in this way attempt to minimize potential conflicts themselves. The profession of nursing involves several types of contractual arrangements, some of which arise explicitly, that is, the individuals' intent to bind their promises, and others in which the nurse has engaged in conduct or words that create a contract from the legal point of view.

Elements of contracts. Regardless of the nature of the agreement or relationship between the parties, four legal requirements must be met for a contract to be binding and enforceable: mutual consent, competent parties, consideration, and a legal purpose. Each of these elements requires further definition.

"Mutual consent" or "meeting of the minds" refers to the understanding of the promises issued by each party. This mutual assent is accomplished through an offer by one individual and an acceptance of that offer by the other. For example, a nurse practitioner is offered a position in a health clinic. This offer includes the terms of employment in either written or oral form. After verbal interchange with the employer regarding these terms, the nurse accepts the position. This may be done either by oral or written consent or by actions, for example, arrival at the clinic on the date specified for commencement of employment.

"Competency of the parties" requires capability of the individuals to understand the consequences of their actions or speech. Agreements made by a person under mental conditions such as insanity, senility, or intoxication are "voidable." The person acting under such disability has the option not to perform the promised activity without legal penalty. A contract made by an infant or by a person induced by fraud or misrepresentation is also voidable. To use the nurse practitioner's situation again, if the employer had offered the position at a specified salary, whereas the actual compensation was less, the nurse has the choice to continue in the employ of the clinic or to disengage from the agreement. Misrepresentation in the mutual assent phase provides the other party with an escape from the contract without incurring liability to the misrepresenting party.

"Consideration" is the binding promise in an agreement. It is the exchange that was bargained for in the offer and acceptance. The hypothetical nurse practitioner, in exchange for the provision of health care for clinic patients, is entitled to salary, which is consideration in that agreement. As in every aspect of law, there are exceptions. If a purely gratuitous offer is made, and the accepting party relies on that promise and incurs responsibility to another individual, the court may find a binding obligation despite the lack of consideration. For example, a physician had promised a donation and the recipient hospital had, in reliance on the gift offer, incurred expenses. When the hospital sued the promisor to obtain the promised gift, the court found the donation intent to be binding on the physician.[17]

The final requirement of a contract is "legality of purpose." It alludes to the subject matter of the agreement. An agreement that a nurse will perform a clearly illegal function, for example, obtaining medications for a requesting patient without prescription, would be neither valid nor enforceable.

Types of contracts. Most contracts need not be written to be binding and enforceable. Legal classifications of contracts are intricate. An "express" contract is one in which all the terms and conditions of the agreement are stated either orally or in written form. In the earlier example, the nurse practitioner entered into employment under this type of contract. An "implied" contract arises from the conduct or words of an individual. When a patient enters a hospital or a person boards a bus, there is an understanding that payment for the services will be made. Another exception in the law appears to complicate seemingly uncomplex principles: oral contracts for a duration of one year or more are not binding or enforceable. A case in point is that which arose when a hospital employed a physician for a period of one year by oral contract. A disagreement arose between the parties after six months, resulting in the doctor's dismissal without a proportionate salary based on the yearly promised income. When the physician sued the hospital to recover the difference in payment, he was without a cause of action or remedy because the contract was oral and for the period of a year.[18]

A breach of contract occurs when a party fails to perform the binding promises. The dismissed physician in this case sued the hospital on the grounds that they had breached the promise to pay a half of the yearly salary. The court disagreed, as there was not a contract. An actual breach occurs when the agreement is binding and enforceable. If, for example, the physician's oral contract contained a six-month commitment, the obligation for appropriate compensation based on the salary would have been granted by the court, since the oral agreement would have been binding on the hospital. The remedy in contract law, which arises from common law, is recovery by the aggrieved party of the actual monetary loss resulting from the breach of contract.

EMPLOYEE-EMPLOYER RELATIONS

From the legal perspective, one very essential element must be present to create the roles of "employee" and "employer": the employer must possess the right to control the employee in the area of employment. Nurses often are engaged in this type of employment when employed by a hospital, institution, public health center, or clinic. This type of employment arrangement is germane both in the area of contract law and tort law.

A few practical considerations with respect to contractual obligations are warranted. Parties who are participants to an employment agreement can minimize potential conflict by clarifying ambiguities in conditions such as salary, hours, and duties. It is also important to discuss unsuitable conditions to arrive at a compromise most suitable to both employee and employer. This arbitration should of course, be done during the formation of the contract rather than subsequent to its creation. It is always beneficial for the reconciled promises to be expressed in writing. A dispute arising after the agreement has been made regarding terms of employment may be readily allayed by reference to the written word so that the parties can bypass the necessity of court intervention.

Some conditions arise in an employment situation by virtue of federal and state laws. In the area of Congressional regulations, the Labor Management Relations Act (LMRA) prohibits unfair labor practices by an employer. Employees of hospitals are entitled to participate in labor organizations that act as collective bargaining representatives for negotiation with the institution in employment and other contractual matters. The LMRA specifically prevents the discharge of an employee for participation in union activities and restrains an employer from supporting any competing unions.[19]

State hospitals are specifically exempted from the LMRA but are subject to state regulations if such regulatory power has been exercised by the legislature. Although most states have not enacted labor relations statutes, those which have protect the collective bargaining process between institutions and employees and specifically create the right for employees to organize, join unions, and bargain collectively in contract negotiations.[20]

The formulation of occupational health and safety standards in the health care field is a matter for state regulation. Some state laws explicitly prescribe safety standards of working premises. This is essentially a preventive measure by statute to coerce an institution into providing safer places for employees before injury occurs. An employer is always obligated to maintain safety on the premises without statutes prescribing safety standards. Coercion is obtained only after an employee is injured and suit for the resulting injuries has been brought against the employer.[21]

Workmen's compensation for an injured employee is a remedy sponsored by state legislatures to circumvent the necessity of a lawsuit and to alleviate the employee's burden in proving negligence of the employer. The scope of this remedial statute varies from state to state, but the normal organization involves a board of commissioners that judges the employee's claim of injury and awards compensation according to a predetermined schedule based on the nature of the personal injury. An example of recovery under workmen's compensation occurred when a public health nurse became infected with beta streptococcus from contact with infected patients. As a result she was unable to continue working. A claim for weekly compensation for the illness was granted by the Industrial Commission.[22] Although the employer had in no way been negligent, the employee was awarded the compensation because the two requisite elements were met: the existence of an employee-employer relationship, and an injury that occurred during the performance of work related duties.

INDEPENDENT CONTRACTOR

An independent contractor, in the opinion of the law, is one who contracts to do something for another but is not controlled by the other, or subject to any right of control in the performance of services. Two professional roles assumed by the nurse are considered of this nature: the special or private duty nurse and the independent nurse practitioner.

In the case of a private duty nurse, the contract of employment exists directly between the nurse and the patient.[23] No dominion or control over the professional services is present, as the patient is presumed to lack the expertise possessed by the nurse. If a special duty nurse is employed by a patient in a hospital or similar setting, the relationship that arises between the institution and nurse is not unlike that with a staff physician. That is, the nurse may be required to comply with the hospital rules to provide services within the institution.[24] On the other hand, the hospital must fulfill some of its implied conditions and promises to an independent contractor, such as providing suitable equipment, safe working premises, and competent co-workers. This exchange of obligations is, however, insufficient to create the relationship of employee and employer due to the absence of the right to control the professional services of the special duty nurse.

When a special duty nurse has entered into a binding agreement with a patient to provide specified care, any subsequent imposition of a condition requires an additional contract. For example, when a patient requests an increase in the nurse's hours or expansion of her duties, additional consideration must be promised. If the nurse assents to an increase in salary in return for added demands, this resulting agreement is enforceable in a court of law, as the elements of mutual consent and consideration have been explicitly fulfilled.

To distinguish this type of employment contract from the employee-employer status, the workmen's compensation provisions do not apply to the independent contractor. Nurses who are employed for short intervals by a patient in a health care institution do not have recourse to recovery for injuries, due to the absence of an employee-employer relationship. However, private duty nurses are not specifically excluded from the Social Security Act; if the hospital coverage permits, voluntary participation by the independent contractor is possible.

Because the independent nurse practitioner provides direct health care and is not subject to the control of an employer, the legal status with the patient is that of an independent contractor.[25] The relationship arises in the form of an implied contract. A patient enters the nursing clinic with an offer to pay for treatment and services by the practitioner. The nurse may either accept this offer by delivering health care or reject the offer by referral to another professional. If care is provided, the patient's promise to pay is binding and enforceable. This option of rejection of course takes on a different hue in an emergency, and the duty to provide immediate attention may preclude the choice to reject the patient's offer.

MALPRACTICE INSURANCE

The value of adequate coverage under a malpractice insurance policy will be displayed through the tort liability of the nurse. Because insurance is a binding set of promises between the issuer and the insured, it deserves explanation as a contract. Through an insurance policy, the company agrees to assume the risks of the insured in exchange for a premium paid by the individual covered by the policy. Professional insurance very basically contains three variables: specific amount of coverage, identification of risks involved, and specified occurrences. Because the nurse may be legally liable for injury or harm arising from the performance of nursing services, it is a wise decision to carry professional liability insurance.

In an employee-employer relationship it is incumbent on the nurse to become familiar with the type and amount of coverage provided through the employer's group liability policy. For the independent contractor, the importance of obtaining professional insurance cannot be overemphasized. Any injuries resulting from nursing services render the independent contractor personally liable for damages to the patient.

TORTS

Professional nursing is a sacrificing and altruistic occupation, promoting and providing health services to society. To discuss conflicting interests that may arise in providing health care is ironic. However, the phenomenal growth of tort actions, particularly in the area of malpractice, necessitates that the practicing nurse be made aware of the possible infringements on the rights of others. An introduction to common law guidelines on interaction with the patient and peers, other than in contractual arrangements, is presented. This area of law is tort liability.

The law engages in protecting individual rights by guarding against unjustifiable and unreasonable conduct by the members of society. Compensation for an infringement on a legally protected right is provided by a cause of action and a remedy of monetary damages for the injured party. This branch of civil law will be more clearly understood by an analysis of the particular rights of the individual and the wrongs that trespass them.

There are two major types of torts: intentional and unintentional. An intentional tort occurs when the wrongdoer (defendant) intends a harmful result of his or her conduct. An unintentional tort results from the actor's conduct despite the absence of an intent to cause the injurious result. Professional malpractice, for example, is an unintentional tort. This definition is based largely on the actor's conduct and will be viewed through an analysis of the particular torts.

The concept of intent does not necessarily presume a hostile action to bring about an injury. It is, rather, the motivation or desire to create a result that invades the interests of another, in a way the law will not permit. A discussion of intentional torts that could arise during the course of performing nursing functions follows:

Battery. Liability can arise when one intentionally and without consent physically touches another. As a result, that person's right to freedom from physical abuse is invaded. In the area of health services, the element of consent to treat a patient is essential to avoid liability for a battery. One might reasonably expect that a patient who enters a hospital is willing to authorize nurses and physicians to proceed with appropriate treatment. However, the patient's right to reject medical recommendations at any time remains absolute. This necessitates a full understanding on the part of the patient to choose acceptance or rejection of the prescribed treatment or, if several alternatives exist, to elect which should be used. It also enables the patient-client to seek further information regarding care. In 1960 a case arose in Kansas when a new and unusual method of treatment was prescribed and implemented without the necessary explanation of potential risks. The patient sued, and the court, in an important judicial determination, decided that the duty to provide the patient with sufficient information which allows him to form an intelligent consent is superior to the duty to treat the patient when an emergency situation does not exist.[26]

This principle of "informed consent" has become firmly embedded in the body of common law governing battery actions brought against health care personnel. The courts in different states promote varying tests to determine whether the informed consent of the patient has been obtained prior to the course of treatment. One of these tests is derived from the community of professionals, that is, how much disclosure is normally made about a particular medical procedure. For example, in Wyoming, the court denied the patient's claim for damages based on findings that information given to the patient regarding possible permanent scarring of the legs from a saphenous vein ligation had not deviated from the amount of disclosure ordinarily given by physicians.[27] Another test of a more subjective nature analyzes the patient's understanding of the explanation of potential risks inherent in a treatment.[28] This element of consent, necessary to avoid liability for battery, can either be "expressed," i.e., when the patient has signed a special consent form or has orally assented to the medical team's explanation of the treatment risks, or "implied" by actions, as the following case indicates. Ocean liner passengers wishing to receive inoculations were instructed to form a line. One passenger who later brought an action based on battery joined the line and offered his arm. The court found that the passenger had implied his consent for injection by joining the line and offering his arm.[29] Two things should be emphasized: the general consent form signed by a patient on admission to the hospital is not necessarily an "informed consent" to all treatment provided later, and the patient can legally withdraw his consent at any time.

The nurse in performing her duties as an integral member of the health care team should be constantly alert to the patient's consent. Normal procedure revolves around the physician's disclosure of treatment information.[30] Contact with the patient when presenting the special consent form should alert the nurse to a patient's uncertainty about a procedure. Explanation regarding injections or preparations for medical treatment should be given, or, if the patient's consternation relates to the performance of the physician's services, the physician should be so apprised.

The only exception to this consent requirement is when a state of emergency exists. Lack of time prevents opportunity to inform the patient of medical procedure. An attempt to gain consent could further endanger a patient's life. Physical entrance to the premises constitutes consent for the provision of emergency care.

Nurses, particularly psychiatric nurses, may find themselves in a situation where their physical well-being is threatened or endangered by a patient. An unauthorized touching, normally forming the basis for the tort of battery, may be necessary for self-protection and thus constitutes a defense to the intentional physical interference with the patient.[31]

Assault. The individual's right to freedom from bodily harm extends to a general fear of losing control of one's whole safety and well-being. In the intentional tort of assault, no actual physical contact is necessary to give the victim a right to a legal remedy. The distinction between these torts is that bodily contact necessary to constitute a battery is absent in an assault, the threat of bodily touch being sufficient to give rise to a cause of action and monetary damages.[32] The threat must be such as to arouse a real apprehension of physical danger. Fear, and fear alone, is insufficient. Hypothetical situations serve as examples. A nurse enters a patient's room and, over the patient's objections, injects medication. He or she is liable in an action brought for battery, as an actual physical contact was made without consent. In an assault situation, the nurse enters the room and, by his or her actions,

creates an atmosphere of physical danger. By analogy, suit brought by an individual against one who shook a fist under the victim's face resulted in an assessment of monetary damages because the action was such as to arouse an ordinary person's apprehension that physical injury would ensue.[33]

False imprisonment. In addition to the individual's right to be free from bodily harm or the immediate threat thereof, the common law reflects the individual's freedom from restraint of movement. An intentional and unlawful limitation of another's personal liberty by physical force, words, or gestures constitutes a violation of this protection and forms the basis for the tort of false imprisonment.

To provide health treatment it is necessary for physicians and nurses to apply varying degrees of confinement to patients-clients. The crucial factor, in avoiding liability for false imprisonment, is that the restraint be reasonable, either for the benefit of the patient or for the protection of society. Examples of this latter reasonable restraint are the isolation of a person with a communicable disease and confinement of a potentially harmful psychiatric patient.[34] To restrict a mentally ill patient who has been sedated, however, might be considered by a court to be an unreasonable infringement on mobility in the absence of proof that the patient continued to be dangerous to himself or others.

The person who desires discharge from a hospital despite the advice of physicians and nurses that further rest or treatment is warranted should not be detained. The individual should, however, be fully apprised of the consequences of an early release. This request for discharge should be noted on the hospital chart, and a form releasing the hospital and staff from liability should be signed by the patient, in the event that complications arise due to the premature release.

Another situation in which restraint on an individual's freedom is unreasonable is the failure of a hospital to release the patient until the medical bill arising from treatment and services is paid.[35] A request that the patient wait until his statement is checked for correct address or insurance information is a contrasting situation; the patient's mobility is not deterred in an unreasonable manner as to violate the freedom of movement.

Invasion of privacy. When a patient requests the services of health care personnel, a relationship of trust arises: trust that treatment will be provided effectively and confidence that information obtained in the course of diagnosis and therapy will not go beyond that relationship. This is an ethical consideration for every practicing nurse; the law protects any individual's private affairs from unwarranted publicity and exposure to public view by providing monetary recompense when this privacy is infringed. A case in point was that brought before the court by the parents of a congenitally deformed child.[36] In contrast to the recently publicized case of Karen Anne Quinlan pertaining to the legal issue of keeping a patient-client alive, the infant's malformation did not draw public visibility. Publicity to this case was stimulated by the physicians and hospital staff who admitted reporters to the hospital room. Monetary damages were granted to the parents who made the legal charge that their privacy had been invaded.

Patients' charts, medical histories, and other information accessible to the nurse should be guarded against intrusion. Divulging such information may subject the nurse and hospital to liability. Some exceptions exist to the invasion of privacy through disclosure of personal matters.

Defamation. A written or oral statement to a third party tending to damage the reputation of the person defamed, is an intentional tort for which the court will award a monetary judgment against the person issuing the communication. Both forms of this tort, that is, slander through writing and libel by oral statement, can arise in a nurse's interactions with patients-clients or peers. The right that the law intends to protect is the individual's freedom from utterance or writings that arouse adverse feelings against the person. A remark or written communication by a nurse that a patient has venereal disease, to someone other than those required to be told, could constitute a defamation. A statement to a third person of an individual's physical deformity or mental condition might be considered by a court of law to be a diminishment of that person's value or esteem.

In Maine a nurse recovered money for harsh and derogatory remarks made by a physician to the hospital administration after she had criticized postoperative procedures used by the physician.[37] The rationale underlying the case is that the statements intentionally made by the physician tended to cause the nurse's disrepute with her employer.

There are, however, defenses to this tort. Analogous to the defense of self-defense in a battery action, the person charged with defamation may have uttered or written damaging statements in the protection of self-interest. A nurse supervisor may, for example, inform the administration of a hospital-agency of a nurse's behavior that would be injurious to the patients-clients or negatively reflect on the supervisor's performance.

Defense of an actionable communication prevails when the relationship is viewed as "privileged" in the eyes of the law. For example, a case arose when a director of nurses wrote a letter to the professional registry requesting that the services of a certain private duty nurse not be performed in that hospital as a result of the loss of narcotics during the times this particular nurse was on duty. The court denied the private duty nurse recovery, specifying the director of nurses' duty to make the communication in the interests of the community. This duty was considered "privileged" communication.[38]

Unintentional torts. The law often has a peculiar viewpoint; criminal liability may arise in the nursing profession despite the fact the actions were well intended. Intentional torts occur when a person's actions intend a harmful result; unintentional torts occur in the area of *avoidable* accidents. No intent that a harmful result would flow from the actor's conduct is present. These torts arise from a complex principle in the common law called "negligence." It is not a state of mind, but a lack of due care to avoid the accident, which gives rise to liability. The court is interested in whether the occurrence that forms the basis of the lawsuit could have been prevented if the actor in the situation had not been negligent. A verbal journey through the elements of negligence is necessary to enlighten the reader as to how liability for negligence is determined. There are four elements in negligence: (1) standard of care, (2) legal duty, (3) causation, and (4) resulting injury.

Malpractice, as a part of negligence, is negligence of a professional in the performance of services. Lawsuits in this area are likely to increase as the professional role of nursing expands. This will be discussed further under vicarious liability.

STANDARD OF CARE. To determine whether a certain action is negligence, a threshold question is posed by the court: "What would the reasonably prudent person acting under similar circumstances do?" The answer given by the court becomes the standard of care required in any given situation. "The reasonably prudent person" is a hypothetical creature of the law and dons some of the characteristics of the accused individual, such as level of educational knowledge and age, but does not assume the peculiarities of that person unless they fall into a category of legal exception. Infancy and insanity are examples of this exception.[39] Conformity to this objective standard of behavior is predicated on a presumption that the actor possesses average intelligence and reasonable prudence. As harsh as it may seem, persons who have less intelligence and wisdom possess these deficits at their own peril.[40]

To add dimension to this abstraction, conduct of a professional nurse is measured against a fictitious "reasonable" nurse. To find negligence in the nurse's actions, it must be proved that there was a failure to meet the standard of care that would have been provided by a nurse exercising "reasonable" and "prudent" professional judgment. In Louisiana a nurse was confronted with an ambiguous medication order entered into a patient's chart. Death resulted from an injection of the medication presumed by the nurse to be the correct one. In that case one of the legal issues revolved around what the ordinary and reasonable nurse would have done when faced with such an ambiguity. Nurses, as expert witnesses, testified in court that the customary procedure would involve clarification of the order by calling the prescribing physician. The nurse's conduct did not meet this standard and she was found liable for negligence in avoiding the accidental death of the patient.[41]

Unfortunately, what constitutes good nursing practice, that is, the standard of care required, is often the subject of differing opinion. A California court was presented with conflicting testimony concerning a nurse who observed swelling or redness at the site of a cutdown. The attending physician stated that the nurse should either contact the physician or turn off the intravenous infusion. Expert testimony from nurses familiar with this aspect of patient care indicated that it would be outside the scope of nursing practice to cut off the flow of the solution, and that notification of the swelling should be given to the physician. The court, after eliciting the divergent testimony regarding the standard of care or reasonable conduct in the factual setting, allowed the jury to determine which of the standards should be applied to measure the nurse's actions.[42]

With regard to a nurse specialist, the standard of care derived from the "ordinary and reasonable" principle reflects the possession of additional knowledge and skills. For example, in 1964 an injury occurred from an injection of thiopental sodium solution by a nurse-anesthetist for a gynecologic surgical procedure. Through introduction of expert testimony into court, it was determined that the use of the anesthesia technique was in accordance with recognized practice of skillful nurse-anesthetists in that community. Because the nurse did not deviate from the customary procedures, the standard of care in preventing the injury was met, and no liability for negligence arose.[43]

The case also implies that the standard of care is derived from practice in the surrounding community. Although this was the method of arriving at the "reasonable man" standard at that time, a Massachusetts case subsequently reversed this traditional approach by using a general professional standard of care for comparison, rather than limiting the standard to the geographic community of professionals.[44] As a consequence, nurses in a rural community would be held to the same standard as would other nurses in urban locations. On the other hand, a greater standard of care is imposed for the treatment and observation in a post-anesthesia room.[45]

LEGAL DUTY. In addition to the standard of care, a court will analyze another aspect of behavior called "legal duty." This element of negligence involves the obligation to foresee the consequences of actions.[46] The standard set for legal duty is whether the ordinary and prudent person would have foreseen the consequences of the particular action. If, from this perspective, the injury was not a foreseeable one, the legal duty is fulfilled.

In the case previously discussed, that is, in which the nurse failed to clarify the prescription, the conduct that did not meet the standard of care owed to the patient gave rise to her legal duty to foresee the consequential harm to the patient. Testimony adduced at trial provided this standard of forseeability. The nurse-witnesses stated it is common professional knowledge that administration of incorrect medication could cause injurious effects. The death of the patient was therefore foreseeable and could have been prevented through exercise of ordinary and reasonable professional discretion.

Another aspect of duty emerges with the Good Samaritan acts. To encourage volunteer medical assistance, state legislatures have enacted statutes that grant some degree of immunity for health professionals who render services in emergency situations. Although no legal duty exists to assist, if one does choose to voluntarily aid, a legal duty to assist with due care arises. Each state grants differing amounts of immunity. A few statutes limit this protection to physicians, but nurses are included in the coverage in forty-five states.[47]

The concept of duty, as applied to hospitals, is demonstrated by a case that arose in the setting of an emergency care unit. A private hospital refused to treat an infant; the nurse on duty instructed the parents of the child to return home and contact their family physician in the morning. The infant's death caused the parents to bring a lawsuit against the hospital for failure to admit and care for their child. The court dictated (1) that it is the duty of the hospital to admit a patient if an emergency clinic is maintained and an exigent (urgent) situation arises and (2) that a duty arises on the part of the nurse to perceive the existence of an emergency. In this case, however, the infant's symptoms were not such as to arouse a person to perceive the circumstances as exigent.[48]

CAUSATION. If the two previous elements are established at trial, that is, the standard of care was not met and the duty to foresee the consequences was unfulfilled, the court will introduce a third element to determine the existence of negligence. The question becomes whether the harm received by the injured party was a result of breach of duty. Referring once more to the case presented on p. 255 wherein the nurse failed to contact the physician, the patient's death was found to be a direct result of the fact that the medication was administered by injection rather than orally. At some point the chain of events becomes so tenuous that it is impossible to attribute causation to failure in meeting the standard of care and breach of legal duty. A hypothetical situation serves as an example of this lack of causation. A nurse gives a patient an injection that induces minor swelling in the arm. The following day the patient stays at home due to the discomfort and incurs an injury from tripping on the stairs. Connection between the events becomes too thin to attribute the action of injection with causation. This situation would probably be deemed by the law to be an unavoidable accident.

Vicarious liability. The employment relationships in the performance of nursing services play an important role in the tort area also. When the employee-employer relationship is formulated, the employer has a right to exercise control over the employee. For this reason, the common law allows an injured party to bring an action against an institution that employs a nurse who acts negligently under the doctrine of "respondeat superior," or "let the master answer." This does not, however, absolve the nurse-employee from liability; it merely entitles the patient to bring legal charges against both the hospital and the nurse. Also, the employer may seek restitution from the nurse for its liability in damages. For example, a general duty nurse continued to inject a saline solution into an unconscious patient after noticing adverse effects. In the case brought by the patient for damages, the hospital was found vicariously liable for the injury through the negligence of its employee.[49]

Under similar theory, certain situations arise in which a nurse in the employ of an institution will be viewed as a "borrowed servant." Under this common law rule, a physician is liable for negligence of an attending nurse when exclusive control and right of direction are in the physician's hands. This type of legal relationship normally occurs in an operating room where the law considers the surgeon the "captain of the ship" and is presumed to have total command of the actions in that room. The rationale for this "loaned servant" doctrine, as stated by a Minnesota court, is that the patient is completely at the mercy of the physician and relies on the surgeon to "guard against any and all avoidable acts that may result in injury to his patient."[50] Because the special duty nurse is not subject to an institution's right of control, the vicarious liability principle does not extend to negligent acts performed by a nurse in this capacity.

Perhaps the most important aspect regarding liability is the increasing independence of the professional nurse. The theory of vicarious liability flows from the conception that nursing is inherently a dependent role. Certainly independent practitioners are beyond this scope of control and are solely answerable for negligent conduct. In this context it is important to realize the value of malpractice insurance, particularly as the profession grows more independent.

CRIMINAL LAW

Certain conduct is considered generally offensive to the members of society. In contrast with the civil law areas of tort and contract, which create individual rights of compensation for injuries caused by another party, both federal and state legislatures have enacted statutes to prohibit such opprobrious behavior and to discipline the actor. Society has an interest in maintaining some semblance of order between its members; limitations on conduct must be set to achieve this ideal. How and why this may be accomplished through law may be summarized as follows: (1) society can physically restrain individuals who endanger civilization as a whole; (2) through the legal process, rehabilitation of violators can be administered; (3) by providing an example of punishment for prohibited demeanor, others may be deterred from engaging in similar conduct; and (4) punitive measures through criminal laws, however primitive they may seem, seek a variety of collective community revenge against society's transgressor.

Depending on the legislative opinion of the grievousness of particular behavior, varying penalties are prescribed to accomplish the purposes mentioned above. Three broad classifications of crime based on the gravity of the offense are (in order of greater to lesser): treason, felony, and misdemeanor. Treason is a warlike act against the United States government or an adherence or provision of aid to its enemies. With the number of nurses employed in government service, even treason becomes a possibility and must be considered. However, this discussion will focus on felonies and misdemeanors as areas of concern for the practicing nurse. If the tort area seemed incongruent with the charitable and genteel nature of the profession, then criminal causes of action will appear all the more incongruous. Regardless of this inconsistency, knowledge of the criminal branch of the law is an important guideline for nursing conduct.

Originally, felony was used to denote those crimes punishable with death or forfeiture of property. Presently it is a classification encompassing any offense punishable by imprisonment. A misdemeanor categorically includes all other crimes carrying lesser sanction, that is, those which provide a penalty of confinement in jail or imposition of a fine. Legislatures, state and federal, have statutorily set forth proscriptions of generally offensive conduct. Murder committed within a state's boundaries, for example, is defined and penalized by that state legislative branch. Thus minor fluctuations are present from state to state.

As some specific examples of prohibited conduct are defined and interpreted in the discussion that follows, there is a common thread weaving through criminal laws. In each is an action that violates some limitation on conduct, and an intent on the part of the actor to commit the forbidden action. As in other areas of the law, the court will analyze the actions and deduce the intent from the point of time and place the crime was undertaken.

Homicide

The taking of another's life, or homicide, is generally a disfavorable act. One may balk at the flippancy of this statement. However, situations exist, for example, in times of war, when killing is apparently justified. Perhaps more palatable exceptions to criminal liability include homicide resulting from self-defense when an individual's life is seriously jeopardized or when a police officer in the line of duty ends a life trying to apprehend an individual committing a serious crime. As characteristic of all legal boundaries and definitions, those governing what is permissible homicide and what is criminal homicide continue to shift. In the case of Roe v. Wade,[51] the Supreme Court authorized an abortion to be performed in the first trimester for a woman on her request; more recently the Supreme Court reversed the decision regarding viability of life by refusing to support termination of life support for Karen Anne Quinlan. The law continues to inquire into the definition of life—when it begins and when it ends. Discussion about homicide in its degrees will focus on those forms that society will not justify: murder, manslaughter, and negligent homicide.

Murder as interpreted by legal principles, is an unlawful killing of one human being by another with "malice aforethought," the latter phrase relating to the actor's state of mind in the commission of the crime. This mental framework is derived from the degree of danger attached to an act in a given state of facts. In a criminal prosecution for murder the court, through the judge or the jury, will reflect on the motivation of the actor deduced from the events as revealed by the testimony of witnesses and introduction of tangible evidence. A simple example follows. When one raises a heavy bar and thrusts it toward another, a deliberate attempt to take an individual's life is presumed from the behavior due to the intensity of danger inherent in such action. Death resulting from a blow on the head with a soft stick would cast doubt on the actor's intent to murder, as the degree of danger is considerably less.[52] The circumstances admit a homicide by an intended action, but without "malice aforethought." This latter classification, a lesser caliber of homicide, is *manslaughter.* The probability that the criminal's action was sponsored by a wicked and malicious motive to kill the victim is slighter, since the motion of the stick would not normally result in the person's death. Consequently, the penalty imposed by law is mitigated.

The third type of inexcusable homicide, *involuntary manslaughter,* is closely akin to the unintentional tort concept of negligence, but is distinguishable from civil liability principles in that the behavior substantially departs from a reasonable man's conduct. The behavior is wanton or reckless with regard to another's life, resulting in an involuntary manslaughter. The law reads into this degree of negligent action the element of intent from the degree of danger, which should have been apparent to the actor from the surrounding circumstances.

To make these distinctions in homicide and to emphasize the importance of the knowledge of this crime for the nursing profession, the following actual cases of criminal prosecutions are provided.

A California chiropractor convinced the parents of a child with a cancerous eye to bypass eye surgery, assuring them that he could cure the disease without surgery. On the death of the child, the state brought murder charges against the chiropractor.[53] Although the case was reversed on appeal, resulting in the chiropractor's emancipation from criminal penalty, it points out the circumstances in which criminal prosecutions for murder do indeed occur. Another example is that of a physician who performed an abortion because the operation had been commonly completed without criminal liability prior to the prosecution.

The following cases are provided as examples of the manslaughter element. A nurse's criminal guilt for the death of a surgical patient was found in the following circumstances. The surgeon ordered the attending nurse to prepare a cocaine solution with Adrenalin for anesthetic purposes in a tonsillectomy. The nurse repeated the order, and after the injection was given the patient died. The physician, it was discovered later, had intended procaine rather than cocaine. The court, after consideration of her training, education, and experience, found the nurse's failure to question the accuracy of the physician's direction of mixture to constitute gross negligence. Obviously the surgeon was also negligent, but the nurse's action caused the patient's demise.[54] The case demonstrates both the occasion of a criminal behavior without wickedness or malice, and also the importance of the intelligent interaction among members of the health care team.

The head nurse of a state institution for the mentally retarded was charged and found guilty of involuntary manslaughter when, under general authorization by a physician at another hospital, paraldehyde was ordered to becalm an obstreperous patient. Although she was unaware of the strength, the dosage was four times that ordinarily prescribed. Illness resulted; the patient was taken to another hospital and died five days later of pneumonia. The nurse's initial conviction of manslaughter was later overturned on the appeal level, as medical evidence indicated that death would have occurred in a matter of hours had the sedative been the cause of the loss of life.[55]

Assault and battery

The attempt or actual infliction of bodily injury forms not only the basis of civil liability for an intentional tort but also may create grounds for criminal liability if accompanied with the requisite criminal intent. The double liability lies in the essence of the classification of laws: the civil liability arises from the victim's right to be compensated for the injury suffered, and the criminal law has at interest the protection of society from conduct harmful to the general welfare. One exception to the similarity of elements exists: for assault to be of a criminal nature, the apprehension of bodily harm must result from actions. Words, which may create a tortious assault from the civil law perspective, are insufficient to raise criminal liability.[56]

In New York a court found the actions of a medical attendant interacting with a patient suffering from dementia praecox to have criminal intent. The medical attendant had used unnecessary and unreasonable force to restrain the patient despite the presence of clear alternatives to achieve physical control. A criminal penalty for battery was imposed.[57]

Criminal prosecution does not preclude the right of an individual to bring a civil law cause of action against the actor, as two rights are infringed. Damages resulting from an assault or battery are recoverable as the victim's right, and society retains the right to control a harmful individual. It is likely that two lawsuits will arise as a result of the dual infringement.

NARCOTICS

The federal Controlled Substances Act was passed by Congress in 1970 to regulate the manufacture, distribution, and dispensing of narcotics, stimulants, depressants, and hallucinogens. Criminal liability is incurred for producing or administering these drugs without a license. In addition to the criminal penalties, the statute contains certain procedures with which every professional nurse should be familiar.

A PRN order for a narcotic drug must be rewritten every seventy-two hours. Physician's standing orders for administration to hospital patients are not adequate to meet this requirement. In an emergency, a physician's oral order for a narcotic is allowed if the nature of the exigency is recorded in the patient's chart by the attending nurse and the physician validates the order within twenty-four hours.[58]

DEFENSES

Since the criminal law is based on the intent of an actor, the following defenses tend to refute the presence of the element recognized by common law.

Insanity

Although the behavioral dynamics of insanity have not been fully unraveled by any discipline, the law recognizes that the mental condition of an actor may negate the element of intent. The law has no rigid rules regarding the nature of insanity; insight about this aspect of an individual is gathered by the court through psychiatric expert witnesses who analyze the psychic content of a person's actions. The law, based on this evidence, draws an inference as to whether the defendant understood the nature and severity of the crime committed. Criminal responsibility depends on whether the actor could discern right from wrong at the time of the action.[59]

Infancy

Criminal intent may be presumed to be absent due to age of an actor. Children are subject to criminal prosecution; however, children under 7 years are conclusively determined to be unable to distinguish right from wrong in the legal sense.[60]

OTHER LEGAL AREAS

Through the voice of its legislative body, a community has an interest in the protection and promotion of the health, education, and welfare of its citizens. Due to the proximity of health professionals to information about conditions that threaten the well-being of the society, the obligation to report such hazards often falls on the nurse. The state statutes that guide disclosure to governmental authorities of otherwise confidential personal history are designed as a vehicle for control and abatement of endangering circumstances.

Child abuse

Physical abuse or neglect of children is perhaps one of society's most serious and complex behavioral problems. In an attempt to eradicate this problem, most states require disclosure of suspected child abuse first by an oral report, followed by a written affirmation to locally designated authorities. Specific information pertaining to the name and address, age, persons responsible for the care of the child, the nature and extent of the observed abuses is often required in the report. Although the details of procedure and substance vary slightly among states, the purposes of establishing both the cause of mistreatment and identity of the perpetrators remain constant. For health professionals within a hospital or other institution, suspicion of child abuse is channeled by statute through the administration. A nurse whose attention is aroused by the possibility of child neglect or abuse should immediately notify the administration.

Phenylketonuria in newborns

State statutes regulating the disclosure of PKU results are an attempt to encourage both testing and treatment of the condition. Physicians or other persons in attendance, confronted with diagnostic symptoms of the disease, are required to report the existence of phenylketonuria.[61]

Communicable diseases

The rationale underlying statutes that require cases of contagious diseases to be reported is to enable quarantine of carriers and treatment to prevent further spread of the disease. An example of this type of regulation is found in the New York Sanitary Code, which requires the physician to report such findings to the local health authority.[62] In the absence of an attending physician, the responsibility falls on other individuals, often the public health nurse.

Births

A state, in maintaining accurate records of births and deaths within its boundaries, relies on the attending physician and nurse to report all births outside a maternity home or hospital. For this purpose, most states have legislated mandatory disclosure provisions for this type of birth.[63]

Wounds inflicted by lethal weapons

Wounds caused by lethal weapons must be reported. Some statutes include automobile accident injuries in this category. For example, New York Penal Law requires incidents to be reported by physicians or nurses in charge of the treatment of wounds.[64] State control of weaponry, coupled with its interest in criminal statistics, forms the basis for reporting injuries to local police authorities by individuals who have access to the information.

Rape

In providing health services, the nurse may encounter victims of the crime of rape. A forced act of carnal knowledge against another individual incurs criminal liability for the transgression.

The role of the nurse, on the discretional approval or request of the victim, is to notify criminal authorities if such an act has occurred. There is a distinction from other disclosure requirements, due to the penumbra of fright and embarrassment that often surrounds the traumatic experience.

Wills

The nurse's duty with respect to a patient's wishes to make a disposition of property on death is twofold: (1) to advise the patient to consult an attorney if time permits and (2) to recognize the responsibilities in serving as a witness when death is imminent and the patient expresses the intention of creating a will orally. Some rudimentary principles pertaining to wills may be helpful to elucidate the functions of the nurse with respect to the maker of the will, the testator.

An individual's property at the time of death is distributed in one of two ways—either pursuant to a will that states the person's desires of allocation to beneficiaries or, if no will has been created, according to a probate statute that provides a formula for automatic distribution. Most individuals prefer to direct their own disbursement of property and it is therefore necessary for the nurse to gain information about the methods of creating a will.

Some elements of a valid will vary from state to state; the number of witnesses required to attest the will, for example, may vary. This summary of principles intends to give insight into the general requirements for a court to recognize and carry out the statements of the testator.

Wills are generally created by written statements of the testator, most often prepared by an attorney in the form of a document. It must be signed by the testator in the presence of witnesses who are not beneficiaries of the disposition. These witnesses affix their signatures as evidence to the statement. A *holographic will* is entirely handwritten by the testator and is a valid directive to the court in some states to effect disposition of property, provided it is signed and dated by the individual making the will.

There is an exception to the requirement that a will be in writing in a select number of states. A *nuncupative will,* or oral statement, will be enforced by the court of those states if the testator is in contemplation of death, provided there is a sufficient number of legally competent witnesses to the oral proclamation. A nurse who gives witness to such declarations should reduce the recitations to writing as soon as possible and, if located in a hospital or other institution, the signed and dated account of the patient's oral will should be sent to the administration immediately. Because the testator may legally alter the disposition of his property until the moment of death, each declaration by the patient warrants this procedure. The sequence and therefore recording of time is essential, as the last words of the testator will control the property allocations to beneficiaries.

With regard to witnessing a written will, it should be understood that attestation may require court appearance and presentation of testimony. The best alternative for a nurse asked to witness the signing of a will may be to suggest that an attorney be called, unless an emergency arises and attestation is needed immediately.

HUMAN EXPERIMENTATION

Scientific research using human subjects in health care and education settings has recently gained public attention because of legal interception. Issues arising from sterilization and contraception have created considerable legal consternation. In 1965 a Connecticut statute prohibited the use of contraceptives. A licensed physician was arrested and convicted of criminal violation by giving contraceptive advice to married persons. The Supreme Court of the United States reversed the decision of the Connecticut state court by holding that the statute violated the right to privacy of married couples.[65] Sterilization has also been seen as a freedom of marital privacy. A court in California looked to the contraception case to find voluntary surgical sterilization legal.[66] The Supreme Court has not yet addressed this particular question but most likely would agree with the state court determination based on the rationale offered in the contraception issue.

Fetal experimentation

A Congressional law passed in 1974 has prohibited further research on a living human fetus before or after the abortion of such fetus.[67] This halt in research is in effect until the National Commission for the Protection of Human Subjects of Biomedical and Behavioral Research has issued recommendations in the area of fetal research. In response to the 1974 legislation, the Department of Health, Education, and Welfare has published guidelines on research supported by federal grants. After exhausting research on animal subjects it is possible to use the human fetus for research, but only after obtaining the mother's consent. This entire area of research will be exciting as it develops.

Transplantation

The transplant of tissue from one area of the body to another or from one person to another raises a legal question. A physician in one case was held liable for battery when a skin graft was performed. The donor was 15, a minor, and gave his consent that the graft be performed. The court found the liability for the tort by dictating that the parents of the minor donor must also provide consent to the procedure.[69]

Anatomical gift laws

During the 1960s a special committee was convened to create a uniform or model version of a law regarding the donation of human bodies. All states had incorporated the essentials of this Uniform Anatomical Gift Act by 1971. The purpose was to remove legal problems that may arise from donation. The state statutes now provide for the method of making such a donation, the rights of surviving relatives of donors, and the liability of physicians and surgeons in the transplant procedure. To date very few courts have had to resolve disputes with regard to donations; perhaps the purpose of the laws has been fulfilled.[70]

LOOK TO THE FUTURE

Fortunately, the contours of legal sanction change with conditions of society and public attitude. Unfortunately, the reflecting modifications, particularly in statutory law, often lag behind the societal mood. Legal aspects with regard to the nursing profession (or perhaps without regard to the profession) are in such an interim period. The rapid expansion in health services provided by professional nurses is not yet reflected in the law. Attention is turned to two particular professional situations and the possibilities of ameliorating the incongruency between practice and law:

1. The dilemma in health care is not a novel or uncommon one: the patient in the coronary care unit undergoes ventricular fibrillation. Without orders directed by a physician, the nurse in attendance institutes closed cardiac massage. As the primary practitioner in the unit, the nurse is in essence engaged in diagnosis and treatment, areas of health care reserved by statute for licensed physicians. The incongruency presents itself as two basic questions of whether the nurse is practicing outside the scope permitted by the nurse practice acts and whether the therapeutic measure of defibrillation is "diagnostic" as defined by law.

Standing orders for coronary care provided by the physician, based on care of previously diagnosed patients, serve to alleviate the incongruency.[71] Not only do questions arise pertaining to the practicality of standing orders in emergency situations, but also courts have not as yet addressed the issue of legality of such delegation of medical practice. It is the tendency and nature of the statutory law to be inflexible, and a court will not issue a decision unless a case is brought based on a violation of the practice acts. Although it is conceivable that a court would defer to the prevalent use of standing orders, the situation greatly evidences the need for legislative reassessment of the medical team and the responsibilities of the members. Only then will recognition of the nurse's professional capabilities be accomplished and assurance be provided that this service in a coronary care unit is legally approved.

2. Earlier in the text the expanded role of the nurse practitioner was discussed. From the responsibilities delineated by the American Nurses' Association and the Nurse Training Act of 1971, it is clear that the registered nurse's health care judgment is often exercised in such capacities as assessment of health status of patients, and evaluation and interpretation of data to implement appropriate nursing intervention. If the distinction between the practice of nursing and the practice of medicine is the degree of diagnostic judgment, the line of demarcation becomes rather tenuous in the services provided by the nurse practitioner. The question is how this new role fits within the outmoded parameters of the practice acts. Perhaps a rationale can be found when the nurse practitioner is in a health clinic and collaborates with licensed physicians. The pitfall of this perspective, of course, is that it keeps the practitioner in a falsely dependent role.

The predicament is more clearly displayed in the case of an independent nurse practitioner clinic. Although there may exist a distant collaboration with physicians, the connection is of a different variety when the physician signs blank prescription forms to be used according to the nurse practitioner's discretion.[72] Of course, a licensed nurse may practice nursing, but the legislative confinement of the practice to the role of dependent health care indicates that the independent nurse practitioner is violating the practice acts. From the legal standpoint, the law must be an integral participant in the evolution of a health care team.

Both the coronary care situation and the nurse's expanded role indicate the necessity for a legal realignment of the professions of nursing and medicine. Among many other innovations in the health services field to bridge the gap between medical care and nursing services, some of the devices that have been created follow. Although their legality has not been tested in the courtroom, some interesting issues of law arise in their usage.

1. *Protocols.* To facilitate primary care by nurses, a schematic approach has been devised to guide a professional nurse in collection of patient data and to implement specific action on these facts. The protocol is a framework for decision-making in the absence of an attending physician. Not only is this method often too confining for the nurse in the provision of health care, but also a problem arises in the legal sphere: Is the use of the approach an unauthorized delegation of diagnostic and therapeutic functions of a physician in violation of the professional practice acts? With the burgeoning use of protocols, judicial analysis could find its legality through an acceptance of the protocol as a prevailing health services custom in the same fashion a court may view the standing orders in the coronary care unit. Additionally, a protocol intends to avoid diagnosis and treatment by the attending nurse, and in this sense it is the protocol that is making the decision.[73] Whatever flaws are inherent in this system, it serves at least as a temporary link between the medical and nurse practice acts.

2. *Joint statements.* Collaborative statements issued by nursing, medical, and hospital associations in California in 1957 were early attempts to circumvent outmoded definitions of practice.[74] Representatives from the organizations combined to produce a written authorization for nurses to start intravenous fluids. Subsequent conferences in other states were held to support the nurse in an extended role in intensive care units. The partnership of the professions in issuing these statements is a valuable exercise in collegial attitude.

The joint statements of authorization are

not law—with the exception of Idaho, which included the possibility of joint statements in the Nurse Practice Act of that state.[75] From the viewpoint of the courts, these joint statements by professional associations may be evidence of professional practice. With many states adhering to the antiquated practice acts, the procedures guided by joint statements still fall outside the ambit of statutory limitations on nursing practice.

3. *Health maintenance organizations.* Congress has enacted a law that encourages the development of health maintenance organizations (HMO's).[76] This legislation is an effort to promote team health care by authorizing public subsidy for the establishment of such organizations. By so doing, Congress has sponsored an approach that promotes and advocates the services of the professional nurse in an expanded role. Conflict with local laws still exists in those states which have not yet amended their practice acts. In spite of the conflict between Congressional legislation and state practice acts, health maintenance organizations have opened an area in which the professional nurse may practice in an expanded role.

4. *Professional Standards Review Organizations.* Professional Standards Review Organizations (PSRO's) are a method to review health care that was legislatively inspired to develop regional norms of care, treatment, and diagnosis provided to patients whose care is paid through federal health programs. The overall plan encourages organization and implementation of criteria for health care practitioners other than physicians. As PSRO's relate to the legal standard of care involved in negligence lawsuits, it has been speculated that the court might view these standards as minimal, while imposing a higher degree of health care as the legal norm.[77]

The most crucial point is the importance of nurse participation in the development of these standards. Whatever legal role these professional review models may serve in the future, it is of ultimate value to "define, lest you be defined," as psychiatrist Thomas Szazz asserts. Intelligent input from the nursing profession may serve a beneficial dual purpose: to provide a basis for judicial interpretation and determination of the function of the practitioner, and to self-direct the profession into those areas which fit the professional nurse in both fulfillment and qualification.

References for unit four

1. For discussion of this topic see McCormick, Charles Tilford: Handbook of the law of evidence, St. Paul, Minn., 1954, West Publishing Co.
2. 4 Wigmore, Evidence, Section 1174 (ed. 3, 1940).
3. 32 Corpus Juris Secundum, Evidence, Section 457 (1964).
4. Prosser, William L.: Handbook of the law of torts, ed. 2, St. Paul, Minn., 1955, West Publishing Co.
5. 8 Wigmore, Evidence, Section 2336 (McNaughton rev., 1961).
6. See, for example, Neb. Rev. Stat. Section 25-1206 (Reissue 1964).
7. Health Law Center: Nursing and the law, ed. 2, Rockville, Md., 1975, Aspen Systems Corp., p. 52.
8. *Ibid.*, p. 53.
9. Kohnke, Mary F., Zimmern, Ann, and Greenidge, Jocelyn A.: The independent nurse practitioner, New York, 1974, Medcom Press, p. 105.
10. Stefanic v. Nursing Educational Committee, 37 A.2d 661 (R.I. 1944).
11. *Ibid.*, Section 5-34-1 (d).
12. Barber v. Reeking, 411 P.2d 861 (Wash. 1966).
13. Bullough, Bonnie, editor: The law and the expanding nursing role, New York, 1975, Appleton-Century-Crofts, p. 87.
14. Idaho Code Section 54-1413.
15. National Commission for the Study of Nursing and Nursing Education: From abstract into action, New York, 1973, McGraw-Hill Book Co., p. 13.
16. Bullough, *op. cit.* ref. 13, p. 16.
17. Cohoes Memorial Hospital v. Mossey, 226 NYS 501 (1966).
18. Parker, Leo T.: Review of hospital lawsuits, Hospital Topics **43**:78 passim, Aug., 1965.
19. Health Law Center, *op. cit.* ref. 7, p. 70.
20. *Ibid.*, p. 74.
21. *Ibid.*, p. 76.
22. Denver v. Pollard, 417 P2D 231 (Colo., 1966).
23. Williams v. Pomona Valley Hospital, 131 P. 888 (Cal. 1913).
24. Creighton, Helen: Law every nurse should know, ed. 3, Philadelphia, 1975, W. B. Saunders Co., p. 63.
25. Kohnke, Zimmern, and Greenidge, *op. cit.* ref. 9, p. 15.
26. Natason v. Kline, 350 P.2d 1093 (Kans. 1960).
27. Govin v. Hunter, 374 P.2d 421 (Wyo. 1962).
28. Russell v. Harwick, 166 So.2d 904 (Fla. 1964).
29. O'Brien v. Cunard Steamship Co., 28 N.E. 266 (Mass. 1891).
30. Hughes, James: The hospital, the physician and informed consent, Hospitals **42**:66-70, June 16, 1968.
31. Prosser, *op. cit.* ref. 4, p. 88.
32. *Ibid.*, p. 34.
33. Plonty v. Murphy, 84 N.W. 1005 (Minn. 1901).
34. Whitree v. State of New York, 290 NYS 2d 486 (1968).
35. Gadsden General Hospital v. Hamilton, 103 So. 553 (Ala. 1925).
36. Bazemore v. Savannah Hospital, et al., 155 S.E. 194 (Ga. 1930).
37. Farrell v. Kramer, 35 A.2d 560 (Maine 1963).
38. Judge v. Rockford Memorial Hospital, 150 N.E.2d 202 (Ill. 1598).
39. Prosser, *op. cit.*, ref. 4, p. 124.
40. Holmes, Oliver Wendell: The common law, Boston, 1963, Little, Brown & Co., p. 43.
41. Norton v. Argonaut Insuance Co., 144 So.2d 249 (La. 1962).
42. Mundt v. Alta Bates Hospital, 223 Cal. App. 2d 413 (1963).
43. Gore v. U.S., 229 F. Supp. 547 (1964).
44. Brune v. Belinkoff, 235 N.E.2d (Mass, 1968).
45. Regan, William: Post-surgical nursing and the law, Regan Report of Nursing Law **13**:1, Oct., 1972.
46. Palsgraf v. Long Island Railway, 162 N.E.99 (N.Y. 1928).
47. Health Law Center, *op. cit.* ref. 7, p. 103.
48. Wilmington General Hospital v. Manlove, 174 A.2d 135 (1961).
49. Parrish v. Clark, 145 So.848 (Fla. 1933).
50. St. Paul-Mercury Indemnity Co. v. St. Joseph Hospital, 4 N.W.2d 637 (Minn. 1942).
51. U.S. Sup. Ct. No. 70-18 (1973).

52. Holmes, *op. cit.,* p. 50.
53. People v. Phillips, 42 Cal. Rptr. 868 (1965).
54. Grennan, Elizabeth M.: The Somera case, International Nursing Review **5:**325-334, 1930.
55. State v. Comstock, 70 S.E.2d 648 (W. Va. 1952).
56. Perkins, Rollin M.: Criminal law, Mineola, N.Y., 1969, The Foundation Press, Inc., p. 132.
57. St. Pierre v. State, 33 NYS 2d 151 (Ct. Cl., 1942).
58. Creighton, *op. cit.,* p. 190.
59. United States v. Freeman, 357 F.2d 606 (2nd cir. 1966).
60. Sutton's Administration v. Woods, 85 S.W. 201 (Ky. 1905).
61. Health Care Center, *op. cit.,* ref. 7, p. 97.
62. Sanitary Code, Ch 2 Reg. 3 (1954).
63. See, for example, North Dakota Cent. Code, Section 50-20-03.
64. New York Statutes, Section 265.25.
65. Griswold v. Connecticut, 381 U.S. 479 (1965).
66. Jessin v. County of Shasta, 274 Cal.App. 2d 737 (1969).
67. Public Law 93-348, National Research Service Award Act.
68. Levy, Charlotte L.: The human body and the law, Dobbs Ferry, N.Y., 1975, Oceana Publications, Inc., p. 49.
69. Bonner v. Moran, 126 F.2d 121 (D.C. Cir. 1941).
70. Levy, *op. cit.,* ref. 68, p. 67.
71. Bullough, *op. cit.* ref. 13, p. 88.
72. Agee, B. C.: Beginning an independent nursing practice, American Journal of Nursing, pp. 636-642, April, 1974.
73. Bullough, *op. cit.,* ref. 13, p. 62.
74. *Ibid.,* p. 17.
75. Idaho Code Section 54-1413.
76. Public Law 93-222, Health Maintenance Organization Act of 1973.
77. Springer, Eric W.: PSRO's: implications for legal liability, Hospital Medical Staff **4:**1, Jan., 1975.

ADDITIONAL REFERENCES

Guinee, Kathleen K.: The professional nurse: orientation, roles and responsibilities, London, 1970, The Macmillan Co., Publishers.
Kling, Samuel G.: The complete guide to everyday law, ed. 3, Chicago, 1973, Follett Publishing Co.
Lesnik, Milton Jack, and Anderson, B. E.: Nursing practice and the law, ed. 2, Philadelphia, 1962, J. B. Lippincott Co.
Mermin, Samuel: Law and the legal system—an introduction, Boston, 1973, Little, Brown & Co.
Murchison, Irene A., and Nichols, Thomas S.: Legal foundations of nursing practice, New York, 1970, The Macmillan Co., Publishers.
Wasmuth, Carl E.: Law and the surgical team, Baltimore, 1969, The Williams & Wilkins Co.

Index